1001
DO-IT-YOURSELF HINTS & TIPS

1001 DO-IT-YOURSELF HINTS & TIPS

Tricks, shortcuts, how-tos, and other nifty ideas for inside, outside, and all around your house

Reader's Digest

The Reader's Digest Association, Inc.
Pleasantville, New York / Montreal

1001 DO-IT-YOURSELF HINTS & TIPS

STAFF

Project Editor
Wayne Kalyn

Project Art Editor
Carol Nehring

Senior Associate Designer
Ed Jacobus

Associate Designer
Robert Steimle

Associate Editor
Troy Dreier

Assistant Editor
Andrew Boorstyn

READER'S DIGEST GENERAL BOOKS

Editor-in-Chief Books and Home Entertainment
Barbara J. Morgan

Editor U.S. General Books
David Palmer

Executive Editor
Gayla Visalli

Managing Editor
Christopher Cavanaugh

CONTRIBUTORS

Senior Associate Editor
Tracey Harden

Researcher
Paula Phelps

Copy Editor
Katherine G. Ness

Associate Editor
Cinda Siler

Writers
Roy Barnhart Step-by-Step Captions
Melanie Hulse Exterior
Edward R. Lipinski *Heating and Cooling; Appliances*
Laura Tringali *Around the Home; Exterior; painting and Wallpapering; Furniture; Stone, Brick, and Concrete; Yard and Garden*
John Warde *Window and Doors; Pluming; Electrical*
Charles Wardell *Interior; Safety and Security*

Photographers
Steven Mays, chief
Robert Brantley
Gene and Katie Hamilton
Joel Musler
Bill Zuehlke

Illustrators
Ian Worpole, chief
Todd Ferris
Robert Steimle

Indexer
Northwind Editorial Services

Library of Congress Cataloging in Publication Data

1001 do-it-yourself hints & tips: tricks, shortcuts, how-tos and other nifty ideas for inside, outside, and all around the house.
p. cm.
At head of title: Reader's digest
ISBN 0-7621-0049-4 (hardcover)
ISBN 978-0-7621-0906-7 (paperback)
1. Houses—Maintenance and repair—Miscellanea.
I. Reader's digest.
TH4817.A18 1998
643'.7—21   97-22347

10 (hardcover)
1 3 5 7 9 10 8 6 4 2 (paperback)

The credits and acknowledgements that appear on page 352 are hereby made a part of this copyright page.

First printing in paperback 2008

Printed in China

We are committed to both the quality of our products and the service we provide to our customers. We value your comments, so please feel free to contact us. Editor, Adult Trade Publishing, c/o Customer Service, Reader's Digest, Pleasantville, NY 10570

ABOUT THIS BOOK

This how-to book is for everybody—from tinkerers whose idea of an all-purpose tool is a butter knife to experienced do-it-yourselfers whose knowledge and equipment verge on the professional.

It is also a different kind of how-to book. Unlike many manuals that are steeped in technical jargon and feature projects only a skilled person could pull off, ours shows you how to tackle 175 of the most common and useful tasks around the home with relative ease. Every job is explained in step-by-step, straightforward language and is accompanied by photographs or illustrations. You'll learn how to do things right the first time, whether you are installing a home satellite dish, clearing a clogged drain, or replacing a deck board.

Best of all, presented alongside each job is a group of related tips and techniques—more than 2,500 in all—for achieving the best results. Gathered from the experts, these hints will save you money and time and will help you avoid the pitfalls that trip up many homeowners.

1001 Do-It-Yourself Hints & Tips is divided into 13 chapters. The first, "Around the Home," is filled with nifty ideas for managing and organizing your household. Here you'll find strategies to simplify and improve your life. Whether you want to set up a home office, double your storage space, or get rid of household pests, there are answers and suggestions galore.

The chapters that follow get down to nuts and bolts, offering a different step-by-step feature on almost every page. If you think that a certain job may be too difficult or time-consuming, check the handy rating system: one symbol indicates a relatively easy task, two signifies one of medium difficulty, and three denotes a more complex job. Nevertheless, none of these projects is beyond the reach of the average do-it-yourselfer.

The book's chapters cover nearly all aspects of home repair and improvement, including interior and exterior repair, windows and doors, painting and wallpapering, furniture repair and refinishing, plumbing and electrical work, home heating and cooling, and appliances and electronics. You'll also get outdoors with sections on gardening and landscaping, as well as patios, walkways, and driveways.

The book concludes with a chapter that addresses everyone's concerns about safety and security. We'll show you how to protect your home, your car, and your family and make your life safer.

Indeed, safety is never far from our minds. For many of the how-to jobs in the book, we offer a laundry list of "Safe and Smart" tips for your protection. We also provide an assortment of special "File It" boxes that you can consult over and over again, whether you are faced with a household emergency like a fire or flood or are trying to figure out how much paint to buy before redoing a bedroom.

We have made **1001 Do-It-Yourself Hints & Tips** practical and accessible. We hope that you will find it fun, inspiring, and useful for years to come.

The Editors

6 CONTENTS

AROUND THE HOME

FILE IT

Emergency shutoffs

Knowing what to turn, pull, or shut off can be a home-saver and lifesaver in the throes of an emergency.

ELECTRICITY

CAUTION: If the floor is damp or the wiring has gotten wet, it is dangerous to touch the main switch box. Have the electricity turned off by the power company.

On a fuse box	Lower or pull the lever to the *Off* position to shut off the power.
On a cartridge-type box	Pull out the plastic boxes holding the cartridge fuses.
On the main circuit breaker box	Flip the one or two main switches to *Off*.
On other circuit breaker boxes	Flip all switches to *Off*.

NATURAL GAS

CAUTION: If you smell gas, open the windows and shut off the main gas valve. Do not light a flame or turn any electrical switch on or off. Don't use your phone. Leave at once and report the leak from a neighbor's phone. If your home uses LP gas, stay out of the basement; LP gas is heavier than air and sinks to lower levels.

The natural-gas shutoff	Turn lever on meter intake pipe so it's perpendicular to pipe.
The bottled-gas shutoff valve	Turn the knob or lever on top of the tank clockwise.

WATER

In a warm-climate home	The main shutoff is often on the outside, where the water pipe enters the house. Turn it clockwise.
In colder areas	The main shutoff is usually in the basement, where the water pipe comes through the wall. Turn it clockwise.
For a broken faucet	The shutoffs—hot and cold water—are usually under or next to the fixture. Turn both clockwise.

Electrical Fixes

To read a plug fuse, look at the window on the fuse in the circuit that has gone out. A blackened window indicates that the cause is a short circuit; a clean window means the circuit is overloaded.

Lights aren't right? Bulbs that burn brightly, then dim before brightening again, indicate that the neutral wire in the line between the utility pole and your home may have become detached. Call your electric company and ask them to check it.

Dimming down. If the lights go dim momentarily whenever several appliances are running at the same time, the circuit might be near full capacity or the electric company is having trouble satisfying the demand for power. Add up the load on the circuit; if the total doesn't come close to full capacity, call your power company for help.

Stop the shock. Never touch a shock victim who is still touching the source of electricity—the current can flow through the body of the victim into yours. Instead, use a wooden object such as a broom handle (never anything metal) to dislodge the victim from the source. Only then should you call for help and perform first aid.

Happy birthday. A simple birthday candle will emit sufficient light during a blackout. To enlarge it and lengthen its life, jab the candle into a jar of petroleum jelly so that only the tip is sticking out; then light it.

Candle power. Make a light during a blackout by pouring a little cooking oil into a glass measuring cup placed in a metal pan; add a short string for a wick. The "lamp" will burn for hours.

Plumbing Fixes

The nose knows. A strong smell of sewage from a fixture in a bathroom, kitchen, or laundry may indicate that the trap in the waste pipe leading away from the fixture has gone dry. Pour some water into the drain and wait to see if the smell goes away. If it doesn't, you may have more serious problems; call in a plumber.

Flood control. When a washer or a dishwasher runs over, build a dam around the spillage with beach towels, old rugs, or other large absorbent materials. The water will be confined to the area, making it easier to mop up.

SAFE AND SMART

If you have a flood, minimize the damage with these do's and don'ts.

➤ Shut off the main water valve if the flood is a result of a broken pipe.

➤ Shut off electricity to the flooded area—if it is possible to reach the main circuit box without touching the water—to prevent electric shock.

➤ If possible, plug a sump pump or wet vac into an outlet protected by a ground fault circuit interrupter (GFCI).

➤ Wear rubber boots and gloves if the leak is in a drain line or has been contaminated with sewage—and disinfect the area thoroughly after it has been cleaned and allowed to dry.

➤ Don't wade through standing water if it has come in contact with electrical outlets or appliances—the water may be electrically charged.

➤ Don't run a gas-powered water pump inside the house. It produces hazardous fumes.

Preventing frozen pipes.
If frigid temperatures threaten a pipe freeze-up, turn on the faucets just a little bit so that water is barely trickling out, and leave them open until the weather warms up. This small amount of running water should keep the ice at bay. Also take into account the wind-chill factor when determining whether temps will fall below freezing.

Work on the right side.
Start thawing the ice in a frozen pipe from the side closest to a faucet, so the ice melt will have somewhere to drain. (The faucet should be opened first, of course.) Gradually work from the faucet side back into the frozen area.

Finding a frozen spot
is all too easy if a pipe has already burst, or is swollen to the point of bursting. But if you're lucky, the frozen section of pipe is simply plugging the water so it can't run. To find the frozen plug, check piping in unheated areas of the house or in exterior walls. Pinpoint the frozen area by swabbing along the pipe with a moist rag; frost will form as you hit the frozen spot.

Slow thaw. When it comes to thawing out pipes, the slower the better. Use a hair dryer set on *High* to elevate the temperature. Never use propane torches—the heat they produce can turn water into steam, which could build up and cause the pipes to explode.

The big turn-off. If pipes have frozen and you must leave the house, be sure to turn the faucets off, or leave them open only a little. If the pipes thaw while you are gone, the pouring water from wide-open faucets might cause a flood.

Down the drain? Don't give up on a piece of jewelry that falls down a sink drain. Instead, use a pipe wrench to open the plug on the U-shaped trap under the sink—or to remove the entire trap if there is no plug. Dump everything from the trap into a bucket, and look for the valuable.

Roofs
Tracking a leak. You've sprung a leak, but where? Trace it back to its source from the inside by looking for water marks on sheathing or framing lumber and for cone-shaped impressions on the surface of fiberglass insulation. Follow the trail upward and mark the uppermost location with a waterproof marker. Check the suspicious spot for dampness or dripping water the next time it rains.

A storm-damaged roof
can be temporarily repaired by covering the hole with plastic sheeting. Fold over the edges of the plastic and staple them to sound roofing shingles surrounding the opening. *Note:* A tarp, particularly a plastic one, is very slippery when wet, so be careful when working with one on a roof.

Wick it away. If water from a leaking roof is flowing down a rafter, it can cause serious moisture damage to the attic joists and the walls below. Divert the water temporarily with a rag "wick" until the leak can be stopped. Tack a long strip of cloth to the rafter in the water's path and set a bucket under it. The strip will redirect the minor river into the bucket.

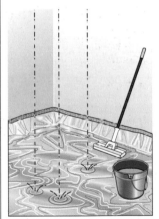

Catch a flood. If leaks are spread over a large area of the roof, capture dripping water in a catch basin made of plastic sheeting, such as painters use for drop cloths. Turn up the sides of the plastic and tape or staple them to the walls to create a large, shallow bowl that can contain the water. Mop up the water frequently so it doesn't overflow.

FILE IT

Fighting fires: The ABC's of fire extinguishers

A quick defense against small home fires, fire extinguishers are rated for use against various types of fires. A multipurpose fire extinguisher, rated ABC, is effective against all of the most common fires in homes and is a good choice if you have only one. Larger models have more capacity. Read the instructions and learn how to use the extinguisher. Check the pressure gauge monthly; if it is low, replace the extinguisher or have it recharged.

	Ordinary combustibles	Designed to fight blazes in wood, paper, rubber, and most plastics. Use near fireplaces, and in living areas and bedrooms.
	Flammable liquids	Contains dry chemicals to smother fires fueled by substances such as oil, solvents, grease, gasoline, kerosene. Use in kitchen, workshop area, and garage.
	Electrical equipment	Contains dry chemicals to smother electrical fires. Use in workshop area and near the electrical service panel.

Fire Prevention

Buyer's guide. A multipurpose fire extinguisher is best if you own only one, but it has a smaller capacity than fire extinguishers designed to fight specific types of fires. You'll have greater fire-fighting power if you keep several types on hand.

Seeing sparks? Disconnect a sparking appliance immediately, and either have it repaired before using it again or replace it. If flames are coming from the appliance, douse them with a Class-C extinguisher or an ABC type. Never try to put out an appliance fire with water, because the splash of water could conduct electricity back to you, resulting in a fatal shock.

Check the bottom line. When using a fire extinguisher, work with a sweeping motion and aim the nozzle at the bottom of the flames, not at the body of the fire or the upper tips of the flames.

Stovetop fires. Resist temptation—don't try to carry a burning pan to the sink. Instead, turn off the range and the exhaust fan, slip on an oven mitt, grab a large pot lid, cookie tray, or pizza pan, and slide it over the fire to smother the flames. Douse range-top flames on grease or oil spills with a generous dollop of baking soda or salt.

Don't peek. Leave the lid on a burning pan for a good, long time, until the material within is completely cool. If the heating element or the oil in the pan is still hot, lifting the lid for just a second can let in enough oxygen to reignite the fire.

Oven fires will eventually die out for lack of oxygen if the door is kept closed. But remember to shut off the oven promptly.

No warning signs. Because flames from a chimney fire usually aren't visible within the house, the first sign may be a call from a neighbor. Other possible tip-offs: unusual heat radiating from the fireplace area, or a loud roaring noise.

To cap or not. Unless you need a chimney cap to remedy problems with water or downdrafts, don't install one. In case of a chimney fire, the cap may direct the flames right down onto the roof.

In case of a chimney fire, evacuate the house immediately. If you have a wood stove, close the damper as you go; if you have a fireplace, close the damper only if you can reach its handle without risk of a burn. After calling the fire department from a neighbor's house, start hosing down the roof.

Steamy solution. Help fight a small chimney fire by throwing 2 cups of water onto the hot coals in the fireplace. The water will turn to steam, which will rise up the stack and help to extinguish the flames.

After a chimney fire, have the chimney professionally cleaned to avoid a flare-up. The creosote in the chimney may not have been completely consumed by the fire.

Propane, Oil, Natural Gas

What's that smell? If you have both natural-gas and propane appliances, here's an easy way to distinguish smells. Sniff around, and if the smell is strongest below nose level, it's propane. Natural gas is lighter and tends to spread through the air; heavier propane tends to settle closer to the floor.

Use your nose. A faint gas odor may signal that a pilot light is out on an appliance—relight it if necessary. Set the control valve to *Off,* then to *Pilot.* Release gas to the pilot light by depressing either the red button or the handle, depending on the appliance model. Light with a match; then keep the button or handle depressed for at least a minute. Release it and set the control to *On.*

A leaky oil tank is bad news, and there is nothing to do but to replace it and have the mess cleaned up. But take action right away. Oil is a serious contaminant, and cleanup just gets worse if it is postponed.

Natural Disasters

Before a thunderstorm, unplug electronic equipment to protect it from high-voltage surges caused by lightning strikes. Or plug items into a quality surge protector. If the lightning is flashing, don't risk a shock by unplugging anything.

Hair standing on end when you're caught outside during a thunderstorm? It's a sign that lightning may be about to strike you. To minimize injury, squat down, lower your head between your knees, and grasp your knees with your hands.

Don't swing in a storm. Golf clubs, fishing rods, aluminum bats, metal batting helmets, and tennis rackets may become lightning rods in a thunderstorm; so when you are stuck outside, ditch them at the first sign of bad weather.

Behind the walls. If lightning strikes your house, evacuate it at once and call the fire department. Even though everything may look fine, an electrical fire could be brewing within the walls. Before reoccupying your home, call an electrician to check the electrical panel, circuits, and receptacles.

Fill that tub. When a major storm is brewing, fill all bathtubs, and any large containers you have, with water. If the power goes off, the water pump won't be working, and you'll need water for sanitary purposes.

Fill that tank. If you have advance notice of a severe storm, go to the gas station and fill all your vehicles with gas. If there's a power outage of any duration, you will not be able to get gas from the electric pumps.

Stormy weather? If you are expecting a hurricane or other spell of bad weather where a power outage is likely, set your refrigerator and freezer to the coldest possible settings. Supercold food will have a better chance of keeping chilled until the power is restored.

Pet protocol. If it's not safe for you to stay in the house, it's not safe for your pets, either. Many public shelters don't allow animals, so find out in advance about motels that accept pets in your evacuation zone; also consider pet shelters and kennels. Make sure you have your pet's carrier, food, ID tag, and vaccination papers.

In the aftermath of a bad storm, check the foundation of your house immediately, and then again at intervals of several weeks. First look for cracks or bulges, both inside and out. During rechecks, add cracked interior walls and sticky doors to the checklist. Any of these problems may indicate that the house is settling because soil has washed out from under the footings.

A cleanup detail. When cleaning up after a bad storm or hurricane, use disinfectant on all floor and wall surfaces. Floodwater can be contaminated with all sorts of bacteria.

Get a contact. Enlist an out-of-state friend to be a family contact. After a disaster, it's easier to call long distance than locally. All family members should call the liaison to let him or her know where they are.

Cabinets and Countertops
A height advantage.
If you're redesigning your kitchen, create counters of varying heights. Some tasks, such as kneading dough, are done more comfortably on a lower surface. If you can't adjust the counter, elevate yourself by standing on a low stool. To raise the workspace, stack several cutting boards on the counter.

Counter intelligence. You don't have to live with a burn or other major blemish in a plastic-laminate countertop. A stainless-steel or cutting-board insert is serviceable and easy to install after you cut away the damaged area to the depth of the insert. Secure a cutting board with sink-rim edging.

Or hide a burned spot with a glazed tile. Glue the tile right over the damaged area and use it as a countertop trivet.

Cut a square hole in a butcher-block counter and store a garbage pail in the cabinet underneath. Push peelings and other counter debris right down the hole. A chopping block or cutting board can be placed over the hole to hide it and cut down on odors.

Store favorite recipes within the plastic pages of a three-ring photo album. The recipes will be easy to see, but shielded from drips and sticky fingers.

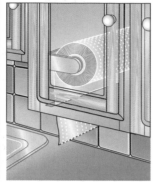

On a roll. Paper towels are always handy—but out of view—when you mount the roll on a holder installed inside a conveniently located cabinet. Cut a slot in the bottom shelf to allow the towels to pass through.

Built-in knife storage.
A long slot cut into a countertop can house kitchen knives close at hand while eliminating the clutter of a knife block. Just make sure that the blades won't cut someone while they're hanging in the stored position.

Flooring
What not to buy. Prefinished laminated or strip flooring with beveled edges doesn't belong in the kitchen. The grooves not only collect crumbs but also make it harder to refinish the floor.

Repair the damage. Fix small tears in vinyl flooring with a dot of tub and tile caulk in a matching color. Level the caulk and remove the excess with a swipe of a damp cloth; then seal.

Damage control. Before trying to dislodge a damaged vinyl floor tile, soften the adhesive with heat (see p. 87). Lay a cloth over the tile; then run a warm iron over it until the tile pries up with a putty knife.

The vinyl solution. When applying wax or finish, give the entire floor one coat and then add a second coat to high-traffic areas, so both areas wear evenly.

Shine. Soap residue can dull a floor no matter how vigorously you mop. Add vinegar to the rinse water to neutralize lingering suds.

Attach felt to the bottom of kitchen chair legs to buffer a tile or vinyl floor from scrapes and nicks. Use weatherstripping, or buy self-adhesive felt pads.

Remodeling
Traffic on trial. When planning a kitchen island, mark out the perimeter of its proposed location with masking or painting tape (painting tape peels up more easily). Count the number of times you step over the tape—after a couple of days, you'll have pinpointed any traffic problems.

Stepped-up island.
If you're planning a kitchen island or peninsula, consider a two-tier design—it separates the snack bar from the workspace and also blocks the view of mealtime clutter from other rooms or areas of the kitchen. A 6-inch step between counter surfaces works nicely.

If you have limited funds, buy the best cabinetry you can afford, and order a plastic laminate rather than a solid-surface countertop. You'll realize savings, and you can upgrade the countertop at a later date. In the meantime, you'll have the basis of a beautiful kitchen.

Appliance outlet stores may sell damaged goods at a great price. If the damage is minor—maybe a gouge on one side or a broken hinge—fixing it will be easy.

Recycling

Pop-out bags. To make a plastic grocery-bag dispenser, cut off the top and bottom of a 2-liter soda bottle with a sharp utility knife, and screw it to a wall or cabinet door. Stuff the bags in through the top, and pull them out through the bottom.

Step on it. To save space in the recycling bin, open the bottom of cans and flatten them with your foot before tossing them in.

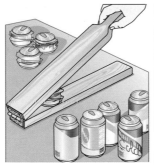

Can crusher. If you want to spare your feet, knock together a can smasher out of a couple of 2 x 4's joined together with a heavy-duty hinge. Shape the end of the top 2 x 4 so it fits comfortably in your hand.

Bulky milk jugs hogging all the room in your recycling bin? Knot one end of a long cord to the handle of one of the jugs; then string the cord through the handles of the other jugs. Tie a loop in the end and suspend the cord on a nail in an out-of-the-way place.

Cleaning Up
Overnight odor eater.
Eliminate refrigerator and freezer smells with a cup of ground coffee. Place the cup inside, close the door, and don't open it until morning. If there are lingering odors, refill the cup with fresh coffee and repeat.

Sterilize the strainer.
To keep your metal sink strainer clean, run it through the dishwasher every time you do a load. The hot water will kill colonies of germs and bacteria that set up home there.

Cushion china and crystal when washing them by spreading a towel on the bottom of the kitchen sink.

Collect food scraps in a colander placed in the kitchen sink. Scrape food into it so the liquid will go down the drain instead of collecting in the bottom of the garbage pail.

Here, kitty. A shake or two of cat litter in the bottom of the kitchen garbage can will absorb any spills and prevent odors. Clean out the litter and replace it weekly.

FILE IT

What's cooking: The new ranges and cooktops
A new range shouldn't be an impulse buy. On average, families purchase a range or cooktop every 15 years. So consider splurging on a self-cleaning model and downdraft ventilation, which eliminates the need for an overhead hood.

Type	Advantages	Disadvantages
Traditional electric coil	Inexpensive; works with all cookware	Drip bowls get soiled easily; difficult to fine-tune heat
Traditional gas burner	Inexpensive; easy to control heat; cooks fast	Drip bowls get soiled easily
Glass ceramic	Easy cleanup; precise heat control	May cook more slowly than other types; must use heavy cookware with flat bottoms; expensive
Solid disc element	Easy cleanup	Cast-iron element must be polished to maintain luster; must use heavy cookware with flat bottoms
Induction unit	Precise heat control; easy to clean	Must use magnetic cookware; very expensive
Sealed gas burner	Easy to clean; even distribution of heat	Somewhat more expensive than a standard gas range

Living Rooms

Focus it. If your living room doesn't have a natural focal point, such as a cozy fireplace or a picture window with a scenic view, create one with an exceptional piece of furniture or a large coffee table arrayed with interesting objects. Wherever the focal point is, surround it closely with seating so that people will not feel as if they are sitting around the fringes of the room.

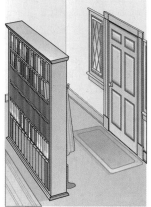

Ease the transition. If the front door of the house opens directly into the living room, create a mini-foyer by installing a tall bookcase or storage unit a few feet back from the door. This visual break will provide a boundary between the entryway and the rest of the room, allowing a more comfortable transition for people coming into the room from outdoors.

Lighter looks bigger. To add a spacious feeling to a small room, use light colors for the walls, rugs, and furniture and a few darker shades for accents. Instead of a dark floor, consider a pickled finish (see "In a Pickle," p. 130)—provided the look fits with the decor.

Installing a floor outlet in the middle of a room allows for more flexible lighting placements—a lamp on a table that isn't set against a wall, for instance, or a floor lamp next to an easy chair in the middle of the room. The alternative—snaking extension cords across the floor—can create electrical hazards or trip up anyone who walks by.

High lights. As an alternative to the space-eating clutter of table lamps or floor lamps, mount lighting fixtures on the walls. Called sconces and available in many styles, these wall fixtures can light a dark corner or illuminate an entryway. Pair them up to enhance a picture or to add importance to a fireplace mantel. Use several to cover a large space such as a long wall.

Open house. When light is bounced off the ceiling, it creates an illusion of openness that can make a small room magically appear larger. For the best effect, install several upward-facing sconces, or a row of lights hidden by a valance or a molding, about 2 feet below the ceiling.

Stairway savvy. When installing sconces along a staircase, pick a style that does not expose the light bulbs, so that they will not be visible to those ascending or descending the stairs.

Moving pictures. If the TV and VCR reside in the living room, place them on a wheeled cart that can be rolled out, or hide them in an elegant cabinet. That way they will not be so intrusive when company comes.

Have a seat. Always have extra chairs on hand when entertaining a larger group by storing a couple of hassocks underneath a long, narrow table set against a wall. Cover the hassocks with a bold, bright fabric if the room needs some color. The table can hold a set of collectibles or a favorite work of art, then double as a dessert or coffee buffet at the end of special meals.

FILE IT

Getting your fiber: A rug roundup

Many people are making the switch from wall-to-wall carpeting to hardwood floors accented with area rugs. Here are some tips to help you choose.

Fiber	Advantages	Expense
Wool	Beautiful, resilient, durable	Most expensive
Nylon	Has great resiliency, extremely durable	Expensive
Olefin	Retains color, resists soil, less durable than nylon	Less expensive
Polyester	Bright colors, but soft fibers are less durable in high-traffic areas	Less expensive

Buying Tips	
Yarns	Look for double twist instead of single twist for superior wearability.
Orientals	In a hand-knotted rug, the more knots per square inch, the higher the quality.
Handwoven test	If the ridges on the back of a rug run parallel to the fringe at either end, it is probably hand-woven. (In a machine-woven rug, the ridges usually run parallel to the rug's length.)

Quality buy. When purchasing upholstered furniture, buy pieces with cushions stuffed with durable high-density material. Hint: Look for cushions that have a domed shape. The dome will flatten eventually, but it does indicate the presence of firm polyfoam inside.

Fireplaces
Installing a new hearth?
Check first with the local building inspector. The dimensions are critical for safety, and are usually specified in the building code. Some local codes require that a hearth extend 8 to 12 inches to each side of the firebox and 16 to 20 inches in front of it.

Fireplace in a hurry.
Zero-clearance wood-burning fireplaces can be installed on any wall of a house with little hassle, usually without building in additional floor support. The prefabs are more energy efficient than their hand-built masonry counterparts, and they are reasonably priced. They also might add value to a home when it is sold—up to 130 percent of the cost.

Natural-gas fires
can add clean, convenient heat and the welcoming look of a cozy hearth to a room where there is no existing fireplace. Prefabricated direct-vent gas fireplaces can be mounted on any wall where there is access to a gas line, and can be vented through a metal chimney channel.

Pellet stoves are a good alternative to traditional wood stoves. Fed with bags of pellets made from sawdust and mill shavings, they do not require the customary supply of cordwood. An additional bonus: the pellets burn more cleanly and leave no wood scraps and bark pieces to litter the hearth.

A face-lift. To spruce up an ugly fireplace, shop for fireplace refacing kits, usually available at fireplace accessory shops. The kits, which are reasonably priced and easy to install, contain faux brick, marble, or slate that can be conveniently glued to the existing fireplace to give it a new look.

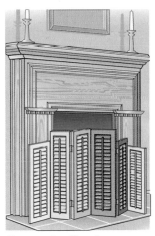

Screen the fireplace
with a funky collection of old shutters gathered from antique stores, garage sales, or salvage warehouses. Paint them different colors and hinge them together so they stand securely.

Hearth plants. Fit a piece of painted lattice in the opening of an unused fireplace, and let an ivy plant or some other vine twine its way through it.

Hide the hearth. Decorate an unused fireplace during summer by planting a container garden in it. Fill the hearth with potted plants from the patio, rotating them so none is deprived of sun for too long. Place saucers under the pots, if necessary, to catch drips.

Dining Rooms
Subtle boundaries.
If you don't have space for a room divider in a living-dining room, create a visual distinction between the two areas by using different flooring materials in each, or by covering the surrounding walls with different wallcoverings or paint.

A simple screen makes a great partition between living and dining spaces—and it can be removed when required. Make one quickly by hinging together three narrow louvered doors. Or use raised-panel doors and decorate them with paint or wallcovering to complement the room's decor. Be sure that the screen won't tip over if accidentally bumped.

Avoid a crush. When outfitting an old dining room table with new seating, measure the new chairs—including the armrests—carefully and match the measurements against the length of the table. Allow about 6 inches of space between the chairs and between chairs and table legs to allow diners to sit down without crowding.

Accessorize a sideboard with drawer pulls made of odd flatware pieces collected at yard sales. Spray them with a coat of lacquer or polyurethane so you won't have to polish them.

Two in one. When the dining room is carved out of the living room space, install a divider to accentuate the different functions each area will serve. A piece of furniture can work; try a sideboard or several low cabinets facing the dining area (they can also store linens and serving ware). Or turn a wide couch to face the living room. Or use both back-to-back if there is room enough.

Electronic armoire. Cloak the clutter of a bedroom TV, VCR, and stereo equipment in a handsome armoire. Look for a piece that has interior electrical outlets, pivoting platforms, and doors that virtually disappear—either into the cabinet itself or flat against its sides when they are opened.

Chic at cost. If you're not up for a major furniture purchase, buy a second-hand armoire and snake the electrical cords through a hole cut out of the back. Just make sure that the shelf can support the weight of the entertainment equipment.

Calm down. Instill calm in a bedroom by installing a dimmer switch. Turn the lights all the way up for reading and turn them down for a little late-night conversation.

No tight spots. When arranging furniture, allow some empty space on each side of the bed for dressing as well as making the bed and vacuuming.

Head of the bed. Don't pass by a great antique headboard just because it's a little narrower than the bed you want to pair it with. Hang the headboard on the wall and snug the bed up close to it.

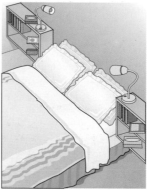

Like to read in bed? Mount a painted rectangular wood box on the wall on either side of the bed and you'll have a place to stash all your reading material, plus a reading lamp. Use dividers to organize stuff.

Molding a headboard. Frame a piece of wallcovering or fabric with base-cap molding for a "headboard" that will add instant drama to a predictable bedroom. A built-up mantel is also a handsome touch—it assembles easily from pieces of prefabricated molding.

Mix and match. When decorating, don't be afraid to combine geometric patterns, stripes, and florals in the same room. If the prints share at least one color, they won't clash.

Size matters. When using a variety of patterns in a decorating scheme, mix big and small. A display of several voluptuous, splashy prints can easily become overwhelming, while a medley of various dainty little prints is bound to be boring.

True to scale. Small patterns look best on the smaller things in the room—lampshades, pillow shams, bedside-table covers, and bed skirts. Larger patterns look great in broad swaths—bedspreads and voluminous window treatments.

Do the twist. Consider the "twist" of each strand of yarn before purchasing a cut-pile carpet for the bedroom. The more times the yarn is twisted, the springier the carpet will be—and the better it will hide footprints.

Guest Rooms

Two for one. A fold-up hideaway wall bed drops down at your convenience but hides the rest of the time, allowing the guest room to be used for other activities. Though these beds aren't cheap, the cost is often offset by the space that you gain.

FILE IT

Room-to-room decorating

Need to decorate a bedroom/bathroom combination? Try these tricks to provide a unified look while preserving the identity of each.

Outfit each room with a different but complementary color of paint; then paint all the trim of both rooms a third color.

Use the same fabric for the window treatments in both rooms, but select a different style of curtain, drape, or shade for each room.

Paint the bathroom the same hue as the dominant accent color in the bedroom.

Wallpaper both rooms in a different pattern from the same color collection—stripes in the bathroom, for example, and a floral in the bedroom.

FILE IT

On the carpet: What will work where

Understanding the differences among types of carpets will help you choose your broad-loom wisely. Here are the common varieties.

Type		Description	Advantages
Cut pile		Each loop of yarn is cut, forming two individual strands.	Wide array of colors and styles. Some types hide footprints.
Loop pile		Surface of carpet is made of uncut, durable loops of yarn.	Very good for areas of high traffic.
Cut and loop pile		Some loops are cut, some aren't, forming patterns and color shadings.	Provides variety, hides soil.

Double your space.
Replace the bed in the guest room with a futon or a daybed with bolsters, and the space can double as a hobby area, TV or computer room, or home office. If you're stuck with the bed, take off the headboard and footboard, push the bed against a wall, and add a lot of throw pillows to minimize the bedroom mind-set.

Blowing in the wind. For a unique window dressing, cut large, kid-appealing shapes from blocks of foam, cover them with pretty fabric, and hang them over a window on a curtain rod. A pattern of two or three interspersed shapes, like stars and moons, looks nice for older kids; a parade of circus or jungle animals will entertain younger ones.

Children's Rooms

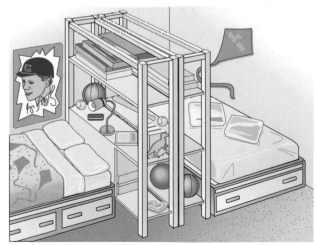

Carve out space for each kid in a double-occupancy room by placing tall bookcases back-to-back as dividers. Not only will the bookcases provide precious privacy, they'll also help children keep their possessions organized.

Kids' pinup. Cover a large section of wall in cork tiles to keep artwork, posters, and mementos off painted walls.

Chalk it up. A coat or two of chalkboard paint (available from home centers) on the back of a door provides little kids with a place to play school and older kids with a built-in organizer to record dates and important things to do.

Buy unpainted furniture that you can paint and decorate in kid-friendly colors now. As your children grow, they can repaint the wood for an entirely new look.

Don't stop with yellow.
Stay away from yellow in kids' rooms. Research shows that even pastel shades of yellow make infants cry more frequently and cause older children to become churlish.

Flying carpet? Bedroom scatter rugs are a treat for chilly tootsies, but they should be skidproof. Either buy rugs with a nonskid backing or place a nonskid pad under each rug. Spring for a thin—between ⅛ and 1/16 inch thick—natural rubber or latex pad, since other types can stain or discolor wood floors.

Playful pulls. Tennis balls cut in half, wooden alphabet letters or blocks, even small animal figurines, all make great drawer pulls. Just remove the existing pull and screw the new one to the drawer.

Mural, mural on the wall.
If your child's taste runs to murals and you live near a local college, call the art department with your specifications. The school may be able to put together a team who can do the job professionally and inexpensively.

Tubs, Tiles, and Vanities

White is right. Not only are white tubs, toilets, and sinks less expensive than their colored counterparts, they never go out of style.

Tile taboos. White grout between floor or wall tiles is tough to keep sparkling; black tiles are a magnet for water and soap marks.

Accessorizing the vanity. For a luxury look at a not-so-luxurious price, choose a stock vanity cabinet from a home center, then upgrade it with a solid-surface countertop and brass fixtures.

More hang-ups. Need more space to hang washcloths and hand towels? Mount long drawer pulls on the false front of your vanity cabinet, and loop the towels through them.

Cut tiling time with a tub surround kit. It includes four tiled and grouted panels that are glued and screwed to the walls, along with special trim pieces that hide the seams.

Remodeling and Upgrading

When replacing a vanity sink with a pedestal sink, make sure the floor under the vanity is finished before you rip it out. Otherwise, you'll have to replace the floor as well as the sink.

Larger than life. Install a chair rail to make a small bath seem bigger. The horizontal line of the rail draws the eye around the perimeter of the room, giving the illusion of greater space. The effect can be amplified by painting the wall under the chair rail the same color as the floor and treating the wall above with a lighter color scheme.

Glass-block walls open up a bathroom but can be hard for do-it-yourselfers to install. An easy alternative is a mortarless or grid system. Mortarless blocks are installed with vinyl channels and silicone; in grid systems, the blocks fit into an aluminum grid and are sealed with silicone.

SAFE AND SMART

When renovating or redesigning a bathroom, here are some tips that will save you money and aggravation.

➤ When adding a bathroom, try to back it up to a kitchen or another bath, so the new bathroom can share the existing plumbing wall.

➤ Move partition walls instead of bearing walls.

➤ When installing a new tub (or a whirlpool), consult an architect or engineer to find out if joists or flooring need to be beefed up to support the added weight.

Adding on. Double your storage space by equipping a vanity cabinet with a lazy susan. Before buying one, measure the interior space of the cabinet, allowing for drainpipe clearances.

Skirt the issue. If you have a freestanding bathroom sink with metal legs, create additional storage space underneath by attaching a fabric skirt to the underside of the sink with Velcro.

FILE IT

Sizing a bathroom

If you're planning to carve a new bathroom out of another space in your house, it will be helpful to know the common sizes.

Type	Size	What it contains
Half bath or powder room	4 x 5 or 3 x 7	Sink and toilet
Three-quarter bath	About 26 square feet	Sink, toilet, stall shower
Full bath combination	5 x 7 feet minimum	Sink, toilet, tub/shower

Done with mirrors. Small bathrooms with windows will look larger if you install a full-wall mirror opposite or adjacent to the window wall. The mirror will effectively double the light, the view, and the size.

Cleanups

It makes cents. After an automatic toilet-bowl cleaning device runs dry, wash the dispenser thoroughly and refill it with ordinary household bleach. The bleach will keep the bowl sparkling while it saves you some money.

Run a squeegee over the walls of the shower enclosure after each use to cut down on soap scum buildup. This is particularly fun for kids to do.

Defogging the mirror. Keep a bathroom mirror from fogging up in cold weather by spreading a little shaving cream on it and wiping it off with a tissue or paper towel.

The tidy bowl. Pouring liquid toilet-bowl cleaner directly into the toilet defeats the purpose. Turn off the water at the supply line and flush; then apply cleaner to a brush and swish around the empty bowl.

The Laundry Room

Location, location. Hook up new laundry appliances near where dirty clothes collect—in the kitchen, a closet in the family room, or on the second floor next to the bedrooms.

Leak control. If your laundry is located on the second floor, prevent water damage to your floor's finish (and the ceilings below) by placing the washer on a specially made fiberglass overflow pan, which is available at most home centers.

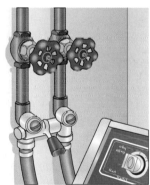

A needed option. When installing a new washer, ask the plumber to outfit it with a single-handle ball-valve lever to prevent potential floods. Depress the lever, and it turns off the water to the machine. Raise it and the water's back on. As a bonus, shutting off the water when you're done with the washer discourages mineral buildup in the water lines, which can restrict water flow.

Save a buck on duct. Situate a clothes dryer on an outside wall, if possible. You'll spend less money on the ductwork needed to vent it to the outside.

The ergonomic dryer. To minimize stooping while loading and removing clothes, set a dryer on a platform about 15 inches tall. If the platform has a built-in drawer, you can stow dryer sheets and other supplies inside.

Stacking up? A full-size stackable washer/dryer combo requires a space 31 inches deep (you have to leave room for the hoses, pipes, and ductwork), 27 inches wide, and 73 inches tall. Smaller models take up less space but do less laundry per load.

Faux softener. If you've run out of fabric softener, a cup of white vinegar added during the rinse cycle will do the job without leaving your clothes smelling sour.

An important bulletin. Hang a cork bulletin board in the laundry space to hold care tags from clothes that need special attention and extra buttons that come with new garments.

Down the hatch. If you're designing or remodeling a house, a built-in laundry chute is a great step-saver. Locate it in a bedroom, bathroom, or hallway. Keep small children safe by raising the opening on the wall and limiting the opening to no more than 12 inches across.

Eliminate a sorting step by using two baskets to double as laundry hampers. Place whites in a white basket and colored clothing in a colored basket.

Detaining drips. Drying clothes on a shower rod often leaves puddles on the floor. Add a second rod over the middle of the tub to confine runoff to the tub.

Save a step. Mount a hanging bar over the dryer, and whisk drip-dry and permanent-press clothes right from the dryer onto hangers to avoid wrinkling.

Drop-down board. Hitch a folding ironing board to the back of a door, and ditch its old bulky counterpart. Some models are hardware-free and just hook over the door—the board is held steady in the drop-down position by suction cups that are pressed against the door.

Setting Up a Home Office

Mark boundaries. If you don't have the luxury of setting up shop in a separate room, create the illusion of having a distinct space by setting off the working area with a barrier made from screens, shelving units, or cabinetry. Arrange the barrier so that it will shield the office as much as possible from the dominant traffic pattern in the rest of the house.

Set apart. When decorating an office-within-a-room, make use of an area rug to help define the space and task lights to distinguish its working atmosphere from the space around it.

Change the pace. Another way to separate a work-space from the rest of the room is to make its surroundings visually distinct. Paint or paper the office walls with a color or pattern that is harmonious with, but different from, what is on the other walls in the room.

FILE IT

Create a floor plan
Here's how to translate space needs and ideas onto paper—and to make sure everything will fit.

1. Measure the proposed space; then draw the walls on ¼-inch graph paper, using a scale of ½ inch to 1 foot. (For larger spaces, you can use a scale of ¼ inch to 1 foot.)

2. Draw in doors, windows, closets, and any existing built-ins.

3. Note outlets, phone jacks, air conditioners, and heaters.

4. Make several copies of the floor plan on a photocopier.

5. Pencil in various floor plans. Include the location of desks, floor lamps, work carts, file cabinets, equipment, couches, and anything else you will need.

6. Make as many revised drawings as necessary until the floor plan looks and feels both comfortable and efficient.

No doze. If possible, keep the office out of your bedroom. Otherwise, whenever you are uneasy about a project or behind schedule, it will be difficult to separate yourself from your work in order to wind down at night.

Think ahead. If you're lucky enough to be adding or remodeling a separate room for your home office, equip it with plenty of electrical outlets. This will make it easier to plug in additional equipment as it is acquired.

A way out. When scouting locations for a home office, consider how often you will host clients and colleagues. If it will be a regular occurrence, try to locate the workspace near an exterior door, so visitors will not have to trot through the main living areas of the house en route to conducting business.

Got only one phone line? You can still conduct business from home by using a phone company service called distinctive ringing. It allows you to set up multiple phone numbers on the same line—each with a different ring pattern. Next time the phone rings, you'll know immediately if it's a personal or a business call.

Phone specs. The phone is a home office lifeline, so plan its position carefully. If you're right-handed, place the phone near your left side as you sit at your desk. Then, if you jot on a pad as you talk, the cord won't pull across your body and your right hand will be free. Left-handers should reverse the position.

The light touch. If you're right-handed, task lighting —which directs light where your vision will be concentrated—should shine over your left shoulder so that your writing hand won't cast shadows on your work. If you're left-handed it should shine over your right shoulder. *Note:* Fluorescent bulbs cast less of a shadow than incandescents.

Save on heating costs. If you are converting an attic or basement space into an office, give the area its own heating source (such as an electric baseboard heater). If the office is to be connected to the central heating, put it on a separate zone so the heat can be shut off at night or when you're out.

Road trip. If you take your office on the road, buy a notebook PC rather than a sub-notebook. The keyboard and display are larger and easier to use.

Furniture and Ergonomics

Desk shapes. The traditional L-shaped work station is efficient for tasks that require spreading out large amounts of paperwork. Keep the computer and other desktop gear on one leg of the "L" and the paperwork, office supplies, and phone on the other.

In the corner. If there is no room for an L-shaped desk, a desk with a corner configuration is a good alternative. The two wings on each side of the main computer area provide space for desktop equipment and paperwork. A corner desk is also great for systems with large monitors, which require extra depth. The downside: You'll always be facing the corner.

Office in a box. Specially designed armoires and credenzas are a good option to consider if your office must "disappear" when you close up shop at night. These all-in-one furniture pieces come in many different styles and contain hidden desks and pull-out keyboard trays. Some even feature fold-away office chairs.

To cut glare, avoid painting office walls white. Instead, choose a pale color that will be easier on the eyes. White is fine for the ceiling, though, since it is out of the field of vision.

At the right angle. Make sure your keyboarding setup is a good fit for you. When seated in your chair, with your feet flat on the floor, do your elbows and knees form right angles? If not, you are inviting discomfort—and possibly debilitating injuries to your back, arms, and legs.

Keyboard keys. Carpal tunnel syndrome is a painful condition that can debilitate the wrists and hands of anyone who does a great deal of keyboarding or other repetitive motions. One key to prevention: Every hour, take a 10-minute break to get away from the keyboard.

Tingle, tingle. It is easy to miss the first symptoms of carpal tunnel syndrome since they usually occur hours after you've finished working. The tip-off is tingling fingers. If this condition occurs at any time, suspect trouble. Untreated, the tingling can turn into stiffness, numbness, and, finally, severe pain.

Take stock. For functional, good-looking storage, combine stock kitchen base and upper cabinets from a home center into a customized wall system. The cost is more reasonable than buying custom office cabinets, and the variety of shelves, drawers, and accessories that are available can be combined into many flexible arrangements.

Down under. Some ergonomists and eye doctors argue that the computer monitor is best placed below—not on top of—the work surface. A few furniture companies are already responding, producing glass-topped desks with a well for the monitor under the glass.

Points of light. When working on a computer, it is important to keep overhead lighting no brighter than the computer screen in order to prevent eyestrain. Fine-tune the overhead light source by installing a dimmer. Turn up the dimmer when reading or doing paperwork, and lower it when working at the screen. Or install task lighting where you need it.

Setting Up an Entertainment Room

Enhance the acoustics of a room by carpeting the floor, bringing in a few cushy pieces of furniture, and hanging canvas paintings on the wall and drapes on the windows. Aside from providing ambiance, these soft surfaces will "capture" sound waves, resulting in clearer, sharper sound quality.

Quick pick. If you have a choice of rooms for a home theater, pick a rectangular one. Sound waves bounce back on themselves in a square room, lowering the acoustic quality.

The dark side. Install light dimmers to make the entertainment room slightly darker than the image on the screen. Also use window treatments to block out outside light.

Go below. Don't bypass the basement when considering locations for a home theater. Below ground level, it is easier to block out the light that can compromise the quality of an image on the screen. To reduce noise interference from living spaces above, install insulation on the walls and ceiling.

Proper placement. The larger the screen, the greater the distance should be between it and the main seating area. For optimal picture quality, plan at least 6 feet between the couch and a screen that is 27 to 31 inches in size, at least 8 feet for a screen that is 32 to 40 inches, and at least 10 feet for a screen that is more than 40 inches.

Back off. Overzealous cleaning of VCR heads can damage them. Some pros suggest you skip a cleanup unless you notice a problem with the tape transmission.

The TV program. Take along a couple of video-cassettes when buying any television, especially a large-screen model. It will give an an accurate idea of what the images will look like on the screen when blown up 5 or 10 times their normal size.

Surrounding sound. It takes six speakers to replicate movie theater sound. The three primary speakers should be placed, facing front, in the center and to the left and right of the TV set. Place the two surround speakers on either side of the room, and the subwoofer on the floor near the TV.

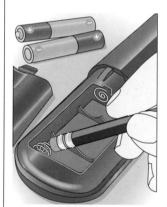

Resurrecting a remote. If new batteries don't bring a dead remote control back to life, try cleaning the contact points gently with an eraser, followed by a spritz of electronic contact cleaner. Reinsert the batteries, and test it again.

Sound Systems
Buyer's guide. If you are on a limited budget, consider a minisystem. If you are building a system with individual components, spend the most on speakers to get the best return on your investment.

FILE IT

Screening those projection TV's
Images on most large-screen TV's (more than 41 inches) are produced by projection instead of by conventional tubes. Models are available with projection from either the front or the rear of the screen.

	Front screen	Rear screen
Ease of installation	Projector hangs from ceiling, so the unit can be installed without ripping out walls.	Space is required behind the screen for the projector, so part of a wall may have to be torn out.
Light level	For the best picture, the room must be totally dark.	The picture remains sharp even if there is some ambient light.
Noise level	Noise from the projector fan can be distracting.	The projector fan noise is muffled by walls or cabinets.

Book smarts. Place books on both sides of bookcase speakers to help balance and absorb the sound.

Assume the position. To maximize the sound, position speakers an equal distance from where you are listening and separate them by at least 6 feet.

Shake it up. Upgrade an average audio system with a subwoofer speaker, which is designed to reproduce the lowest frequencies. Any compact disc or tape will spring to life once you add it to the mix.

CD clean. When cleaning a CD by hand, don't wipe in a circular motion, as is done with vinyl records. It scores the mirrorlike playing surface with dust particles and can cause the laser to read the scratch rather than the music. Wipe outward from the CD's center toward the rim for scratch-free cleaning.

Decks

Building basics. Purchasing pressure-treated wood 2 weeks before building will give the lumber time to dry out and adjust to moisture conditions in the yard. Wood will eventually crack if it is nailed or screwed in place while it is wet.

Vent a deck. To prevent mildew, peeling paint, ice buildup, and rot underneath the roof's drip line, install a roof gutter (see p. 54) or place vents where water dripping from the edge of the roof hits the deck.

A popped nail can be hammered back in, but it will just work its way out again. Instead, remove the nail. Then hammer in a new nail at a slightly different angle, or for a more effective fix, install a galvanized deck screw in the old nail hole.

Spacing out. Align new decking perfectly by placing a nylon felling wedge, used to split logs and firewood, on a joist between the boards. The wedge, available in stores that sell chain saws and related equipment, has smooth sides that won't mar the softest of woods.

Recycling deck boards. If the damage is confined to the top surface of the boards, save money on replacements by flipping the boards over. Use galvanized deck screws to reattach the flip-flopped boards.

Deck Finishes

If you prefer a finish on a wooden deck, select a semi-transparent deck stain. Look for one made to withstand foot traffic (check the label before buying). One coat is usually enough; a second coat may create a film on the surface that will eventually crack and wear away.

Before finishing new deck wood, test to find out if the wood is dry enough to accept stain by applying some to a small spot in an inconspicuous area. After about 15 minutes, most of the stain should be absorbed. If any of the stain beads up, wait a few days and then repeat the test.

Accessorizing the Deck
Light up outdoor steps with low-voltage deck lighting. Simply screw or clip the housings in place on the stairway and run the cord to a transformer that is plugged into an outdoor outlet. For safety's sake, the outlet must be protected by a ground-fault circuit interrupter (GFCI).

Mosquitoes invading your screened-in porch or deck? They could be coming up between the floorboards. If there are cracks between the boards, cut screening to fit joist-to-joist underneath; then staple the edges to both joists and decking.

Continue lighting down the path that leads from the deck by installing solar-powered outdoor lighting. The new models are wireless—just push them into the ground wherever light is needed. The solar energy gathered by their small collection panels during the day is automatically released after dark as a bright, steady beam that will shine for about 6 hours.

Add a lattice "corral" under a deck for storing lawn-care eyesores out of view. Pass by the cheap ¼-inch panels—they are too flimsy. Instead go for ⅜-inch or thicker panels.

Before remodeling the basement, be sure to consult a local building inspector. Building codes vary from region to region, and must be followed carefully in order to avoid unsafe procedures, expensive repairs, and fines. Also review all proposed changes to structural walls with a professional before beginning work, to avoid compromising the house's foundation.

Clever disguise. As an alternative to boxing in steel support posts with wallboard, disguise them with PoleWrap, a covering of slatted oak attached to a fabric backing. Available at most home centers, the covering is good-looking and a snap to install. Stick it onto the posts with construction adhesive.

Design detours. The potential living space in a basement can be chock-full of obstructions such as overhead pipes, ductwork, columns, and posts. Don't be discouraged. Design around the obstructions, fashioning unusual architectural details to hide them. Or paint the offending features in various bright colors to emphasize their own sculptural forms.

Divide and conquer. Depending on the size and condition of your basement, you may choose to remodel only a portion of it instead of the whole area. Concentrate on the section that has the best light and easy access.

Step-by-step remodeling. Details may vary, but basement work is usually done in the following order:
(1) diagnosing and fixing all water/moisture problems
(2) adding outside windows or doors
(3) nailing up framing
(4) installing rough plumbing, heating, and wiring
(5) adding insulation
(6) applying wallboard
(7) finishing ceiling and floor
(8) completing plumbing, heating, and wiring
(9) assembling shelves, cabinets, or built-ins.

Leftover lattice? Turn two pieces of garden lattice into a storage rack by nailing each of them to a pair of basement ceiling joists and anchoring them to the adjoining wall studs. Store long, narrow lightweight objects such as molding or spare pipes by inserting them through the openings in the lattice.

Wine cellar. A basement corner is a perfect place to create storage for wine. Build racks from pieces of plywood or pine, tilted so that the bottles can be stored on their sides. This allows the corks to stay wet and swollen so air won't leak in and spoil the wine. For an authentic touch, trim the racks with the end panels of wooden wine crates.

To be floored. If the basement slab is dry and level, brush on a chemical sealer, then lay tiles—asphalt or vinyl—directly on the slab.

Hardware help. Always attach fasteners for storage units or brackets to solid masonry, not to the mortar in between. Toggle bolts or very short plugs work well on cement block foundations, which are hollow.

FILE IT

The underground: Fixing basement problems

Space below ground level sometimes can be less than comfortable. The following pointers will help to improve the livability of a new basement room.

Access	A window or door on an outside wall is preferable (most codes require at least a window for a bedroom). A walkout can provide daylight and solar heat as well as easy access.
Dampness	Divert outdoor runoff by improving the efficiency of gutters and increasing the angle of the ground slope away from the foundation. Halt groundwater seepage by building a perimeter drainage system around the foundation. (If the area is used only for storage, a sump pump might be the best solution.)
Headroom	Codes for minimum ceiling heights vary, but the most common allowance is 7½ feet.
Heating	A separate system of electric baseboard heating is recommended, since the additional space may overload a central heating system. The thermostat can be turned down when the room is not in use.
Insulation	Insulate the walls and floor to keep basement rooms dry and comfortable.
Lighting	For natural lighting, deepen window wells or enlarge existing windows where possible. For electric lighting, consult an electrician to ensure that wiring plans meet safety specifications.

Look up for storage. If your garage has a high ceiling, attach a storage loft to the wall plates. Use the loft to stash away all the objects that usually lean against the walls and spill out onto the floor. A clearance of at least 96 inches above the floor allows adults—not to mention a minivan—plenty of headroom.

Safe climbing. Decrease the chance of falling by climbing up to an overhead garage loft on a extension ladder, not vertical steps attached to the wall.

Folding workbench. If there is no extra room anywhere for a workshop, install a fold-down workbench in the garage. The bench top can be made from a plain-surface solid-core door. Fasten it to the wall with a piano hinge approximately 3 feet above the floor (or whatever height falls midway between your own waist and hips). For legs, attach two 2 x 4's to the outside corners with door hinges so that they can be tucked underneath the bench when it folds down.

Cleaning up concrete. A sealed concrete floor in the garage usually requires only an annual cleaning and a new coat of sealer. If you choose to paint the floor, use acrylic latex paint, not an oil-base masonry paint.

Follow the yellow lines. Need help staying uncluttered? Organize everything in the garage the way you want it, then spray-paint yellow "parking space" outlines around the items on the garage floor and against the walls. The outlines will remind you—and the rest of the family—where everything goes.

Catcher in the carport. Until a leaking car can be fixed, protect the garage floor with a drip pan made by laying a sheet of corrugated cardboard on a large cookie sheet or jelly-roll pan. Slide the pan under the site of the leak, and replace the cardboard as needed.

Auto diagnosis. Line the garage floor with newspaper before pulling in the car. The next time you back it out, check the papers for drips and stains that may reveal leaks in the car's various systems. Dark greasy droplets mean an oil leak; clear oily stains may be brake fluid; red drips could come from transmission fluid; and those greenish puddles are most likely to be coolant.

Night moves. Inspect your car's front and rear lights every time you head out for a nighttime drive by setting up one mirror at an inside front corner of the garage and another at the inside back corner. Position them so you can see a pair of lights in each mirror.

Bumper room. Nail scraps of carpet or pieces of an old tire to posts and other obstructions that the car or its flung open doors—might inadvertently crash into or scrape against.

Easy entry. When purchasing an automatic garage door opener, consider buying a model that has a built-in keypad entry feature. You won't need a transmitter or key to get bikes, gardening tools, or pool accessories out of the garage; instead, you simply punch in a code on the keypad to open the door.

Pinup board. Instead of throwing away an old dartboard, target it for the garage. It makes a great communications center for any family that is constantly coming and going by car. Tack up messages with the darts; they won't get lost the way pushpins do.

FILE IT

Smooth operation: Fixing a sluggish garage door
When the door won't open smoothly, check the following elements—one of them is likely to be the culprit.

Hardware	Have the bolts or screws on the rollers worked loose? This could cause the door to get stuck or to wobble in its track.
Rollers	Have the rollers jumped the overhead track? The track may be bent.
Lubrication	Are the hinges, rollers, or other moving parts corroded? Try oiling them lightly.
Springs	Have the springs lost tension? Have the doors serviced professionally.

Increase storage space by decreasing the number of things you have to store. Use the 2-year rule to help: If you haven't worn or used it in 2 years, out it goes.

Less luggage. Save space when storing luggage by placing smaller pieces inside larger ones.

Loaded luggage. Pack away off-season clothing in pieces of luggage and slide them under the bed. If you take a trip, temporarily unpack the clothing and stack it in laundry baskets.

Create a junk pile. Open mail by the garbage can or recycling pile and drop junk mail right in.

Windowsill solution. Attach both ends of a curtain rod to the casing several inches above the sill, and you have a window box for potted plants.

A paper trail. Buy a roll of paper towels or toilet paper in a color you don't use and place it at the back of a cabinet. If that roll shows up in the bathroom or kitchen, it's time to stock up.

Declutter a hall or kitchen by storing children's school notices, bills, and other pending paperwork out of sight in a vertical file (or even in a retired napkin holder). Stash the file in a convenient base cabinet.

Up against the wall. Whether it's miniature chairs, dishware, or salt and pepper shakers, save space by mounting collectibles directly on the wall. Use shadow boxes, hooks, pegs, or shelves.

Open up a drawer. Install dividers and organizers in drawers to keep things in order. Items won't shift around or get mixed up when the drawer is opened and closed.

Going undercover. Store extra blankets or furniture throws between the mattress and the bedspring.

Furniture fixes. When shopping for furniture, look for ottomans with removable tops, coffee and end tables with built-in magazine storage and slide-out surfaces for drinks, headboards that double as storage trunks or bookcases, and pine benches with lift-up seats for hats and gloves.

Extend hallway storage by replacing a console table with a credenza. The look is equally handsome, but the credenza lets you conceal a multitude of items, including keys, hats, gloves, umbrellas, and mail. Topping the credenza with a hutch or rack provides even more storage.

Bathrooms

Towel basket. If you have an empty corner in the bathroom, fill it with a large basket loaded with rolled towels. Not only is this arrangement pretty and convenient, it frees up lots of space in the linen closet.

Separate but equal. If several people use the same bathroom, assign each individual his or her own vanity drawer. This will keep clutter down and encourage everyone to be responsible for replacing his or her own possessions.

Overhead storage. Increase bathroom space easily with over-the-toilet shelving. Inexpensive units made of wood, wicker, plastic, or steel are perfect for holding towels and grooming products.

All hung up. Many grooming gadgets, such as electric shavers and hair dryers, have hooks for hanging. To free up drawer space yet keep the bathroom organized, install a rack made from a wood backing strip and cup hooks. Then hang up the appliances.

Old kitchen cabinets are wonderful storage vehicles for attics, basements, or garages. The combination of drawers, shelves, and cabinet space will hold many different types of household items.

Store bathroom items in vinyl shoe pouches, wire-coated baskets, and shower caddies mounted directly on the bathroom wall instead of in the shower.

Bag bath toys. If small children and adults share the same bathroom, store bathroom toys in a mesh bag with a drawstring. Hook the string of the bag over the shower head, and the water from the toys will drip right down the drain.

Bedrooms

Down under. Install four rollers on an old dresser drawer, fill it up, and roll it under the bed.

Adding a bar. Install a rod on a bedroom door and hang your bath towel on it to dry. The rod eliminates clutter, reduces bathroom moisture, and humidifies the bedroom.

Head of the bed. For attractive, ample storage, move out a headboard and night tables and move in a combination of stock cabinets and open shelving units. Available through many home centers, the cabinets can be combined to meet individual needs and are less expensive than custom built-ins.

Shelving

Bolstering a bookcase. Installing a wall-length floor-to-ceiling bookcase? You may have to strengthen the floor first. The average floor is built to withstand a load of 50 pounds per square foot, but the load of a filled bookcase is easily greater. Talk to a building inspector, carpenter, or an engineer before proceeding.

Good support. To prevent shelving from collapsing, a good rule of thumb is to add a support every 30 inches along the length of a ¾-inch-thick shelf. The heavier the load, the closer the supports should be.

Neat knobs. Make a unique coat, hat, and umbrella holder for an entryway by attaching several decorative doorknobs to a piece of wood. Insert a dowel into the shank of each knob, drill the wood to accept the dowels, then glue the dowels in place.

FILE IT

Shelf lives: How the materials stack up

Here are some common shelving materials. Each has pros and cons. Hardwood is always more expensive than softwood, in both solid and plywood forms. If you use plywood, remember that you'll have to cut the shelving out of 4 x 8 sheets. Particleboard is generally not recommended for shelving.

Type	Advantages	Disadvantages
No. 2 pine boards	Easy to work with; accepts paint well (seal knots before painting).	Boards may be warped. Hand-pick flat, straight ones with few knots.
Clear pine	Same as No. 2, but no knots.	More expensive than No. 2.
Hardwood boards	Attractive, especially when stained or finished with clear finish. Birch and maple may also be painted.	Harder to work with than softwood.
Birch plywood	Easy to work with; can be painted or coated with clear finish.	Hard to stain. Raw edges must be covered with either molding or veneer tape.
Oak plywood	Easy to work with; easy to stain.	Difficult to paint. Must cover exposed raw edges as above.
Fir plywood	Easy to work with. Grade AB can be painted or stained. Rougher grades (CD) are cheaper.	CD grades don't accept finishes well. Edges must be covered as above.

Kitchens

Antique armoires make great storage units in kitchens with a period or country style. Make sure that the shelves within can withstand the new loads they will have to bear.

Wine cellar in a cabinet. Take out the shelving from an existing cabinet (pick one that's well away from any heat source or cooking appliance). Install in its place two pieces of plywood, each slotted halfway through and assembled diagonally so that they form an X. Each quarter of the cabinet can then hold bottles lying horizontally.

Cookbook collectors can save space by looking for visible—but out-of-the-way—places to store little-used volumes. One solution is to mount shelves above doorways and windows.

Avoid nesting. Stacking pots or mixing bowls within each other may save space, but it takes too much time to dig them out when any item except the one on top is needed. In the most efficient kitchens, containers are stored where they can be grasped immediately.

Proper placement. When stocking kitchen cabinets, think creatively. Why store all the cookware in the same place? Stash the pasta pot—and any other pot routinely filled with water—near the sink instead of the stove.

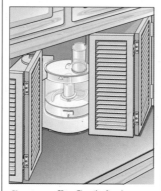

Custom fit. Can't find an appliance garage to suit your needs? Paint several small shutters, hinge them together, and hide the appliances behind them.

Light the way. In a tall, deep pantry closet, a door-operated switch is the ultimate convenience. The light automatically comes on when the door is opened. Best of all, when your hands are full, the closing door hits the button and automatically switches off the light.

Number it. Number-code those pile-ups of plastic container tops and bottoms so they can be put together in a flash.

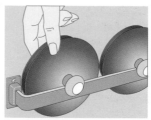

Putting a lid in it. If pot and pan lids are creating a mess in a cabinet, mount an ordinary towel rack on the back of the cabinet door and organize the lids in a nice neat row.

Spin the wheel. For tough-to-reach corners in a cupboard, a lazy susan will do the trick. You won't have to pull out half the cupboard's contents to locate an item.

Free up drawer space by placing aluminum foil, wax paper, and plastic wrap under the sink in a six- or eight-pack plastic soda holder, or beneath an upper cabinet in a tilt-out drawer.

Drawer space at a minimum? Put utensils in a large heavy pitcher rather than in a jumble in the drawer. A lightweight pitcher will tumble over every time you remove an item.

Wire wall storage. A vinyl-coated wire grid wall system is not only waterproof—a handy characteristic in a kitchen—it is snazzier than plain old perfboard. Equip it with a variety of handy hooks, baskets, and other clip-on accessories.

Bag it. Stuff those plastic fruit and vegetable bags from the grocer's into an empty paper towel tube. The tube looks a lot neater than a pile of bags, and you'll be surprised at how many it holds.

How to brown bag it? To organize a bevy of brown grocery bags, clamp them in an old wooden pants hanger and hang them in a closet.

Closets

Plan first. Weed out a closet before reorganizing it. Measure everything that needs to fit back in, then translate these measurements into a design on graph paper. Then, and only then, go out and purchase a closet organizing system.

Hang time. Store holiday decorations out of the way by hanging them inside a closet, above the closet door.

Don't make the cut. Many wire shelving systems are based on a 12-foot shelf module. Don't try to cut down shelves that are too long for your closet with a hacksaw; you'll wind up with sharp, jagged ends. Ask your supplier to cut the units to the right length.

What's included? Not all closet organizing systems include the mounting hardware in the price. When comparing prices, find out exactly what you will get for your money.

Fold what you can. Folding clothing, in most cases, will save space. Fold all the clothing you can, stack it in piles, then measure the piles to determine the amount of shelving needed to accommodate them.

Smart hang-ups. Attach a piece of Velcro to the end of a hanger to keep thin straps from sliding off it. Sew a big loop at the neck of kids' jackets to increase the odds that they will be hung up rather than finding a home on the floor or a newel post.

The eyes have it. Save time by placing the most frequently used items in a closet at eye level.

A favorable reflection. Glue a square mirror tile on a closet's ceiling to inspect the top shelf without climbing a stepladder.

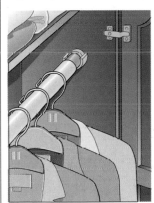

Relieving the load. When the clothes rod in a closet sags under too much weight, replace it with a length of galvanized pipe placed inside PVC piping. Remove the manufacturer's name from the PVC pipe with lacquer thinner.

Color-coded linens. Select a different color or pattern of bed linen for each family member. Whenever a fresh set of linens is needed, it will be easy to pick out the pieces for a particular bed from the linen closet.

SAFE AND SMART

➤ Locate closet drawers below eye level so you can see the contents at a glance.

➤ Use clear plastic bins and boxes in closets so you'll be able to see the contents without having to open them.

➤ Place unused hangers on one end of the clothing rod to make them easy to locate.

➤ Remove empty dry-cleaning bags and hangers to save space.

Weatherproof closets. Cope with wet stuff in an entry closet by installing a boot tray over a plastic pan. Hang wicker or wire containers on the closet door; they allow ventilation for faster drying of damp gloves and hats. (Some baskets can be folded up when they're not in use.) Install a grille in the closet door to increase ventilation, or replace it with a louvered door.

Neat clothes. If you want to keep clothes uncluttered, file tiny notches about 1 inch apart in a wooden clothing rod; the hangers won't slide together.

Basements

Stud space. Use the empty spaces between wall studs in a basement to house narrow shelves for small items. Place the shelves on wooden cleats nailed to the studs. Since moisture can be a problem in many basements, don't store things there that can be damaged by dampness.

For deeper, wider shelves between studs, notch out a piece of ¾-inch plywood to fit around two or three studs; then support the plywood with brackets made from 2 x 4's. Be sure to use drywall screws to secure the whole assembly.

Dampness protection. To protect a storage cabinet in the basement from moisture, elevate it on blocks of pressure-treated wood. In addition, attach 1 x 2 furring strips to the concrete wall, so the cabinet will not be nailed directly to the wall. Finally, place a sheet of polyethylene behind and under the cabinet before securing it in place.

Step-up storage. The under-the-stair area of the basement is often underutilized. Divide the space into bays; then equip each bay with organizers or drawers. Try to use the whole depth of the stairs.

Steps open at the back? Mount plastic bins or dishpans on wooden guides in the small spaces right underneath the stair treads. Use the bins to store small fasteners. Just make sure the front of the bin is set well back from the tread.

The long view. The space between basement ceiling joists is perfect for storing long lengths of leftover building materials. Nail racks, made from pieces of scrap lumber, to the joists.

Strip of tools. Organize tools in your workshop space on a magnetic knife holder. Press chisels and other small metal tools onto the holder to keep them out of the workbench shuffle.

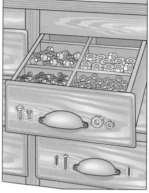

Proper ID. A multidrawer organizer can hold all those nuts and bolts, but how do you know what is in each drawer? Just tape or glue one of the items to the outside front of the drawer, and the contents can be identified at a glance.

Staying put. If your perfboard hooks fall out of their holes easily, solve the annoying fallout with two-piece perfboard hangers. Constructed of a hook and an anchor, the improved hangers, available in home centers, stay put when the tools are pulled off.

Rules for tools. Those who do a lot of woodworking should forgo perfboard and open-rack storage systems and store those tools behind cabinet doors. Tools left out in the open pick up a coating of sawdust and need to be cleaned frequently.

Laundry logistics. If the washing machine is in the cellar, prevent loose buttons from becoming lost in the dungeon by storing them in a magnetic key box (available at auto supply stores). Stick the box on the side of the washer, and every time a stray shows up, pop it in.

Garages

Centralizing stuff. When tackling the next garage cleanup, don't just stick things where they happen to fit. Try reorganizing the space into "centers," the way a kitchen is organized. Group together all the items used for specific activities, like sports, car repair, gardening, and woodworking.

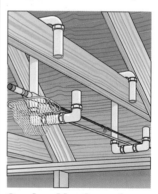

Overhead hooks made from glued-together pieces of PVC pipe make cumbersome items like gardening tools and fishing rods go up, up, and out of the way. Suspend a hook over a tie beam, or attach it to a rope from the ceiling.

Banking a bike. Store a lightweight bike off the garage floor with a couple of screw hooks attached to studs or joists. A long winter's nap on cold concrete could result in cracked, flat tires in the spring.

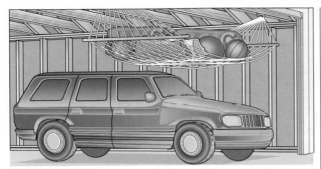

An old hammock strung over the car in a garage bay can be a clever resting place for sports balls, empty duffel bags, and other bulky lightweight items. Attach the hammock with screw eyes that are secured to the joists.

Reel organization. Cut two notches in a length of 2 x 4, mount it on a garage wall, push on a couple of hose reels, and there will be no more games of jump rope with long extension cords again. The cords unroll smoothly from the reels when needed, held in place by the notches. Or the reel can be popped off and moved to a new location.

Got a hang-up? Create space by hanging a shoe bag on the garage wall or on the inside door of a cabinet to store miscellaneous items. You can also use the spine of a three-ring loose-leaf binder as a catchall: the rings can be opened and closed for hanging smaller, lighter items.

Velcro rescue. Sets of self-adhesive strips of strong Velcro are designed to hang various hand tools or larger items—there's even a set made for gardening tools. Put up a few in the garage and watch clutter disappear.

Hosing reel. Turn an empty 5-gallon paint bucket into a garden hose reel. Just screw the bottom of the bucket to the garage wall; then wrap the hose around it.

Go-go storage. Mount heavy-duty casters on tool carts, workbenches, potting benches, and other in-garage cabinet modules. Snuggle those modules against the wall while the cars are inside, then roll them out for use after the cars have been driven out.

Corraling garbage cans. Prevent garbage cans from blowing or tipping over by securing them to the side of the garage with bungee cords. Install two screw eyes into the wall on either side of the can. Then wrap the cord around the middle of the can, hooking each end of the cord into the eyes.

Attics

Attic sense. Since the basement and garage are usually easier to get to than the attic, store frequently used items in those more accessible spaces. Save all the seasonal items, or those items that you will probably never use but can't bear to throw out, for the attic.

Plastic storage bins are the best choice for storing clothing in an attic, and not just because they allow the contents to be seen at a glance. Cardboard boxes and trash bags make a good home for vacationing mice.

Miles of aisles. Don't just heap stuff in piles in the attic. Instead, make boxes and bins more accessible by arranging them in rows perpendicular to the attic ceiling. Leave enough aisle space between rows for easy maneuvering. And label everything so that when a container is needed, it can be easily identified.

Highs and lows. Temperature swings tend to be more pronounced in the attic, since it is usually above the house's insulation. These fluctuations will devastate books, videos, and photographs, so find another place for them.

FILE IT

The well-designed garage
When planning or rethinking garage storage, here are some points to store away.

Minimum clearance. There should a minimum of 3 feet between cars in a two-car garage, 3 feet between a car and the side walls, 2 feet between the car and the garage door, and 1 foot between the car and the front wall.

Maximum storage. Build hanging shelves or wall-mounted cabinets around the contour of your car's hood and roof. For safe parking, fasten a rubber ball to a cord with a screw eye, and hang the ball so that it will bounce against your windshield when the car is in the right place.

An open-and-shut case. When space is at a minimum in a garage, think tilt-out bins, roll-down window shades (installed on the front of cabinets or other furniture), or sliding doors instead of conventional doors.

FILE IT

Tool time: How to fill up a toolbox

The tools below make a good starter set; add the italicized tools as finances allow.

Measuring and marking	Hammering and prying
25-ft. tape measure	16-oz. curved-claw hammer
Combination square	Rubber mallet
Carpenter's level	1/32- and 3/32-in. nail sets
Chalk line	Flat pry bar
Awl	20-oz. framing hammer
Steel framing square	Cat's-paw nail puller
Plumb bob	Crowbar
100-ft. steel tape measure	

Cutting and shaping	Fastening
Utility knife	Standard and Phillips screwdrivers
Crosscut saw	6-in. long-nose pliers
Hacksaw	5- and 8-in. adjustable wrenches
Coping saw	Allen wrench set
Block plane	Socket wrench set
1/2-in. wood chisel	Several clamps
Sandpaper	Groove-joint pliers
Flat file	Diagonal-cutting pliers
1¼-in. putty knife	Electric drill
5- or 6-in. taping knife	Locking pliers
Caulking gun	Staple gun
Wire brush	3/16- and 1/2-in. nut drivers
Sharpening stone and oil	More clamps (you can never have too many)
1- and 1½-in. wood chisels	Open-end and box wrenches
Wider taping knives	Deep sockets for socket wrench

Hand Tools

Discourage rust. Throw some charcoal or a couple of pieces of chalk into a toolbox to absorb moisture and discourage rust.

Just one look. Store nails, screws, and countless other fasteners in clear glass jars, rather than cans, so you can see what you have at a quick glance.

Powder power. Dip a screwdriver tip in some scouring powder before attacking a screw. The powder gives the tool increased holding power in a slick screw slot.

Power steering. Slip a slit tennis ball over a screwdriver handle for extra turning power.

Keeping a handle on it. When replacing a loose wooden handle with a new one, place the new handle in a warm oven to dry the wood. Then install it; moisture from the air will cause it to swell for a tight fit.

Get it straight. Keep a nailhead straight when driving it home by placing one end of a horseshoe magnet right next to it. The attraction between metal and magnet will allow you to hammer it straight in.

Pulling a long nail is easier if you rest the hammerhead on a block of wood. The wood provides necessary leverage to withdraw the nail.

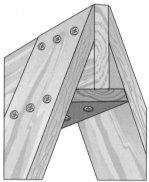

Space-saving sawhorses. Knock together a few stacking sawhorses from ¾-inch-thick lumber, drywall screws, and yellow glue. Add a hardwood block as shown to strengthen the joint.

Buttering up a saw. Apply a light coat of paste wax to a handsaw blade. It protects the metal teeth and eases them through wood.

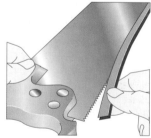

To keep saw teeth out of harm's way, slide plastic report-cover spines over the blades of your handsaws.

Finger-tight. Tighten a hacksaw blade with your fingers, not with pliers or a wrench; if the blade is too tight, it will break in the cut.

Wrenching experience.
When loosening a very tight nut or bolt, push the wrench with your open palm rather than grasping it with your hand. If the nut suddenly loosens or the tool slips off, you won't smash or scrape your knuckles.

Getting leverage. Place a small piece of pipe over the handle of an adjustable wrench to provide more length and leverage on a stubborn job.

On the level. Lengthen a level by attaching a straight board to it with a piece of electrical tape (duct tape will cause bumps).

Pencil it in. Mark off 1-inch increments on a carpenter's pencil to make rough measurements quickly. It's more accurate than eyeballing, yet faster than dragging out a tape measure or ruler.

Short cuts. Cut string, rope, or tape in a jiffy by running them over a handy cutting strip. Cut off the metal strip from a box of plastic wrap and tack it to the end of a workbench. Just make sure the tips of the teeth are flush with the tabletop.

Power Tools

No accident. Tape the chuck key of a drill near the plug. You'll always know where it is and will virtually eliminate accidents because you'll have to pull the plug when changing drill bits.

In the can. Secure an empty 35mm film canister next to the plug of an extension cord to hold a grounding plug. The adapter will be nearby if you have to plug into a two-slot outlet.

Tight fit. If the plug of a power tool cord comes unplugged from an extension cord, bend in one prong a little to snug up the fit.

Seamless sanding. If the belt on a sander breaks apart at its seam because it was installed backward, give one of the new seamless belts a spin. It's designed to work no matter which way it's installed.

Shop vac not sucking up?
Increase the vacuum's suction with a piece of self-adhesive weatherstripping placed on the inside of the lid where it joins the tank edge. Use weatherstripping that is ⅜ inch wide and ¼ inch thick.

To drill an angled hole, first drill through a block of hardwood, then cut the bottom of the block to the desired angle. Hold the guide on the wood with one hand and drill through it with the other.

In the bag. Cut down on cleanup when drilling through plaster or wallboard by taping a garbage bag below the area in which you'll be drilling. Then drill above the tape, and the debris will fall right into the bag, not on the floor.

For a perfectly vertical hole every time, use a drill guide made by nailing together two ¾-inch wood blocks measuring 1½ inches high and 2 inches long. When drilling, just run the bit down the inside corner.

Straight-on drilling.
Keep a bit straight when drilling horizontally by mounting a ¼ inch washer on the shank of the bit. If the washer slides up or down, you know you're off course.

Save the bit. Hardwood must be predrilled before inserting nails or screws, to prevent the wood from splitting. Save wear and tear on drill bits by predrilling with a nail of the same size (a 4d or 6d finishing nail, for example). Before you chuck the nail in the drill, trim off the head with nippers.

Cord control. Corral the loops on a long power tool cord by slipping a piece of PVC pipe over it to hold the loops in place.

Stingers and Biters

Dry out. Depopulate mosquitoes by clearing away anything that can hold stagnant water—empty flowerpots, wheelbarrows, sandbox covers, wading pools, old tires, and so on.

Pesty puddles. If your property remains puddly for a few days after a heavy rainstorm, you're inviting a mosquito infestation. Either build up the low areas with clean fill, then cover with topsoil and seed, or contaminate the puddles with a few drops of dish detergent—which will kill any mosquito eggs that are laid there.

Sleep well. To prevent mosquitoes from stinging you while you're asleep, dab a little citronella oil on the headboard of the bed.

To remove a small wasp nest from under a roof eave, wait until night, when the insects are inactive; then knock down the nest with a long pole. The wasps will look for a new home.

Sweetening up wasps. Cut a little hole into the lid of an empty margarine container, pour in a little sugar water, snap on the lid, and set the tub a good distance away from the picnic table. Wasps will be attracted to the sweet water and will get stuck inside the tub.

Destroying the colony. A potful of hot, soapy water poured down the hole of an in-ground yellow jacket nest will effectively destroy the colony. But here again, do your work after dark, to make sure all the insects are inside the nest.

Pesky Pests

Blowing off flies. To keep flies out of a room, aim a house fan at the doorway. Houseflies have hairs on their bodies that are ultra-sensitive to air currents, and they usually won't risk traveling through moving air.

Smart swatting. During takeoff, a housefly travels slightly backward, so aim the swatter just behind the fly. As the frightened fly takes flight, it will likely run right into the swatter.

In mothballs. Placing a few mothballs in the bottom of a garbage can will send flies packing.

A cedar lining. Facing a closet interior with cedar will protect its contents from moth damage and provide a fresh whiff of cedar smell every time you open the door. For the quickest job, use roll cedar—it's thin and can be cut to size with regular scissors, then glued to the walls with contact cement or yellow carpenter's glue.

The smell of success. If you can no longer smell cedar when opening a cedar closet, rub some sandpaper over the wood to open the pores and release a fresh moth-repelling whiff.

Pest repellents. Turning away pest and insects at the door is easier than evicting them once they've moved into your home. Below are the most likely ports of entry; plug them up with caulk, siding or sheet metal, or metal screening.

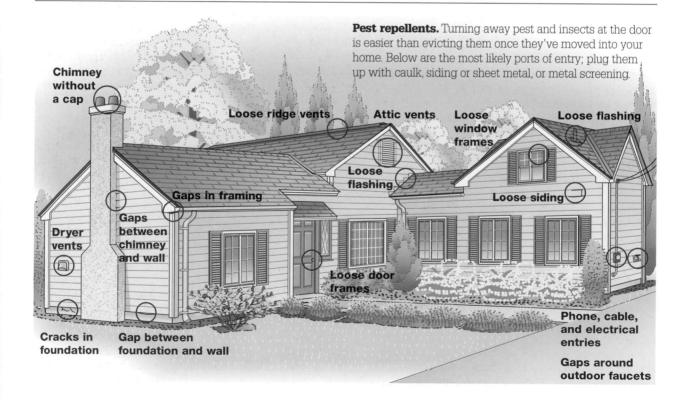

Chimney without a cap

Loose ridge vents

Attic vents

Loose window frames

Loose flashing

Loose flashing

Gaps in framing

Loose siding

Gaps between chimney and wall

Dryer vents

Loose door frames

Cracks in foundation

Gap between foundation and wall

Phone, cable, and electrical entries

Gaps around outdoor faucets

SAFE AND SMART

What's your poison? No matter what you use, there is a protocol to keep it from poisoning your family or your food.

➤ Store poison on a high shelf away from food and clothing or in a locked cabinet, not under the kitchen sink.

➤ Make sure food and utensils don't get contaminated with mist when spraying.

➤ Wear a respirator mask and protective clothing. Wash all exposed skin immediately after spraying.

➤ Place all bait-type poisons out of the reach of pets and children.

➤ Extinguish the pilot light on a gas stove before activating an insect bomb.

Bag it. Don't store empty grocery bags (or cardboard boxes), or you risk stocking your shelves with cockroaches as well as groceries. Because roaches thrive on paper and glue, the bags are often infested with eggs, if not with live roaches.

Jar roaches. An empty jam jar filled with a little beer, a few banana slices, and a couple of drops of anise extract makes an effective roach trap. Wrap the outside of the jar with masking tape to help the roaches climb up, and smear a line of petroleum jelly around the inside of the rim to keep them from climbing out.

Go fishing. Build a trap that lures and kills silverfish. Press a strip of adhesive tape onto the side of a small straight-walled glass, then shake about ¼ cup of flour into the glass. The insects will walk up the tape, drop into the flour, and get stuck there.

To debug houseplants, press a garlic clove into the soil at the root of the plant. Cut the shoots back if the garlic sprouts.

Home Wreckers

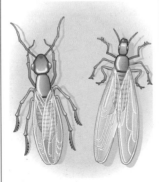

Identifying the invader. Carpenter ants and winged termites are both black, but it's easy to tell the difference. Carpenter ants (left) have segmented bodies and elbowed antennae; termites (right) look like black rice grains with legs and sport straight antennas.

The first line of defense against carpenter ants or termites is to repair any roof or plumbing leaks that could add moisture to your home. Neither pest will take up residence in your home without a source of moisture to invite them in.

No entry. A carpenter ant problem can often be brought under control by cutting off the entry point to your home. For a nontoxic detour, try a line of chili powder, bonemeal, or powdered charcoal as a barrier.

The last supper. Treat worker carpenter ants to a tasty meal, and they will unwittingly poison their entire colony. On an index card, mix a sprinkling of boric acid into a spoonful of mint-apple jelly; then place the card out of the reach of pets and children (but near the colony, if you know its location). Within a couple of days, you should notice fewer ants.

Raccoons and Rodents

Banish bandits. Raccoons hate the smell of ammonia. Before locking down the lid of garbage cans on garbage night, sprinkle some ammonia over the trash bags. Raccoons will think twice before scavenging at your house.

Squirrel zapper. If squirrels continually invade the bird feeder, invest in a feeder that penalizes greedy rodents with a mild battery-powered electric shock. The birds don't get shocked, and the zapped squirrels don't suffer lasting harm.

Squirrel in the chimney? Fill a large flat pan with ammonia and position it inside the hearth so the fumes can waft upward. This should drive out the intruder (and any offspring). Cap the chimney to prevent future invasions.

A clean trap. Wash a mousetrap with water and let it dry for 24 hours. Then, to keep the human scent off the trap, wear rubber gloves when baiting it.

Take the bait. Set a few mousetraps and bait boxes close to the wall so the mice will see them as they scurry by. Because they have limited vision, mice hug the walls while traveling, where the feel of their long hairs brushing against the wall keeps them on track.

Spicing up the bait. Peanut butter, gumdrops, and pieces of crisp bacon are tempting bait for mice. For extra appeal, sprinkle the bait with a little oatmeal or cornmeal.

Pet Pests

The pill for pests. Veterinarians are prescribing new oral medications to deflea pets. When fleas dine on your pet's blood, they consume some of the medication, which renders them infertile. Since the pests can't breed, they eventually die off. The prescribed dosage is based on the weight of your pet.

Collared! A weekly vacuuming of rugs and floors is an effective way to keep fleas under control. For extra punch, toss a piece of flea collar into the bag of the vacuum cleaner to kill any fleas before they can multiply. Make sure to stretch the collar first, to activate it.

Starve 'em. During ant season, place a pet's food dish in the center of a pie pan filled with water to keep ants out of the food.

Pick a tick. If you live in a tick-infested area, spot-check your pet for ticks every night before you go to bed (and don't let the animal accompany you there). Animals get Lyme disease, too, and to prevent serious illness, it's important to remove ticks promptly.

Killer brew. Keep a small cup of household bleach nearby when you're deticking your pet. Depositing the ticks in the cup as they're removed will kill them on the spot.

Stains and Smells

A deodorizing brew.
To remove pet odors from a room, warm some ground coffee over low heat in a cast-iron frying pan until the scent of it fills the air; then immediately move the pan to a trivet in the smelly room. When the coffee cools, the odor should be gone.

When a pet gets skunked, deodorize him with a bath of equal parts white vinegar and warm water instead of the usual tomato juice concoction. Vinegar is a lot cheaper and works just as well at removing odors.

The hard truth. Locate litter boxes, guinea pig cages, and other domiciles for small animals in a room with a hard floor. Carpeting will absorb pet odors—tile, wood, and linoleum won't.

Floor exercise. If a pet relieves itself on a wood floor sealed with penetrating stain (not polyurethane-covered floors), rub the spot with a rag dampened in white vinegar. Then rub it gently with fine steel wool. Apply a floor wax (in a color that matches the floor), and buff with a flannel cloth. Repeat as needed.

Grooming and Caring

Burrs are easier to remove from long cat and dog hair if you massage in a little light oil around the burr first. Let the oil sit for a while, then comb out the burrs with a wide-tooth comb—the wider, the better.

Sucking it up. If a pet doesn't mind the noise, remove loose hair from a dog or cat with the upholstery attachment of a vacuum. Just stay away from the animal's face and ears.

Dry-cleaning your pet.
If a pet is jittery about water, try dry-cleaning the animal by briskly rubbing baking soda over its coat, getting down to the skin. Then brush out the animal's hair thoroughly.

Sweet rinse. Add some baking soda to the rinse water after bathing the pet and you'll end up with a better-smelling animal.

The well-insured pet.
Some vets now offer an HMO plan that, for an annual fee, provides services either free or at a discount. While contracted between you and the vet, the plan is actually administered by an HMO company.

New babies in the house?
House a new litter of puppies or kittens in a child's plastic wading pool. Pad it well with old towels or rags.

The right medicine.
To prevent scratches while administering pills, wrap a cat in a towel, securing its paws firmly. After you've poked the pill to the back of the cat's mouth, gently blow in its face—the startled cat will reflexively swallow the pill.

One-stop feeding. Hungry animals will often push an unweighted dish around the kitchen floor as they eat. To keep it in one place, put the dish on a rubber mat.

Shelter from the storm.
Protect doghouse denizens from wind and rain by hanging a rubber doormat, cut into strips, along the top of the entrance. The dog will be able to enter and exit the house, but will be snug and dry once inside.

Grounding a bird. If your tweetie has escaped from its cage, draw the drapes and turn off all the lights in the room—birds usually don't fly in the dark. The bird should stay in one spot so you can easily apprehend it.

Breaking Bad Habits

Chew no more. To stop a pet from gnawing on its paws, tail, or fur, paint the spot with oil of cloves, available at drugstores. The horrible taste will discourage chewing.

The hole thing. Fed up with a dog repeatedly digging up the same spot in the yard? Send the dog packing by scattering a crumbled cake of toilet freshener over the area—the smell will keep the dog away.

Fruitful solution. Stockpile orange, grapefruit, and lemon rinds in the freezer over the winter. In the spring and summer, poke the rinds into the soil of flower and vegetable gardens, then cover them with a light dusting of soil. This will keep your cats from digging up the young plants.

A fragrant reminder. A cat who has forsaken its litter box for another location in the house can be gently redirected with some lemon juice on a cotton ball. Put the ball into a lidded tea strainer and hang it where the cat has chosen to urinate—the smell should discourage the cat and send it boxward.

In case of accidents. After cleaning up a cat "accident," wipe the area with a cloth moistened with ammonia. The pungent odor will kill the smell of cat urine and will prevent the cat from returning to the same spot to relieve itself.

Tape trick. Place strips of double-sided adhesive tape on tables and other surfaces that are off-limits to your cat. Cats hate the feel of the adhesive on their paws, and will soon learn to keep off.

Stay off the couch. Keep cats away from the sofa by covering its pillows in aluminum foil.

FILE IT

Pet tricks: Finding a lost animal

Outfit your pets, especially dogs, with ID and rabies tags. This will help whoever finds the lost animal to contact you—and prevent the pound from putting it to sleep.

Distribute flyers with a picture and description of the animal, your phone number, and an offer of a reward throughout your neighborhood. Cover an area that is twice as large as your dog's normal stomping ground.

Take the flyers to local vets, pet supply stores, animal shelters, laundromats, the neighborhood Y, and other places that have community bulletin boards.

Check the local animal shelter frequently, and don't forget to visit shelters in nearby towns and cities.

Ask the mailman and garbagemen if they've seen your pet.

Put up posters near elementary schools. Kids seem to be very aware of animals they encounter, and they tend to be out and about in the neighborhood.

EXTERIOR REPAIRS AND IMPROVEMENTS

Job ratings: Easy   Medium   Complex

Steady as she goes. To prevent a ladder from being blown over by a gust, secure it with rope to a screw eye in a fascia board or to a tree on the opposite side of the house.

Weighty matters. Ladders are rated for load capacity. Load includes the weight of the user *plus* tools, materials, and equipment. Be certain that any ladder you use is rated for the weight you need to support.

Solid footing. To give a ladder skid-free traction on smooth surfaces, simply set the feet into an old pair of rubber boots.

If the ground is soft, keep the ladder from sinking by setting its feet on a piece of ¾-inch plywood about 8 inches wider and deeper than the ladder's base. Stake the board on four sides so it doesn't shift.

Secure the base of an extension ladder with sandbags or by tying it to a stake or another immovable object. A garden fork driven into the ground at the same angle as the ladder can also serve as an anchor. Never secure it to something that might move.

Damage control. To prevent a ladder from scarring shingles or siding, cover the top of the rails with old socks, gloves, or mittens secured with string.

Weather wise. Don't climb a ladder in inclement or windy weather. Also take extra care to secure a ladder that's set on frozen ground. If it thaws, the softer turf could destabilize the ladder's feet.

Don't be shocked. Working near power lines with an aluminum or damp wood ladder is dangerous since both can conduct electrical current. If you must work near electricity, use a non-conductive fiberglass ladder.

No way out. When putting up a ladder near a door, lock or brace the door first. Alert your family and also tape up a sign as a reminder. Cover glass-paneled doors with a blanket to avoid accidental damage from falling objects.

Designated help. Always tell a friend or family member that you will be working on a ladder—and for approximately how long. If the ladder falls or, even worse, if you do, you know that someone will come to your aid.

No snags. Wear a side- or rear-hanging tool belt to avoid snagging the ladder's rungs when climbing up.

An elevating thought. Don't climb a ladder with your hands full of tools. Place tools in a bucket, tie a rope to the handle, and hoist them up and down.

Use cordless tools when working on a roof or ladder to sidestep trip-ups on long extension cords.

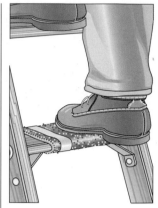

Giving the slip to slips. A piece of outdoor carpet wrapped around a ladder's bottom stair or rung is a handy mat for muddy feet when climbing up—and a timely reminder that you've reached the last rung when climbing down. Use another scrap of carpet to cushion your shins from bumping up against a troublesome rung.

SAFE AND SMART

➤ Dress for success by wearing dry, clean softsoled shoes with good traction, and a longsleeved shirt and pants to prevent scratches.

➤ For roof work, make sure the ladder extends three or four rungs above the roof line. The extension provides a safe handhold for getting on and off the roof. The two sections of the ladder should overlap by at least four rungs.

➤ Use both hands to steady yourself as you climb. Keep your weight centered between the side rails at all times—most accidents are caused by overreaching.

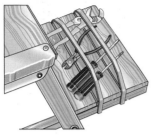

Always dropping tools while up on a stepladder? Hold them tightly in place with large rubber bands stretched across the folding tool shelf.

Glue a strip magnet to the top step or rung of a ladder to prevent screws and other small hardware from taking a swan dive.

Security first. Storing a ladder outside is an added enticement for a burglar. If you must leave a ladder out in the elements, be sure to chain it to a tree or secure it to a sturdy wall with locking brackets.

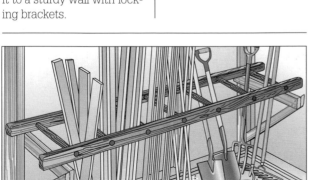

Instant storage. Use an out-of-commission wooden ladder as a storage bin by securing its rail to a workshop wall. The space between rungs can be used to sort short lengths of lumber or to store long-handled tools.

Inspect a ladder that is stored outside for loose rungs, cracks, dents, rot, rust, frayed rope, and weakened hinges before climbing it. Repair damage or replace parts as needed.

Hidden deficits. Painting a wood ladder can hide structural defects that could lead to a nasty fall. Instead, protect the wood with clear polyurethane, scuffing the treads with sandpaper to increase traction.

Tightening the belt. Hanging a ladder horizontally on nails is a space saver. For extra holding power, screw an old belt into the wall and buckle it tightly around the ladder's middle. The ladder will stay put, no matter how hard it's jolted.

If you're short on space, use a stepladder to hold plants or other household items. Just open the ladder, position it in the corner of the room, and place flowerpots or knickknacks right on the steps.

Setting up an extension ladder

WHAT YOU'LL NEED

Extension ladder

1 To raise an extension ladder, place its feet against the base of the wall. Lift the top rung and walk the ladder up, rung by rung, until it is vertical. Then pull its feet out from the wall. Extend it at least 3 ft. above working level and lock the extension.

2 Set the feet of the ladder at about a 75° angle to the ground on a solid, level surface. You should be able to stand with toes touching the feet of the ladder, arms and back straight, and hands on the rungs at shoulder height.

3 To move the ladder, unlock the extension and lower it, rung by rung, until it is all the way down. Carry the ladder parallel to the ground to the new location, and set it up as before.

Seen from afar. Inspect the roof in spring and fall and after severe storms. A quick inspection with binoculars often does the trick. For a close look, raise a ladder and inspect the surface from the eaves.

Sun spots. Pay special attention to south- or west-facing roof surfaces. They receive the lion's share of sun and storm damage.

Fire away. Extend the life of a wood-shingle roof by applying a wood preservative and fire retardant to the shingles every 3 to 5 years.

Coming unglued. To pry apart asphalt shingles without damaging them, slip a trowel, putty knife, or pry bar under the edge and tap it gently with a hammer.

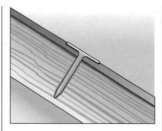

Being flush. Be certain that the nailhead is flush against the shingle (top)—an angled head (below) can cut the shingle, leaving it vulnerable to tearing and sudden liftoff in a high wind.

Flash repairs. To stop a leak quickly, slip a piece of flashing or sheet metal under the broken shingle and secure it with roofing cement. Try this with a tile or slate roof only if you can reach the leak without walking on the tiles. These fragile materials can crack when weight is applied.

Signs of trouble. Piles of mineral granules in gutters or under downspouts are signs of shingle wear. Shingle edges that are curled or coated with mold, mildew, or algae are additional trouble spots. Replace curled or balding shingles as soon as you can. Glue down slightly warped edges with roofing cement before they turn into a major leak.

Don't walk. Treading on roof shingles in temperatures above 80°F can loosen the gravel from softened asphalt. Temperatures below 50°F make shingles brittle and prone to cracking.

Are you square? Standard 3-tab asphalt or fiberglass roof shingles come in bundles of 27; three bundles make up a square and cover 100 square feet. To estimate how many squares you'll need to reshingle, calculate the square footage of the roof and divide by 100. Then add 10 percent for waste.

Tools and hardware always slipping down a pitched roof? Put on the brakes by placing everything on sheets of white plastic foam packing.

Drive new nails through the old nail holes when replacing a shingle. If you can't, seal up the old openings with roof cement.

The right angle. Set new nails and also reseat loosened ones by slipping the flat end of a pry bar under the shingle above it and onto the nailhead. Hammer the bar near the edge of the shingle; the bar's angle will transfer the impact to the nail without damaging the wood or the asphalt.

Stop-gap measures. For maximum leak prevention, dab roofing cement on the nail shaft before hammering it into the shingle. Cover the head as well.

Head start. Hammer nails partway into the replacement shake before setting it in place. Locate the nails so that when hammered home, they will be shielded by 1½ inches of the overlapping shake.

Drip detection. Standing in the attic, follow the path of the drip back to its source—which on a sloped roof is often upstream from the leak. Then push a nail through the damage so you have a marker when you're up on the roof ready to make the repair.

Coming clean. If a leak has stained the ceiling, remove the spots with equal parts of water and chlorine bleach. Dab the stains with a moistened sponge until they're gone. If the ceiling doesn't come clean, seal the ugly spots with primer or a special stain-killing paint, then apply a coat of ceiling paint.

Soda shakes. To antique new shakes instantly to match old ones, dip or brush them with a solution of 1 pound of baking soda dissolved in ½ gallon of water. They will "weather" to gray in a few hours. Finish up the job by brushing on a wood preservative before installing the shakes on the roof.

Good bye to fungi. If your wood roof is furry with fungi, here is the perfect solution. Mix 3 ounces of trisodium phosphate, 1 ounce of laundry detergent, a quart of 5 percent liquid laundry bleach, and 3 quarts of warm water. Brush it on, let it stand for 5 to 10 minutes, and hose away stains and fungi.

Plant fruit and nut trees away from the house. A steady bombardment of heavy apples or chestnuts isn't good for the roof and can tempt squirrels to set up residence in your house to be nearer a free meal.

Trim tree limbs that overhang the roof. Shaded shingles will develop mildew, shortening their life.

SAFE AND SMART

➤ Always balance shingles on your shoulder when carrying them up a ladder.

➤ Asphalt shingles without cutouts are faster to install and usually last longer. The cutout is the first place to wear on 3-tab shingles.

➤ Be sure to wear thick gloves when installing red cedar roof shingles. Shingle splinters can cause severe infections in some people.

➤ Wood shingles aren't perfectly flat on both sides; one side is slightly convex. Eyeball the surface of each shingle for a curve, and install it curved side up.

➤ Dry roof tar is murder to remove from tools. Use a paint stirrer or a split piece of wood as a tar paddle and toss it when you're finished.

Replacing an asphalt shingle

WHAT YOU'LL NEED

Safety goggles

Flat pry bar

New asphalt shingle

Claw hammer

Galvanized roofing nails

Work gloves

Caulk gun and tube of roofing cement

1 Wearing goggles, remove the damaged shingle, using a flat pry bar to pull it out. Be careful not to damage the surrounding shingles.

2 Slide a new asphalt shingle into place. Line it up with adjacent shingles, and then secure it with roofing nails.

3 Dab roofing cement under the tabs of the new shingle and of any other shingle that might have been loosened. Press down the tabs firmly to seal the cement.

A great ending. For a smooth, wrinkle-free roll-roofing job, install roofing from one end of the roof to the other, never from the center to the ends.

Unwind and relax. Roll roofing should be unrolled 24 hours before it is installed so that the curl will relax and the sheets can lie flat. Coiled roofing may buckle after installation.

A new top coat. Revive a roof that needs more than spot repairs with black asphalt roof coating. Brush it on, working from the highest to the lowest point.

Listen up. Press gently on blistered roofing and listen for a squish. If you hear one, the blister is wet and you need to patch it (see "Blister relief," below). If all is quiet, leave the blister alone.

Broad brushstrokes. If you can't pinpoint the source of a leak, cover the general area with roof tar. Scrape the area clean of gravel before applying the tar, and replace the granules once the tar has set.

Shingle sunblock. Deter UV damage by painting the roof with reflective asphalt aluminum paint. It lubricates and reseals the roofing membrane in one swipe.

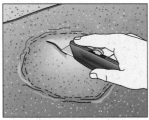

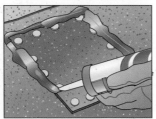

Blister relief. To repair blistered roofing, slit the bubble with a utility knife, let it dry, and pack roofing cement under it; then smooth the roofing flat. Secure the repair with nails on both sides of the slit. Apply roofing cement on the slit and nailheads; then nail on a patch of roofing 2 inches larger than the slit itself. Seal the edges with roofing cement.

Patching a flat roof

WHAT YOU'LL NEED

Brush

Utility knife and straightedge

Asphalt-saturated cotton fabric

Roofing cement

Putty knife

1 Brush the entire area clean; then cut out the damaged section of roofing with a utility knife. Use this piece as a template to cut a piece of asphalt-saturated cotton fabric 2 in. wider on all sides than the damaged area.

2 Apply roofing cement to the exposed area with a putty knife. First work the adhesive under the cut edges with the putty knife; then coat the center section generously.

3 Place the patch on the exposed area, and smooth it down. Apply roofing cement over the patch, spreading the cement 2 in. beyond the edges.

A safe perch. The ideal position for sitting on a roof is with one leg bent back flush along the roof and the other bent up, with the sole of your shoe on the shingles. This position centers you and prevents you from leaning dangerously.

Keep off the flashing. Avoid applying pressure directly to or within 12 inches of the flashing. The weight can tear or crack the joints beneath the roofing.

Rust buster. Pinholes or rust in metal flashing can be repaired by scrubbing away corrosion with a wire brush and applying rust-resistant primer. After it dries, apply a coat of caulk or sealant, press a layer of fiberglass mesh into the caulk, and then top with a second application of sealant.

Cap roof vents with hardware cloth. This heavy-duty mesh will keep out curious animals and airborne debris. Press the cloth down over the sides, and glue it with roofing cement.

Stop a leak in soft lead flashing by tapping it lightly with a hammer. Apply roofing cement or a shot of automotive undercoating to seal any gaps that remain.

Shingle savvy. Install new shingles at the same time that you repair the flashing. Old shingles can develop cracks and punctures during the repair, which, if left untreated, can lead to major leaks later on.

SAFE AND SMART

➤ Flashing on older houses may contain lead. Wear gloves, and wash your hands well afterward.

➤ Always keep roofing cement and a caulking gun handy when going up on the roof. You can make those small repairs on the spot rather than struggling to find them again later.

Replacing vent flashing

WHAT YOU'LL NEED

Work gloves

Pry bar

Putty knife

New vent flashing

Roofing nails

Hammer

Roofing cement

1 Wearing work gloves, carefully bend back the shingles above and on both sides of the vent with a pry bar. Scrape out any old adhesive with a putty knife. Then gently pull up the old flashing, making sure not to crack the shingles.

2 Slip the new flashing over the vent. The neck of the sleeve should fit the vent pipe tightly. Lift the shingles above and on both sides of the vent, and slide the new flashing underneath. Rotating the flashing as you lower it will ease the the installation.

3 Nail the flashing on the top and sides, making sure the nails will be covered by the shingles. Seal the nailheads with roofing cement. Nail the bottom edge of the flashing; it should lie on top of the shingles below it. Seal around the flashing with more cement.

Elbow crease. For ease of installation, bend sheet flashing to conform to the shape of the roof. Crease flashing by bending it over a thick straightedge, such as the side of a 2 x 12, sawhorse, or workbench.

Right 'round the bend.
The undulating curves of corrugated roofing pose a challenge when you're reflashing a chimney. The best bet is to buy preshaped flashing for these types of joints. A local hardware store or home center should be able to order the flashing if they don't carry it.

Cut and paste. Before removing old flashing, trace its shape on a piece of paper to get an exact fit for its replacement. Old flashing may break apart when it is chiseled away.

Corrosion caution. Make sure the nails used to secure flashing are made of the same metal. Different metals interact with each other, speeding corrosion.

Are they compatible?
Flashing should be compatible with gutters. Copper flashing, for example, can corrode aluminum gutters.

Chimney cricket.
A chimney leak that can't be fixed with a patch may be due to trapped water pooling behind the chimney. Installing a cricket—a peaked wood insert—will divert the water to the sides, where it can run off. Seal the cricket with flashing followed by roofing cement.

A repellent act. Seal out moisture from exterior chimney bricks by brushing on a vapor-permeable water repellent designed for masonry surfaces. Be careful not to use foundation or masonry sealer. Both prevent the bricks from breathing, locking in moisture from burning wood.

Capping moisture.
A missing or damaged chimney cap can result in moisture down below. An easy way to check a cap without getting up on the roof is to place a single piece of newspaper at the base of the flue the next time it rains. If the paper becomes a soggy mess, chances are the cap needs to be repaired or replaced.

Replacing metal chimney flashing

WHAT YOU'LL NEED

Work gloves

Safety goggles

Masonry chisel

Hammer or pry bar

Flashing material

Metal snips

Galvanized roofing nails

Mortar and trowel

Silicone roofing cement

Replacement shingles

1 Remove the old flashing and the surrounding shingles if they are worn. Chisel out the mortar along the chimney, leaving a 1½-in. groove. Using a hammer or pry bar, remove the nails holding the flashing in place.

 Aluminum flashing is softer and easier to work with; galvanized sheet metal is harder and more durable.

2 Cut new flashing identical to the old, using the old flashing as a template. Lay out the new flashing and cut it with metal snips to the correct shape. Flashing may come in one piece or may be done as base flashing, which attaches to the roof, and counterflashing, which attaches to the chimney.

'Tis the season. Clean your chimney in spring, before the accumulated deposits have hardened.

Select a chimney brush that is the same diameter as or slightly larger than the flue. Steel-bristle brushes are ideal for tile-lined chimneys, while polypropylene models clean metal linings with hardly a scratch.

The upside-down fire. To limit creosote buildup, place the larger logs on the bottom of the fire and graduate upward with the smaller logs and kindling. Light the fire from the top and it will burn downward.

Wise crack. If a room fills with smoke when you start a fire, cracking open a window near the fireplace will help reverse the flow of air back up the chimney.

Cold prevention. To warm up a cold chimney and prevent wintery drafts from chilling the room before a fire is lit, light one end of a piece of newspaper and hold it high in the damper opening. The warm gases will quickly counteract cold air flowing down.

SAFE AND SMART

➤ Some chimney leaks may be repaired by repointing the mortar rather than replacing the flashing. If the flashing is sound, chisel out the old mortar; then mix some new mortar and press it into the joint.

➤ To detect a blocked or damaged chimney, install a carbon monoxide detector in the same room as the fireplace to warn you of a buildup of harmful gases.

➤ Troubleshoot fire hazards by looking for hot spots, cracks, and leaking smoke where the chimney is exposed in the attic.

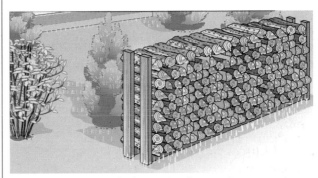

Cut chimney deposits by storing firewood uncovered in a sunny area to dry out. Keep the logs off the ground and drape a tarpaulin over them when it rains or snows.

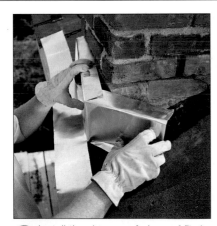

3 Install the down-roof piece of flashing first. For one-piece flashing, slide the edges into the groove created by chiseling out the mortar, and nail the sides down securely. If shingles are still in place, then nail the flashing underneath them.

! **Cut flashing can be razor-sharp. Protect your hands with heavy work gloves.**

4 Attach the side flashing next, following the same procedure as with the down-roof flashing. Repeat on the other side of the chimney. If the chimney has flashing and counterflashing, start with the down-roof base flashing, then install the base flashing for each side. Work from bottom to top, overlapping each piece on the one below it. With either kind of flashing, install the up-roof piece last.

5 Finish by sealing the flashing into the chimney groove with fresh mortar, using a hand trowel. Depending on the configuration of the flashing, you may have to mortar as you go. For added water protection, apply roofing cement to the vertical flashing edges that cannot be mortared in. Replace any shingles that were removed, making sure they overlap the nails securing the flashing.

To pinpoint a sag, pour a bucket of water into the high end of the gutter and look for puddles to form at the low points; then adjust the slope as necessary.

Firm it up. Correct sagging gutters with a simple adjustment of the metal brackets. Gently bend up the brackets with pliers to level out a slumping gutter.

Inside job. If the joints between gutter sections leak, seal them from the inside with silicone caulk or gutter sealant. Then smooth the caulk to eliminate any ridges that could slow the flow of water.

Plugging a hole. To prevent caulk from pushing through a hole before it cures, temporarily seal the hole from the outside with a scrap of plastic sandwich bag secured with tape.

Fix a leaky steel gutter by applying a liberal coat of roofing cement over the hole, followed by a piece of heavy-duty aluminum foil. Repeat the steps and top with a third coat of cement.

A leaky elbow that connects to a downspout doesn't necessarily signal trouble at the joint. Check for a blockage farther down the pipe, where water may be backing up.

A fresh start. Replace, don't patch, a perforated downspout. The force of falling water will blow out even the snuggest plug.

FILE IT

Leaky gutters: Quick ways to stem the tide

For minor repairs, try a leak-sealing compound in an aerosol can. Clean the rusty area first, and then simply spray some sealer on it.

For more substantial repairs, use metal patching compound. Mix the liquid polymer with powdered cement and fillers, and apply it over the fiberglass cloth supplied with the kit.

To cut down on future leaks, use flexible plastic gutter lining made of polyvinyl chloride—the same material used in plastic plumbing pipe. Clean the gutter and cement the lining to it with the adhesive supplied. The material comes in long rolls to minimize seams.

Repairing a leaky gutter

WHAT YOU'LL NEED

Wire brush or sandpaper	Work gloves (optional)
Clean rags and paint thinner	
Fiberglass or metal patch	
Scissors or tin snips	
Fiberglass resin, polyurethane caulk, or gutter seal	
Paintbrush or putty knife	
Blind rivets and rivet gun (for metal patches)	

1 Clean dirt or rust from the area with a wire brush or sandpaper. Wear gloves if there are sharp edges. With a rag, wipe the area with paint thinner and let dry. Cut a patch to cover the area plus 2 in. all around if using fiberglass; 2 in. longer for metal.

2 For a fiberglass patch, apply a thin coat of mixed resin to the gutter with a paintbrush, as shown here. Be careful not to touch the resin. For a metal patch, spread a 1/8-in. layer of caulk or gutter seal with a putty knife.

3 Press the patch into the adhesive with a rag. For fiberglass, apply a thin coat of resin over the patch, wait 24 hours, sand, and apply another coat. For metal, rivet the patch at both ends; then spread caulk or gutter seal over the edges and let it dry.

De-clutter the gutter. Speed up cleanup by making a scraper from a piece of scrap hardboard or plastic. Cut it to the exact width of the gutter to push debris and silt into easy-to-remove piles.

When cleaning gutters, plug the top of the downspout with a rag first. This will prevent a mess from going down the drain.

Pick the bucket. Scoop up the heaped debris with a small plastic sand shovel or garden trowel and toss it into a bucket. Ladling the debris over the gutter's edge can soil the siding.

Attach a long rope to the handle of the bucket and lower loads of debris to the ground so you have both hands free for going down the ladder.

Metal ladder hooks for paint buckets are also a convenient way to hold the bucket near the job site; or make a hook by bending a piece of heavy coat hanger wire into an S-shape.

If pine needles are the source of a gutter clog, don't count on screens to help. The needles can get through the mesh but your fingers can't, making for a time-consuming cleanup.

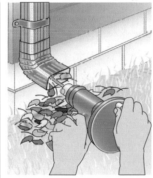

Blocked downspout? Instead of hassling with a ladder, use a plumber's snake, working from the bottom up. Feed in some coil, turn the handle until the coil moves easily, then feed in some more. Repeat until the blockage is removed.

Water power. A blast from a garden hose can loosen tough clogs from a downspout. Just enlist a helper to feed the hose up to you.

Homemade leaf guards can be made from strips of galvanized wire mesh with holes no more than ¼ inch wide. Nail gutter-size lengths of mesh underneath the lower course of the roofing, and extend them across the entire gutter.

Installing gutter guards or screens

WHAT YOU'LL NEED

Tape measure

Gutter guards or screens

Metal snips

1 Make sure the gutters are leak-free and clean and the downspouts are clear and draining properly. Measure the gutters and purchase the needed guard footage. If the gutters have metal spikes or other obstructions, measure between them.

2 Cut the screens or guards to fit the length of the gutters. If there are metal spikes, it's likely that you can cut notches in the screens to accommodate them. If there are overhanging clips, cut screens in lengths to fit between them.

3 Install the inside edge of the screen under the bottom row of the roof shingles, and depending on the type of screen, snap the outer edge under or onto the outer edge of the gutter.

Strung out. If a tape measure isn't long enough to run the length of the gutter, measure it with a length of string instead. Fold the string in half to measure and mark halfway points.

Hang time. Gutter brackets should mount on a surface perpendicular to the ground. If the fascia board is slanted, use a triangular spacer to position each bracket at the right angle.

Go long. Use a 6-inch-long Phillips screwdriver bit in an electric drill when installing gutter brackets. The extra length will go the distance from the front edge of the gutter to the fascia.

Dip a putty knife in some mineral spirits before smoothing out sticky butyl caulk to prevent it from gunking up the blade.

Let it slide. Gutters positioned too close to the last row of roof shingles will catch snow and ice as it slides off the roof and suffer damage. Lower the gutters just enough to clear the projected snow line.

Stay in shape. To prevent gutters from deforming while cutting them, place a 2 x 4 spacer block in one end for support.

If cutting vinyl gutter, use a hacksaw with a fine-tooth blade to avoid a sloppy cut. Whisk off burrs with a file or fine sandpaper.

Going with vinyl? If so, don't seal expansion joints, where a straight section turns a corner, with caulking compound. They need to expand and contract with changing temperatures.

Vinyl is final. Gutters made of vinyl are easy to put up, moderately priced, and require no painting. Though aluminum gutters have many advantages, they can leak if the joints aren't riveted by a professional.

Leftover vinyl gutter makes a great storage rack for scraps of lumber and pipe. Screw the mounting brackets to studs in a wall and snap in the gutters.

Working with wood. Treat wood gutters with two coats of wood preservative every 5 years. Just be sure the trough is dry and sanded smooth before applying the sealer. Also, sand and repaint the outside of the gutter with two coats of exterior house paint.

Installing a gutter and downspout

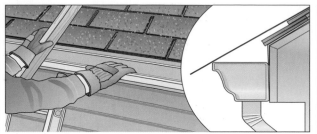

WHAT YOU'LL NEED

Ladder
Level
Chalk line
String
Brackets and top clips
Hammer or screwdriver
Nails, screws, or masonry fasteners
New gutter, downspout(s), and elbows
Caulk
Tape measure
Metal snips or a hacksaw
Straps or brackets
Splash block

1 Take down the old gutter. Inspect and repair the fascia if needed. Snap a level chalk line across the top of the fascia for reference. Run a string to mark the slope from the high end of the run to the drop outlet site. Allow for a gutter pitch of ¼ in. per 10 ft. Attach brackets every 30 in. along the sloped line. Runs of 35 ft. or longer should slope from a high point at the middle of the run to outlets at each end.

2 Connect the gutter pieces on the ground before installing them, starting with the drop outlet piece. Put on the end cap; then connect the drop outlet to one of the long gutter pieces using a special gutter connector with a gasketlike seal. To make the seal more watertight, apply a small bead of caulk to the inside surface of the connector and the end cap.

The wrong channel.
Make sure downspouts don't deposit water on or near sidewalks. Wading through a rushing stream during a rainstorm is a nuisance, and slipping on an ice patch if the temperature suddenly drops below freezing is downright dangerous.

Hang on to hangers.
They make handy hooks for extension cords, coils of wire, and garden hoses.

The rain in the drain. To keep water out of a basement or crawl space—and foundation soil from eroding—channel rainwater several feet away from the house with a piece of downspout, positioning a splash block underneath it.

Shovel out the block.
Clear splash blocks of ice and snow in winter so that water will be deflected away from the house, not toward it. Deposit snow a good distance from the foundation to prevent basement leaks.

Live in a drought area?
Recycle any precipitation by positioning a rain barrel (some are sold with taps) under a downspout that is outfitted with a handy fold-down diverter.

SAFE AND SMART

➤ Old gutters may be hard to handle, so enlist an extra pair of hands to remove them. Provide a helper with a separate ladder or scaffold from which to work.

➤ Lower old gutters to the ground with a rope or carry them down. Tossing them from on high could accidentally jar the ladder or hit someone on the ground.

➤ Butyl caulk is ideal for sealing together aluminum gutter sections.

➤ Simple spikes and ferrules can provide a quick fix for sagging gutters. Drive them through the lip of the gutter and straight into the roof rafters or the fascia for instant support.

3 Measure the length of the run from the high point to the outlet. Cut the gutter piece, with the drop outlet attached, to fit the length. Use metal snips or a hacksaw, keeping the edges straight so they will fit into the connector, if needed, or the end cap. Mount the gutter on the brackets, and caulk the inside of the connecting pieces. Snap the clips on top of the brackets.

4 Attach an elbow to the drop outlet and one to the downspout. Have someone on the ground hold the downspout against the wall of the house, then measure the distance between the two elbows. Cut a piece of downspout to fit, attaching it to the elbows by sliding it over the elbow coming from the drop outlet and inside the elbow coming from the downspout. Do most of the assembly on the ground.

5 Fasten the downspout to the wall with straps or brackets spaced 6–8 ft. apart and held in place by screws, nails, or masonry fasteners. Attach an elbow and a piece of pipe to the bottom of the downspout to direct water away from the foundation. A splash block placed beneath the spout helps disperse the water and keeps it from washing away the soil.

Look for trouble. Stroll around the perimeter of your home periodically to target pockets of rotted wood. Insert a screwdriver or awl into the rot to determine the depth of the decay, and make any necessary repairs before small problems turn into larger ones.

To minimize wood rot, make sure new plants and shrubs are positioned at least 18 inches from the house, and trim back established ones that are touching the siding.

No-splash zone. Rotted siding near the base of a wall is often caused by rain running off the roof and splashing up onto the siding. Before replacing the siding, fix clogged or leaky gutters so raindrops are caught and channeled away from vulnerable wood.

If more than 25 percent of the siding on a wall must be replaced, it's probably easier and cheaper to do the entire wall.

Crack attack. A shot of waterproof glue can often be enough to mend split or cracked siding. Gently lever the crack open with a putty knife, squeeze in the glue, and nail or temporarily tape the wood on both sides of the crack. Remove any oozes with a damp rag.

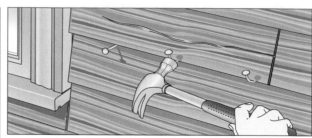

Put on the squeeze. When fixing a horizontal crack, apply glue, then tack several small finishing nails at an angle under the siding piece along the length of the repair. Bend them up to hold the wood pieces together while the glue sets; then remove them when it has dried.

Going with the grain. After filling holes or cracks with exterior wood putty, duplicate the look of the wood grain by lightly raking the repair with a wire brush or the tip of a putty knife.

Bee careful. Don't plug a carpenter-bee hole in siding until the bee has evacuated. The frantic insect may drill into your living room.

Use narrow shingles when replacing wood near a corner or window casing. Wide shingles will shrink too much, leaving gaps.

If a popped nail doesn't hold when hammered, the sheathing behind the siding could be rotten or infested with insects. Correct the underlying problem before repairing the siding.

Replacing wood siding

WHAT YOU'LL NEED

Hammer

Small wedges of scrap wood

Backsaw

Keyhole saw

Pry bar

Plunge-cutting hacksaw

New clapboard

Saw

Wood preservative

Drill

Galvanized siding nails

Caulk or putty

Exterior-grade primer

Exterior-grade paint

Paintbrush

1 Drive small wedges of scrap wood beneath the damaged board. Then use a backsaw to cut across the exposed portion of the clapboard on each side of the damaged area.

When replacing more than one piece of clapboard siding, work from the bottom up.

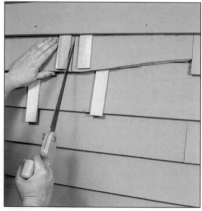

2 Use two wedges to raise the clapboard overlapping the damaged board; finish off the cut with a keyhole saw, holding it with the blade's teeth pointed out. Make the cuts square so the new board will fit evenly. Then remove the wedges.

Hammering for one.

To sink a nail that can't be reached with both hands (one to hold the nail, one to hold the hammer), tuck the nail, point side out, into the hammer's claw. Wearing goggles, reach up and start the nail with a swing. Then reverse the hammer and drive it home.

Being blunt. To stop splits when nailing wood siding, blunt the sharp end of the nail with a blow of a hammer. This won't work for the end of the board: always predrill those holes first.

Patching paper cuts.

It's easy to pierce the building paper under the siding when pulling off damaged boards. Seal punctures promptly with a generous slather of black asphalt roofing cement.

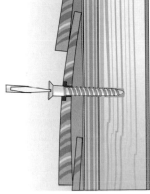

Flatten warped boards with long screws inserted into the studs. To avoid splitting the siding, drill pilot holes and countersinks. Cover the screwheads with exterior-grade wood putty.

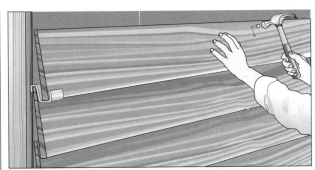

S is for support. When installing new siding, hold long boards in place for nailing with a nifty S-shaped clip you can make out of a 4-inch piece of sheet metal. One curve hangs on the prior course of siding while the other supports the next course firmly until you can secure it with a few nails.

Making the cut. Keep work areas clear. Throw away cut ends of siding into a scrap pile. Stumbling over blocks while sawing is not only aggravating but also dangerous. Also, never leave a block of wood with a nail sticking through it on the ground. Bend the nail over or pull it.

Get a grip. When sawing nails behind siding, wrap duct tape around one end of the hacksaw blade for a safe and comfortable grip.

Don't trash old siding that has been cut to fit around an opening, fixture, or obstruction; use it as a template for its replacement.

3 To remove exposed nails, pry up the board slightly with a pry bar resting on a scrap block. Then gently tap the pry bar to push the siding back down, leaving the nailhead exposed. Pry out the nail.

4 To remove hidden nails, gain access to them by inserting two wedges under the course above the damaged board. Then slip a plunge-cutting hacksaw under the board, and cut the nails flush with the board beneath; take out the damaged piece.

5 Cut a replacement board, treat the sawed edges with wood preservative, and drive the board into place with a hammer and scrap block. Predrill the nail holes, and secure the board with galvanized siding nails in the same way the surrounding siding is attached. Caulk or putty the nail holes and the seams between new and old siding; then prime and paint.

Wait for the warmth. Never attempt repairs to vinyl when the temperature sinks below freezing. Vinyl becomes brittle in cold weather and can crack when nailed.

Sizing it up. Don't skimp on the patch size when repairing vinyl siding, or you'll just wind up doing it again. As a general rule of thumb, the patch should be at least an inch wider and longer than the crack that is being repaired.

Can't find scrap vinyl to repair a crack? Cut out a patch from a plastic milk jug or laundry detergent bottle. It does the job, and you can't beat the price.

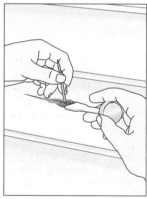

Repair shallow cracks without removing the siding. Gently lever up one side of the crack with a toothpick, apply some adhesive from a vinyl-siding repair kit, and then press the crack closed.

Match game. Minimize color discrepancies when replacing damaged siding by using a piece of weathered siding cut from an inconspicuous area. Install the new piece in the out-of-sight area.

Smooth operator. Get a smooth cut when trimming vinyl with tin or aviation snips by using the first two-thirds of the blades on each stroke. Pressing them closed will create ragged edges.

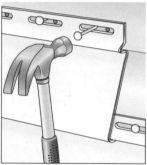

A holding pattern. When attaching a piece of replacement siding, nail as close as possible to the center of the preformed nailing slot, but outside the original nailing holes. This will allow the fasteners to bite into fresh wood, giving them better holding power.

Painting vinyl? Sand it lightly first to bolster paint adhesion, and use an acrylic latex paint with a high solids content.

A light touch. When painting vinyl siding, choose a color that is at least as light as the original. Darker shades absorb more heat, which can cause overheating and warping.

Repairing cracked vinyl siding

WHAT YOU'LL NEED

Zip tool

Hammer or pry bar

PVC cleaner

Scrap vinyl

PVC cement

1½-in. galvanized or aluminum nails

1 To remove the damaged section, insert a zip tool (which can be purchased from a siding supplier) beneath the bottom edge of the overlapping section. Pull down while sliding the tool horizontally. Then remove the nails with a hammer or pry bar.

2 Clean the back of the panel with a PVC cleaner. Cut a section of scrap vinyl to cover the tear. Glue the scrap, finished side down, to the prepared surface with PVC cement.

3 Nail the repaired panel in place. Relock the siding by pulling down the bottom edge of the overlapping siding with the zip tool and, with your other hand, pressing the edge of the top panel over the ridge of the bottom one.

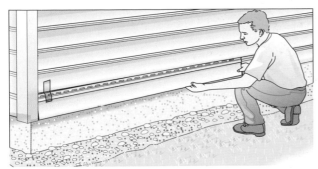

Going solo. If you can't rustle up a helper when installing hard-to-handle pieces of replacement siding, secure one end with duct tape and start the installation at the other end.

Repairing dented aluminum siding

WHAT YOU'LL NEED

Drill
Sheet-metal screws with flat washers
Pliers
Two-part auto-body filler and plastic spreading tool
Fine sandpaper
Oil-base metal primer
Acrylic latex paint and paintbrush

Disguise small scratches in aluminum siding with a dab of acrylic latex paint. Sand the scratch gently with fine steel wool first; then prime with an oil-base metal primer before applying a finish coat.

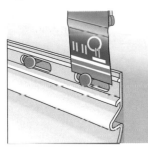

The gap. Leave a little space—about the thickness of a matchbook cover—between the siding and the nailheads when replacing aluminum or vinyl. While a tight fit may seem ideal, it can cause the siding to buckle over time.

Chalk talk. Powdery white residue on aluminum siding, called chalking, is caused by the natural self-cleaning action of the finish. Rain usually washes it away, but you can lend a helping hand with a soft rag and a solution of ⅓ cup of household detergent in a gallon of water.

Salt-air cautions. Although durable and virtually maintenance-free in almost every region, aluminum siding is a poor choice in coastal locations. Salt air can cause dark, blistery areas of corrosion, which can become a real maintenance headache.

For dented, pitted siding, use a flat-finish paint to help hide the imperfections.

Wax on, wax off. Give small areas of dull aluminum a sheen with a coat of liquid car wax. Wash the siding with dishwashing liquid and water, let it dry, and then apply the wax with a damp sponge. Buff it with a soft cloth for siding that glows.

1 When repairing large dents, start out by making them smaller. Drill ⅛-in. holes into the deepest parts of the dent. (If fixing a small dent, skip to Step 3.)

2 Next, insert sheet-metal screws with flat washers on them into the drilled holes. Use pliers to pull out the screws slightly, gripping the washers. This will raise the dented area. Now remove the screws.

3 Apply a two-part auto-body filler to the dents. Level it off with the plastic spreading tool that comes with the filler, and let it harden. After sanding the spot, apply an oil-base metal primer. Finish with two coats of acrylic latex paint.

Sill strategy. A badly damaged sill can be sheathed in aluminum after being repaired. Make a template with brown wrapping paper, scratch the outline onto standard aluminum flashing, and bend the metal onto the sill. Secure it with aluminum nails.

Boiled linseed oil is a less expensive alternative to commercial wood preservatives. Thin the oil by half with turpentine or mineral spirits for the first coat, and mix a thicker brew of 2 parts oil to 1 part spirits for additional coats.

Can this sill be saved? Plunge a screwdriver or awl into the rotted area: If it penetrates more than 2 inches or so, you need to replace the sill; if you hit sound wood sooner, you can probably salvage it.

SAFE AND SMART

➤ Wear safety glasses when working with wood preservatives, and even then keep your hands away from your face. The chemicals are highly irritating to eyes.

➤ To avoid spontaneous combustion, saturate oil-soaked rags in a water-filled container and dispose of them properly.

Beat the clock. Many wood-repair products harden in 15 minutes, so read the label before using. To avoid waste, apply only as much filler as you can work with in that narrow time frame.

Take the powder. Powder fillers have a long shelf life and won't dry up in the can like many ready-made ones. Mix up a batch of filler as you need it, being careful to add water slowly—a little goes a long way.

A smooth operation. To level wood filler with the sill, cover the repair with plastic, then run a block of wood over it. Touch up as necessary with sandpaper after the repair is dry.

Large areas of decay? Save money on costly filling products by recycling slivers of dry scrap wood to fill up the hole. Coat the cavity with wood filler, pack in the wood, and then cover with additional filler.

Filling in rotted wood

WHAT YOU'LL NEED

Hammer	Exterior wood filler
Chisel	Putty knife
Electric drill and 3/16-in. bit	Sandpaper
Epoxy consolidant	Primer
Disposable brush or squeeze bottle	Paint
Rubber gloves	Paintbrush

1 Cut areas of rotted wood from the sill with a hammer and chisel. Let the wood dry; this can take a few weeks, and you must cover the sill if it rains. Then drill a honeycomb pattern of 3/16-in. holes into the damaged area, holding the drill at an angle.

2 Saturate the damaged area with epoxy consolidant, using a disposable brush or a squeeze bottle. Protect your hands with rubber gloves. Let the consolidant dry thoroughly.

3 Apply exterior wood filler to the damaged area with a putty knife. Smooth the filler so it is level with the sill. Let it dry; then sand, prime, and paint.

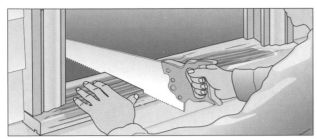

Three easy pieces. Cut a standard sill into three pieces, removing the middle section first with a pry bar and then wiggling the side pieces free from the window frame. Butt the pieces together and use as a template for the new sill.

Replacing a windowsill

WHAT YOU'LL NEED

Work gloves and safety goggles	Galvanized finishing nails
Hammer and chisel	Nail set
Pry bar	Wood putty
Hacksaw blade	Exterior caulk
Windowsill stock	Primer
Sandpaper	Paint
Wood preservative	Paintbrush

Removing the inner sill?
The best way is to drive any nails holding it completely through with a hammer and nail set and then gently pry it off from the outside.

Hacksaw helper. Place a hacksaw blade in a holder to make quick work of cutting hard-to-reach nails in tight places like jambs.

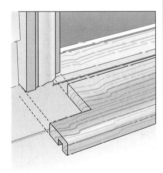

When buying a new sill, choose stock that is notched with a drip groove. Install it so that the groove is on the outside edge to prevent water from following the underside of the sill.

Before installing a sill, brush it with two coats of preservative like copper or zinc naphthenate. Both accept paint and will add years to the wood's life.

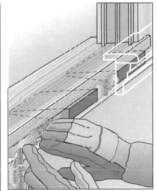

Bridge the gap. Support the new windowsill by hammering thin wood wedges or pieces of scrap wood shingles between it and the rough sill. Stuff fiberglass insulation around the shims to minimize heat loss; then caulk.

Salvage operation. Search second-hand building supply yards for older, hard-to-find trim. It's easier on the wallet than commissioning a millwork outfit to duplicate an out-of-stock design.

Can't find the right sill?
Use a 2 x 6 and notch a drip groove into it with a table or circular saw.

For a tight fit and easy installation, always bevel the ends of the sill that go into the jambs.

1 Remove the windowsill with a hammer and chisel. You may have to separate it from other window parts with a pry bar. Here, the sill rests beneath the window frame. It may also be necessary to cut the nails that hold the sill in place with a hacksaw blade.

2 Using the old sill as a guide, cut a new sill from windowsill stock. Choose stock with the same thickness as that of the sills in your house. Sand the new sill, rounding the edges. Treat the sill and any exposed surfaces with wood preservative.

3 Slide the sill into position and secure it with galvanized finishing nails as needed. Sink the nailheads, and fill the holes with wood putty. Fill gaps with paintable exterior caulk. Then prime and paint the sill.

Test old caulk by poking it with a screwdriver. If it cracks, scrape it out and squeeze in a fresh bead.

Improve your metal. To get the tightest seal when caulking aluminum, bronze, or galvanized steel, wipe down the surface with a common solvent such as methyl ethyl ketone, which removes protective coatings and oily deposits.

Lube job. A few spritzes of silicone lubricant on the metal plunger eases caulk removal and makes for speedier insertion and disposal of cartridges.

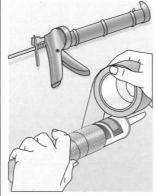

No overruns. Wrapping the caulk tube with duct tape before inserting it into the gun will nip a messy overflow in the bud. The tape prevents the cartridge from swelling and collapsing as pressure is applied.

Save your knees and back when caulking the gap between a house's foundation and siding—a significant source of heat loss—by propping an old mirror on a piece of wood. You'll have a worm's-eye view of the job at hand.

Climate-control caulk by swaddling the tube in a heating pad before working in cooler weather; refrigerate the tube for 15 or 20 minutes on a hot day.

Make it stick. For maximum adhesion in cool weather, "prime" the crack with a blast from a hair dryer before caulking.

Is it paintable? Always check the tube label to see if the caulk will accept paint. Some silicone caulks have exceptional adhesion and elasticity but will resist a coat of paint.

Pushing it. Pushing, not pulling, the caulking gun along the crack will allow you to fill and smooth in a single step.

Caulking the exterior

WHAT YOU'LL NEED

Screwdriver

Putty knife

Siliconized acrylic latex caulk

Small wire brush

Sandpaper

Naphtha

Paintbrush

Open-cell polyethylene foam backer rod

Butyl rubber caulk

Elastomeric sealant

1 Seal around wall penetrations, like spigots. Loosen the screws, if any, holding the spigot in place; then scrape out the old caulk with a putty knife. Squeeze new siliconized acrylic latex caulk behind the mounting plate, and screw the plate back in place. Smooth the caulk with a putty knife.

2 If you have a brick or masonry house, scrape out the old brittle caulk between the brick, stone, or concrete and the wood trim, and remove caulking residue with a small wire brush; blow off any remaining dust. Then apply a siliconized acrylic latex caulk to the gap between the wood and the brick. Smooth with a putty knife.

Point and shoot. To caulk in very tight spaces, tape the tip of a flexible drinking straw to the tube's nozzle and pull the trigger. You'll hit the mark every time.

Potato fingers. Pieces of potato carved to the right joint shape are a nifty way to smooth caulk—and the juice prevents the caulk from sticking. Keep the potato pieces moist in a plastic bag until you're ready to use them.

Putting on the squeeze. When caulk runs low, place a short piece of dowel between the cartridge and the plunger to force the last drop through the nozzle.

Let it weep. When caulking on the outside of a brick house, don't fill the small, regularly spaced holes or mortarless joints located above the foundation, doors, and windows. These "weep holes" allow moisture to escape from the wall.

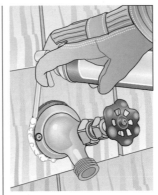

Use polyurethane foam rather than caulk for cracks wider than ½ inch. Because foam expands from 10 to 30 percent once it leaves the can, a few squirts can also silence squeaky stairs and pad pipes that rattle against the house frame. Always wear gloves and goggles.

Tee time. A golf tee makes a nifty stopper for an open tube of caulk. The diameter of the shank fits the cartridge nozzle to a T.

Screw it. If you've been using a nail to seal a caulk tube, switch to a screw. The threads on the shaft form a tighter seal, and it won't slide out on its own.

Caulk tube clogging? Push a folded-up twist tie into the tip. Next time you caulk, simply pull out the tie and that troublesome dried caulk plug along with it.

3 If you have wood siding, scrape out loose caulk and loose paint; sand the area smooth. Wipe the painted area clean with naphtha; then apply a siliconized acrylic latex caulk.

! **Don't paint caulk that doesn't require it. Caulk's normal shrinkage and expansion can cause paint to crack.**

4 Seal the gap between the house's siding and the foundation. Scrape away loose material and old caulk. If the resulting gap is more than ½-in. wide or ½-in. deep, insert an open-cell polyethylene foam backer rod into the gap first. Then apply butyl rubber caulk.

5 Seal any exposed nails in the roof or the vent flashing; also check for cracks around the vent and chimney flashing. Use a dab of solvent-base elastomeric sealant, and smooth the edges with a putty knife to eliminate ridges that would impede drainage.

Follow the sun. Power-wash on the shady side of the house, keeping the nozzle about 2 feet away from the siding (always wear goggles). Washing in sunlight can dry the dirt onto the siding before you've had a chance to rinse it off.

Bottom up. Always power-wash a house from the bottom up; working from the top leaves hard-to-remove streaks on unwashed walls below. When rinsing off, reverse directions.

Listen closely. A sharp paint scraper produces a mellow cutting sound during use; a dull one gives out a shrill screech. In general, carbide-tipped scrapers stay sharper longer.

Horse sense. A horse's curry comb, found in farm and some pet supply stores, makes an unusual but effective paint scraper. What's more, the shaped handle is very comfortable to hold, preventing fatigue when you're working for extended periods of time.

Express scraping. A sharpened garden hoe will make short work of large areas of peeling paint. Finish up with a paint scraper before priming. Don a pair of safety goggles when scraping.

Direct deposit. To clean off scrapings from a putty knife and dispose of them too, run the blade through a slit cut in the side of an old coffee can. The scrapings accumulate in the can and the blade exits clean as a whistle.

A glass act. Use steel wool, not sandpaper, when removing old paint from a window frame. If you accidentally swipe the glass, the steel wool won't scratch it the way sandpaper can.

Preparing wood siding

WHAT YOU'LL NEED

Power washer or garden hose

Household detergent

Long-handled scraper

Dust mask

Electric sander

Extra-coarse and medium-grade sandpaper

Awl

Epoxy wood filler (optional)

Putty knife

Oil or acrylic latex primer

Paintable caulk

Paintbrush

1 Wash the surface to remove dirt and loose paint. For best results, use a power washer that delivers up to 2,000 lb. per sq. in. of water, and add detergent to the water. If the siding shows signs of mildew, remove it with a detergent/bleach solution. Don't shoot water under lap siding. For minimal dirt and debris, washing with a garden hose will probably be sufficient.

2 If you still have areas of loose paint, remove it with a long-handled scraper. Then, wearing a high-quality dust mask, use an electric sander to feather the edges or smooth any cracked and alligatored paint. Start with an extra-coarse grade of sandpaper and move to a medium grade.

Prime time. Before painting aluminum doors, windows, leaders, or gutters, scrape off rust spots with a wire brush, then wipe down the metal with a rag soaked in white vinegar. It removes oxidation and also boosts paint adhesion.

Stick to it. For a nonslip grip on sandpaper when working on rounded or irregular surfaces, run a strip of double-sided adhesive tape down the back of it. Place your hand on the tape and sand as usual.

Buckle up. When painting trim work at the top of the house, create a caddy to carry up a bevy of brushes. Cut off the top of an old plastic clothes detergent container, make two slits in the back, and thread an old belt through them. Buckle on the caddy and pack in the brushes.

A great coverup. A few sheets of heavy-duty aluminum foil make a tough "tarp" for exterior hardware. The foil molds around even irregular shapes and stays in place if you knock into it with a brush or roller.

Easy-peel tape. Wax up both sides of a roll of tape with a candle stub before masking off areas you want to protect. The tape will be a breeze to remove and you won't rip off any old paint along with it.

Slip a paint tray inside a plastic grocery bag before pouring in the paint. If the bag has print on it, turn it inside out to prevent the ink from tainting the paint. When you're finished, just trash the bag.

SAFE AND SMART

➤ To avoid damage to wood siding when power washing, move the wand continuously and maintain about a 24-inch distance from the wood.

➤ Paint applied before 1978 may contain dangerous lead. Leave removal to a pro, if possible. If you remove it, wear a lead-filtering face mask and clothes that can be thrown away. Catch the scrapings on drop cloths, and dispose of them as specified by your local health department.

3 Check for rotting wood, especially along the trim or under water spigots. Use an awl to determine how deep the damage is. With light damage, simply sand until you reach solid wood. Deeper areas of rot need to be hollowed out and left to dry (see p. 60), then filled with an epoxy wood filler. Sand after the epoxy has dried.

4 Remove crumbling caulk around doors and windows with a putty knife. Sand and brush out dust or paint particles, and prime the wood. Then refill with a paintable caulk.

5 Prime bare wood or newly sanded areas. Select a primer that will work well with the paint you are using. You may want to have the primer tinted the same color as the paint. Paint within 2 weeks of priming.

 Before priming, apply a wood preservative to problem areas to make wood last longer.

Will an accent color clash with the main house color? Cut a cardboard "shutter" or "door" to the exact size, paint it the color in question, and prop or tack it in place. Step back and you'll quickly have your answer.

Name that paint. To find out if the paint on your house is latex or oil-base, dampen a cotton ball with rubbing alcohol and run it across an out-of-the-way corner. Latex paint will come off; oil paint won't.

Color correction. No two cans of paint are exactly the same color, but there is a way to minimize the difference. When the open can starts to get low, top it off with paint from the new can and mix well. This "transition" paint will average out any color difference.

Loading up. Use an old plastic dishwashing detergent bottle to load up a paint pad. Shake the bottle now and then to mix the paint or stain—making sure to pop the top down first.

A clean pour. Before pouring paint from a can, tuck a "rope" of paper toweling into the circular groove at the top to prevent paint pools and drips down the side. Toss the toweling after you're done and the lid will fit like new.

Don't go natural. Use a synthetic-bristle brush when applying latex. Water-base paint will swell natural bristles, causing frizzy ends and sloppy strokes.

Stem the flow. To prevent stain and paint from dripping down your arm when working overhead, turn up a cuff on a rubber dishwashing glove and pack it full of toilet tissue. The tissue stops dribbles in their tracks.

A free hand. If you prefer to keep your brushing fingers free, slice off the toe of an old tube sock, then cut a small hole through the side of the sock for your thumb. Pull the sock down your arm, place your thumb in the hole, and button your shirt cuff over the sock.

Whitening trick. To stop white paint from yellowing, add several drops of black paint in for every quart of white paint.

Applying the paint

WHAT YOU'LL NEED

Canvas drop cloths
Sheets of plastic
Ladder or scaffold
Paintbrush
Paint pad
Paint sprayer

1 Working on a dry, windless day, cover surfaces below the work area, such as a lower roof, with canvas drop cloths. Protect an air conditioner or mailbox with sheets of plastic; tie back or trim overgrown shrubs.

 Always paint in the shade. Painting in the sun will cause the paint to dry too quickly, leaving brush marks.

2 Remove any shutters and paint them at your leisure. Paint from the top of the house to the bottom, working in self-contained sections to avoid seams. For example, paint the entire area between two windows, then move on to a different section. Siding is painted first, then trim and windows, doors and porch railings, and finally thresholds, porch floors, and steps.

Don't get bugged. Keep pesky flying insects from ruining a brand-new paint job by stirring several drops of citronella oil into a gallon of paint. It won't affect the paint—just the bugs.

Painting a porch? Stir a little sand into the paint can to provide traction and to prevent slips and slides in wet weather.

Keep track of both the amount of remaining paint and the color by marking the can with a brush mark before putting on the lid.

When soaking a brush, suspend it in a container to prevent splayed bristles. Cut an X in the middle of a plastic coffee-can lid, push the brush handle through from the inside, and relid.

Overnight stay. Store a brush filled with oil paint overnight in a can or jar of water. The water keeps the bristles from stiffening and minimizes prep time the next day. Just swipe the brush against a piece of cardboard several times to wick off the water, and you're ready to go.

Tired of stiff brushes? A quick soak in a table-spoon of hair conditioner mixed with a pint of warm water will soften them up.

To revive a brush that is hardened with dried oil base paint, give it a vinegar bath. Place it in a pot of white vinegar and simmer for 10 minutes. Rinse the bristles with water, and hang the brush until it dries.

A sweeping strategy. Use a soft synthetic-bristle broom to sweep paint on porch or decks. It's faster and whisks paint into hard-to-reach gaps between boards.

A brassy finish. To get exterior brass light fixtures to look as good as a freshly painted house, apply a layer of clear-coat car wax and buff with a soft rag.

3 For wood siding, paint the under-side of the clapboard first. Apply the paint in short strokes, spreading out the paint with smooth, even ones. Press the brush bristles against cracks and rough surfaces to force paint in. Check periodically for missed spots and drips as you go.

4 If you are using a paint pad, load one side of the pad and, as with the brush, paint the bottom edges of the siding first. Then pull the pad slowly but firmly along the length of each board. If the pad is narrower than the siding, overlap strokes so that you won't create a seam in the middle of the board. Check periodically for missed spots and drips as you go.

5 If you are using a paint sprayer, hold the gun horizontally about 10–12 in. from the siding and spray up and under the bottom edge of each board. Then hold the nozzle in an upright position and paint each board in a series of even, parallel strokes, overlapping each strip of paint by about 1 in. Go a little beyond the edges of the area before starting the return pass. Strive for a thin, even coat.

Rot begets rot. If you discover rot or infestation in one piece of wood, chances are some nearby boards are similarly affected. Before making repairs, inspect every support post, joist, and deck board for damage.

Put a coat on. To minimize further decay in a joist with some rot, dig out the rot, let it dry, and brush on two coats of deck preservative.

Undressed wood. Never cover the ends of deck boards with trim or nosing. That will prevent moisture from evaporating from the end grain—an open invitation to rot and insects.

To discourage warping, lay new boards bark-side up, so the semicircles of wood grain on the ends of the boards curve downward.

Can't grab a nail? Gouge around it with a wood chisel until the head is exposed. Then pull it.

Pull out popped nails in deck boards; then secure the boards with 16d nails. Better yet, use 3-inch decking screws, which can be easily removed. If nailing, insert the new nails into the old holes, driving them at an angle so they bite into fresh joist wood below.

Stain-free hardware. Use hot-dipped galvanized or stainless-steel fasteners when doing deck repairs. They're rust-resistant and won't stain the wood.

Heavy rains seep through the spaces between deck boards and can wash out the soil below—especially on a slope. To minimize erosion, cover the soil with a thick layer of gravel.

Lattice panels are a great way to beautify an unsightly area under the deck. To cut the delicate lattice to fit without giving yourself fits, use a jigsaw rather than a circular saw and cut slowly.

Built-in planters. Using the bottom of a paint can as a guide, draw a circle on the deck boards where you'd like a floral display. Cut the circle out of the decking with a saber saw, and insert a clay flowerpot.

Replacing a deck board

WHAT YOU'LL NEED

Work gloves	Galvanized nails or deck screws
Pry bar or screwdriver	Epoxy wood filler
Hammer and wood chisel	Saw
Reciprocating saw or hacksaw blade (optional)	Lag bolts
Pressure-treated decking lumber	
Water-repellent staining sealer	

1 Take out the damaged deck board, using a pry bar to remove nails or a screwdriver to remove screws. If you can't get the nails or screws out, try cutting them from underneath the deck board using a reciprocating saw or hacksaw blade.

2 Inspect the underlying joist, and with a hammer and chisel, remove any rotted wood. If the wood is wet, let it dry; then apply the wood filler. Cut a reinforcing joist from pressure-treated lumber, and secure it to the damaged joist with lag bolts.

3 Cut the new deck board to the exact length and width of the existing decking. Treat it with a water-repellent staining sealer. When it is dry, put the new board in place and attach it to the joists with galvanized nails or deck screws.

Time to reseal? Splash a glass of water on the deck boards. If beads form, the wood is still water-repellent; if the water is sucked up, prepare to seal.

Sap stains on wood will be even more visible when coated with a clear or semi-transparent deck stain. Remove them with mineral spirits; then apply the finish.

When replacing a board, upgrade the appearance of the old wood with deck brightener, and let the new wood grow old with it.

Simple solution. For a low-maintenance deck, leave the floor untreated and simply power-wash it each spring to give it a fresh face. Use detergent if the wood is truly soiled.

Paint a rug. If weathered decking doesn't suit your taste, paint a bold design on the deck floor with colorful exterior polyurethane paint.

Spray on deck finish with a pump-type garden sprayer. It's quicker, and the spray will penetrate between the deck boards. Just pick a still, windless day to work.

Double coverage. Always brush a second coat of staining sealer on the coarse ends of the deck boards, since they absorb more than the tops and bottoms.

Jump on puddles. Brush out pools or puddles of stain thoroughly. They can stay sticky for weeks, finally solidify, and then peel.

When brushing on deck stain, always work to a wet edge to avoid unsightly overlap marks. Start each new brushload from an unfinished area, moving toward the wet edge. Then brush back to where you began.

Weatherproofing a deck

WHAT YOU'LL NEED

Dust mask	Paint sprayer (optional)
Garden hose	Safety goggles
Pail of household bleach and water or deck cleaner	Broom
Belt sander or medium sandpaper	
Water-repellent staining sealer	
Paintbrush	

1 Clean the wood with a dilute solution of household bleach or with a deck cleaner, and hose it off. Wearing a dust mask, sand any rough areas as needed, and sweep away the sawdust.

2 Wearing safety goggles, apply a clear or staining sealer with a brush or sprayer. If using a brush, work with the grain and drive the bristles into the crevices between boards. Also seal the underside of the boards and the joists, beams, and posts.

3 With a paintbrush, carefully smooth any drips at the ends of the boards. If using a sprayer, back-brush the surface.

Take it slow. Eliminate the need to sprint under a closing garage door by installing a push button near the entry door of the house and another button near the garage door.

Busting rust. Brush a light machine oil on both extension springs once a year to silence squeaks and prevent rust from getting a toehold. For maximium lubrication, raise the door completely to relax the springs before applying the oil.

FILE IT

Before you can press the button...
You may need to do some groundwork for the installation of a garage door opener.

Power supply	Be sure you have a standard 120-volt grounded (3-prong) receptacle within reach of the power unit (usually 3 to 6 feet).
Locks	Deactivate or remove the garage door bar lock. An opener's motor can burn out if laboring against an inadvertently locked door.
Reinforcement	If your door is made of lightweight fiber-glass or aluminum, strengthen the top section with metal bars.

Open-and-shut case. To keep a garage door from crashing down when you're making a repair, wedge a 2 x 4 between the floor and the door's corner, then attach a C-clamp or locking pliers to the door track just ahead of the top roller.

Garage door binding? Use a carpenter's level to make sure the bottom sections are plumb. Reposition the brackets if they aren't.

Both extension springs should be replaced on a garage door, even if only one is faulty. It will keep the door in balance and prevent premature wear and tear.

Plug the leaks. Sectional roll-up doors leak air through the panel joints, increasing energy bills in heated garages and turning unheated spaces into wind tunnels. Close the door on drafts by tacking a neoprene gasket across the length of each joint.

Tuning up a garage door opener

WHAT YOU'LL NEED

20-weight nondetergent motor oil
Pump can with flexible spout
Rag
White lithium spray lubricant (optional)
Open-end wrench
Tape measure
Epoxy (optional)
Replacement sensor bulbs and batteries for remote (optional)

1 Pull the manual release cord and open and close the door by hand a few times to check for obstructions. Unless the owner's manual tells you differently, lubricate the chain with 20-weight nondetergent motor oil, using a pump can with a flexible spout. Then moisten a rag with oil and wipe it across the wheel tracks, or coat them with white lithium spray lubricant.

2 Tighten the garage door's hinge bolts, as well as any loose roller mounts, with an open-end wrench, making sure the rollers fit properly inside their tracks. Lubricate the rollers by putting a few drops of motor oil on their center points or by spraying them with white lithium lubricant.

On track. Tracks that aren't precisely parallel on top can cause a garage door to bind. Take measurements between the tracks at several locations and adjust if needed.

Foam pipe insulation will create a tight seal against even an irregular floor, shutting out drafts and leaks down under. Tack a piece, slit side down, to the door's bottom, about ½ inch from the door's front edge, to keep it well out of sight when the door is closed.

Can you dig it? Shovel snow away from the bottom of your garage door immediately. Solar heat reflected by the door can melt unshoveled snow in a hurry, creating a small lake inside the garage and freezing the door to the ground when the temperature drops.

Keep out seeps. The long joint between the bottom horizontal rail and the garage door panels is especially vulnerable to seepage. Run a bead of paintable caulk along it, and test it periodically for wear.

Spray-on antifreeze. A few spritzes of silicone lubricant on the rubber weatherstripping at the bottom of the garage door will help prevent snow and ice from sticking to it.

SAFE AND SMART

➤ Call a professional to fix a faulty torsion spring—the type attached to the top of the door and running parallel to it. These springs have dangerously high tension and can cause serious injury.

➤ Never run your car or lawn mower inside a closed garage. A tightly weatherstripped door locks in not only warm air but also deadly carbon monoxide gas.

Heading on vacation? To burglar-proof your garage, go back to basics: unplug the door opener and reactivate the manual lock on the door. Many newer openers come with vacation switches that automatically disengage the units.

3 Check that the door fits tightly against the frame and stop but doesn't press or bind against them. Moisture damage and foundation settling can affect the door's fit. To adjust the fit, loosen the nuts, move the track by hand, then retighten.

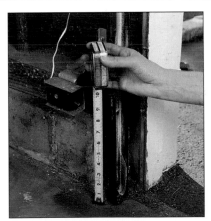

4 Newer garage door openers have photoelectric sensors that stop the door from closing when the light beam is obstructed. If your door doesn't stop, use a tape measure to make sure the sensors are properly aligned. Replace the bulb if it has burned out. If the sensors' housing is cracked, repair it with epoxy.

5 To test the opener's sensitivity, close the door on an empty cardboard box: When it touches the box, it should reverse. If the remote isn't working, try replacing the battery or shifting the antenna that sticks down out of the motor housing. Finally, check the motor for loose wires, making sure that all connections are snug.

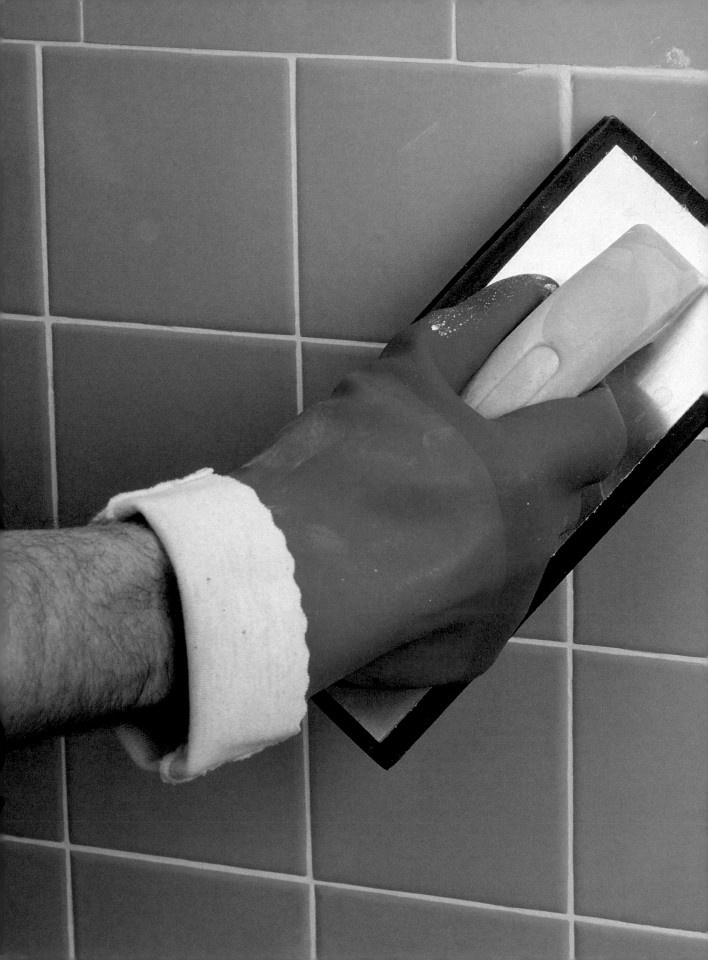

INTERIOR REPAIRS AND IMPROVEMENTS

Job ratings: Easy   Medium   Complex

Molding math. To allow for cutting waste, measure each wall, add at least 2 or 3 inches to the number, and round up to the next highest foot in molding stock. For a 5-foot 6-inch wall, for instance, buy a 6-foot length of molding. Or, for a 5-foot 11-inch wall, order an 8-foot length.

Sizing it up. Better yet, buy molding in lengths that allow you to use a single piece for every side of the room. It avoids waste and having to splice short pieces together later.

Instead of wood molding, use preformed polystyrene molding. It's easy to cut and install and can also be painted. Some molding systems come with formed corner blocks, eliminating the need for miter cuts.

Remove existing molding carefully to avoid damaging the wall behind it. Use a stud locator to find and mark the points where the molding has been fastened to the wall. At each mark slip a wide-blade putty knife behind the molding and loosen it slightly from the wall. Then hold a thin scrap of wood against the wall and wedge a flat pry bar between the scrap and the molding. The scrap will protect the wall while the bar levers away the molding.

Conduct a probe. If you don't have a stud finder, sink finishing nails at various points along the wall to locate the studs. Probe in the strip of wall that will be covered by the molding so the test holes will be covered when the installation is complete. Once a stud is located, the remaining ones are likely to be spaced every 16 inches from that point.

Stain or paint? It depends on the wood you are using. Oak and walnut accept stain uniformly; other hardwoods, such as cherry and maple, and softwoods like pine absorb finishes unevenly and appear blotchy when stained—unless you use a sealer first. An alternative is to skip the stain and finish the wood with a clear varnish.

Mismatched profiles? If you get stuck with two strips of molding with slightly mismatched profiles, join them on straight runs only, and patch the differences with joint compound. Never use mismatched profiles when making corners; in fact, experienced carpenters cut both sides of a corner out of the same piece of molding to ensure the best fit.

Installing crown molding

WHAT YOU'LL NEED

Tape measure and pencil
¾-in. plywood
Circular saw
Screw gun and 1½-in. drywall screws
Molding
Paint and paintbrush
Trim screws or 8d finishing nails
Hammer and goggles (if nailing)
Caulk (if needed)
Miter saw and extension table
Coping saw
Utility knife
4d finishing nails

1 Cut strips of ¾-in. plywood backing just wide enough to fit under the molding. Mark the ceiling joist locations, and for the sides of the room where the joists run perpendicular to the wall, screw the plywood into the joists. For the other sides, install the screws at an angle so they penetrate the top plate behind the wallboard. On the short walls, leave a gap at each corner so the molding will clear the plywood.

2 Paint the molding and let it dry. With a scrap of molding, mark throughout the room where the bottom edge of the molding will sit on the wall. Cut the first piece of molding square and to the length of the longest wall. Install it with trim screws (above) or 8d finishing nails (wear goggles if hammering). The screws or nails should penetrate the plywood strips.

Avoiding split ends.
Driving nails near the end of a strip of molding can cause the wood to split. Pre-drill these nail holes, using a bit that is slightly smaller than the nails. This also ensures that the nails will be in the correct location.

Finish first. It's always a smart move to paint or stain the ceiling molding before installing it. Instead of spending hours on a ladder, all you have to do then is countersink the brads, fill the holes, and touch them up quickly with paint.

Tweaking the trim.
Mitered cuts for outside corners often need a little tweaking to make them tight. If there is a gap in the fit, use a block plane to carefully trim the miter-cut edges so that their surfaces meet cleanly.

Smart shims. Small shims can help wedge together miters on the inside corners of walls. Glue each joint with carpenter's glue, tap a shim into the joint with a hammer, and then cut off the shim with a chisel when the glue dries.

Corner work. Apply a thin coating of yellow glue (carpenter's aliphatic resin) to the mitered cuts of outside corners after predrilling the nail holes. Fasten the tips of the miter joint to the wall by tapping finishing nails through the holes into the wall. Once the glue sets, lightly sand the outside corner with 120-grit sandpaper.

Closing the gaps. If a gap appears between a straight run of crown molding and the ceiling, try edging the molding upward slightly to cover the valley before fastening it. If the molding looks too crooked that way, fill the gap with siliconized latex caulk instead, and paint it.

Prop it up. Handling a long piece of chair rail or crown molding while trying to tighten a joint at one end can be a challenge. If no one is available to hold the molding in place, drive a finishing nail partway into the wall near the opposite end and prop the molding on it. After securing the joint, work toward the propped-up end.

3 For long walls, you may need to use two pieces of molding. Join them midway with a 45° compound miter. If the ceiling is not flat, you may need to caulk the gaps.

4 For the next piece of trim, make a coped joint to fit snugly against the first piece. Cut the molding at a 45° angle; then make 60°-angle back-cuts along the cut edges with a coping saw. Fine-tune the fit with a utility knife.

5 Outside corners must be com-pound mitered, so the miter slopes toward the corner. Cut samples first, adjusting the fit as needed. Fasten the molding to the walls and ceiling, and cross-nail with 4d finishing nails.

 A scrap of molding, placed upside down on the piece you are cutting, makes a good clamping block.

 Cut outside miters a little long and trim them once or twice to fit.

Panels are easier. Instead of tongue-and-groove planks, consider using precut panels for wainscoting. They come in a variety of styles and can be installed much faster.

Panel points. When designing a layout, center the panels beneath windows, using narrow ones so you won't have to cut larger panels into an L-shape to fit around the window. Also make sure that electrical outlets don't fall near the edge of a panel. If they do, move the outlets closer to the panel's center.

Solid backup. Install wainscoting only over solid wallboard or plastered walls. Wainscoting installed directly to the wall studs is more likely to warp or crack due to the difference in moisture levels. Also, always remove existing baseboards so the wainscoting can lie flat all the way to the floor.

Beware of bowing. Look carefully at wainscoting stock when you're shopping, and buy the flattest you can find. Warped or bowed tongue-and-groove planking or panels will never look right when installed.

Straighten up. It is crucial to align the first panel or tongue-and-groove plank perfectly. Take the time necessary to check it with a plumb line.

In damp areas such as bathrooms, kitchens, and wet basements, avoid using plywood panels for wainscoting; the moisture in those rooms may eventually cause the laminated layers to separate. Instead, use solid tongue-and-groove planks that have been thoroughly primed on both sides as well as on all four edges.

Drying out. Planks or panels should be thoroughly dry before they are installed. Otherwise they may shrink, leaving gaps. Knotty wood retains moisture more than wood with minimal knots. Stack the lumber indoors (near where it will be installed) for at least a week to acclimate it.

Disappearing seams. Paint or stain the tongues of tongue-and-groove planking before installing, or their unfinished surface may show as the planks shrink.

Installing wainscoting

WHAT YOU'LL NEED

Pry bar

Tape measure and pencil

Chalk line and level

Precut wainscot planks, baseboard, and cap

Block plane (if needed)

Caulking gun and adhesive

Eye protection

Hammer and color-matched paneling nails or 6d finishing nails

Scribe

Saber saw

Screw gun and screws (optional)

Backsaw and miter box, or electric miter saw

Electric drill and bits

1 Pry off the baseboard. Use a tape measure and pencil to mark where you want the top of the wainscoting to fall (usually 40 to 48 in. above the floor). Snap a chalk line at the desired height, and then use a level to make sure that it's even.

 If you're doing this alone, tap in a nail to hold one end of the chalk line.

2 Locate the studs and mark their locations above the chalk line. Set a plank with its top along the line and a side at a door or corner; if necessary, plane the edge for a tight fit. Apply a vertical ribbon of adhesive to the wall for each plank. Where planks are over studs, nail them to the studs at the top, bottom, and midpoint of the plank (wear goggles). Continue with more planks, fitting them together tightly as you go.

Hide the nails. Drive finishing nails through the tongue of each plank at the top, center, and bottom, angling them back slightly toward the center of the plank. Because the groove of the next plank will cover the nails, they won't have to be countersunk and covered with putty.

Give it a rest. If possible, delay installing the baseboards for about 24 hours, until the adhesive has set and the planks or panels have settled a bit.

Which direction? When installing tongue-and-groove wainscoting, right-handers will find nailing easier if they start on the left end of a wall and work toward the right. Lefties should do the reverse.

Built-in with paint. Painting a corner cabinet the same color as the wainscoting can make the cabinet seem like a permanent part of the room, whether it is built in or not.

Replacing a plank. To replace a single tongue-and-groove plank, remove it and then chisel off the back lip of the new plank's groove. Push the new plank's tongue into the adjoining plank; then nail the groove side into place.

Fix a warp in a new plank or in existing wainscoting by screwing it into a stud at the top, center, and bottom of the plank. Fill the holes with wood plugs and finish them to match the rest of the wainscoting.

Do it with wallpaper. Instead of wood wainscoting, install a chair rail and washable prepasted wallpaper along the bottom third of a wall. Wallpaper costs less than wood, is easier to apply, needs no new baseboard, and offers an unlimited number of patterns to choose from. If the walls don't need protection from chairs, use a wallpaper border in place of the chair rail.

3 When you approach a window, do not install the last full plank. Instead, mark above the chalk line where the edge of the plank (not including the tongue) will fall. Then place another plank against the sill, and set a scribe to the width between the mark and the edge of the plank (inset). With the point of the scribe against the window side casing, draw a guideline down the plank, scribing around the sill.

4 Using a saber saw, cut the marked plank. Install the full plank and the cut plank; then continue around the window, scribing as needed. If you plan to paint or finish the wainscoting planks, cap, and baseboard, do it now (see "Disappearing Seams," above). Set the baseboard in place, mark where one end must be trimmed, and wearing eye protection, cut it with a saber saw. Fasten the baseboard to the studs.

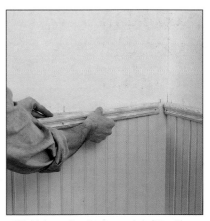

5 Using a backsaw and a miter box or an electric miter saw, cut one end of the wainscoting cap at a 45° angle. Set it in place, with the angled end in a corner, and mark where the other end must be trimmed and where the studs fall. Cut off the end and drill pilot holes on the stud marks. Screw or nail the cap to the studs. The fasteners must be long enough to penetrate the studs.

Be a cautious buyer. Buy several square feet of the tile you like, and lay them out in a patch in the room where they will be installed (or in a place where the lighting is similar). If you're happy with your choice of tile after living with it for a few days, then go back and place the whole order.

Tile-sizing a room. Always consider the size of the tiles in relation to the room where they will be installed. Using small-scale tiles can make a room seem larger.

Dirt devils. Tiles that are very light or very dark will show dirt, dust, and crumbs. Tiles that mask dirt best are mid-range solid colors, smoky fume glazes, granite, or variegated patterns that simulate stone.

Slippery clean. Smooth, glossy tiles are easy to clean, but they can be dangerously slick when wet. Textured tiles provide great slip resistance but are harder to keep looking spic-and-span. A compromise is a tile with a glaze or a matte finish that is slip-resistant but cleans up well.

Save money or time? Unglazed tiles are less expensive than glazed but can be tough to keep clean. They have to be coated with a tile sealer after installation, and then resealed every year if they are in a high-traffic area.

Roughed up. When tiling a wall, install backer board with the rough side facing out. It gives the adhesive a textured surface to grab onto, resulting in a stronger bond with the tile.

Solid backing. When installing backer board, leave a narrow expansion gap between the bottom edge of the panel and the sink, tub, or counter that the board adjoins. The gap can be filled with flexible caulk after the tile is in place. Maintain the gap while the backer board is being installed by using temporary spacer strips or shims under the edges.

Tile over tile. You can tile over an old tiled surface if it is sound and flat. Rub down the glazed surface with silicon carbide paper to prepare it to receive the new tile adhesive. Some home-repair stores carry kits for covering old tile.

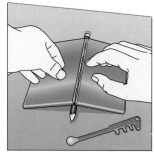

Quick cuts. Simply score the glazed side of the tile with a glass cutter. Then lay the tile on top of a pencil that is positioned directly below the scored line. Carefully press both sides of the tile to snap it in half.

Replacing damaged ceramic tile

WHAT YOU'LL NEED

Grout saw or cordless tile saw

Gloves

Hammer and cold chisel

Broom and dustpan

Stiff-bladed putty knife or old chisel

Replacement tile

Latex tile adhesive

Grout

Rubber grout float

Large sponge

Penetrating sealer

1 Use a grout saw or a cordless tile saw to remove the grout from around the damaged tile.

2 Wearing gloves, carefully crack the tile with a hammer and cold chisel, and remove the pieces. Sweep up all tile pieces from the counter and floor, making sure not to touch the shards with your bare hands.

Be precise. When cutting tile to an irregular shape around a door frame, create a template with a piece of solder. Press the solder into the area to form the shape; then use it as a template to mark the cut.

Light grout can ruin the look of a beautiful kitchen because it tends to stain and will discolor over time. Consider a darker grout. Darker tiles also may look better with a tinted grout.

Protect grout with a penetrating sealer. Apply the sealer with a narrow paintbrush when the grout has fully cured, about 2–3 weeks after installation. Avoid heavy use until it is sealed. Refresh the sealant every other year.

When repairing tile, take extra time to test grout color mixes first. Make up several color samples, noting the proportion of tint to grout required for each one. Allow the samples to dry for 3 days before choosing one.

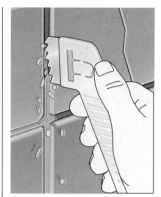

Grout out. Removing damaged grout is a breeze with a grout saw, available at hardware stores. It is the size of a utility knife, but its stiff blade has a sawtooth edge. Some models can be fitted with larger blades to clean out grout more efficiently from wider joints.

Strengthening the bond. Mix drying retarder into the grout to extend the drying time. The longer the drying time, the stronger the cure.

Softening the slams. Seams near doors should be caulked rather than grouted. The flexible caulk will stand up to the vibrations from slamming doors better than brittle grout will.

Hiding gaps. Install shoe molding over the baseboard to cover the gap where the tile and baseboard meet.

Planning for the future. Buy extra tiles when you start a project, and carefully wrap them to guard against breakage. Mark the package with the brand, color name, date, source, and the room where the tiles are installed. Also set aside some grout of the same type and color, and store it in a tightly sealed container near the tiles. The tile and grout will be invaluable for future repairs.

3 Scrape the remaining adhesive off the wall with a stiff-bladed putty knife or an old chisel. If working on wallboard, try not to remove any layers of the board. If you do, smooth the areas by trimming the torn layers.

4 Butter the back of the replacement tile with latex tile adhesive. Then press the tile firmly into place. Check for proper spacing, and allow the tile to sit overnight, undisturbed.

5 Force grout into the joints with a float (above). Hold the tool at an angle and draw it across the tile diagonally. Immediately remove excess grout with a damp sponge (inset); repeat when the grout dries to a haze. Wait at least 24 hr. before touching. Seal the grout after a few weeks.

Layout logic. Make a scale drawing of the project first, allowing for the grouting space between the tiles, typically 1/16 to 1/8 inch. During the planning, try to minimize the number of tiles that will need to be cut and avoid using narrow strips of tile. Take along the drawing when buying the tiles.

Color cognizant. If a backsplash design includes both plain and decorative tiles, buy both at the same time, along with any edging you'll be using. You'll be sure to get the perfect color match.

Buyer's guide. Ceramic tile is classified by its porosity. *Nonvitreous* is highly porous; *semi-vitreous* is moderately porous; *vitreous* is least porous, making it the perfect choice for a kitchen backsplash or a bathroom.

Solid backup. Though you can apply tiles directly to the wall, a cement backer board offers a better setting surface. Made for tile, it resists water and moisture. Don't use plywood backing.

Tapering off. When a counter extends beyond the cabinets above it, taper off a backsplash from the height of the cabinets by stepping down the tiles from the side of the cabinet to the end of the countertop.

Top it off. If the backsplash doesn't extend right up to the overhanging cabinets, finish it off with bull-nose tile trim in a matching or contrasting color, a wooden molding, or a shallow spice rack. If wood is used, seal it with a durable waterproof finish; it will need to be wiped down more often than regular woodwork.

Visual aid. If you can't visualize how a pattern will look, make color photocopies of the tile and tape them to the wall. Rearrange until you have the right look.

A pressed-tin backsplash combines style and function without grout maintenance hassles. Apply construction adhesive to a precut sheet of tin, place it against the wall to fit, and nail it in place. Paint it with oil-base primer and two coats of oil-base enamel.

Installing a ceramic tile backsplash

WHAT YOU'LL NEED

Masking tape and sandpaper

Carpenter's level

Pencil and permanent marker

Tile spacers and straightedge

Tiles

Tile wet saw or snap cutter

Tile nippers (if needed)

Electric drill and hole saw (if needed)

Notched trowel

Tile adhesive

Unsanded grout and grout trowel

Sponge and towel or scouring pad

Silicone sealant and angled foam brush

Caulk and caulking gun

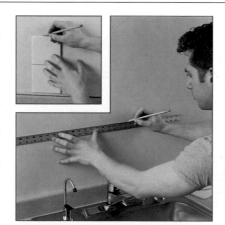

1 Plan your backsplash to be at least 8 in. high. Turn off the power to the receptacles and switches, and tape over the outlets to protect them from tile adhesive. Make sure the walls are clean and sound; sand glossy painted surfaces. Check the countertop for level, and plan the tile layout carefully to minimize the need for cutting (inset). Pencil layout marks on the wall as needed to guide the installation.

2 Mark cut lines on tiles with a permanent marker. If you must make many straight cuts, rent a tile wet saw; otherwise, use a snap cutter. Make curved cuts with tile nippers, and make holes with a carbide-tipped hole saw in an electric drill. Allow tiles that were wet-cut to dry before installation.

 Buy extra tiles—cutting them neatly takes practice.

Missing tiles. If you've miscalculated the number of tiles—or want to change the design—get the extra tiles right away. Buying soon after the purchase date of the first batch increases the chances of finding a close match in the second batch.

A final check. Before gluing the tiles onto the wall, assemble them on a worktable or on the counter directly below the area where they will be installed. Space the tiles to allow for the width of the grout joints, and review the final layout and color scheme.

Loosen electrical outlets so the tile fits underneath the outlet ears, making the outlet flush with the tile. Use electrical box extensions if required by code.

Fragile beauty. Use fragile decorative tiles on a wall or backsplash, but not on a countertop. They may crack under the heavy traffic of plates and pans.

Bottom to top. When tiling a backsplash, always start at the countertop and work up. Maintain an even space between the counter and the backsplash by using shims underneath the edges of the lowest row of tiles.

Before the adhesive dries on the back of the tiles, level the surface by tapping the tiles with a rubber mallet. To avoid breakage, place a thin board wrapped in carpet over the tiles before tapping. Clean away any adhesive that squeezes through between the tiles.

Finger work. Use your finger to fill grout joints on an inside corner. You can sense just when the joint is full.

Go with the flow. Moisture and temperature changes can crack a grout joint between a countertop and a backsplash, or between a backsplash and wood trim or a cabinet. To avoid a breakup, fill these joints with flexible caulk, which is made to survive such fluctuations.

Tools of the trade. A squeegee is a handy tool for compressing grout and cleaning it off tile surfaces; a popsicle stick or a toothbrush handle is great for packing grout into a joint.

After grouting, wipe the tile surfaces twice with a damp sponge, once in each diagonal direction, to avoid removing fresh grout from the joints.

3 Using the smooth edge of a notched trowel, spread adhesive at about two-thirds the thickness of the tile; then comb it out with the notched edge. Use only as much as can be covered in 20 min. or so. Comb adhesive over the wall evenly, spreading it up to but not over any layout marks. Be sure to keep the adhesive away from the countertop—this area will be filled later with caulk.

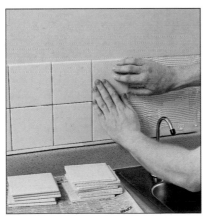

4 Press the tiles into place with a slight twisting motion, starting at the bottom of the wall and working up. Once several tiles are in place, use a straightedge to check the alignment and to make sure the surface of each tile is in the same plane. Allow the adhesive to cure for at least 48 hr.

5 Mix unsanded grout, and force it into the joints by spreading it diagonally across the tiles with a rubber-faced grout trowel. Wait 15 min., and then remove excess grout with a damp sponge. When a dry haze forms on the tiles, remove it with a clean dry towel or nylon scouring pad. Caulk between the countertop and the backsplash several days later. After a week, apply silicone sealant to the grout.

Use it or lose it. When working with patching plaster, pace yourself by mixing only as much as you think you can apply in 20 minutes or less. It's always better to throw out plaster that has already begun to set than to try to reconstitute it with more water, which will affect its appearance.

Material difference. Use a gypsum plaster–perlite mixture when patching plaster. It's cheap and available at most hardware stores and some lumber-yards. Ask for the *regular* formulation. Perlite, a pulverized volcanic glass, makes the mixture light. When dry, it's rock-hard.

Mix it up. If you need a little more durability than joint compound offers, mix some patching plaster into the compound. As a bonus, the blend won't dry out as fast.

A smooth finish. Finish up any plaster repair with a top coat of joint compound. It'll be easier to sand the repair flush with the wall.

Is this crack serious? A crack that is large, recessed, and uneven in width generally is caused by a structural problem. Get professional help to remedy what might be wrong with the house's structure before attempting to fix the crack in the plaster. A crack—usually small—that affects only the surface of the wall or the plaster material itself is probably a superficial fissure that can be easily repaired with joint compound.

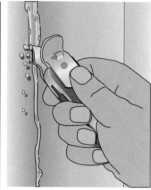

Go wide. To repair a thin crack in plaster, use a can opener to widen it to about ⅛ inch. Then blow out the dust and bits of old paint with a hair dryer. Dampen the crack with a sponge and fill it with patching plaster.

A putty spatula. Patch tiny cracks and nail holes with a small rubber kitchen spatula. It's more flexible and easier to use than a putty knife.

FILE IT

Filling a hole in the wall
Each patching compound has its strengths and weaknesses. Keep them in mind the next time you attempt to mend a hole in plaster or wallboard.

Type	Advantages	Disadvantages
Joint compound	Applies smoothly and sands easily	Takes 24 hours to dry; shrinks
Spackling compound	Dries fast; minimal shrinkage	Harder to sand smooth
Patching plaster	Dries in 2 hours; doesn't shrink; durable	Difficult to sand

Repairing damaged plaster

WHAT YOU'LL NEED

Drop cloths

Dust mask, work gloves, and goggles

Painter's tool

Spray bottle with water

Latex bonder

Hawk or plywood scrap (to hold plaster)

Plaster of Paris and joint compound

4-in. and 10-in. taping knives

Sanding block

Primer and paint

Putty knife

80-grit flint sandpaper

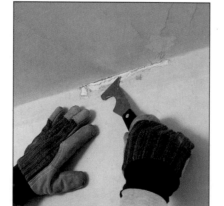

1 To repair a plaster crack, first move furniture out of the area and put down drop cloths. Wearing a dust mask, some form of eye protection, and work gloves, scrape out loose material with a painter's tool.

2 Dust out the inside of the crack and lightly mist with water (top); wait a few minutes until the plaster absorbs the water. Apply a latex bonder, which bonds the new plaster to the plaster wall; allow about 45 min. drying time. Fill the crack with plaster, joint compound, or a mixture of the two. Sand when it is completely dry. Spot-prime and paint.

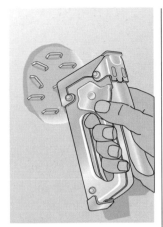

Staple a crater. Prepare a large, shallow wall crater for plaster by driving staples partway into the surface being covered. The staples provide anchor points to hold the filling compound until it makes a secure bond. Make sure the level of the staples is slightly below the surrounding wall surface so they won't show through the new plaster.

In a hole? When a hole in a plaster wall is too large to be filled by joint compound alone but isn't exactly a crater, apply self-adhesive fiberglass mesh tape (used for wallboard) in a crisscross pattern over it. Finish off with two or three coats of joint compound.

Putty knife too narrow? A hole filled with joint compound can look messy if it is wider than the putty knife. Instead of gouging the compound with the corners of the knife, use a wider smoothing tool or hold a metal ruler on edge and pass it across the patch.

Blow dry. Encourage small patches of joint compound to dry with a hair dryer set on a low temperature. Apply the heat evenly to keep the compound from cracking.

Wallboard over plaster. When covering an old plaster wall with wallboard, find the underlying studs and mark their location. Align the edges of the wallboard over the studs, and fasten it to the plaster and studs with 2-inch drywall screws. Tape and fill the seams as you normally would; then finish off the job with paint.

On the surface. An old plaster wall or ceiling often has a distinctive texture that needs to be matched when it is patched. While the plaster patch is still damp, use a comb, sponge, or stiff brush to replicate the texture. It may help to make a practice patch on a board first to ensure a better match with the wall texture.

Sand art. When making a patch in plaster with a sandy texture, fill the hole with plaster until it's nearly flush with the surface. Then seal the patch with latex primer, and finish it with paint laced with sand.

For a smooth finish, clean the putty knife frequently by running it over a clean scrap of wood. This prevents dried bits of compound from getting into the fresh stuff and marring the final coat.

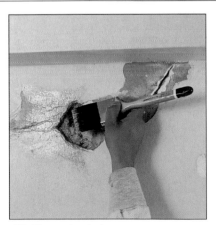

3 To repair a hole, remove any loose or crumbling plaster with a painter's tool. Dust out the inside of the hole and lightly mist with water; wait a few minutes until the plaster absorbs the water. Apply a latex bonder, and allow about 45 min. to dry.

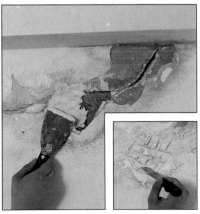

4 Mix enough plaster of Paris to fill the hole. Using a 4-in. taping knife, fill the hole from the center out, to a depth just below the wall surface (above). Before the plaster sets, scratch the surface in a crosshatch pattern with a putty knife. This improves adhesion of the final coat. Let the plaster dry.

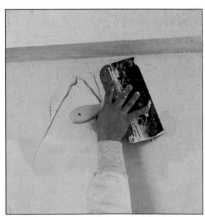

5 Using a 10-in. taping knife, apply a finish coat of joint compound. Check the wall to make sure the surface is level and that there are no indentations caused by air bubbles. If necessary, apply another thin coat of compound. When the patch is dry, sand lightly with 80-grit flint sandpaper.

Odd sizes. Before ordering wallboard, ask about the different sizes of panels that can be ordered. Covering walls that are 9 feet tall with 4-foot panels would require taping two horizontal seams on each wall. Some companies make 4 ½-foot panels, which would require only one taping per wall.

A good screw-up. You should fasten wallboard panels to studs with screws instead of nails whenever possible. You'll save a lot of hammer swinging, and down the road you won't have to fuss with nailheads that inevitably pop out.

A tight fit. Successful fastening requires setting the screws at the proper depth within the wallboard: recessed enough to allow taping compound to hide the screwhead from view but not so deep that the screw punches a hole in the paper and pulverizes the gypsum core.

Nails popping out? Drive additional nails about 2 inches above and below the popped head. Then, holding the wallboard tight to the stud, hammer all the nails until recessed dimples show around the heads. Don't break the paper face. Dust off loose paint and plaster, and fill the dimples with joint compound using a 6-inch taping knife. When the joint compound is dry, sand with fine sandpaper and then paint.

Cutting corners. To cut wallboard that runs past the outside corner of a wall, hold the panel in place and use a utility knife to score the back side of the sheet, using the corner's edge as a guide. Then snap the section forward and complete the cut from the front side.

Heady help. It's common to prop up wallboard with your head before nailing it to a ceiling. To cushion your head and reduce neck strain, wear a hat with padding inside it.

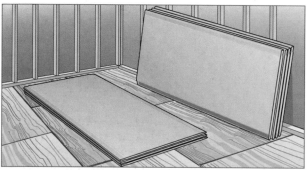

Proper storage. Store wallboard panels in a cool place that has good air circulation and low humidity. Stack the panels flat, or place them on their long edges. And don't forget: wallboard panels are heavy, so lighten the load on floor joists by dividing large groups into several smaller stacks.

Repairing damaged wallboard

WHAT YOU'LL NEED

Square, straightedge, and tape measure
Pencil and level
Wallboard saw (optional)
Utility knife
Scrap wood for nailers
Phillips screwdriver or electric drill
Wallboard screws (varying lengths)
Scrap wallboard for patch
Rasp (optional)
Joint compound and wallboard tape
6-in. taping knife
Fine sandpaper and sanding block

1 You'll need to remove a rectangular section of wallboard larger than the hole and reaching to the edges of the studs on both sides. Mark cut lines with a pencil and a level. Use a square to make sure corners are 90°.

 Enlarge the hole if necessary to locate the studs and any wiring or pipes.

2 Cut the wallboard with a wallboard saw or a utility knife and straightedge. Cut the nailers slightly longer than the opening, and fasten them to the studs with drywall screws.

Support system. When working alone, nail blocks to the studs to support a wallboard panel. For partition walls, tighten a C clamp to a stud and lift the panel onto the clamp.

Inside jobs. On inside corners, apply joint compound in two steps. If you finish both sides at once, the knife will foul the first side while you work on the second.

Making the connection. Rub chalk on the face of an electrical box. Lightly rest the panel to be fastened against the wall and electrical box; then tap the panel firmly with your fist, and the outline of the box will appear on the backing. Pierce the center of the outline with a wallboard saw, and use the outline as a guide to cut the opening.

Mix the mix. Get rid of air bubbles in premixed joint compound by blending it with a clean stirring stick or utensil. Otherwise, the bubbles might show up where you don't want them—on the wall.

Visual effects. When sanding overhead, seal out dust with a pair of ordinary swim goggles. They are airtight and lightweight, and they provide plenty of visibility.

Leave the dust behind. Joint compound is water-soluble, so edges can be feathered with a wet wallboard sponge (available at hardware stores) instead of a sanding block. Dip the sponge in water, squeeze out the excess, then use it like a sanding block, being careful not to soak the paper face of the wallboard; it rips when wet.

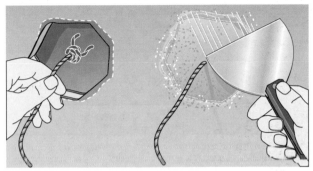

The hole story. Repairing holes in wallboard can be tricky, since there is usually no backing behind them. This technique works well for holes up to 2 inches wide: Cut a piece of firm cardboard slightly larger than the hole. Insert a piece of strong string through the cardboard, and knot it at the back. Push the cardboard through the hole and pull it tight to form a backing. Apply fast-drying joint compound to the hole. When the patch dries, cut the string flush against the wall with a knife. Score the surface of the patch. Apply more compound and smooth it out; then sand and paint.

3 Measure and cut a wallboard patch with a utility knife and straightedge. If possible, use the removed piece of wallboard as a template. Position the new piece of wallboard in the opening, trimming it with a utility knife or rasp as necessary. Fasten it with 1¼-in. drywall screws. Trim any loose paper or gypsum that projects above the surface with a utility knife.

4 Apply a coat of joint compound over all seams (top) with a 6-in. taping knife. Embed paper joint tape in the compound by drawing the knife across the tape at an angle and squeezing out most, but not all, of the compound (bottom).

 Avoid overlapping the tape at the corners.

5 When the first coat dries (usually overnight), apply a second coat that extends 6 in. beyond the first coat. When that coat dries, scrape off any bumps or ridges; apply a third coat that extends another 6 in. beyond. When dry, sand lightly with fine sandpaper; sweep and vacuum to remove all dust before you prime and paint.

Get thin. If you've never installed sheet vinyl, choose one of the thinner, less expensive vinyl products; they are easier to install than the thicker ones. If you prefer a thicker, higher-quality vinyl, hire a professional to install it.

No cover-up. Before putting down new vinyl, make sure the subflooring is free of dirt, polish, paint spills, and plaster bits. Imperfections will cause the vinyl to deteriorate from the underside.

Don't remove old vinyl. Flooring laid before 1982 may contain asbestos fibers, and removing it may release them into the air. Lay new flooring over the old instead. If the old flooring has to be removed, it's time to call in a professional.

Strip down to bare wood. To remove sheet vinyl from a floor, use a sharp knife to cut it into strips 10 inches wide. Wrap one end of each strip around a rolling pin, and peel up the vinyl by rolling the pin back along the strip. Roll up the other strips until all are removed. If felt backing remains on the subflooring, moisten the backing with warm soapy water and scrape it off with a floor scraper.

First, flatten it. Tightly rolled vinyl can be a chore to flatten out before it's fitted into a room. Tame its springiness by spreading the flooring on the front lawn or driveway for a while; the warm sunlight will relax it.

Then, let it acclimate. After the vinyl flooring has relaxed, roll it out in the room where it will be installed and let it sit for at least an hour. This will give the vinyl time to adjust to the room's temperature.

Out-of-the-way seams. If vinyl must be seamed, plan so that the seams do not fall directly in doorways. In addition, seams in the vinyl should be positioned at least 6 inches away from seams in the subflooring.

Roll out the bubbles. To flatten out pesky air bubbles when pressing the vinyl into the adhesive, run a floor roller across the newly laid flooring. You can usually rent one from the store where you purchased the vinyl.

Storing rolled vinyl? Lay it on the floor. If it's stored on end, the weight of the roll may cause the flooring to crack or warp.

Patching vinyl flooring

WHAT YOU'LL NEED

Scrap vinyl flooring	Toothed trowel or plastic applicator
Utility knife	Damp cloth
Masking tape	Heavy weight
Straightedge	
Stiff-bladed putty knife or scraper	
Flooring adhesive	

1 Cut an oversize patch from the scrap. Place it over the damaged area, align the pattern, and tape it in place. Simultaneously cut the patch and the flooring beneath with a utility knife (held vertically) and straightedge.

2 Remove the top (new) piece of vinyl and set it aside. Peel up the damaged flooring. Scrape off the old adhesive from the underlayment with a stiff-bladed putty knife or scraper.

3 Apply flooring adhesive to underlayment with a toothed trowel or plastic applicator (left). If vinyl was installed with perimeter adhesive, spread adhesive under cut edges. Press patch in place and clean off adhesive. Apply weight for 24 hr.

Vinyl tiles can work nicely in the kitchen, but sheet vinyl works better in a bathroom. Fewer seams means less water leaking through in case of a flood.

To secure a loose tile, apply adhesive beneath the edges, then drive one finishing nail into each corner and an additional one along each seam. Fill the nail dimples with matching caulk.

Cool tool cleaner. To remove dried flooring adhesive from the surface of a tool, set it in the freezer overnight. The next morning the adhesive will be hard as a rock and can be chipped off easily. Wear safety goggles when doing this.

SAFE AND SMART

➤ Sponge-mop vinyl flooring with a solution of warm water and clear ammonia to minimize dulling films.

➤ Remove scuff marks from vinyl flooring by rubbing them with a soft abrasive pad using a circular motion. Shine with a wool-felt or lamb's-wool pad.

➤ Prevent floor damage by supporting heavy appliances on wide rust-proof floor protectors.

A smooth way in. At the entrance to a room with vinyl floor covering, bind the edge of the flooring with a metal threshold strip to prevent the vinyl from curling. The strip will also form a smooth transition to the flooring in the adjacent room, preventing people from tripping over the edge.

The best of both. Liven up a dull floor by laying decorative tiles into cutouts made in a sheet vinyl floor that is the same thickness as the tiles. Note: This won't work for perimeter-laid floors (adhesive only at the edges).

Top coat. Scuffing and scraping will wear off the clear top layer of vinyl tiles. Restore the deteriorating areas with vinyl sealant, available at flooring outlets and home centers.

Leave no soap. Rinse off soapy floor cleaners well, or they will leave a thin film that attracts dirt and clouds any polish that is put on top of it. Designate a separate mop for rinsing.

Store vinyl tiles flat, in their box. Tiles that have been removed from their box may curl, making them hard to install. Weight down loose tiles to prevent them from curling up.

Replacing a vinyl tile

WHAT YOU'LL NEED

Hair dryer, or steam iron and toweling	Rubber mallet or hammer
Stiff-bladed putty knife or scraper	Wood block
Latex tile adhesive	Damp cloth (if needed)
Notched applicator	Board and heavy weight
Replacement tile	

1 Warm the damaged tile with a hair dryer to soften it and the adhesive. Or lay a towel over the tile and apply heat with an iron. Starting at a corner, work a stiff-bladed putty knife under the tile and gently pry it up.

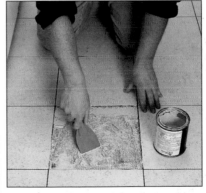

2 Scrape off all adhesive residue from the underlayment, being careful not to damage the edges of the remaining tiles. Apply a uniform coat of flooring adhesive with a disposable notched applicator. Do not get the adhesive on your hands.

3 Warm the replacement tile as in step 1. Align one edge and lower it into place. Tap with a mallet and wood block to seat it. Wipe off any adhesive with a damp cloth. Lay a board over the entire tile and weight it down for 24 hr.

Price the job first. Add up the cost of all the materials and then contact a few flooring installers. They may be getting the same materials wholesale, making their whole-job price more attractive than you anticipated.

Check the real thing. Never choose prefinished flooring from photographs alone. Visit a flooring dealer and compare various products. Place several pieces of flooring together so you can check edge details such as beveling.

How moist? Install wood flooring when the moisture content is between 6 and 9 percent (measure the stock with a moisture meter). Properly dried flooring will minimize warping, swelling, and shrinking later.

Install a vapor barrier. Lay down a protective layer between the subflooring and the wood flooring to prevent moisture from seeping into the wood from below. For best results, install a layer of 15-pound felt.

To fasten strip flooring, nail through the tongue of each board at intervals of 8 inches, angling the nails back toward the board. When the adjoining board is fitted over the tongue, the nailheads will be covered.

Nail it. Floorboards need to be independently fastened in place so they can shrink and expand separately from one another. As the boards shrink, gaps will form around each one, but they're so tiny that they're seldom noticeable.

Wide-plank flooring (4 inches wide or more) must be screwed into the joists and subflooring, in addition to being nailed through the tongue, to prevent excessive shrinkage. Finish the screwheads by sinking them slightly and then covering them with wood putty or wood plugs.

The match game. Before filling nail holes or covering screwheads in a wood floor, custom-color the putty. Mix dust from the final sanding of the floor with a sufficient amount of sealer to form a sticky paste. Then use a putty knife to force the paste down into cracks and nail holes, scraping off the excess. After the paste has dried on the surface, use 100-grit sandpaper to smooth the filled areas by hand.

Repairing a damaged floorboard

WHAT YOU'LL NEED

Square and pencil
Electric drill with bits
¾-in. spade bit
Wood chisel and hammer
Pry bar
Nail puller and nail set
Saw
Spiral flooring nails
Wood block and mallet
Wood putty, sander, and sandpaper
Wood finish and applicator

1 To remove a damaged floorboard, draw a line square across the width of the board. Using a drill with a ¾-in. spade bit, bore several holes along the line, on the damaged side of the line. Carefully chisel along the line so that the edge is square.

2 Bore several holes along the centerline of the damaged floorboard, with no more than 1 ft. between holes. Drive a chisel along the center of the floorboard to split it lengthwise. Chisel as needed to break up the board, and remove the waste with a pry bar. (Repeat steps 1 and 2 to remove adjacent floorboards, if necessary.)

Finish up. Before refinishing, determine the kind of finish originally applied. Use a sharp edge to scratch the floor in an obscure spot. If flakes form, a surface finish was probably applied. No flakes means it was likely a penetrating sealant. Next, try smudging an inconspicuous spot with a dry sponge. A smudge indicates wax, which means that the floor will have to be sanded to bare wood.

Gauge the finish. Lightly draw a pencil mark across a few floorboards in a high-traffic area before applying the protective finishing coat. When the pencil mark begins to wear off, it's time to apply another coat.

SAFE AND SMART

➤ Fill dents in a wood floor with clear nail polish or shellac. The floor's color shows through, so the dents won't stand out.

➤ Paint ceilings and walls before refinishing floors. You'll avoid drips on the finish and scratches from rearranging furniture and the inevitable dropped putty knives.

➤ When refinishing a floor, temporarily seal adjacent doorways with clear plastic sheets to collect sawdust and prevent it from invading other rooms.

Move quickly. Work as fast as possible when applying clear finishes to floors. The coat can dry quickly, causing streaks to emerge and spoiling the look.

Slow-cured coating. A water-base polyurethane floor coating lasts longer if it is allowed to cure slowly. Minimize air movement in the room by turning off the heating or air conditioning and closing the windows and doors. Wear a respirator.

Creaking and squeaking floors can often be silenced by driving shims into the gaps between the joists and the subflooring. Brush both sides of the shim with construction adhesive; then tap it firmly into the gap.

Gluing squeaks. Use hot-melt glue or construction adhesive to silence a squeaky floor. As a helper walks on the floor above, mark the spots that squeak from below. Inject the glue between the subflooring and the joist at each mark, running the glue along both sides of the joist.

3 Pull nails, being careful not to break any tongues or grooves on remaining boards. If it is difficult to remove some nails, sink them with a nail set. Cut the replacement board to fit snugly. (If you've removed more than one board, start replacing on the side where tongues are exposed. Fasten boards with flooring nails driven into the tongues at a 45° angle every 8 in.)

4 Chisel off the lower lip of the groove on the replacement board so that it will fit over the exposed tongue. (If you have removed more than one board, do this on only the last replacement board.) You may also have to bevel or back-cut the upper lip slightly. Place the board in position, cover it with a wood block, and strike it with a mallet until it is flush.

5 Drill pilot holes for the flooring nails every 12 in. on the groove side of the replacement board (just the last board, if you have replaced more than one), ½ in. from the edge. To avoid splitting hardwood, use a slightly larger bit to drill a ⅛-in.-deep well for the nailhead in addition to the pilot hole. Sink nails with a nail set. Fill the nail holes. Sand and finish the boards to match the existing flooring.

FILE IT

Step by step: Anatomy of a staircase

Knowing the different components of a staircase is very helpful, especially when you need to make repairs.

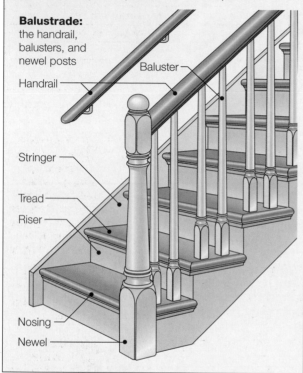

Balustrade:
the handrail, balusters, and newel posts

- Handrail
- Baluster
- Stringer
- Tread
- Riser
- Nosing
- Newel

Foam fix. Quiet squeaky stairs that are open from behind with polyurethane foam sealant. Squirt the foam along the open space between the tread and riser; as it dries, it expands to fill the gap. Don't squirt too much foam or it could leak through the front.

A little dab will do it. When you can't get under the stairs, one of the quickest ways to silence a musical step is by running a bead of caulk under the nose, cushioning the joint where the tread meets the riser.

Nail it down. To fix a squeak from above, fasten the treads to the stringers and risers with spiral-shank flooring nails that are 3 times as long as the thickness of the tread. Fill the nail or screw holes with wood putty; then lightly sand them. Paint or stain.

Work in pairs. For extra bite, drill pilot holes slightly smaller than the nails you're going to install. Pairs of nails, placed several inches apart and angled toward each other, will hold better than single nails.

Step on it. It helps to have someone stand on the step while you drive a screw from the tread into the riser.

Fastener facts. If you are installing screws in a tread or riser, drill pilot holes with a profile bit that matches the screw size. It widens the entrance to the screw hole, so that the screwhead can be sunk below the surface and covered with putty.

The hiding game. If a baluster in a prominent spot becomes damaged, swap it with one from a less visible part of the same stairway. Fasten it in its new spot with glue, if possible, or with a few finishing nails run from the top of the baluster into the rail and from the bottom into the tread.

Search for replacements. Sometimes matching balusters can be found in a salvage yard. If not, consider ordering a custom-made baluster. Remove a sample baluster and take it to a millworking firm that specializes in stairways.

Fasten loose balusters. As a house settles, once-snug handrails and balusters can become loose. Tighten them by drilling a hole at an angle through each baluster into the handrail and screwing the baluster to the rail.

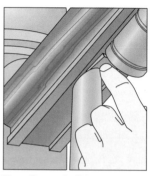

Very loose balusters can be tightened with shims. Tap each one in place with a block and a mallet; then carefully trim the edges with a utility knife. Finish the edges that show so that they are uniform with the rest of the woodwork.

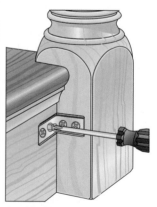

Renewing a newel. A loose newel post can be tightened up by screwing small angle brackets to the base of the post on both sides and fixing them to the staircase. To make the repair less conspicuous, chisel out a 1/8-inch recess for the bracket; then cover it with wood filler, sand it, and paint or stain.

If a tread needs replacing, look for stock at a lumber-yard, matching the shape and thickness of a worn or damaged tread as closely as possible. Better yet, see if the tread might be usable if it is turned over.

Tread tips. When replacing a tread, pine is usually the wood of choice if you're going to cover it with carpet. Go with oak if the tread will be exposed and stained.

Removing old carpeting from stairs usually means pulling up loads of tacks An old screwdriver with a sharp end makes a wonderful tack puller. Wearing goggles, simply slip it under the head of each tack and give it a gentle twist. The tack should lift out of the carpet without causing damage.

Worn carpeting on a stairway need not be discarded. Carpeting wears out most quickly on the nosings of the stair treads. To make the carpet look almost like new, move it an inch or two along the length of the stairway so that the worn spots are in a less conspicuous place. Another option is to switch the carpet around, top to bottom.

Conceal staples on a long-napped stair runner by brushing the nap over the staples. If the runner has a short nap, use an artist's brush to touch up the staples carefully with matching paint.

Estimate a stair runner by measuring a tread and a riser, and multiplying the sum of the measurements by the number of steps in the stair. Add a few extra feet for fitting, and a few more for repairing any sections that might be damaged later on.

Steep basement stairs? Apply a coat of white or yellow paint to the top and bottom steps to help people spot them at a glance. Run a strip of fluorescent tape or neon paint on treads that aren't well lighted.

A good foothold. Give stairs some extra traction by installing V-shaped metal or vinyl "nosing" guards over the edge of the steps. The top is ridged, so you don't slide on the stair's edge. Metal guards are screwed on; vinyl ones are pasted on with contact cement.

Fixing squeaky stair treads

WHAT YOU'LL NEED

Wooden wedges	Various drill bits
Hammer	Wooden blocks and screws
Wood glue	
Metal L-shaped shelf brackets and screws	
Electric drill	

1 To silence a squeaky stair tread, try tapping wooden wedges into the joints until they are just snug. You may want to coat the wedges with wood glue and inject some additional glue into the joint from either behind or above.

2 Metal L-shaped shelf brackets can also hush a creaky stair tread. Install two brackets, positioning them underneath the tread and behind the riser. Space them on either side, each about a third of the way from the stringers.

3 Another option for silencing a squeak is to secure wood blocks beneath the stairs where the tread meets the riser. Glue both surfaces, place each block about a third of the way from the stringers, and drive screws into the tread and the riser.

Start with the roof.

To keep a basement dry, install gutters, downspouts, and extensions to channel rain away from the house. This prevents puddling around the foundation and seepage into the basement.

Watershed experience.

The ground around a foundation should slope away from the house at a rate of 6 inches for every 10 feet. To ensure that the slope sheds water rather than absorbing it, put a layer of clay beneath the topsoil or sod.

Cracks are big trouble.

Open cracks along the basement floor, or vertical cracks along a basement wall that are wider at the top than at the bottom, indicate a possible problem with the footings beneath the foundation. Consult a structural engineer for advice.

Clear drainpipes.

Roof drainpipes that go into the ground should be free of clogs. A clogged drainpipe can inject water into the ground next to the foundation, sending it back to the basement.

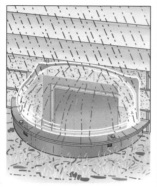

Window-well cover-ups.

During a heavy rain, a basement window well can fill up with water, which can then seep into the basement. Cover up basement window wells with clear plastic domes.

Divining dampness.

To find the source of moisture, use a hair dryer to dry out a patch of wall about 15 inches square. Then tape a 12-inch-square sheet of plastic in the center of the dry area. Check the plastic after 2 days. If the underside is wet, the problem is seepage from the outside. If the top side is wet, it's condensation from the inside.

Before you paint

a basement wall with waterproofing paint, treat any leakage problems. Though an interior waterproofing paint can reduce dampness from seepage, it can also contribute to serious water damage if it masks a leak.

Coatings aren't all wet.

Oil-base epoxies provide the most water resistance when brushed on an interior wall. Less expensive alternatives are oil paints specially made for waterproofing. Two coats provide a good seal.

Cut condensation

in a basement by insulating cold-water pipes and air-conditioning ducts and by venting clothes dryers. Use a dehumidifier during the summer. If the basement is finished, an air conditioner can also remove excess moisture.

Fixing a leak in a basement wall

WHAT YOU'LL NEED

Eye protection, dust mask, and gloves

Cold chisel

Small sledge- or mason's hammer

Stiff-bristle brush, water, and buckets

Vacuum (optional)

Hydraulic cement

Pointed trowel

Wood block (optional)

Shovel and tarp

Sand and masonry cement (if needed)

Foundation sealant

Paintbrushes

Exterior paint

Topsoil and splash block (optional)

1 When patching a minor leak from the inside, wear eye protection, a dust mask, and heavy gloves. With a cold chisel and a small sledge- or mason's hammer, remove any loose or crumbling material. Chisel at an angle to undercut the crack (this will lock in the patching material when it hardens). Brush or vacuum the area to remove all debris and dust; then dampen the area, unless it is saturated from leakage.

2 Mix hydraulic cement according to the manufacturer's instructions; as it cures, the material expands for a better bond, even under water. Apply the cement, using two layers for deep holes. Press it into the cavity with a pointed trowel, slightly overfilling. Then level and smooth the patch, using the trowel or a block of wood in a circular motion. Wash the tools immediately, before the cement cures.

Test the joints. Leakage often occurs along the joint where a porch, patio, driveway, or walkway meets the foundation. Fill the joint with a high-quality sealant such as silicone. Then check the drainage pitch to see if the water can be encouraged to run off faster, or in a different place.

Drainage check. To see if the subgrade drain system is working, disconnect the downspouts that run into it. Then add an elbow to the existing pipe and attach it to a 4-foot length of drainpipe. Direct this pipe away from the house. If the basement remains dry after a heavy rainstorm, the problem is in the subgrade system.

Get a good grade. Faulty grading may be the cause of a wet basement. To find out, tape a sheet of plastic to the siding and slope it to the ground at least 4 feet away from the foundation. If the basement stays dry after a rain, regrade the ground around the foundation so that it slopes more sharply.

Install an interior drain when water accumulation in the basement is caused by a high water table. Hire a contractor to do the job. The drain should lead to a sump pump that moves water outside the home.

Back up a sump pump. To prevent water from rising in the basement during a power outage, install a battery-operated sump pump as a backup.

Lighten up. Reflect sunlight into a dark basement by filling window wells with white crushed rock.

A clean finish. To keep basement dirt and dust from being tracked upstairs, park a nonslip mat near the bottom of the stairs so that anyone heading upstairs will have to walk over it.

Swale away. To avoid regrading around the foundation, dig a shallow trench, called a swale, to direct water away from the house. Place the swale 6 feet from the house. Slope the trench downward, leading away from the house, 1 inch per foot. Reseed the trench with grass, or in areas where there is heavy runoff, line it with gravel.

3 If the foundation wall is accessible, patch the crack from the outside. Dig a trench several feet deep, piling the soil on a tarp. Scrape off dirt from the wall with a metal trowel, and scrub it with a stiff-bristle brush and water; then let the wall dry.

! **Don't clean the wall with spray from a garden hose—it will take too long to dry.**

4 Chisel out the crack as in step 1. Narrow cracks need only to be sealed; cracks wider than 1/8 in. should be filled with a mixture of 70% sand and 30% masonry cement. Brush on a sealant, extending it 6 in. on all sides of the crack. Allow the sealant to dry (some require a day of drying time); then apply a second coat and let it dry.

5 Paint over the sealant, covering an entire section of the foundation wall, if possible, to ensure a uniform finish. Refill the trench, adding new topsoil if necessary, so that the soil slopes away from the house. To prevent future leaks, replant any flowers or shrubs at least 4 ft. from the house. As another safeguard, place a splash block beneath the downspout to divert water away from the house.

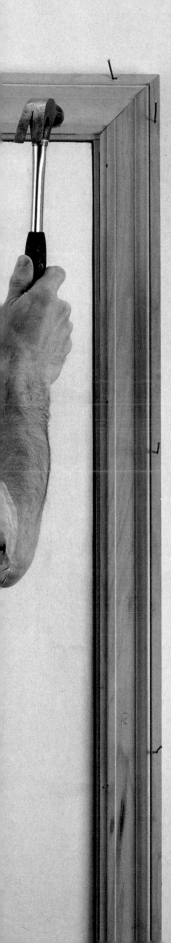

WINDOWS AND DOORS

Job ratings:　　Easy　　Medium　　Complex

Seal cracked glass temporarily or plug up a small hole in a flash by brushing the breach with clear shellac or nail polish.

Erase shallow scratches on glass by dabbing them with a little toothpaste and then polishing the area vigorously for a minute or two. "Extra-whitening" brands usually work best because they contain higher levels of abrasives.

Removing cracked glass? Wear safety goggles and thick gloves, and work from the top down—if a stray piece of glass drops, it won't fall on your hand.

A good scrape. Lift glazier's points easily from wooden sashes by scraping them out with a small hook scraper, used by painters. The scraper will also remove any loose putty and paint in the same motion.

Becoming soft. Remove stubborn window putty with a heat gun or hair dryer. Wave the appliance back and forth along a 4-inch length of putty, being careful not to scorch the frame or overheat the glass. When the putty softens, slide a putty knife underneath it and pry upward.

A buyer's guide. Take a shard of broken glass with you to the hardware store when buying a replacement pane. Most glass for ordinary-size windows (not picture windows) is either single-strength ($3/32$ inch thick) or double-strength ($1/8$ inch thick), available in two grades: A (superior) or B (standard). Choose double-strength for storm windows and for panes in vulnerable locations.

Wear rubber gloves when handling new glass. They provide a sure grip and won't leave fingerprints on the pane—not to mention cutting down on nicks.

Carry large pieces of glass vertically; they can break under their own weight when carried horizontally.

Replacing a broken pane in a wooden window

WHAT YOU'LL NEED

Duct tape

Heavy gloves and goggles

Hammer and stiff putty knife

Old chisel (optional)

Needle-nose pliers

Paint primer or other sealer

Tape measure

Glazing compound

Replacement glass

Glazier's points

Screwdriver (optional)

Exterior paint and brush

1 Wearing gloves and goggles, use a hammer and putty knife or chisel to remove the glazing compound. Pull out the glazier's points—thin metal wedges that hold the glass in the frame—with pliers; remove the glass. It may be easier to remove the sash first.

 Tape over cracked glass to prevent it from falling apart during removal.

2 Scrape out all old compound; paint any unfinished wood with primer or with a sealer such as linseed oil. Have new glass cut to order; use the old glass as a pattern, or carefully measure the opening and deduct $1/8$ in. from both dimensions.

An easy score. Scoring glass neatly with a glass cutter is easier if you start the cut on a piece of scrap glass placed against the top edge of the pane you want to cut. Draw the cutter smoothly, scoring the glass from top to bottom in a single stroke.

A slick trick. When you're glazing, lightly grease the putty knife with boiled linseed oil to avoid pulling out the glazing compound on the final pass.

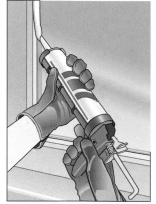

Good move. Caulk-style glazing compound (window putty) is even easier to apply than the canned variety. Using a caulking gun, apply a ribbon of compound around the inside window opening before installing the glass. Afterward, apply another ribbon to the glass. Trim the compound and let it harden before painting it.

Stay out of the sun. Wash windows on cloudy days for a dazzling shine. Bright sunlight dries window cleaner too rapidly, causing streaks. Also, use vertical strokes on one side of the glass and horizontal strokes on the other to allow you to pinpoint any streaks that do form.

Frames before panes. Clean painted wood or metal window frames before cleaning the glass to avoid re-spotting clean panes.

Vacuum natural wood window frames rather than washing them with harsh, dulling detergents. When cleaning is necessary, use a wood cleaner labeled for use on natural wood finishes.

Unpainted aluminum window frames quickly develop a gray coating of natural oxides that protects the metal against corrosion. Restore the shine by polishing the frame with very fine steel wool and applying a clear lacquer to preserve the glow.

Security matters. For impact-resistant windows, replace vulnerable panes with polycarbonate plastic, which can be cut with a saw and installed like window glass. The downside? Polycarbonate is expensive and scratches easily.

3 Using a putty knife, apply glazing compound to the channel all around the opening. Depending on how firm the glazing compound is, you can also roll it out with your hand to form a thin rope, then press the rope all around the opening. Position the new glass and press it firmly against the glazing compound.

4 To set the glass securely, press glazier's points into the muntins and against the glass with a screwdriver or stiff putty knife. Use at least two per side, spacing them every 4–6 in. When finished, scrape off excess glazing compound from the inside with a putty knife.

5 Apply glazing compound over the edges of the glass with a putty knife, or roll out a ⅜-in.-diameter rope of glazing compound and press it against the perimeter of the glass. Hold a putty knife at an angle and draw it across the compound, pressing firmly and working out from the corners. The compound should not be visible from indoors. Let it cure before painting.

When buying windows, mind your R's and U's. R-value gauges a window's resistance to heat flow and U-value measures the conductance of heat. The best windows will have high R numbers and low U's.

Moisture or cloudiness between the panes of an insulated sash means that water vapor has leaked into the sealed space. Check your owner's warranty; chances are the faulty sash will have to be replaced with a new one.

Super sealant. Standard oil-base putty can dissolve the all-important sealant between the panes of insulated sashes. Instead use specially made sealants that are recommended by the manufacturer.

Go to the film. Clear or tinted insulating window film can chop winter heating and summer cooling bills. Make sure the film is labeled "low-e" for low emissivity. Tinted film reduces summer heat more than clear film, but you may not need it in areas with moderate summer temperatures.

Clean window film with a solution of dishwashing soap and water. Harsh ammonia-base cleansers can damage it.

Window film cracking? To remove it, try spraying it with a solution of water mixed with a few drops of liquid dishwashing detergent. Apply one coat, let it soak in for 10 to 15 minutes, and spray it again. Then scrape off the damaged film with a 2-inch stiff-bladed plastic putty knife.

From the inside out. To improve window performance without the high cost of replacing old windows or installing exterior storm-and-screen combinations, try inside storm windows. Most interior storm windows are held in place with easy-to-install magnetic strips or Velcro for quick removal.

Installing new sashes

WHAT YOU'LL NEED

Utility knife

Trim pry bar or putty knife

Cutting pliers (if chain)

Screwdriver

Yardstick or similar rod

Fiberglass insulation

Replacement sashes

Nail puller

Hammer and 4d finishing nails

Nail set

Caulk and touch-up paint

1 Pry off the interior stops and save for reuse, if necessary. Raise the lower sash and angle it out of the opening, making sure not to damage the casing trim. Cut the sash cords (or chain), if any, and lift out the sash. Do the same for the upper sash.

 Cut paint between the stop and jamb with a utility knife before prying off the stops.

2 Unscrew and remove the pulley and any other track hardware from the jamb, and open the access panel; remove the sash weights, and using a yardstick, stuff the cavity with fiberglass insulation. Reinstall the access panel.

Storms won't close?

Chances are the sashes and screens aren't in the correct tracks. The upper sash usually fits in the frame's outermost track, the lower sash in the intermediate track, and the screen, if there is one, in the innermost track.

Don't force it. Forcing storm sashes up and down can twist the frames, making a small problem worse. To free up a sticking sash, spray silicone lubricant on the track whenever the problem occurs.

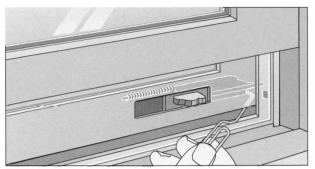

Use a large paper clip to retract a broken slide in an aluminum-frame storm window. Open the clip partway, and use pliers to bend it to form a right angle about ¼ inch from the end. Insert the hook in the sash, snare the slide from underneath, and pull it toward the center of the window to free it.

Naturally cool. Before investing in a houseful of thermal windows to beat the heat, try planting a tree where it can deflect the prevailing summer winds to keep the house cool.

Window treatment. Awnings can block up to 80 percent of the solar heat that would otherwise strike a window, and they don't obstruct the view. Acrylic fabric generally requires the least maintenance and keeps its color the longest.

SAFE AND SMART

➤ Insulation-enhancing gases sealed between the panes of double-glazed windows are safe if the glass breaks and the gases leak out.

➤ Use a metal wire to clean out any debris from the weep holes at the base of aluminum-frame storm windows. The holes allow condensation to escape from between the primary windows and the storms.

➤ When washing a window, shake out the cleaning cloth frequently. The dirty grit that collects on the rag can scratch the panes.

➤ Paint strippers and wet cement can dull glass; protect panes when using them.

3 Install the jamb liner brackets. Follow the manufacturer's instructions for the number of clips needed for each liner and the required spacing between clips. Follow any insulating, weatherstripping, or exterior caulking instructions. If required, remove the parting bead from the head jamb using a pair of locking pliers and install the supplied one.

4 Snap the vinyl jamb liner in place over the brackets according to the manufacturer's instructions. This provides an airtight track for the upper and lower sashes.

5 Install the new sashes, starting with the top sash. If reinstalling the interior stops, remove any remaining nails, pulling them from the back side to avoid marring the exposed surface. Reinstall the stops, pressing them lightly against the liners; secure temporarily with 4d finishing nails. Test for smooth operation of the sashes, adjusting the stops before setting the nails. Fill nail holes, and touch up with paint.

Buyer's guide. Choose miniblinds that match the color of the walls or trim, or that are a neutral shade. When you make those inevitable changes in decor, the blinds will fit right in.

The decorator's corner. Mounting blinds between window jambs emphasizes the trim; mounting them outside the jambs alters a window's appearance, often for the better in a room with clean, contemporary lines.

White-glove treatment. Dust blinds by donning cotton gloves and wiping the slats with your fingers. It's faster and more effective than vacuuming or using a duster. Dampen the gloves slightly to remove thick dust from dirtier slats.

Pinning your progress. Keep a clothespin handy when dusting blinds. If you have to stop in the middle, clip the pin to the last slat you've cleaned.

Restore the magic. If the blind's rotating plastic wand doesn't do its job, take the blind down and inspect and lubricate the screw assembly inside the head-box. Also make sure the tape or string that holds the slats is attached to the horizontal tilt tube.

A clean start. Conceal stained, grimy hems on shades by reversing the shade on the roller. Take the shade down, remove the staples holding the fabric to the roller, then undo the hem and remove the slat. Switch the material end for end, staple it to the roller, and stitch a new hem with the slat inside. To ensure that the shade is aligned, keep the long edges of the fabric perpendicular to the roller when stapling.

Shade won't roll up? Take a slack window shade down and roll it up by hand about halfway. Rehang the shade and test it for tension. If it still doesn't roll up in a snap, take it down again and roll it up a little more.

Relax a shade that is wound too tight by taking it down and twisting the flat-sided pin clockwise a quarter or half turn with pliers. This should release the pawl inside the roller, letting the spring unwind when the pliers are released.

Installing a miniblind

WHAT YOU'LL NEED

Tape measure

Miniblind (correct width)

Pry bar (if needed)

Drill and 1/16-in. bit

Screwdriver

Knife or scissors

1 Determine if you want a surface-of-casing or an inside-the-frame mount. For an inside-the-frame mount, you may want to mount the brackets on the side jambs or on the head jamb, depending on the window width. Attach brackets with screws.

2 Insert the headrail into the brackets. Some models have a hinged front that opens and closes around the headrail. Attach the mounting clips to the decorative valance, and then attach the valance to the front of the headrail.

3 To shorten a blind, take out pull cords and cut ladders at a point 2 in. longer than planned length. Take off bottom rail (cord is secured to rail with clips or a plug) and slide out slats. Replace bottom rail, and knot pull cords at proper length.

A waiting period. Once you've tied the new rope or chain to the sash weights, make sure there's enough slack to raise and lower the window before trimming any excess rope.

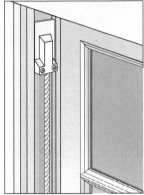

Dodging the drafts. Cut down on cold air at the sash pulley holes by attaching a seal over them. Pull the sash rope away from the jamb and slip the cover over the rope. Then position the seal over the sash pulley holes and push it tight against the jamb. The adhesive backed gasket and screws will hold the seal firmly in place.

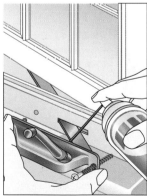

Crank it up. A sluggish casement window might mean a dirty crank mechanism. Apply a silicone spray or light oil to the crank works for ease of operation.

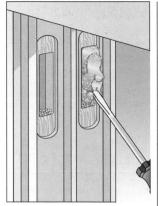

Fill 'er up. If you're not using the sash-weight system but the drafty cavities still remain, pour vermiculite or loose-fill cellulose through the pulley hole at the top of the jamb. Fill the top of the pocket with unfaced fiberglass batt insulation.

In newer houses, sluggish sashes are often due to too much fiberglass insulation between the wall framing and the window jamb. Wearing a dust mask and gloves, remove the window trim to expose the jamb and dig out any extra fiberglass with a long, sturdy screwdriver.

To free up most sashes, gently slice through any paint film along the tracks with a utility knife. If that doesn't work, place a block of scrap wood along the window sash. Tap the wood lightly with a hammer to free the window.

For slick sashes, rub the window tracks with a candle end or a piece of bar soap. While you're at it, scrape away lumps of dried paint and remove dust and debris from the corners and the bottom of the tracks.

Replacing a window sash chain or cord

WHAT YOU'LL NEED

4d finishing nails
Hammer
Utility knife
Trim pry bar
Nail puller or pliers
String
Sash chain or cord

Nail —

1 To raise sash weight, pull chain or cord and secure it with a nail. Remove window stop, take out sash, and disconnect chain or cord. Open weight cavity access panel and pull out sash weight. Carefully detach chain or cord from weight.

2 Tie a string to the top end of the old chain or cord, then pull it through the access hole. Use string to thread new chain or cord through the pulley and out the access hole. Attach new chain or cord to the sash weight. Replace weight cavity access panels.

3 Pull the sash weight to the top, and secure it by putting a nail through the chain or cord. Rest the sash on the stool and attach the chain or cord to the sash channel. Leave about 2 in. slack to allow the window to close completely.

Minimal maintenance.
The only upkeep required for a door closer is wiping the rod with a lightly oiled cloth once a year.

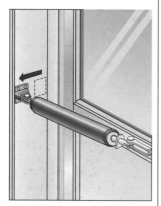

A quick finale. If you want a storm door to shut quicker but have already adjusted the door closer to the maximum speed, position the closer bracket on the door frame farther from the door. This increases the angle between the tube and the door, speeding up closure.

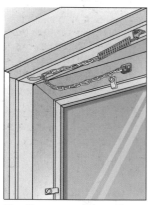

Don't come unhinged.
To prevent a storm door from blowing off the hinges in high winds, install a chain retainer. Attach one end to the head jamb, open the door as far as you want it to reach, and stretch the chain to the door frame to determine where to secure it.

Screws loose in the closer bracket? Snug them up by replacing old screws with wider ones, or drill out the holes with the next-size drill bit and glue solid wood plugs into the holes. Install the bracket screws directly into the wood plugs for a secure fit.

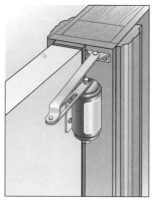

A flame retarder. Attaching a hydraulic door closer to an interior door, particularly one leading into a garage, can prevent fire from spreading into the house.

Latch on to a solution.
When a screen door doesn't stay shut, the latch is usually out of alignment with the latch plate. Check the wear marks on the plate and observe how the latch hits the plate as the door closes. Filing the latch hole slightly larger is often a quick fix for the problem.

Steady a sagging door with a turnbuckle and equal lengths of picture wire or cable. With the turnbuckle fully open, wire one end to the top corner of the screen door on the hinge side, the other end to the bottom corner on the latch side. Then tighten the turnbuckle until the sag is gone.

Replacing a screen door closer

WHAT YOU'LL NEED

Phillips screwdriver

New door closer, bracket, and screws

Tape (for template)

Pencil

Electric drill and bits

Hammer and metal punch (for metal jamb)

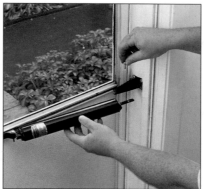

1 Close the door and remove the pin that secures the closer arm to the jamb bracket. If replacing only the cylinder, disconnect it from the door bracket; reverse the procedure to install a new cylinder. Otherwise, take out screws and remove closer assembly.

2 Use a template (if supplied) or use the bracket as a template, and mark the screw locations with a pencil. Drill pilot holes, and secure the bracket with the screws. If moving the closer to the bottom of the door, be sure it doesn't interfere with the threshold.

3 With the door closed, secure the cylinder arm to the jamb bracket with the pin. Hold the door bracket against the door, and mark the screw locations. Drill pilot holes and attach the bracket. Turn cylinder adjustment screw to adjust closing speed.

SCREENS

Improve your metal.
Preserve galvanized metal screens by cleaning them and lightly spraying them with spar varnish each year.

Screen saver. Washing dirty screens at least every year extends their life. Lean the screens against a wall, fence, or tree, and dampen them with fine spray from a garden hose. Then scrub both sides gently with a scrub brush dipped in hot soapy water. Wash the frames with a sponge. Rinse well with the hose, then let the screens air-dry.

Easy riders. For screens that slide with ease, wrap a strip of sudsy cloth around a ruler or screwdriver and insert it into the narrow slots. Rinse out the cloth in clean water and then reinsert it to get rid of any soap residue. Wipe the slots dry.

SAFE AND SMART

➤ If a screen is torn near the frame, replace the screen instead of bothering to patch it.

➤ Always replace metal screens with the same metal as the frame.

➤ Tighten the mitered corners of wood-frame screens with corner reinforcements or chevrons.

All at once. If all of your window screens appear shabby, replace them as a group to avoid a house that looks like a crazy quilt.

Winter storage. Before storing the screens for the winter, wrap each one in newspaper or brown wrapping paper and seal with tape to keep them from gathering dust. Or use a big sheet of plastic, like an old shower curtain or tablecloth.

Sunscreen for windows.
Fiberglass or plastic screens filter out both bugs and the sun's rays, keeping the house cooler and upholstery and carpeting from fading.

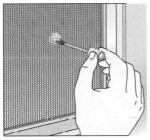

Mending the mesh. Use clear nail polish or clear epoxy glue to repair small tears and holes in screens. First straighten the torn strands with a toothpick; then apply polish or epoxy to the area, and spread it with a cotton swab. Open clogged mesh by pricking the cells with a clean toothpick before the polish or epoxy hardens. Repeat several times if necessary to build up a thick layer.

Patching a screen on a flat surface is easier than mending it in place. You can reach and support both sides with your hands and can avoid unsightly runs if applying epoxy or nail polish.

Replacing a metal-frame screen

WHAT YOU'LL NEED

Awl or nail

Utility knife

Screening

Spline roller and spline

Wide-blade screwdriver

1 Pry out old spline with awl or point of a nail; remove spline and screen. (Save metal spline for reuse; replace vinyl spline.) Using a utility knife, cut new screening 2 in. larger than frame on four sides. Align weave with frame.

2 Roll screening into groove with a spline roller's convex wheel; maintain tension by pulling screening taut on opposite side. Then roll in spline, using concave wheel. Fiberglass screening and spline are rolled in at the same time.

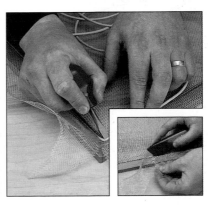

3 As you near each corner, cut screening at a 45° angle to corner. Press spline into and around corner with tip of a screwdriver. Continue rolling spline around frame. Trim excess screening with utility knife angled toward outside of frame.

If it moves, strip it.

Weatherstripping is great for sealing parts that move, like window sashes and doors; use caulk around fixed frames, such as window and door trim, and around the glass in skylights.

Digital detection. Dampen the back of your hand and move it all around a door or window. Your skin will feel cooler when you near a leak. If no breeze is blowing, enlist a helper to stand outside and aim a hair dryer at window or door seams.

SAFE AND SMART

➤ If drafts persist around a weatherstripped window, apply caulk between the wall and the inside trim. Pay attention to the apron, located beneath the sill.

➤ Forsake short-lived foam and felt weatherstripping for more durable and better looking vinyl or metal.

➤ Seal metal casement windows with grooved gaskets that slip over the window frames. Similar gaskets are made for individual panes on jalousie windows.

Anticipate the need.

You'll lose heat if you apply weatherstripping when wintry winds are blowing—and self-stick types don't adhere well when the temperature drops below 50°F.

Make it stick. Before applying self-stick weatherstripping, wash the surfaces with trisodium phosphate (TSP) or wipe them with deglosser, available in paint stores. Rinse with a cloth or sponge dipped in clear water, then towel-dry.

Leaky window or storm? To determine which is the leaky party, here is the rule of thumb: If moisture forms on the windowpane, cold air is leaking past the storm sash. If moisture appears on the storm window, then warm air is leaking around the inside window.

Barring drafts. Custom-seal the bottom of a badly warped double-hung window by opening the lower sash and applying a ribbon of caulk on the sill. Lay plastic wrap over the caulk, lower the window, and lock it. When the caulk dries, raise the window and remove the plastic wrap for a perfect weatherstrip.

Weatherstripping a window

WHAT YOU'LL NEED

Tape measure
1⅛-in. spring bronze weatherstrip
Metal shears or tin snips
Claw hammer
Screwdriver

1 Cut strips of 1⅛-in. spring weatherstrip to fit bottom of lower sash and bottom face of upper sash. Attach to bottom of lower sash with nailing edge toward the inside. Attach to bottom face of upper sash with nailing edge toward the top.

2 To seal channels, cut weatherstripping about 1 in. longer than the lower sash. Raise the sash and slip the end of the strip between the sash and the channel; fasten it to the channel with the nailing edge toward the inside. Repeat for the upper sash.

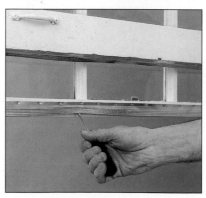

3 To set the spring tension, insert a screwdriver under the open edge; lift and slide the tool back and forth to bend the strip at the hinge line. If the sash was already tight, it may have to be removed (see p. 98) so the edges can be planed or sanded.

Weatherstrip watch.
Check exterior doors every year for a weatherstrip upgrade. As your house shifts and settles with age, the weatherstripping may need to be adjusted or replaced in order to block out new sources of moisture and drafts.

Factory failure. If a door has factory-installed interlocking weatherstripping, repair it when necessary by opening any crimped areas with a putty knife or pliers, or by striking them with a wood block and hammer.

Carpet care. An automatic door sweep makes it easier to open and close a door over a carpet and spares the fibers from premature wear and tear. When the door is opened, the end of the sweep presses against a metal strike plate attached to the door frame, causing the sweep to rise above the carpet; when the door is closed, a spring inside the sweep lowers it again.

Are you a nail dropper?
Get a tight grip on those little nails supplied with metal weatherstripping by holding them with long-nose pliers instead of your fingers.

Shifting insulation strips can cause a door to bind or to close with difficulty. Loosen or reposition the weatherstripping on the jamb, making sure you can slide a credit card between the weatherstripping and the door when it is closed. Then reinspect the insulation to be sure it contacts the door for an effective, draft-killing seal.

Don't forget. Weatherstrip around a full-size or drop-down attic door. For hatchways covered only by a square of plywood, attach foam or vinyl tubing around all four sides of the opening so the hatch board rests on top of the strips.

Weatherstripping a door

WHAT YOU'LL NEED

Nail-on vinyl or butyl rubber ½-in.-dia. tubing
Tape measure and utility knife
Hammer
Nails (usually included; if not, use ¾-in. wire nails)
Door sweep and screws for installing
Hacksaw
Screwdriver and awl

1 Make sure the doorjamb is clean. Measure the head and hinge sides of the doorjamb at the inside stop; cut lengths of weatherstripping to fit. Starting on the hinge side, nail strip to jamb with tubular part flush against stop.

2 Along the top and latch sides, nail the strip to the stop, with the tubular part extending slightly over the edge so that it just touches the door when it is closed.

3 Install a sweep on the inside door bottom. Cut it to length if needed, using a hacksaw on the metal and a utility knife on the vinyl gasket. With door closed, position sweep so it touches threshold; mark screw holes with awl and install.

Buyer's guide. Quality weatherstripping—magnetic or foam—should be an integral part of any prehung entry door you buy. Doors with large expanses of glass reduce the insulation value and security of a door.

Preserve the old. Remove a wooden threshold by cutting the old one into three pieces with a backsaw and then carefully prying it out from beneath the door jambs. Use the pieces to trace a pattern for a new threshold on heavy paper.

Quiet a banging door by applying two or three ¼-inch dabs of clear silicone caulk to the edges of the door stops. They create a cushion for the door and are just about invisible. Or dot the door jamb with a few self-sticking felt pads.

Door need a face-lift? Grab the biggest screwdriver that will fit the screwheads and give each of the hinge screws a healthy twist clockwise. Even tightening the screws a quarter turn can often straighten up a sagging door.

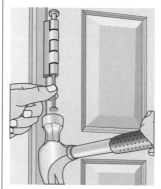

Use a hammer and nail to remove stubborn hinge pins that are open on the bottom. Insert the nail underneath the pin and drive it upward with the hammer to force the pin out of the hinge.

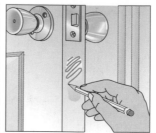

If a door binds, mark where you think it's rubbing with chalk or pencil. Close the door, reopen it, and look for smeared marks. Then plane or sand them away.

Prevent splintering when planing or sanding door edges by always working from an edge or end toward the center. Going in the other direction will chip the wood when the tool passes over the outer edge.

Planing or sanding a door? Straddle it to keep it steady. If the door is too wide to straddle comfortably, wedge the forward end into a corner of the room.

Installing a threshold in a doorway

WHAT YOU'LL NEED

Safety goggles

Tape measure and pencil

Adjustable metal threshold

Jigsaw with a metal-cutting blade or a hacksaw

Metal file

Saw (optional)

Utility knife

Drill with ⅛-in. bit

Screwdriver

1 Kneeling down indoors, measure the inside width of the door frame. Then purchase an adjustable metal threshold.

 An adjustable threshold is more forgiving and can be adjusted for both a tight fit and easy operation.

2 Wearing goggles, cut the threshold with a jigsaw equipped with a metal-cutting blade or with a hacksaw. Use a metal file to smooth the edges. If the door doesn't clear the threshold and adjusting the threshold doesn't solve the problem, you will have to trim the bottom of the door.

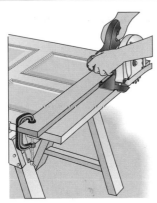

To trim a door bottom, use a straightedge as a guide and score a cut line with a utility knife to prevent the wood from splintering. Clamp a board along the line to guide the saw, placing wood scraps beneath each clamp to prevent them from marring the door. If you use a circular saw with a fine-tooth carbide blade, place the most prominent side of the door down when cutting; if using a handsaw, place the prominent side up.

Making the cut. When trimming the bottom of a hollow-core door, be sure to save the cutoff that contains the bottom crosspiece. Carefully chisel off the veneer on both sides; then reinstall the crosspiece in the bottom of the door, using wood glue and clamps.

Hollow victory. Fill a hole in a hollow door with spray foam insulation, coat it with drywall compound when dry, then sand and paint.

When space is tight, install a pocket door to replace a swinging one. Carpenters usually enclose a pocket door inside a specially built wall, but it is relatively simple to surface-mount the door's overhead frame instead and enclose it with decorative molding.

Left is left, right? When purchasing a new interior door, determine whether the old one is right-handed (knob on the right as the door opens toward you) or left-handed (knob on the left). Exterior doors that open into the house follow the same rule. Outside doors that swing away are either left-handed reverse (knob on the right as the door opens toward you) or right-handed reverse (knob on the left).

No entry. Strengthen a door against break-ins by reinforcing the frame so it can't be pried away from the latch. Remove the molding from the latch side of the door frame, and fill the space between frame and wall stud with strips of plywood or with a 2 x 4. Don't bow the frame, or the door won't close. Reattach the molding.

3 For a one-piece rabbeted jamb, notch the threshold to fit the narrower exterior dimension of the door frame. If the jamb has a removable exterior stop, cut the stop to accommodate the threshold; remove the stop for cutting, if necessary.

4 Using a utility knife, cut both the vinyl feet and the weatherstripping insert about ½ in. longer than the threshold to accommodate shrinkage. Replace the vinyl feet and position threshold in the doorway.

5 With the insert in place, position the adjustable portion at the proper height to create a seal with the door's bottom edge. Remove the vinyl insert to install screws into predrilled pilot holes. Replace the vinyl insert, pushing the excess ½ in. toward the center. Other models vary; follow the manufacturer's instructions.

Buyer's guide. If you want a traditional look and a wider ledge at the base of the window, incorporate a stool in your trim design (see "Anatomy of a Window," p. 116). You can buy stool stock already milled to fit over the sill. Or for a simpler look, add a fourth piece of trim beneath the window.

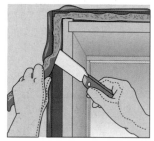

When installing trim, kill drafts for good by filling any gaps around the window with foam or fiberglass insulation or with caulking. Be careful not to bow the jambs inward by installing too much filler.

Support system. Free your hands when installing apron molding by bracing it with a batten of strong flexible wood. Cut the brace slightly longer than the distance between the bottom of the apron and the floor, and wedge it in place. The batten snugs the apron against the stool while you nail it. Place scrap carpet under the batten to protect the floor.

Evening out the odds. If one face of a mitered joint is higher than the other, pare down the excess with a razor-sharp chisel or drive a thin wedge behind the low side to extend it from the wall. Saw the wedge flush, and fill the gap behind the casing with caulk.

Cutting corners. Instead of struggling with miters, use decorative blocks at the top corners of window trim, and run side and head casings right into them.

For tight miter joints, bevel the rear edge of each piece with a sharp utility knife or a block plane, which allows the front face of the mitered pieces to press tightly against each other. Also apply some glue to the joint before nailing it.

Close up an open miter by running a sharp backsaw over the seam between the two boards. Saw between them, removing a tiny amount of waste from each board. Then reposition the boards by pressing them together and nailing each one near its mitered end.

Installing window trim

WHAT YOU'LL NEED

Trim

Combination square or metal rule

Tape measure

Pencil

Coping saw (optional)

Miter box and backsaw

Power miter box (optional)

Scribe (compass)

Wood rasp

Sandpaper (various grits)

4d, 6d, and 8d finishing nails

Hammer

Drill and 1/16-in. bit

Level

1 Begin by sketching out the plan on paper, and consult it as you work. Next, using a straightedge or a combination square set to the desired reveal (typically 3/16 in.), pencil in reveal marks at the ends and middle of the jambs and the head casing. (For combination square method, see p. 110.)

2 Measure the width of the window, side trim included, and cut the stool about 1½ in. longer on each side. Center the stool, and scribe it to the lower sash, leaving sufficient space for window clearance; cut notches. Shape the ends to match the front profile using a rasp and sandpaper. Fit in place, check level, and secure it to the rough sill with 8d nails.

Sanding contoured trim?

Make a customized sanding block that fits the pattern precisely. Mix water putty or plastic auto-body filler in a plastic bag, pressing the bag against the molding before the putty hardens so the mix conforms to the surface. When the putty hardens, remove the plastic bag and shape the sides of the block with a saw or rasp for easy gripping. Now wrap a piece of sandpaper around the block and get to work.

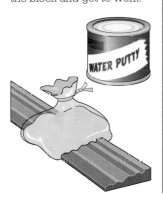

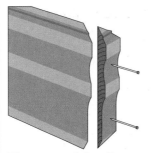

The return ticket. Returns give aprons and stools a finished look and cover porous end grain, which shows darker beneath a natural finish. Miter the ends of the stool and apron inward; then miter the waste pieces and reattach them (mitered edge to mitered edge) to their respective boards with glue and brads to form a right angle. If you think that brads will split the wood, glue the mitered return into place and use tape to hold it there while the glue dries.

Picture this. Picture-frame casing is easy on blinds, shades, and curtains and a breeze to make. Start by mitering both ends of the head casing and fitting the side casing to it. Cut the bottom casing about 2 inches too long, mitering one end to fit the miter at the bottom of a side piece. Then mark the remaining end and trim it until it fits against the other side piece.

Interior shutters are a perfect way to window-dress new trim and to let in light without sacrificing privacy. Trim them to fit, if necessary, by sawing equal amounts off the top, bottom, and sides. *Note:* Don't trim off more than 1 inch in overall width or 1½ inches in overall height.

Fill the gaps. If window trim doesn't sit flush against an uneven wall, don't try to pound it into shape. Fill the gap with a paintable caulk (or white caulk if the walls are white). Smooth it, and when dry, paint it to match the molding.

The right fit. Before buying interior shutters, measure the height and width of the window at three different points. Go with the narrowest measurement as a guide for trimming the shutters.

Minor adjustments. If you have less than ⅛ inch to trim off the shutter, plane it rather than sawing it.

3 Place the side casing on the stool and mark where it meets the reveal line along the head jamb. Cut the casing using a straight cut if using corner blocks, a mitered cut if not using corner blocks. Align casing with reveal marks; use 4d finishing nails to anchor it to the jamb and 6d nails to anchor it to the framing through the wallboard. Install the opposite-side casing in the same way.

4 Corner blocks should be slightly wider and thicker than the head and side casing. Predrill the holes and install with 6d nails.

 To avoid splitting the wood, drill pilot holes for nails placed near the end of a trim board.

5 Measure and cut head casing. Fit it into place between corner blocks, aligning it with reveal marks. Secure head casing to jamb and wallboard using same method as with side casing. Install the apron. Cut it to equal the outside casing-to-casing dimension. Shape ends with a coping saw or, for a more finished look, make a return (see "The Return Ticket," above). Secure apron with 6d nails. Set all nails and fill holes.

Guaranteed fit. Prehung interior door units usually include mitered trim molding as part of the package. If you square up the door frame when you install it, the corners should fit.

Before installing trim, make sure the wall surfaces beneath the trim joints are level. Use joint compound to level out irregularities, or sand them away.

Losing the edge. Remove the light, fuzzy splinters on freshly cut trim with a few light passes of fine sandpaper. Splinters can collect clumps of paint, making an otherwise perfect mitered joint look clumsy.

Fantastic plastic. Use plastic or vinyl door trim in damp locations like bathrooms. It resists moisture better than wood and won't expand and contract, which can cause joints to fall out of alignment.

Mood-altering trim. Create classic or contemporary designs by combining different molding shapes. Deeply fluted molding suggests formality; predominantly flat surfaces, a more informal welcome.

Stable situation. Moisture loss and gain causes wood to contract and expand, throwing once-tight miter joints out of whack. The movement is greatest across a board's width; so if a casing is to be wider than 4 inches, build it up with pieces of narrower trim. Also, consider using woods like cherry, red oak, and white pine, which stay put more than beech and maple.

Last but not least. Install baseboard molding last, after all vertical door molding, wainscoting, if there is any, and finish flooring is in place. This way, the baseboard can be fitted directly to the standing trim and the finished floor with fewer chances of gaps.

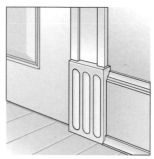

Get a tight fit where baseboards meet thinner door casings either by beveling the ends of protruding contours back at a 45° angle or by installing plinth blocks that are thicker than the baseboard molding.

Installing door trim

WHAT YOU'LL NEED

Level

Framing square

Shims (if needed)

Combination square and pencil

Casing and hinges

Miter saw and box

Tape measure

Electric drill and 1/16-in. bit

Hammer and nail set

2d, 4d, and 6d finishing nails

Sanding block, rasp, or block plane

Sandpaper

Paintable caulk

1 First make sure the head jamb is level. Then, using a framing square, verify that the side jambs are square to the head jamb. (Reshim the jambs as necessary.) Hold the side trim against the hinge to determine how big the reveal should be. Mark the reveal in four places along the length of each side jamb.

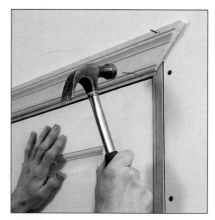

2 Cut a miter on one end of the head trim. Position the piece at the reveal intersection and mark the length at the other reveal intersection; then cut that miter. Drill pilot holes at the end of the trim, and tack it to the jamb with 4d finishing nails. Then tack 6d finishing nails along the top of the trim through the wallboard and into the wall studs. Don't drive the nails flush yet.

Like a pro. When installing molding in more than one room, consider renting a power miter saw (also called a chop saw) for the task. Not only does this tool save time, it also enables amateurs to achieve professional results after only minimal practice.

Cleanup detail. After cutting and mitering trim, whisk away sawdust from the workbench with an ordinary car snow brush. It's thin enough to get into crevices easily, and sawdust and wood particles don't stick to the stiff bristles.

Reviving old trim? Scrub it with a fine/medium grit sanding sponge dipped in mineral spirits to clean and sand it at the same time. An added bonus: The sponge hugs the curves and contours of the trim.

For more detailed trim, use a stiff-bristle toothbrush dipped in mineral spirits to clean it up.

Don't dent delicate trim. Create an instant mallet with a piece of heavy kitchen sponge. Wet the sponge, wring it out well, then wrap it around a hammerhead and secure it with a rubber band.

To erase dents in wood trim, heat the head of a hammer with a hair dryer, place a damp cloth over the dent, and then press the hammer against it. Move the hammer around gently to swell the crushed fibers.

Protect outside door trim with an overhang or awning. The overhead protection can triple the door's life span—and makes searching for house keys in a downpour more tolerable.

Architectural details. Dress up a plain flush door by tacking on thin strips of molding to create handsome rectangular panels.

3 Measure from the floor to the top corner of the head trim; transfer this measurement to the trim stock. Make the cuts with a miter saw, and tack the trim into place as with the head trim. Then repeat the procedure for the trim on the opposite side.

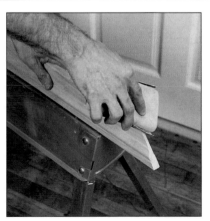

4 If a joint is uneven, sand the edge of the miter on the side trim as needed, using coarse sandpaper on a sanding block. If the side trim is cut too long and a second cut is required, it is generally better to cut from the bottom.

5 Hammer and set the nails all around the trim. Fill gaps between wall and trim with paintable caulk. Lock the miters by driving 4d finishing nails into the top and side of the trim about ½ in. from the corners; set the nails and fill.

! On wider trim, glue the miters before nailing in the trim. This ensures a longer-lasting fit.

A quick release. The secret to removing a doorknob from an entry-door lockset is to locate the small slot or hole covering the hidden clasp in the base of the knob. Insert a screwdriver or nail into the opening and press hard while pulling the doorknob at the same time. In most cases, the knob will slide off easily.

Lubricate a jammed lock with powdered graphite, available in small squeeze bottles. Oil or grease attracts dirt and becomes sticky.

Frozen out? Open a frozen lock by heating the key's teeth with a match or lighter before inserting it. (Wear gloves when doing this.) Spray deicer may also help.

Easy open. Replace door-knobs with lever handles to easily open a kitchen, pantry, or laundry room door when your hands are full.

Restore a worn hinge without removing it by removing the pin and placing metal washers between the lower barrels of the hinge leaves.

Quick fix. You can some-times change a lock without replacing the latch and knob by replacing the old lock cylinder with a new one. New cylinders and keys are less expensive than replacing the assembly.

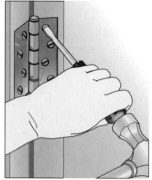

Turn, turn, turn. To ease the turning of hinge screws, loosen the paint in the screw slots first. Rap the handle of an old screwdriver with a hammer, driving the tip into the slot and giving it some bite.

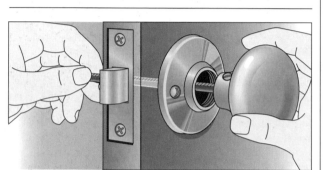

Older doorknobs can be tightened by simply adjusting the spindle. Loosen the setscrews holding the knobs, and center the spindle so it extends equally on both sides of the door. Then reposition the knobs so they fit snugly against the door but do not bind.

Installing a new lockset and knob

WHAT YOU'LL NEED

Lockset with template

Tape measure

Tape

Awl

Pencil

Electric drill, 2⅛-in. hole saw, and 1-in. spade bit

Chisel

Wooden mallet

C-clamps

Phillips screwdriver

Lipstick (optional)

1 Fold and tape the manufacturer-supplied template to the door so the holes will be centered 37–40 in. above the floor (see directions). Mark the hole centers with an awl or a sharp pencil point or nail; remove the template.

2 Use a power drill with a hole saw (usually 2⅛-in.-dia.) to bore the lockset hole. Drill the latch-bolt hole with a 1-in. spade bit. Insert the latch-bolt assembly, and trace the outline of the latch-bolt plate on the edge of the door.

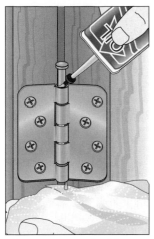

Silence a squeaky hinge

by lubricating it with a drop or two of light household oil. Raise the hinge pin slightly so you can drip oil onto the shaft above the hinge's upper barrel. Then swing the door back and forth a few times to distribute the lubrication along the entire length of the hinge pin. Hold a paper towel under the hinge to catch drips.

Don't pry. Slide hinges free from their notches (called mortises) when removing them from wooden doors. Prying them upward will chip the wood. If a hinge sticks in a notch after you've removed the screws, gently tap it sideways with a hammer to free it.

Night vision. If you have trouble finding the front door lock in the dark, dab a few drops of luminous paint around the keyhole for increased visibility.

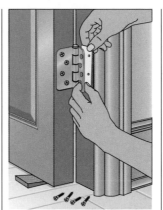

Get out of a bind. If a door binds at the top or bottom corner, try tightening the hinges. No luck? Then remove the hinge from the doorjamb diagonally opposite the binding corner and place a shim of cardboard, about the thickness of two playing cards, behind it in the notch. Refasten the hinge and test the door. Add a second or third shim if necessary to square the door in the opening.

Quiet a rattling door

by moving the doorstop tighter against the door at the bottom. Cut through the paint on both sides of the stop with a utility knife so it can break free. Then tap the stop in the direction of the door with a wood block and hammer. Anchor it in position with finishing nails.

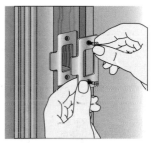

Double up. If the latch on an old interior door no longer extends far enough past the strike plate to keep the door from swinging open, install a second plate over the first.

3 Holding chisel perpendicular with bevel side in, make a ⅛-in.-deep cut around the perimeter. Then angle chisel and undercut perimeter. Make repeated cuts to chisel out wood until plate fits flush. Clamp scrap wood to door edges to prevent splintering. To install latch bolt, drill pilot holes and fasten with screws. Insert exterior handle, then interior knob and rose plate. Align holes and secure with screws provided.

4 Cover the end of the latch with lipstick or pencil lead dust. Turn the knob to retract the latch, close the door, and holding it closed, release and retract the latch several times to mark its exact position on the jamb. Open the door (with latch retracted). Align the strike plate over the marks, and trace the outline of the plate and the hole; you can turn over the strike plate for tracing.

5 Bore a ⅞-in.-dia. by ½-in.-deep hole for the latch. Then mortise the strike plate as done for the latch-bolt plate, but with shallower cuts to accommodate the thinner plate. Using an awl, mark the center holes; then drill pilot holes. Attach the strike plate with the screws provided.

FILE IT

Anatomy of a door

Know your panels from plinths with this door-at-a-glance.

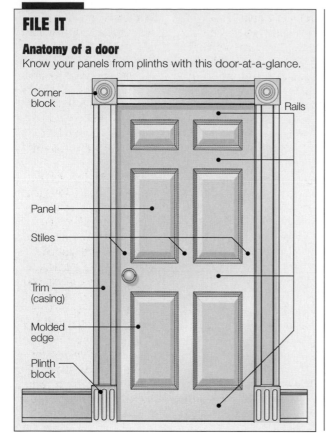

- Corner block
- Rails
- Panel
- Stiles
- Trim (casing)
- Molded edge
- Plinth block

Getting the edge. Sand a door's edges before repainting the door. Too much paint may cause the door to stick in the frame.

Mess-free scraping. When removing old paint or stain from a door, keep the messy remnants from sticking to the scraper by periodically applying nonstick cooking spray to the blade.

Before painting, straighten out minor warping in a door by adding an extra hinge. Or remove the door, place it on sawhorses, and lay a heavy weight on the bowed section to correct the curvature.

Sparkling hardware.
To clean door hardware of old paint without resorting to chemical strippers, place it in a pan of cold water and add 4 tablespoons of baking soda per quart of water. Let the solution simmer for 30 minutes. Remove the hardware with tongs, and wearing rubber gloves, scrub off the paint with steel wool.

For paint-free hardware, cover each hinge leaf with a piece of clear package-sealing tape, trim the excess, and then paint without spatters or runs.

Painting a door

WHAT YOU'LL NEED

120-grit sandpaper

Lint-free cloth

Primer (if needed) and paint

Small mirror

Hammer and screwdrivers

Paintbrushes (1-in. and 3-in.)

Paint roller, "smooth-surface" cover, and tray

1 Remove lockset hardware (see pp. 112–113), sand door with 120-grit paper to dull glossy paint, then wipe away any dust. Clean the door with a lint-free cloth, and prime it if necessary.

2 Use a mirror to inspect the bottom edge of the door to be sure that it has been painted or sealed. If not, take out the hinge pins, remove the door, and apply a sealer. Paint the door's edges first, using a 1-in. brush.

Carry-all. Take the old door hardware with you when buying replacements. You can match the exact length of the latch-bolt shaft and the size of the hinges.

Battered doors? Fill dents and holes with wallboard joint compound before painting. Patch exterior doors, especially metal ones, with auto-body filler.

Don't shake it up. Gently stir clear finishes such as polyurethane or varnish. Shaking them will create hundreds of tiny air bubbles that will pit the finish as it dries. If you've accidentally shaken a can of varnish, let the container rest for a few days; the bubbles will gradually disappear.

The wet look. To keep a wet edge wet in warmer weather, cool the can of varnish to about 55°. Cooler solvents evaporate more slowly. On an especially warm day, place the can in a makeshift ice bucket.

Bottom up. To paint the bottom edge of a door without removing it, apply a generous swath of paint to a scrap of carpeting wide enough to hold comfortably with both hands. Then slide the carpet under the door and rub it back and forth to coat the bottom edge.

Baby the paint. Dust magnetic weatherstripping with talcum powder before painting a door to which it is attached to prevent the magnetic strip from marring the fresh paint.

Color correct. Paint the door edge the color of the room into which it opens.

Drip control. When staining or applying a clear finish to a door, lay the door flat to discourage runs. Take special care near the edges by applying the stain or finish with a rag or having one handy to catch runs that could flow around the door and discolor the other side.

Great grain. Give a door eye appeal by adding graining to the finish. Paint the wood a flat background color, such as beige or light olive. When the base coat has dried, dip a graining tool in darker paint thinned with linseed oil, and drag it over the surface to create a wood-grain pattern. Afterward, protect the paint with a coat of clear sealer. Graining kits are available in crafts stores, or you can use a soft-bristle paintbrush to achieve the same effect.

3 Paint a panel door, one side at a time, in the following order: First paint the molded edges of the panels (using a 1-in. brush), and then paint the panels themselves (using a 3-in. brush).

 When painting sliding doors, complete one door before starting the other. With flush doors, work from top down.

4 Use a clean rag to wipe off excess paint that has dripped onto the vertical stiles and horizontal rails. Using a 3-in. brush, paint the center stile next, but only the areas between panels. Then paint the rails, feathering the edges where you meet a previously painted area. Finish with the two outside stiles.

5 When the door has dried, paint the trim with a 1-in. brush. On the in-swinging side, paint the casing and the jamb up to the stops the color of the in-swinging side of the door. On the opposite side, paint the second color on the casing, the remaining jamb, and the stops themselves.

FILE IT

Anatomy of a window

Whether repairing or painting a window, it's helpful to know sashes from stops. Below is a window-at-a-glance.

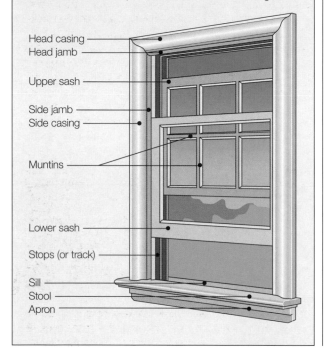

- Head casing
- Head jamb
- Upper sash
- Side jamb
- Side casing
- Muntins
- Lower sash
- Stops (or track)
- Sill
- Stool
- Apron

Order of importance.

If you are painting windows, doors, and baseboard, start early in the day and do the windows first, followed by the doors, so they will be dry before you need to close them at night. Paint the baseboard last, so any dust picked up on the brush from the floor won't be spread to other surfaces.

Prep work.
Fill the seams in casing trim with caulk before painting. To avoid a mess, pierce a very small hole, about ⅛ inch in diameter, in the caulking tube.

If painting in sunlight,
don't use ordinary masking tape to mask off windows. For a less sticky bond, use drafting tape or the special masking tape used for painting automobiles.

Save time when painting multipane windows by "masking" them with lip balm instead of masking tape. Rub the balm around the edges of the glass, next to the trim, leaving a border of bare glass about ¹⁄₁₆ inch wide for a good seal. Any paint on the coated surface will be easy to remove when the paint is dry.

Painting a window

WHAT YOU'LL NEED

- Canvas drop cloth
- Vacuum
- Bucket, sponge, and mild detergent
- Window scraper
- Sanding block and fine sandpaper
- Screwdriver (usually Phillips)
- Primer or stain-killing paint (if required)
- Masking tape, paint edger, or lip balm
- Painting tape
- Paint
- Angled sash brush

1 Lay down a drop cloth, and first vacuum and then wash the window glass, frames, and trim to remove all dirt; use a scraper or fine sandpaper to remove any loose paint. Take off locking hardware with a screwdriver; apply primer to any bare wood, or stain-killing paint if the wood needs it.

2 For double-hung windows, open both sashes partway. Use masking tape, an edger, or lip balm to protect the glass, and painting tape to protect the wall surface. Paint as much of the upper sash as possible, reverse the sash positions, and paint the lower parts of the upper sash. Paint vertical surfaces first, then horizontal ones. Work from the inside of the window surface out. Allow the paint to overlap the glass by ¹⁄₁₆ in.

A thin argument. Be sparing when painting window channels; too much paint causes the sashes to bind.

Split the difference. Hold a rag against the wall as you paint window trim to absorb any streaks of paint that could slop onto the wall. A neat demarcation is important because of the visible difference between flat wall paint and the semigloss or glossy enamel used for washable trim.

Remove a stray bristle from a window frame by stabbing at it with the tip of the brush and lifting up. Wipe the brush on a newspaper to get rid of the annoying bristle for good.

Paint remover. Use a window scraper to remove dry paint from the panes. After scoring the paint with a sharp utility knife (use a ruler as a guide), hold the scraper at a right angle to the scored line and push the tool toward it against the excess paint, making sure to stop at the line.

The delicate cycle. For scratch-free sanding on delicate casing or other molding that will be brushed with clear finish, sand with the grain up to the joints at the corners—not across them.

Gently remove stains from vinyl or vinyl-clad windows by dabbing them with mineral spirits or rubbing them with a hand cleaner that contains lanolin. Don't use steel wool or sandpaper.

The unvarnished truth. Avoid using exterior spar varnish on interior wood. It takes longer to dry, increasing the chances of attracting both dirt and dust. One exception: Brush it on interior windowsills located on the south side of the house. Exterior spar varnish contains UV inhibitors that prevent sunlight from destroying the protective varnish-to-wood bond.

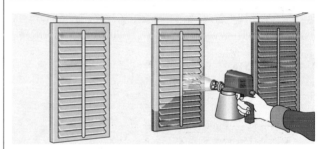

Spray-paint shutters by hanging them on an outdoor or indoor clothesline. Mount two screw hooks at one edge of the shutter, hang it, and spray all sides without flipping it.

3 Paint the lower sash in an open position; again do vertical surfaces first and work from the inside out. Use exterior paint on the bottom edge of the lower sash and the top edge of the upper sash. Check the sash corners and muntin intersections for paint buildup and drips, and remove them by gently dabbing with a dry brush. When the sashes are dry to the touch, slide them up and down a couple of times.

4 Paint the casing, then the apron and stool. Paint the window jambs last, if at all. Sash channels should not be painted more than once. If you must paint them a second time, sand well or use paint remover to take off old paint. Wait until the window is completely dry, and then lower both sashes all the way. Paint the upper jamb; when that is dry, raise the sashes and do the lower jamb.

5 Remove the masking tape and painting tape. Scrape excess paint off the window glass, using a window scraper. After the paint is dry, reinstall the window hardware.

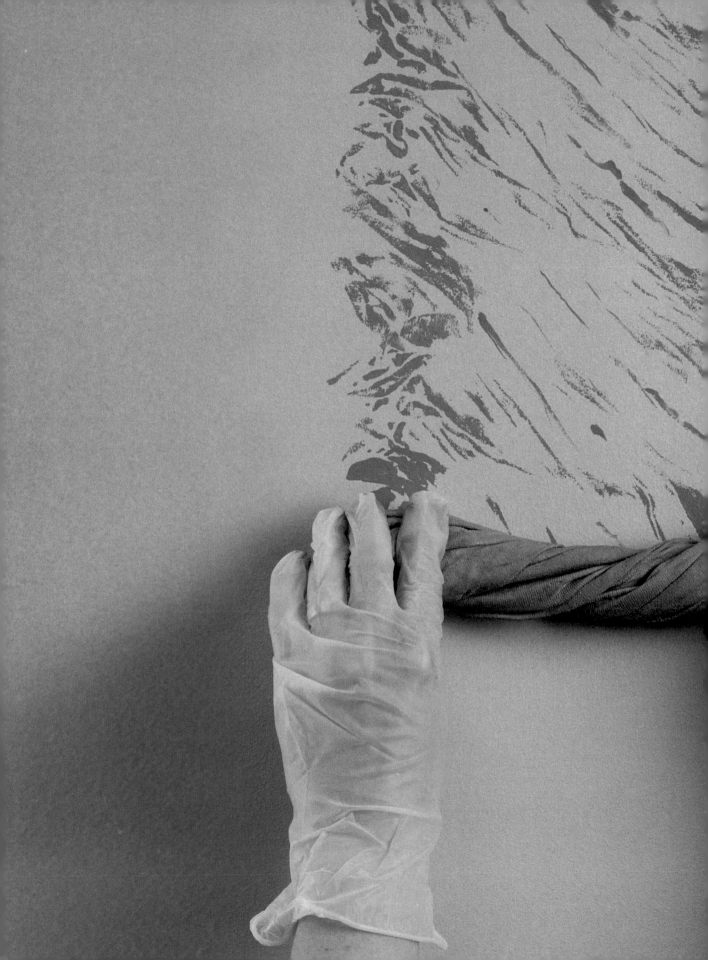

PAINTING AND WALLPAPERING

Job ratings: Easy   Medium   Complex

No fan of drips. When freshening up a ceiling, prevent paint from speckling ceiling fan blades by covering them with those plastic bags your daily newspaper comes in. The width of the bag is just right for most fans.

I.D. your hardware. Right after you remove each piece of hardware from a window, door, or cabinet, flag it with a little piece of masking tape marked with its location. This way, you'll be able to replace everything with a minimum of fuss when the job is done.

Mop and go. If you have to completely wash down a ceiling, save time by using a squeeze sponge mop. Start in a corner and progress across the ceiling. This is a drippy job, so wear safety goggles, cover the floor, and drape any furniture before beginning.

Under cover. Wet paper can really reduce the mess when painting windows. Cut the paper to fit and press it in place—it will cling to the glass.

Before painting, don't damage the wall by ripping out old anchors and mollies that you're no longer using. Tap them into the wall instead and fill in the holes with joint compound.

Makeup for walls. If you discover brown water spots on the ceiling or wall, determine the source of the leak and fix it. Use a stain-blocking primer to cover up the offending spots. When preparing wood for painting, dab clear shellac on any knots to prevent them from bleeding through.

Caulk is a good choice for filling cracks, gouges, and seams in plaster and wallboard. Use water-base acrylic caulk that can be painted. Apply it with a caulking gun or straight from the tube, and smooth it with a wet fingertip, wearing latex surgical gloves.

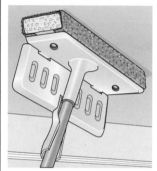

Upwardly mobile. Instead of buying a pole sander for high, hard-to-reach areas, make a sanding stick. Just take the pad off a sponge mop, cover it with sandpaper, and slide it into place.

Preparing the surface

WHAT YOU'LL NEED

Latex surgical gloves and rubber gloves

Screwdriver

No-rinse detergent with TSP (trisodium phosphate)

Clean rags and sponges

Household bleach and mild detergent

Paint scraper

Sandpaper

Putty knife and joint compound

Hammer (if needed)

Pole sander

Dust mask, goggles, and respirator

Deglosser (optional)

Plastic drop cloths and masking tape

Primer or sealant

1 Use a screwdriver to remove all door locksets, light switch covers, and outlet covers from the area to be painted. Wash the walls and moldings with a no-rinse detergent solution, such as water and TSP. Remove any mildew with a solution of water, bleach, and mild nonammonia detergent. Use a rag saturated with cleaning solution to wash around outlets and light switches.

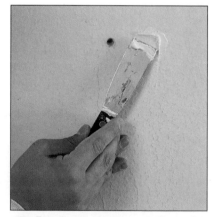

2 Remove any loose or peeling paint with a scraper, and feather the edges with sandpaper. Fill large, uneven areas or deep gaps in the paint with joint compound. Do the same for nail holes (see "Before Painting," above). Level any areas you have filled, and once dry, sand smooth.

Food for thought. When preparing a kitchen for repainting, don't forget to tape around the door seals of refrigerators and freezers. This will prevent spackle and paint dust from tainting the food inside.

Both sides now. Use double-sided painter's tape to hang thin plastic drop cloths when closing off a room for spackling and sanding. The adhesive on one side clings to walls or woodwork; the opposite side is tackier, for a better grip on the drop cloths.

Draw! Crayon marks on walls will bleed through a fresh coat of paint. Remove them by rubbing them with a dab of toothpaste on a damp cloth, then rinsing with water. If some marks remain, cover with a shellac-base stain-blocking primer.

For spatter-free doors. Slip an easy-to-make plastic sleeve over doors before painting, and they'll stay nice and clean. Measure and cut two large pieces of polyethylene film to size, apply masking tape to the edges, and staple them together on three sides. Allow some extra room for the doorknob, and to slide the sleeve on and off.

Call waiting. When priming or painting, leave the telephone in an accessible place and cover the handle of the handset with a plastic bag. You'll be able to grab it if it rings without smearing it with paint.

Shoe saver. Slip an old pair of cotton socks over your sneakers or shoes before you paint. The fabric will absorb drips and spatters and save on cleanup work.

A good coverup. To provide a foundation for paint, prime walls that contain dirt, rust, or smoke residue with a stain-blocking primer.

Mildew mistake. Using a household cleanser to remove mold could leave oil on the area and prevent the paint from adhering well. Use a mildew killer or a 1:2 solution of bleach and water.

Get a good seal. When using masking tape to protect wood trim, firmly press down its edge with a flexible putty knife. This will prevent paint from seeping behind the tape.

Moisture barrier. When preparing walls in a damp area, such as a kitchen or bathroom, apply a primer with a vapor barrier before putting on the top coat.

3 Sand glossy surfaces with fine-grit paper and a pole sander. Wear a dust mask and goggles (above). Or apply a commercial deglosser, following the manufacturer's directions. Ventilate the room and wear a respirator.

! **Paint that was applied before 1978 should always be tested for lead. Test kits are available at hardware and paint stores.**

4 After sanding, be sure to brush away dust. The surface must also be free of dirt, crayon, and grease, which could bleed through the paint. Dusting will suffice for most ceilings. The exceptions are kitchen and bathroom ceilings, which may be greasy or stained with mildew. Spot-clean these surfaces (see "Mildew Mistake," above). You can also buy primers and paints with antimildew agents.

5 Mask and cover any hard-to-remove light fixtures or thermostats with tape and plastic sheeting. Seal or prime raw wood. Also spot-prime any newly patched areas on the wall. Ask the clerk at your paint store to help you choose a primer appropriate for the type of paint you will be using for the finish coat. You may want to tint the primer to cut down on the number of finish coats that will be necessary.

The well-groomed brush. Always wash a new paintbrush before you use it. Any loose hairs will be flushed away before they can mar your finish.

No-shed roller. To keep fibers from a new roller sleeve from embedding in your paint job, wrap the sleeve in masking tape, then immediately zip it off. The fuzz should pull off with the tape.

Chalk up a good mark. Because the paint usually doesn't match exactly, it can be hard to disguise small water spots or other marks on white ceiling tiles. So skip the paint and try some white chalk. Rub on the chalk, blow away the excess, then rub on a little more if necessary.

Spatter matters. Prevent splashes when stirring paint with an electric drill and mixing attachment by covering the can with a paper plate. Punch a small hole in the plate to allow the mixer stem through.

Ceiling shield. To keep drips off your arm when painting overhead, use a plastic lid from a coffee can. Slit the plastic in the center, then push your brush through the slit. The lid will catch the drips.

Flipping your lid. Keep the tops on paint cans while you work. Leaving them open is an invitation for dust and foreign objects to settle in the paint. And open paint cans pose a hazard to small children and pets who may wander into the room while you're painting.

Kid stuff. While painting, protect electrical outlets with childproof outlet caps. Remove the cover plate (make sure the power is off), insert the caps, and roll the paint right over the outlets.

Smart stairs. Don't give up the use of your stairs during a paint job. Just paint every other step and let the paint dry before painting the alternate steps. You'll always be able to make it up and down the stairs—even when some of the paint is wet.

Dislike that paint smell? Chop a big unpeeled onion into large chunks, and toss them into a container of cold water. That odor of brand-new paint will disappear.

Hate taping? Save yourself time and effort by using a paint shield instead. These handy tools, about a foot in length, are held tight against moldings, trim, or other edges while you paint. Once you get the hang of using a paint shield, cutting in goes like lightning.

Pour and store. Funnel leftover paint into clean gallon milk jugs at the end of a job. You can see the color through the plastic, and it's easy to pour the paint from the jug into a tray without making a mess.

Applying the paint

WHAT YOU'LL NEED

Gloves, hat, and eye protection

Canvas and/or plastic drop cloths

Latex paint (semigloss for trim; eggshell or flat finish for walls and ceiling)

Coffee can

Roller tray

Painting tape

Paintbrushes

Paint roller, cover, and extension handle

Wheeled paint pad

Broad knife or paint shield

Bucket and water or mineral spirits

Roller scraper or painting-tool spinner

Garbage can and plastic liner (optional)

1 Stir paint before using. If paint is old, have a local retailer check that it is still usable and spin the container. Pour paint into a coffee can for trim work and cutting in, or a roller tray for ceilings and walls. Paint ceiling, walls, then trim. As you work, tape off areas with painting tape.

 Buy a spout for the paint can; it will keep the rim neat.

2 Use top-quality nylon/polyester filament brushes for latex; natural China bristle for oil paint. A 1-in. or 2½-in. angular sash brush is good for details and cutting in; a 2½-in. straight brush, for wide trim. Buy quality rollers —short nap for smooth surfaces and minimum ½–1in. nap for textured walls. Tape off the ceiling, then cut in all around it (see step 3). Paint ceiling with a roller, using a sturdy extension handle.

Close at hand. Keep track of your home's color scheme by making color wands from regular wooden paint stirrers. Just dip a stirrer in each can of different-colored paint, let it dry, and label the other end with the room or area to which it corresponds. Consult these wands when choosing a new paint color, and take them with you when shopping for fabric, wallcoverings, or accessories. They give you a more accurate sample than paint chips.

A colorful reminder. Take the time during repainting to write the color and brand of the paint you used on the inside of a switchplate or outlet cover. It will be easy to match the paint at a later date.

Blow hard. Take a deep breath and exhale into a partially full paint can before snapping on the lid. The carbon dioxide you blow out will prevent the paint from oxidizing and forming a skin.

FILE IT

You're covered: Estimating the paint you'll need

Figuring out how much paint you need can be one of the trickiest parts of the job. The following formula can help you get it right. The final figure is for one coat; double it if you plan on applying two. The spread rate (typical coverage) for a U.S. gallon of paint is generally 400 square feet. Read the label to see if your brand differs.

1. _____ × _____ = _____
Width of all walls added together   Height of ceiling   Total wall surface

2. _____ × _____ = _____
Height of window   Width of window   Window surface

3. Repeat line 2 for each window and add together

4. _____ × _____ = _____
Height of door   Width of door   Door surface

5. Repeat line 4 for each door and add together

6. _____ + _____ = _____
Total from line 3   Total from line 5   Surface not to be painted

7. _____ − _____ = _____
Total from line 1   Total from line 6   Total surface to be painted

8. _____ ÷ _____ = _____
Total from line 7   Spread rate   Gallons of paint for each coat

3 Let the ceiling paint dry thoroughly; then prepare to paint the walls. Choose a wall to begin with and cut in on this wall only. First cut in around the ceiling, floor, doorways, windows, and trim. A wheeled paint pad is easy to use, requires no taping, and better matches a roller's texture. Still, a sash brush may be needed in places. If working alone, cut in edges for only as large an area as you can go over before cut-in area dries.

4 Immediately after cutting in, roll that area with paint. Apply paint in an N pattern to the upper part of the wall and roll it out. Repeat for the lower part, blending areas to avoid lap marks. Be sure to work with wet edges to avoid a "bordered" look. Depending on the color and type of paint, you may need one or two coats. Tinting the primer to half the formula of the finish paint can reduce the number of required coats.

5 Finally, paint the trim. Tape it off or use a broad knife, paint shield, or other straightedge to keep edges neat. (For detailed instructions on painting a door, see pp. 114–115; a window, pp. 116–117.) Clean applicators when they become overfull or messy and after use. Options for cleaning include rinsing, running the roller over a plastic roller scraper, or spinning with a painting-tool spinner held over a lined garbage can.

To make a stencil, trace a pattern from a book or use a copy machine to copy a fabric design, enlarging or reducing it as necessary. Pencil a level line 1 inch from the bottom of the design as a guide, and trace the final result onto pieces of clear acetate. Make several stencils for each color. Tape one of the acetates to a cutting board, and using a mat knife, cut out the areas for one color. Do this for all the colors; then tag the stencils to indicate up, down, right and left.

Background check. Any type of paint can serve as a background for stenciling, but the most workable finish is eggshell. Surfaces should be clean and free of cracks, and the background paint should be completely dry.

Test your color combo. Do a color proof on paper before committing yourself to stenciling the wall. If the colors you've chosen don't work well with the pattern, it's better to find out now.

When weaker is better. When securing a stencil to the wall, avoid masking tape, which can pull off the existing finish. Use drafting tape or painter's masking tape—they have a weaker adhesive. Or spray the back of the stencil with artist's adhesive (to keep things neat, spray inside a box or other contained area).

Pounce on it. The rapid bouncing of the tips of the brush bristles against the stencil is called "pouncing," and it produces that characteristic stenciled look. Pounce from the edges to the center of the stencil.

Protect the design and allow for cleaning by covering the stenciled finish with a coat of extra-pale matte varnish. The shinier grades of varnish—eggshell or gloss, for example—give more protection.

No-lag stenciling. Choose fast-drying stencil paints or artist's acrylics when executing a multicolor design. This will allow you to maintain the momentum while you work.

Up with stencils. Don't limit your stenciling opportunities to broad surfaces such as walls. Stair risers and other unusual locations can also be beautified, as can many furniture pieces. Make sure you do the proper prep work for whatever surface you choose to stencil, and take measures to protect the finished design.

Stenciling a room

WHAT YOU'LL NEED

Ready-made stencils

Latex surgical gloves

Tape measure, chalk line, and level

Artist's chalk

Drafting tape or painter's masking tape

Removable spray adhesive (optional)

Stencil paint or artist's acrylics

Paint tray or disposable plastic plate

Stencil brushes

Paper towels

Water and rags for cleanup

1 Many stencil designs can be purchased at craft stores; you can also make your own (see "To Make a Stencil," above). Ready-made stencils often have guidelines to help you position the stencil correctly. Plan to start stenciling from a corner of the room, if possible. Measure down from the ceiling, and mark the wall with artist's chalk at points that correspond with the guideline on the stencil.

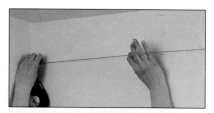

2 Snap a chalk line from mark to mark, and make sure it is level. Align the guides on the stencil with the chalk line, and tape the stencil to the wall; do not tape over any cutouts.

 For neater results, lightly spray the back of the stencil with artist's adhesive. Test first to make sure the adhesive leaves no residue.

Canvas the area. If you don't want to paint the floor, consider stenciling a canvas floorcloth. Buy a stiff piece of canvas and turn under the cut ends. Paint it the desired background color; then stencil away. Protect the cloth with a few light coats of spray-on polyurethane.

Move it outdoors. Stenciling the mailbox or front door can help perk up your house's exterior. Just make sure you use paint formulated for outdoor use, and finish with nonyellowing, super-hard polyurethane.

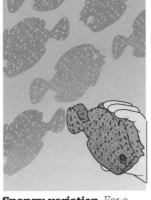

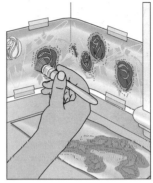

Spongy variation. For a look similar to that produced by stenciling, try sponge-stamping. Either cut synthetic cleaning sponges into the desired shape or buy precut sponges at craft stores. It sounds simple—just dip the sponge in paint, blot, and press on the wall—but there's definitely a knack to this, so practice on cardboard first

Take the long view. When selecting a precut stencil, step back and make sure it looks good from a distance. A pattern that is attractive up close may be unreadable from 10 feet away.

No cutting corners. For a continuous design, make sure you wrap the stencil around corners. It's crucial that the stencil remain level as you start on the abutting wall, since corners can be uneven.

Cut a rug. Turn a drab floor into a knockout by stenciling a "rug" directly on it. Just make sure to coat the floor with a hard, durable finish after the stencil paint has dried. A nonyellowing, super-hard polyurethane is a good choice.

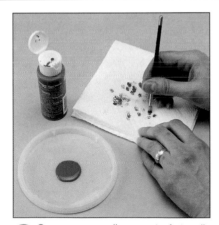

3 Squeeze a small amount of stencil paint (about the size of a nickel) onto a paint tray or disposable plastic plate (the lid from a take-out container will work perfectly). Dab the tip of your stencil brush into the paint. Blot it on paper towels to disperse the paint evenly on the brush and to remove any excess paint. The brush should be almost dry before you start.

4 Work one color at a time. Hold the brush perpendicular to the wall and lightly dab all the cutouts that use the first color. Work from the outer edges of each cutout toward the center; this helps keep the design neat. Carefully lift the stencil, clean it, and reposition it. Continue to stencil the entire room with the first color.

5 Wash out the stencil brush and prepare to start the second color. Lightly touch the wall to make sure the first color has dried. Put the stencil back in position, realigning the guidelines to make sure the pattern is straight. Apply the second color in the same manner as the first, working all around the room. Continue this way until the design is completed.

A wall in its prime.
Always coat new wallboard with a primer before applying a paint finish. Otherwise, the colors will be sucked into the porous surface.

When choosing colors,
it's best for beginners to err on the side of subtlety. Keep them light or neutral, and consider choosing two or more shades from the same color card to play it safe.

Only the best.
Use top-quality latex paint for sponge painting and most other decorative finishes. It is easy to apply, cleans up with soap and water, and poses no problems with harmful fumes. And by adding an extender to the paint, you can prolong the drying time, so you can work the surface if required.

Sponging light over dark
gives an illusion of depth. Applying a dark color over a lighter one produces a more defined, textured look. If you are sponging on more than one color and are using latex paint, wait until each application is dry to the touch before you start applying the next color.

Handling tight corners.
Sponge-paint in corners and around trim by using a small piece of sponge ripped off the main one. You'll be able to dab this mini-sponge right up to the line. If you do use the big sponge in corners and around trim, make sure you thoroughly tape off these areas first, since sea sponges have naturally ragged, messy edges.

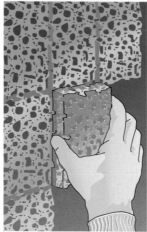

Be square. For a pattern that resembles gold leaf, use soft colors and a square or rectangular sponge instead of a sea sponge. Overlap the edges of each print. A smooth-surface foam sponge will impart an even print; a coarser synthetic sponge will add texture to the finished design.

You need perspective.
Step back from your work every so often and assess the overall look of the job. If there are heavy areas of paint, lighten them by sponging on a little base color once the paint dries.

No interruptions, please.
It's easy to continue the same pattern and produce a consistent finish if you complete the entire room before taking a break. If this isn't possible, work up to a natural break, such as a chair rail or corner, before stopping.

Faster, easier marble.
Sponge-on marbleizing kits allow you to achieve the look of marble in three easy steps. You swirl several colors together on a paper plate, sponge the paint onto the surface, then draw on the marble veins with the edge of a feather.

Sponge-painting a wall

WHAT YOU'LL NEED

Flat or eggshell-finish latex paint for base coat

Paintbrush (for small areas) or paint roller and cover (for large surfaces only)

Latex surgical gloves

Natural sea sponge

Eggshell-finish latex for sponging

Paint tray

Water-base polyurethane (optional)

Paint extender

Bucket and water

1 In sponging, paint is applied to a dry base paint using a natural sea sponge (see step 5 for how to sponge off). To sponge on, apply a base coat with a brush or roller and let it dry. Immerse a sea sponge in water and wring it out so the sponge is damp. Pour the second-color paint into a paint tray. Rotate the sponge in the paint; it should be evenly and lightly coated.

2 Repeatedly and lightly dab the surface with the sponge in a random pattern. It's best to practice your technique first on cardboard or paper. Some things to keep in mind: Dip the sponge in more paint as needed, and vary the pressure depending on how much paint is on the sponge. Occasionally rotate the sponge to vary the pattern somewhat.

Stone from a can. Not all faux stone finishes require time, special materials, and artistic ability. If you want the look without the fuss, try aerosol "granite." It's easy and fast to apply and works great on mantelpieces, hearths, and tabletops.

On the dot. For a stippled finish without a stippling brush, gently dip the bristles of a dust or shoe brush into paint and apply to a tabletop, wall, etc. The paint will break up into dots, creating a soft, suede-like finish.

Nice lines. Use a window-cleaning squeegee to create a decorative combed finish. Trim it to the desired width, then cut ½-inch-wide notches in the blade, leaving ¼ inch between notches. Draw the comb through the paint in either straight or curvy lines.

Don't stop with walls. Furniture pieces, especially country-style ones, are perfect candidates for sponging. Paint the piece a light or dark base color, and sponge with different colors. Be sure to protect the surface with a nonyellowing, super-hard polyurethane.

All that glitters. If you want gold accents, buy a small bottle of gold-leaf paint and lightly sponge it on top of a base coat on the wall. For a more subtle effect, sponge gold paint on trim and molding, after first applying a base coat.

Instant aging. Using a technique known as wiping off, you can add the look of age to ornately carved architectural elements or furniture. Make a glaze by thinning alkyd enamel undercoat with an equal part of mineral spirits. Brush the glaze on the carved area, then quickly wipe it off with a lint-free rag, leaving paint in the crevices. Use light paint on a dark background, darker paint on a light background.

3 Work in a 2- x 2-ft. area, starting at the top of the wall and working your way down. Always maintain a wet edge to keep the pattern consistent. Overlap the pattern slightly; every mark should blend with the next.

 If the painted area needs to be protected, apply a nonyellowing water-base polyurethane.

4 Once you have completed the entire area in one color, you may want to sponge on a second color. This adds richness and texture to the finish. The second color could be different but complementary; it could also be a variation on the first color. One way to achieve this is by simply adding white to the first color.

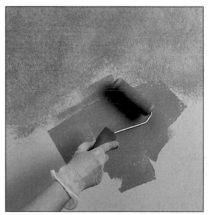

5 To sponge off, apply a base coat and let it dry. The second color should be a different but complementary color or a variation of the first color. Before applying second color, add paint extender to paint to lengthen the drying time. Apply paint with a roller in a crisscross fashion. Moving quickly before the paint dries, use a clean, damp sea sponge to lift off areas of color. Rinse and wring sponge often.

Try something different. In addition to old undershirts and sheets, test a few unconventional fabrics for rag-rolling—you might like the textures and effects they impart. Experiment with lace, cheesecloth, burlap, linen, etc. Just make sure the cloths are lint-free.

More than enough. Whatever fabric you choose for ragging on your finish, make sure you have plenty of it. The rags become unusable as they get saturated with paint, and you will have to substitute fresh ones.

Prep your rags. Be sure to trim cheesecloth before you rag-roll to prevent threads from becoming embedded in the paint. When using fabric from the rag bag, wash it first and, likewise, remove all loose threads with a snip of the scissors.

Merrily we roll along. If you have trouble rolling the rag down the wall without skidding, wrap it around a 10-inch length of 1-inch-diameter wooden dowel. Hold the rag on the dowel tightly with your fingers, and the dowel will roll with ease.

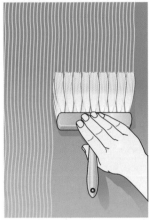

What a drag. Dragging a lighter color of paint over a darker shade creates an interesting tone-on-tone texture. A 6-inch-wide wallpaper paste brush makes a good dragger—it will produce a handsome "textured stripe" look.

Take it off. As with sponging, you can also rag-roll paint off the wall. However, this technique requires two people—one to apply the base, the other to roll the paint off before it dries. To roll off the paint, use the same technique as for rolling on, but after every few strips, dip the cloth in water and wring it out thoroughly. Overlap the strips slightly, and don't backtrack.

Rag-rolling and ragging a room

WHAT YOU'LL NEED

Flat or eggshell-finish latex paint for base coat

Paintbrush or paint roller and tray

Latex surgical gloves

Cotton rags

Eggshell-finish latex paint for ragging

1 First, apply a base coat and let it dry. Wearing latex gloves, saturate a rag in paint and wring out the excess. Fold and roll up the rag so it is loosely twisted.

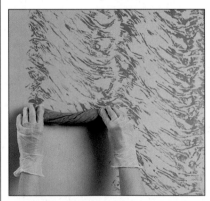

2 Grasp the roll at each end, place the rag on the wall just below the ceiling, and roll it straight down the wall. Reroll the rag, and redip it in paint as needed for a uniform look. Vertical strips should just touch each other, not overlap.

3 To create a plain ragged finish, do not roll the rag. Instead, bunch it in your hand and press on the paint; the ridges will create a pleasingly wrinkled pattern. Rearrange the rag in your hand as you paint to vary the finish. Be careful of loose, floppy ends.

Don't waste time. Color-washing requires quick hand motions. So keep moving, make your gestures as broad as possible, and try not to rework the surface. Practicing ahead of time on heavy cardboard will help you get the effect you want.

On hot days, brush water on the wall with a paintbrush before starting to color-wash. This will help the paint brush on better and flow more easily as you work it.

A little help. Adding an acrylic gel extender to the paint slows down the drying time considerably, giving you more time to work the surface of the paint to get the effect you want.

A spattering of color. For a completely different look, try spattering, in which splashes of color are literally thrown on top of a base coat. You can spatter by hitting a paintbrush against a wooden stick or brush handle. Or, for a finer spray, load the end of a wider brush and run a palette knife or your thumb over the edge. Wear latex surgical gloves, goggles, and plenty of protective clothing, because spattering makes a mess. Protect other parts of the room, too.

Silhouettes on the wall. Before spattering a wall, spray mount tree leaves or shapes cut from paper. After the paint dries and you remove the leaves or paper, the silhouettes will remain.

Color-washing a wall

WHAT YOU'LL NEED

Latex surgical gloves

Painting tape

Eggshell-finish latex paint

Paint tray

Water

Sponge brush, nylon brush, or sea sponge

1 First, tape off all moldings. Pour the paint into a tray and mix it with water to obtain a milky consistency. With a 3-in. sponge brush, start painting at a corner, making large crisscross strokes. Don't overlap. The coat should be translucent, with some darker areas.

2 For a different effect, use a sea sponge instead of a sponge brush. Prepare the paint as above; then rub it on using circular motions. Be sure to blend the edges slightly. For added texture, let it dry, then add a second coat of the same paint.

3 Another technique is to use a 3-in. nylon paintbrush and create visible, textured brush strokes. Prepare the paint as above and work in large crisscross strokes. Don't overwork an area; doing this successfully depends on knowing when to stop.

Ink blot technique. The term "inking" color off means to blot it off the surface. You can use the same crisscross motion as with color-washing and achieve much the same effect. Just apply the watered-down paint to the wall with a brush or roller. Then bunch the cheesecloth in your hand and lightly pull it across the wall, using broad crisscross strokes. As with any "pulling off" technique, this goes quicker if you enlist a helper to apply the paint right before you pull it off. Work one small section at a time, and watch that the paint is not so thin that it runs and drips.

To paint, or not to paint.
If you have older wood paneling that needs a new look, the options range from cleaning it to staining it to painting it. If you're not sure, try cleaning it first. Use a mild detergent that is safe for whatever finish is on the paneling—wax, oil, or polyurethane, for example.

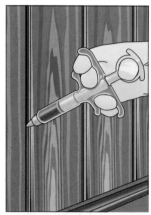

The staining solution.
A fresh coat of stain can often spruce up wood paneling. However, be aware that the wood can shrink when exposed to dry air, causing lighter unstained wood to appear at the joint lines. You can dab at the joints with a brush, but it's easier and quicker to use a glue injector loaded with stain.

In a pickle. It's easy to apply a translucent, whitish finish—called pickling—to unfinished paneling. Wash the paneling with water and no-rinse detergent. Then thin white alkyd enamel undercoat with an equal part of mineral spirits, and brush it on the wood. Wipe off quickly with a lint-free rag for an understated finish; wait longer for a bolder look.

Tint your primer, and you may be able to cut down on the number of finish coats needed to fully cover the old color of your paneling. Ask your local paint store to adjust the primer to half the color density of the final shade.

The real thing. Paint won't adhere to vinyl or plastic paneling. If you can't tell whether your panels are made of wood, sand a small area—vinyl or plastic will shred and flake off.

Groove-y accents. If you decide to paint the paneling, you can spackle the grooves for a seamless finished look. Or just skip the spackle if you want a look that's a little more "country."

In the right order. For the neatest job when finishing paneling with raised or recessed panels, paint the molding around each panel first. Then paint the flat panel in the center. Finish with the frame. Working in this order will allow you to even out all runs and drips as you work.

Painting wood paneling

WHAT YOU'LL NEED

No-rinse detergent (TSP) mixed with water	Medium (80-grit) sandpaper
Bucket, sponges, and towels	Window exhaust fan (optional)
Spackle and spackle knife	Acrylic primer (with optional tinting)
Goggles and dust mask	Interior acrylic latex paint

1 Wash the paneling with a solution of warm water and no-rinse detergent, such as TSP. If a finished look is desired, fill in the grooves with spackle. Also fill in any holes or indentations with spackle. Let the spackle dry thoroughly.

2 Wearing goggles and a dust mask, sand spackled surfaces until smooth. A window exhaust fan helps move dust out of the room. Rewash the surface with no-rinse detergent and let it dry thoroughly. Open the windows to speed drying.

3 Apply acrylic primer to the entire area and let it dry. Apply the desired finish paint, using one or two coats as necessary.

Clean up your act. Walls don't have to be in good shape to hang a wall liner, but they do have to be clean. Wash them well with warm water and a no-rinse detergent; then apply acrylic primer. If the primer beads up, you know there is still grease or oil on the wall. In that case, wash the walls down again, let dry, and reapply the primer.

Great for fabric. If you will be hanging fabric on the wall, it's a good idea to put up a wall liner first. Fabric needs an especially smooth wall surface, and a wall liner is the quickest, and usually the easiest, way to achieve this.

Peeling paint? If the damage is slight, just spot-scrape and prime; then put up the wallcovering. But if there are multiple layers of peeling paint, sand off the loose paint and go for the wall liner. Wallcovering won't adhere well to paint that is poorly bonded to the wall—and it certainly won't look good when installed.

Lead paint? Wall liner is the perfect cover-up for walls coated with hazardous lead-base paint.

Other cover-ups. Some other interior surfaces that can be camouflaged by wall liner include brick, concrete, and stucco walls.

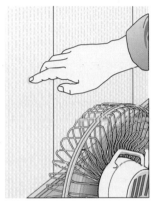

Press test. To test if the wall liner is thoroughly dry, press it lightly with your finger. If it doesn't indent, you can proceed to paint or hang wallcovering on top of it. If the wall liner does indent, it needs more time to dry. To speed things along, aim a fan at the wall and check again in a few hours.

Good for borders, too. Wallpaper borders also need a smooth wall surface. If you are planning to hang a border and your walls are in less than perfect shape, glue a strip of wall liner beneath the border. Cut the liner slightly narrower than the border, and apply it with heavy-duty wallcovering adhesive. Let it dry thoroughly; then apply primer before hanging the border.

Installing wall liner

WHAT YOU'LL NEED

No-rinse detergent (TSP) mixed with water	Heavy-duty wallcovering adhesive
Bucket and sponges	Roller or wallpaper paste brush
Spackle and spackle knife	Broad knife or other straightedge
High-quality acrylic primer	Utility knife
Lining paper	

1 Wash the paneling with a solution of warm water and no-rinse detergent, such as TSP, to remove all dirt and grease. Spackle grooves and any imperfections (see facing page). Apply a good-quality acrylic primer and let it dry thoroughly.

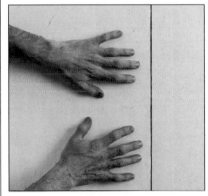

2 Hang the wall liner as you would wallpaper (see pp. 134–135). Apply a heavy-duty wallcovering adhesive with a roller or paste brush. If you will be installing wallcovering, hang liner horizontally. If you will be painting, hang liner vertically.

3 Cut around the windows and doors with a utility knife, using a straightedge to hold the liner against the molding. Smooth the liner with a brush or sponge. Wait 48 hr.; then apply the primer before painting or applying the wallcovering.

Vinegary glue remover.
A solution of equal parts of white vinegar and hot water does a good job of softening the adhesive behind old wallpaper—and it's much cheaper than a chemical remover. Even though the vinegar is nontoxic, its pungent smell can be irritating, so open the windows.

Glue removal II. Remove any remaining adhesive with a nylon brush or pot scrubber. Dip the brush or scrubber in hot water regularly to keep it clean.

Messy business. When removing wallpaper or washing down walls, make sure you cover the entire floor surface with protective drop cloths. And because plastic is not absorbent, it's better to use canvas drop cloths or plastic drop cloths that are backed with paper.

Getting steamed off.
A steamer can be awkward and even dangerous to use, but sometimes it's the only tool that will remove a stubborn, old, nonstrippable wallcovering or multiple layers of wallcovering from plaster walls. (Note: Never steam a wallboard surface, because the moisture from the steamer can damage the paper covering.)

Go straight to the top.
When using a steamer, start at the upper part of the wall. Any steam that condenses and runs down the wall will accelerate the glue-loosening process on lower sections.

Take off glue residue. Use a window squeegee dipped in hot water to remove leftover wallcovering paste from stripped walls. Wipe the gunk off the blade frequently with a clean rag.

Off the floor. When removing old wallcovering, be sure to place it on a drop cloth, not on the floor. The solutions used to remove wallcovering can cause dyes to run, staining floors and other surfaces.

Neatness counts. Whatever tool you use for scraping off old wallcovering, take care not to damage the wall surface beneath. Any scratches or gouges that you accidentally make while scraping will have to be repaired prior to painting or hanging new wallcovering.

Make a power peeler out of a power paint roller by using it with a solution of soap and hot water. The suds will be pumped through the tube to the roller. For vinyl and other impenetrable papers, first score the surface (step 4).

Removing old wallcovering

WHAT YOU'LL NEED

Drop cloth and masking tape

Plastic for covering outlets

Mops and towels

Rubber gloves and latex surgical gloves

Stiff putty knife

Hot water and liquid dishwashing detergent

Wetting agent such as chemical wallpaper remover (optional)

5-gal. garden sprayer

Safety goggles (if using chemicals)

6-in. wallboard taping knife

Wallpaper stripper

Scoring tool

Bucket and sponges

Acrylic primer

1 Strippable wallcoverings can be entirely removed without leaving any backing on the wall. Peelable wallcoverings come off in two layers—the top vinyl coating, which peels off, and the paper backing, which is left on the wall. To remove peelable wallcovering, pry under a lower corner with a stiff putty knife. Then gently peel upward until the entire vinyl coating is removed, leaving the paper backing behind.

2 To remove the paper backing—and many wallcoverings—from the wall, spray the wall surface with a mixture of hot water and a small amount of liquid dishwashing detergent, or with chemical wallpaper remover. Use a 5-gal. garden sprayer and wear eye protection if using chemicals. Spray walls from ceiling to floor, letting solution soak in. Continue until the paper bubbles up or separates from the wall.

Mark the spot. To make it easy to reinstall hardware—and to prevent drilling more holes in the walls—fill the fastener holes for pictures, mirrors, and drapery brackets with a toothpick before installing wallcovering. Take out the toothpick when covering the area, then push it through before proceeding to the next section.

Cover-up test. If there is only one layer of untextured wallcovering on the wall and it's still adhering tightly, you may be able to leave it in place and just hang the new wallcovering over it. One way to test the old wallcovering is by running your fingers over it; if you hear a crackling noise, the covering is loose and should be removed. Also check the edges and corners by prying them up with a putty knife. If large sections lift off, plan on removing the covering.

Covering coverings. If the old covering passes all the above tests and you decide to cover it over, first check for any loose areas and glue them down with wallcovering adhesive. Then wash the surface with detergent or a mild solution of bleach and water. Apply a primer made for use under wallcoverings.

Tie those apron strings. To prevent countless trips up and down the step ladder, wear an inexpensive carpenter's apron when removing or installing wallcovering. A measuring tape, seam roller, and other small tools will easily fit within the commodious apron pockets, where they'll always be close at hand.

Step by step. Paint the ceiling and any trim after removing the old wallcovering and before installing the new. It's easy to remove wallcovering paste from woodwork and painted surfaces, but it's almost impossible to remove paint from new wallcovering.

3 Once the paper has bubbled up or separated from the wall, start scraping it off with a 6-in. wallboard taping knife. If the wallpaper is hard to remove, use a wallpaper stripper; don't gouge wallboard walls.

! Before wetting walls, cover the floor, turn off the power, and tape over and around electrical and telephone outlets.

4 Some wallcoverings can be difficult to strip dry and are hard to penetrate with the wetting solution. If this is the case, score the wallcovering's surface in a crisscross pattern with a scoring tool. Then spray with the wetting solution as before, letting it soak in and waiting until the paper starts to bubble up or separate. Scrape the surface with a wallboard taping knife or a wallpaper stripper.

5 After all the wallcovering and backing material has been scraped off, wash the walls with hot water and liquid dishwashing detergent or chemical wallpaper remover. You can also use a solution of ¼ cup bleach in 2 gal. of hot water. Continue washing until all glue residue is removed. Before painting or hanging new wallcovering, apply a good-quality acrylic primer to the walls, and let it dry for 24 hr.

Unseamly edges. To hide the white seam edge that is often visible on dark papers, run an indelible marking pen around the ends of the roll. Use a pen with a color that is close to the paper's background color, and err on the side of being too light. Always let the ink dry before wetting the paper.

Cover damaged walls with heavily embossed wallpaper, which is good for hiding cracks. Or use a wall liner (see p. 131).

Filling the gaps. If you are installing a wallpaper with a pastel background, before papering, coat the wall with a primer tinted to match the background. This ensures that any seam gap will be virtually invisible.

Imperfect walls? Before installing wallcovering, check the walls one last time by shining a flashlight at an angle across them. Irregularities that need to be sanded will cast shadows.

Get the strips straight. Here's how to keep patterns with a horizontal repeat on the straight and narrow: After hanging a strip, place a carpenter's level along a design element and draw a perfectly horizontal line across the wall where you plan to hang the next strip. Align the new strip with the line. Do this for each strip.

Put the process on hold. Can't hang a strip you've already wet? Fold it as described below in step 2. Then roll the strip up loosely and seal in a plastic garbage bag. This will keep the adhesive moist for an hour.

To find wall anchors, place a short finishing nail, with the point sticking out, in each anchor hole before applying a new wallcovering. The nail will pierce the paper and let you spot the anchor once the paper is up.

Cutting corners. For the neatest results, cut the last partial strip on the first wall ¼ inch wider than the space left so it wraps around the corner. For the abutting wall, measure the width of the cut-off piece and mark a new plumb line for it (see step 1, below) that distance from the corner.

Installing wallcovering

WHAT YOU'LL NEED

Wallcovering

Canvas drop cloths

Stepladder

Yardstick and pencil

Carpenter's level

Long scissors

Bucket

Water tray

Table

Large sponge

Wide wallboard taping knife

Utility knife with extra blades

Seam roller

1 Starting in a corner or at a doorway, measure out ½ in. less than the wallcovering width and make a mark. This is where the first seam will fall. Using a carpenter's level as a guide, draw a perfectly vertical line at this point and extend it from ceiling to floor. Measure the wall height, and align the desired pattern of the wallpaper at the ceiling line. Then cut a strip that is 4 in. longer than the wall.

2 Roll up strip loosely, paste-side out, and soak it briefly in water tray; see maker's instructions for exact time. Pull strip face-down onto a table. Fold upper two-thirds over itself, paste-side in, taking care not to crease it. Fold lower third over itself.

 Change the water every two or three strips. Each dip leaves residue in the water.

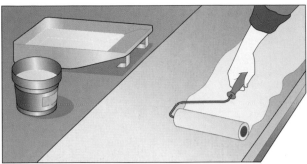

Make it stick. Use paste activator instead of plain water to wet prepasted paper. Put the activator in a clean paint tray and apply it with a clean medium-nap paint roller. Don't submerge the paper in activator; it can leave an ugly slick coating on the finished side. Test a single strip first.

Remove a spot from a delicate wallcovering by gently rubbing it with a piece of balled-up rye bread.

Papering a switchplate?
Keep these tips in mind: Start with a metal plate; it's flatter than a plastic one. Clip the corners of the covering diagonally to prevent bunching. Use vinyl-on-vinyl adhesive; prepaste or glue won't hold well. At a screw hole, make a small slit. When securing the plate to the wall, lift the edges of the wallcovering, insert the screw, and then smooth the edges flat over the screw.

SAFE AND SMART

➤ Don't use plastic drop cloths on the floor. They are slippery when wet.

➤ Open a stepladder fully and lock its braces. Climb no higher than the second step from the top. Don't lean to the side or reach out too far.

➤ Turn off the power to outlets at the main service panel before removing the cover plates and papering over them.

Recycling the leftovers.
After finishing a job, use wallcovering scraps to cover wastebaskets, lampshades, picture frames, window shades, shelves, books, and photo albums.

A clean cut. To avoid expensive tears in wallcovering, change cutting blades often—every two or three cuts. Use a knife with a break-off blade or (with care) a single-edge razor blade. For intricate cuts along molding, a craft knife is the best bet.

When papering a ceiling, ensure a strong bond by pressing each strip against the ceiling with a dry paint roller. Work from the middle of the strip out toward both ends. Better yet, use self-adhesive paper.

3 Unfold the top of the strip and smooth it in place. Overlap the ceiling by about 2 in. and align the strip along the marked line, not the corner or the door frame. Then open and smooth the bottom fold. Use a wet sponge to wipe off any excess glue.

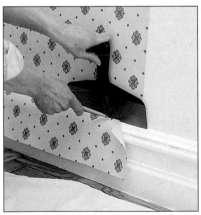

4 Using a wide wallboard taping knife as a guide, trim the top and bottom of the strip with a sharp utility knife. Cut at a shallow angle and don't lift the blade. Trim around door or window molding the same way; if the covering tends to bunch up at a molding corner, make a cut into the waste area before trimming, or try a new sharp blade.

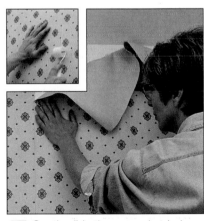

5 Gently slide the second strip in place next to the first, and align the patterns. Make sure the edges just touch along the seam. After 10 to 15 min., flatten the edges with a seam roller (inset).

 Pressing a seam roller too hard may squeeze out the adhesive from the wallpaper.

FILE IT

Wallcovering why's and where's

In addition to aesthetics, you need to consider how and where a wallcovering will be used before making a choice. Here is a guide to the most common wallcoverings.

Type	Applications
Standard paper	This wallpaper consists of an inexpensive paper backing with a decorative print directly applied to it. It has a very thin vinyl coating that is not very effective at repelling grease and excess moisture. Best for use in areas that do not get heavy use, such as bedrooms and dining rooms. It is generally prepasted.
Solid sheet vinyl	This wallpaper has a paper backing laminated to a solid vinyl decorative surface. It is durable and generally well suited to areas that receive heavy use, as well as kitchens and bathrooms. It is usually prepasted.
String cloth (naturals)	This wallpaper is made of fine vertical threads laminated to a paper backing. It can be tricky to apply and does not wash very well. Thus it is best for areas that do not get heavy use. The texture of the string cloth can help hide imperfections in the wall beneath.
Moiré	This decorative wallpaper has a silky, watermarked look that can be both formal and elegant. The pattern is generally printed on a paper backing. This type of wallcovering is washable and is generally suited to formal rooms in the home.
Fabric-backed	The pattern on this wallcovering is printed onto a fabric backing made of scrim or cotton. This woven backing is extremely durable. The covering may be scrubbed clean and also can be removed in a one-step process. For this reason, it is ideal for areas that get heavy use. It is available in many varieties, including commercial.
Commercial	This heavy-duty wallcovering is generally sold in widths of 48 to 54 inches, and is available in various weights, depending on the proposed use. It is scrubbable and dry-strippable, meaning it can be removed in a one-step process. It is well suited to commercial spaces and to residential areas that get heavy use, such as children's playrooms.

The more, the better.
As a rule of thumb, match the number of border treatments to the size of the room. A single run of border at the ceiling will be overwhelmed by a cavernous room. The room will look more pulled together with additional borders at the baseboard or trimwork.

Border-line savings.
To cut the cost of wallcovering by about half, use strips of border to fashion a "chair rail"; then hang the covering either above or below the "rail." Paint the other area of the wall with a complementary color.

Coping with kids. Since it's usually easier to remove fingerprints, crayon, and other marks from paint than from wallcovering, in young children's rooms it makes good sense to hang a border at chair-rail height and install the wallcovering out of reach above it.

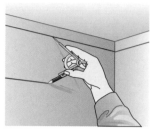

Level it. If you need to mark the width of the border on the wall, use a drawing compass. It goes quickly and you'll get an accurate line. Just be sure to work from a level top line.

Scuff up glossy paint on walls before applying strips of border—otherwise, they won't adhere tightly. Use fine- or medium-grit sandpaper, and make sure to wipe away or vacuum up all the dust. Then roll on a coat of wallcovering primer.

A little help from friends.
Try to work with a helper when hanging a border at ceiling height. You stand on the stepladder and press the border in place while your assistant feeds you fresh border from the accordion-folded pile.

Pick the right adhesive.
When hanging vinyl border over vinyl wallcovering, make sure to use vinyl-to-vinyl adhesive. Otherwise, the border won't stick.

Cosmetic surgery.
Lengthen the look of a room's doors and windows by overlapping wallpaper borders. Hang the horizontal strip first, and top it off with the vertical layers.

Lower your ceiling.
To reproportion a high-ceilinged room, hang matching wide borders at the top and bottom of the walls. The borders will visually reduce the height of the room, making it appear cozier.

Loose ends? Use white household glue to repair a loose border edge. Dab the glue on the underside of the paper with a long artist's brush, then coat the wall surface with glue. Roll the repair with a seam roller.

Simple valances over windows hide unsightly hardware and add a decorator touch to plain rooms. They can be fun or formal—execute your ideas in cardboard and place each design over the window to see which looks best before cutting the valance out of plywood. Finish up by covering the valance with matching wallcovering.

For a stenciled look, trim the edges from the wallpaper border and hang just the interior motif. The design will look as if it's been painted on.

Make your own. To transform your leftover wallcovering—or that roll or two you picked up cheap at the home center—into a lovely border, just mark the width, then cut the covering on a long worktable with a sharp utility knife. Use firm pressure and go slowly, or the covering could tear.

An embossed border can add architectural detail to an otherwise plain painted room. If you like, you can decorate the border with any good-quality paint to match your color scheme.

Rectangular "panels" made from border suggest the sumptuousness of wood paneling and add a formal accent to living room or even dining room walls. If you are a wallcovering novice, the job will go more smoothly if you select a border with a nondirectional overall pattern.

Installing a border

WHAT YOU'LL NEED

Tape measure or level and straightedge	Bucket and paste brush
Pencil or chalk line	Smoothing brush or large sponge
Wallpaper border	Utility knife

Wallpaper paste or vinyl-to-vinyl adhesive (for installing a border on top of wallcovering)

1 To locate position lines, use a level and straightedge. You can measure from a fixed point, such as the ceiling or molding; however, make sure the border is level, as the ceiling line can be uneven. Mark position lines with a pencil, or snap a chalk line.

2 Brush on paste or adhesive, or soak prepasted paper. Fold the paper paste-to-paste, accordion-style. Carry it to the wall, position it against the line, and smooth it with a smoothing brush or other tool or a large sponge (see pp. 134–135).

3 To make a tight seam, position the second piece so that the pattern lines up and overlaps the first piece by 2 in. Cut through both layers with a utility knife and straightedge. Remove the cut-off ends. Smooth; then roll the seam.

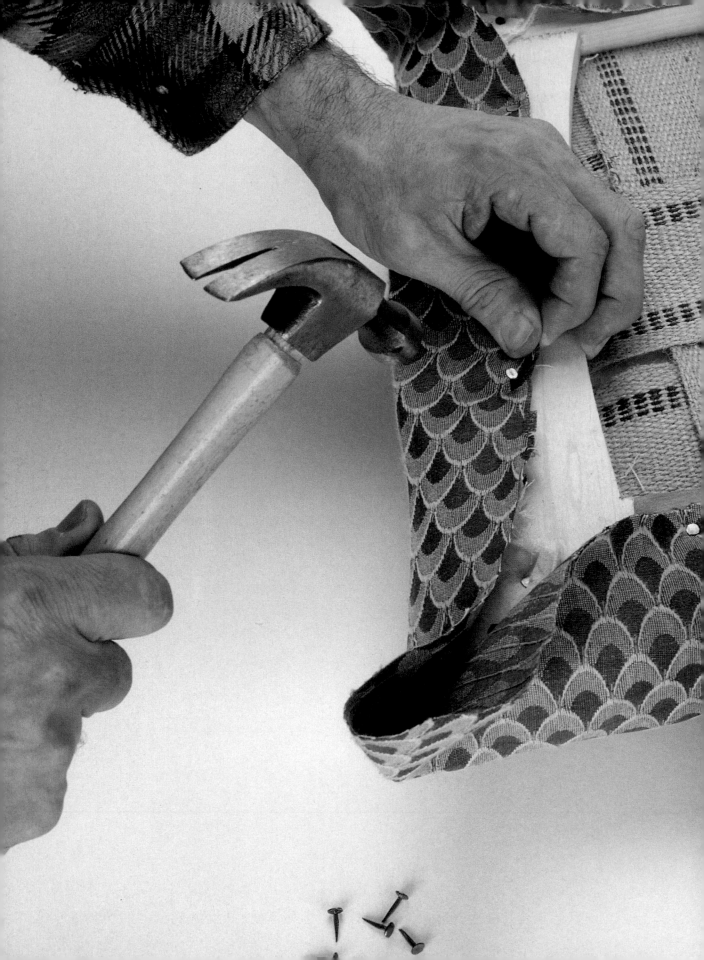

FURNITURE REPAIRS AND REFINISHING

Job ratings: Easy   Medium   Complex

Cut the fuzz. For fine antiques, use a methylene chloride-base stripper instead of one of the newer "safer" strippers. Not only can the water in these strippers make the wood fibers fuzz up, which will add another sanding step to your labors, it can cause delicate veneers to delaminate.

Weighing your decision. When purchasing a methylene chloride stripper, choose the product that contains the most methylene chloride. Since manufacturers usually don't list ingredients by percentages on the can, you'll have to compare weights. Holding a same-size can in each hand, simply go with the one that feels heavier.

Don't take it off. Try a furniture refinisher before resorting to time-consuming strippers. Refinishers work by dissolving a thin layer of existing finish and replacing it with a film of fresh finish. They preserve the patina of the piece, as well as your money and time.

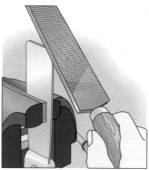

Real smooth. Because strippers soften the wood, round off the sharp corners of a putty knife with a file before using it to remove the stripper. This way you won't gouge the wood.

Out of the kitchen. A plastic spatula is a good substitute for a metal scraper when removing softened finish. Hold it upside down and push it away from you—there's no danger that the flat, flexible blade will scratch the wood.

Spray away. Sticky, gooey stripper scrapings will slide off a putty knife with ease if you occasionally lubricate the blade with a spritz of nonstick cooking spray.

All plugged up. After removing a piece's hardware, plug its screw and key holes with newspaper twists. The paper plugs will prevent the openings from collecting stripper gunk, which becomes rock-hard and difficult to remove once it dries.

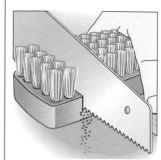

Little big brush. For a mini-brush with terrific potential, saw off a 2-row-wide section of a stiff-bristle scrub brush. Use it to work stripper into tight spots and to scour off the dissolved finish afterward.

Stripping wood

WHAT YOU'LL NEED

Goggles

Respirator

Chemical-resistant gloves or two pairs of rubber gloves

Paint-and-varnish remover

2-in. paintbrush

Plastic scraper or putty knife

Brass brush or old toothbrush

No. 2 and No. 00 steel wool

Mineral spirits or paint thinner

Pointed tool, such as an old screwdriver

Clean lint-free cloth

Vacuum with brush attachment

1 Wear goggles, a respirator, and chemical-resistant gloves or two pairs of rubber gloves when applying the stripper. Brush on a liberal coating, and avoid going over any given area with more than one brushstroke. Work from top to bottom, one section at a time. Reposition the piece of furniture as needed.

2 When the finish has bubbled up, use a plastic scraper or a putty knife to remove it from large flat surfaces. Use a brass brush or an old toothbrush to remove the finish from crevices. Repeat the process until all the finish has been scraped away. Use No. 2 steel wool for the final removal, making sure to wipe with the grain to avoid scratching the wood.

Plane talk. Clean loosened finish from carvings and other irregular surfaces with a handful of planer or jointer shavings (available for free from most woodshops). The stripper sludge will grab onto the shavings, making it easier to remove.

Sticky stripper. A handful of sawdust sprinkled atop a fresh coating of liquid stripper will keep it from dripping off the wood surface. The bad news: Since the sawdust absorbs stripper, you'll have to use more of it.

Too hot for comfort. Wear cloth gardening gloves when stripping paint with a heat gun. The hot stream of air, along with the molten paint, can easily damage or burn through rubber or plastic gloves—and very likely the skin within.

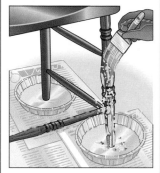

Do the pan-pan. When refinishing chairs, tables, or anything with legs, place a disposable pie pan under each leg. The pan will catch stripper drips as well as the softened finish as you scrape it off.

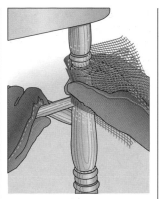

Net gain. After a stripping job, use some nylon netting from supermarket produce bags to clean up around legs and spindles.

Don't cry over milk paint. Try household ammonia if stripper won't budge a milk-paint finish. But remember, your antique will be worth more with the original finish, even if it's worn or damaged, than with a pristine refinishing job.

Stoke and soak. To loosen water-base paint on hardware, soak it in boiling water. For oil-base paint, immerse the hardware overnight in a bucket containing ½ pound of wood fireplace ashes mixed with 2 gallons of water. Wear rubber gloves when reaching into the bucket.

Out, damned spot. There's no need to refinish an entire piece just to remove white water spots. Rub a paper towel dipped in cigarette ashes gently over the damaged areas, and the spots should disappear.

Another spot remover. To treat a large expanse of water damage, smear on a generous coat of petroleum jelly and let it stand overnight. When you wipe the surface clean, the finish should be rejuvenated.

3 Brush the stripper on vertical surfaces one section at a time. Remove the stripper and dissolved finish from turned pieces and small surfaces with No. 2 steel wool. For best results, unravel the steel wool from the pad and rinse it often in mineral spirits.

For easier access, place the furniture on a steady table or a workbench.

4 Crevices usually require additional attention. Let the stripper do the work. Force it into crevices with the tip of a brush, wait, then use a pointed tool, such as an old screwdriver or a tool for removing grout (as shown here), to carefully scrape the dissolved finish from the crevices.

5 To neutralize the stripping chemical and remove any residue, rub the entire piece with No. 00 steel wool dipped in mineral spirits. Rinse the pad often. Never use water, which can raise the grain of the wood. Wipe the piece with a clean lint-free cloth; then vacuum it with the brush attachment.

Natural or not? When deciding whether to stain wood, it helps to moisten a small area with a cloth dampened in mineral spirits. The darkened color will approximate how the unstained wood will look under a clear finish.

If you pine for stain but want to avoid the typical blotchiness that occurs with coniferous woods, use a gel stain instead. Gels are thicker and don't penetrate the wood as deeply, resulting in a more uniform color.

Sealant at the right price. As an alternative to pricier commercial sealing products, dab a bit of mineral oil on the end grain of the wood to prevent it from guzzling the stain.

Two for one. A thinned coat of final finish makes an excellent sealer. Just dilute it with the recommended solvent to an easily flowable consistency. Remember that penetrating-oil finish doesn't require sealer—the whole point of this type of finish is to get down into the pores.

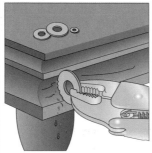

Handling the curves. Scrape out small inside curves with a washer clamped in locking pliers. Chances are you can find a washer that will fit the curve almost exactly. You may need to file it a little.

Take a shine to it. Check to see if wood needs a second application of filler by raking a flashlight across the surface 24 hours after the first coat has dried. If the sheen is even, with no highlights or flat areas, one coat will do it.

Moisturize your filler. To keep filler workable until the next job, dip a small piece of sponge in the same solvent used in the filler and store it inside the can. The sponge should be damp, not soaking wet.

Get organized. File your sandpaper sheets by size, type, and grit in the pockets of an accordian file. You'll never have to waste time hunting for the right abrasive again.

Reuse that belt. Instead of retiring used sander belts, cut them into thin, long strips and use them to sand spindles and other turnings. Work the strip back and forth like a shoeshine cloth.

Preparing the surface

WHAT YOU'LL NEED

Sandpaper (various grits)

Damp sponge (optional)

Clean lint-free cloths

Mineral spirits

Rubber gloves

Penetrating resin sealer

Stain

2-in. brushes

Paste filler

Putty knife or plastic scraper

1 Unfinished furniture should be sanded with progressively finer sandpapers up to at least 180-grit paper. If you plan to use a water-base stain, wipe the furniture with a damp sponge, then sand it to remove the raised wood fibers. Clean the wood with a lint-free cloth sprinkled with mineral spirits.

2 Wearing rubber gloves, apply a sealer to softwood and to all end grain to ensure even staining. Then apply the stain with a brush or a lint-free cloth, following the manufacturer's instructions and making sure all areas are covered. Lightly wipe or brush over any overlapping strokes immediately to obtain a uniform color, especially on large flat surfaces.

Hose job. For short-radius inside curves, wrap sandpaper around a sanding block made from a 6-inch length of garden hose. Slit all but 1 inch of the hose with a sharp knife, slip the edge of the sandpaper into the slit, then wrap the paper around the hose with the grit facing out.

Sander pad worn out? Replace it with a piece of computer mouse pad. Attach the pad with rubber cement; then trim the edges flush with a utility knife.

FILE IT

Sandpaper by the numbers

Sandpaper is classified by a number reflecting the size of its grit particles. Higher numbers indicate smaller grains for finer sanding. Here are the common grades of sandpaper with their grit numbers and uses.

Grit	Texture	Use
50–60	Coarse	Rough sanding and shaping; removing paint.
80–100	Medium	Intermediate sanding after rough sanding; sanding on previously painted surfaces.
120–150	Fine	Final sanding before applying finish.
160–240	Very fine	Smoothing primer and paint.
280–320	Extra-fine	Smoothing between undercoats.
360–600	Superfine	Wet-sanding varnish or lacquer for an ultrasmooth finish.

Curve ball. For smooth inside curves, sand them with a tennis ball wrapped in sandpaper.

Stronger sandpaper. Your abrasives will last longer if you give each sheet a duct-tape backing.

Sanding board. It's easier to rub small objects against the sandpaper than it is to rub the paper against the object. Hold the sandpaper steady with a clipboard, fastening it at the sides with spring clips if necessary.

A peeling sanding block. Self-adhesive sandpaper is convenient, but it can get stuck to wooden sanding blocks. Glue a thin layer of cork to the block's bottom, and the paper will peel right off every time.

3 Most stains should be wiped several minutes after they've been applied. For those that are applied and left to dry, apply the stain and then, using the same brush, even out the stain's surface using long, overlapping strokes with the grain.

4 To avoid drips or uneven coloring, don't oversaturate the applicator when applying the stain to turned or detailed sections. Wipe off any excess immediately.

5 To fill the open pores of woods such as oak, mahogany, or ash, brush on a paste wood filler after staining. When the material hazes over, use a plastic scraper at a 45° angle to the grain to remove the excess. Then buff with a soft cloth.

No-mess pouring. Hold the opening of an oblong container at the top when decanting the finish into a smaller container. This causes the liquid to flow in a steady stream, cutting down on drips and runs.

Keep it warm. Store cans of finish on shelves, not on a concrete floor. A chilly concrete floor could damage the stain, affecting the uniformity of the finish when you brush it on.

Take a break. Since varnish and polyurethane finishes stay tacky for hours, airborne dust specks can easily become trapped in the finish. After thoroughly vacuuming the room, give any remaining dust some time to settle before applying the finishing material.

Neat knob finishing. With a spring clothespin, grasp the knob by its screw and balance the assembly in an upright position. You'll be able to apply the finish to every area without messing your hands.

Elevate furniture legs for easy finishing by driving a screw into the bottom of each one. Adjust the screws as needed to keep the piece from rocking while brushing on the finish coat.

Dust for fingerprints. Before handling sanded unfinished wood, scrub your hands with a fistful of sawdust to scour off natural skin oils. They can leave telltale marks on the wood, flawing the final finish.

Tooth tiny. An old toothbrush can be useful for working finish into crevices and other hard-to-reach areas. The soft-bristle kind is best for most jobs.

Working small. Stain small, intricate areas of furniture with a cotton swab. The swab not only gets into tiny crevices but also absorbs a lot of finish, making quick work of finely detailed staining jobs.

FILE IT

The finishing touch: Common furniture finishes

When using any finish, be sure to follow label directions and observe any precautions about safe handling or flammability. Lacquer, polyurethane, and most varnishes come in satin, semigloss, and glossy finishes.

Finish	Solvent	Characteristics	How to Apply
Acrylic varnish	Water (before the varnish dries)	Thin, hard film with no amber tones. Moderate resistance to wear and spills.	Spray or brush on two or three thin coats. Usually comes in a spray can.
Alkyd varnish	Mineral spirits	Hard warm-toned film. Moderate to good resistance to wear and spills.	Brush on two to three coats. Easy to recoat but hard to spot-repair. Sand between coats.
Lacquer	Lacquer thinner	Thin, hard film. Very good spill and wear resistance. Used on commercial furniture.	Spray on two or three coats with professional gear; brush on slow-to-dry type. Don't use over other finishes.
Penetrating oil	Mineral spirits	Soaks into wood fibers for natural-looking finish. Tung oil is the most durable type.	Wipe or brush on, let stand for 30 minutes, then rub vigorously. Usually three coats are required; wet-sand the third coat.
Polyurethane	Turpentine, mineral spirits	Very hard warm-toned film. Excellent resistance to wear and spills.	Brush on two coats. Hard to spot-repair. Recoat within specified time. Don't use over shellac.
Shellac (white or orange)	Denatured alcohol	Thin, lustrous clear or amber surface film. Wears well but is easily marred by spills.	Brush on two or three thin coats. Easy to spot-repair. Also use to seal wood for other finishes.

People prefer paper. Apply and wipe off penetrating oils with paper towels, not rags. Rags can leave lint embedded in the finish, while the paper toweling won't. Just place oil-sodden paper towels outside to dry before throwing them in the trash or they could spontaneously combust.

Baby the brushes. Between coats of finish, store the brush in a pull-out baby-wipes container full of the recommended solvent. The slits in the top will grip the handle, allowing the bristles to hang suspended in the solvent without bending.

In the bag. Pop a foam applicator into a self-locking plastic freezer bag until you're ready to apply the second coat. The airtight seal will prevent the finish from hardening the foam.

Extra paint roller? Put it to use as a stain applicator. Cut a clean, dry 9-inch thick-nap paint roller into three equal sections. Hold one piece in your hand to wipe on the stain. The roller will absorb more stain than a brush and will apply it more evenly than a cloth.

Homemade dust magnet. No need to buy a tack cloth when it's so easy to make your own. Just wet a cloth with mineral spirits and add a little varnish. Fold the cloth and squeeze it to spread the varnish throughout and to wring out excess thinner. Store the rag in a can with a lid.

Blue-jean sheen. Buff the last coat of a dried oil or varnish finish with polishing cloths cut from old jeans (avoid seams). The denim will leave a lovely luster.

Hot wax. A coat of paste wax can make furniture gleam. Warm up the wood first, though, with a hair dryer set on low to ease the spreading of the wax and to encourage deeper penetration into the wood.

SAFE AND SMART

➤ Wear a respirator (indoors), thick gloves, and eye protection when applying finishes. Make sure to work in a well-ventilated room.

➤ When using a clamp to hold refinished wood, tape a 35mm film container lid to the mouth of the clamp to avoid marring the finish.

Applying the finish

WHAT YOU'LL NEED

Rubber gloves

Lint-free tack cloth and mineral spirits

2-in. paintbrush

Wood sealer (if required)

220-grit sandpaper

Wood finish

1 Use a tack cloth to clean the wood. Brush on a sealer if it is recommended by the finish manufacturer. When it dries, smooth the surface with 220-grit sandpaper. Wipe off dust with a tack cloth.

2 Apply the finish from top to bottom, one section at a time, following the wood's grain. When applying polyurethane or varnish, brush just enough to level the finish. When applying a penetrating finish, wipe off any excess before it dries.

3 Some types of finishes require some sanding between coats. After each coat dries, sand the surface with 220-grit paper. Remove dust with a tack cloth. Let the final coat dry for 48 hr. and wax if desired.

The sound of soundness. You can tell veneer is loose if it makes a hollow sound when you tap it with your fingernail. If it resonates with a dull tone, chances are it is solidly adhered to the core stock.

Shopping tip. When buying mail-order veneer for a small repair, it's often more economical to purchase a sample kit containing a variety of species instead of a larger amount of material sight unseen. There will usually be a piece in the kit that approximates the look of the original wood.

Location, location. To better match the grain of highly figured veneers such as crotch or burl wood, use a paper frame cut to the size of the repair. Move the frame around on the patching veneer until you locate the area that best complements the grain pattern of the original veneer.

Antique furniture sometimes has a veneer that is no longer available. If you need to make a repair in a conspicuous place and can't find a matching veneer, take a piece from a less visible area on the furniture and use that for your patching veneer. Match the less visible area as best you can.

Fatten it up. Flesh out a piece of too-thin patching veneer by gluing it to a second veneer piece—sand the bottom veneer to the right thickness before gluing. Position the bottom veneer so its grain runs opposite to that of the top layer.

Bubble trouble. To flatten a veneer bubble, carefully slit it in the direction of the grain with a sharp razor or craft knife. With a glue injector, shoot glue beneath the veneer. Press the repair flat, and weight it down with a brick or heavy book for at least 12 hours.

Iron out problems. If the veneer still bubbles after you slit and reglue it, cover the area with aluminum foil and press it with an iron set on low. Apply heat for no more than 10 seconds at a time and check for scorching. Clamp the repair overnight.

Patching veneer on furniture

WHAT YOU'LL NEED

Veneer	Wallpaper roller or block of wood the size of your hand
Veneer saw or sharp utility knife	Stain and finish to match
Metal ruler	Furniture putty stick to match
Contact cement and small disposable paintbrush	Sandpaper

1 Choose a patch of same wood with grain that matches area to be replaced. Using veneer saw or sharp utility knife and metal ruler, cut around damaged portion of veneer down to core stock. Pry up veneer and scrape away adhesive residue.

2 Cut a piece of veneer in the same shape but slightly larger than the area to be replaced. Apply two coats of contact cement to the back of the patch and to the core stock with a disposable paintbrush or supplied brush. Let each coat dry until tacky.

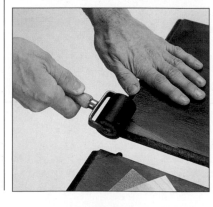

3 Lay patch in place. Apply pressure with wallpaper roller or block of wood. Sand any overhanging veneer off edges. Sand surface flush. Stain new veneer to match old. Fill seams with furniture putty stick; if needed, stain again. Apply finish to the entire surface.

Leave the lead on. If the piece you're painting is over 10 years old, the original paint may contain lead. Before repainting, dull the shine with a liquid deglosser instead of sanding the paint to give it "tooth." This way you won't be exposed to lead-contaminated dust.

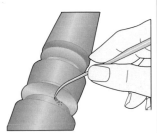

Dental picks work wonders cleaning out old stain from small crevices and intricate ornamentation.

Beat it. The best way to mix paint is with a beater from an electric kitchen mixer chucked into a variable-speed drill. Keep the speed slow but steady; mixing too briskly can cause air bubbles to form in the paint. You can pick up cheap beaters at flea markets.

Avoid a sticky situation. When priming and painting drawers, coat only drawer fronts and their edges. Applying paint to the sides or edges of the drawers will make them stick in the carcass. Use clear finish instead.

Particleboard primer. For a really smooth finish on porous particleboard edges, coat them before painting with a filler made of latex wood putty thinned with water to the consistency of cream. Lightly sand the edges before you apply it and once again after it dries.

Flawless painting. Don't pick out stray brush bristles, dust, or lint from a painted surface once a skin has started to form. Instead, wait for the surface to dry, then buff out the blemish with a damp paper towel.

Spraying, warmly. Aerosol spray paint will perform better if you place the can in a container of warm water for about 5 minutes before using. It will spray out in a finer mist for even coverage.

Contain the spray. Place a small piece of furniture in a large cardboard appliance box when spray-painting it to minimize the mess.

Keep your distance. To keep a spray can the right distance from the work—all the time—tape a gauge made from a length of dowel to the spray can. Cut the dowel about an inch shorter than the desired distance so you don't accidentally scrape the freshly sprayed paint.

Painting furniture

WHAT YOU'LL NEED

Mineral spirits and cotton cloths	Sanding block or finishing sander
150- and 220-grit sandpaper	Primer
Tack cloths	Paintbrushes
Wood filler	Paint
Putty knife	
Spackle (optional)	

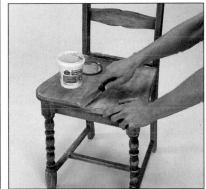

1 Wipe wood with mineral spirits to clean. Sand it with fine sandpaper to dull all shine; wipe with a tack cloth. Repair any damaged areas with wood filler. If the wood is open-grain and you don't want to see grain through the paint, rub in some spackle.

2 Sand the filler lightly with 150-grit sandpaper on a sanding block. Wipe with a tack cloth. Apply a primer. First turn chair upside down and paint areas that are hard to reach. Then turn it right side up and paint from top down.

3 When primer has dried, sand surface lightly with 220-grit sandpaper. Wipe with tack cloth. Apply two or more coats of alkyd or latex enamel. Allow each coat to dry. If paint is glossy, sand between coats with 220-grit sandpaper; clean with tack cloth.

Turn some tape. A few winds of Teflon pipe-thread tape turned around the threads of a screw-on cap will ensure that the lid will always twist right off the glue bottle—even after periods of long storage. As a bonus, the tape will tighten the seal, keeping the glue from hardening.

Let it flow. If yellow glue has hardened in the bottle, you can soften it up with a little white vinegar. Add a few drops, let it sit for a while, then shake. Repeat as necessary.

Store and pour. Move glue bottles inside for the winter. Both white and yellow glues can usually withstand one or two freeze/thaw cycles, but any more could turn them lumpy.

Loose chair rungs? First try injecting the joints with a wood-swelling product before disassembling and gluing them. If you do decide to glue them, make sure they fit snugly. For a tight fit, wrap thread around the dowel end, then soak it in glue.

A larger dowel is the best solution for a joint that is really loose. Cut the new dowel to a length equal to the depth of both sockets, minus ⅛ inch for glue. It should fit snugly, with no gaps around the sides.

Shrink oversize dowels down to the right size. A quick zap in the microwave will diminish a dowel's diameter just enough to allow it to fit a hole that's slightly too small. Set the microwave for a minute at a time, and don't exceed a total of 3 minutes.

Knead epoxy? For no-mess mixing, put both epoxy components in the corner of a plastic sandwich bag and knead until smooth. Cut the corner off and dispense the adhesive right from the bag.

Bridge game. Two-part epoxies are messy, but for situations where you must bridge the gap between loose-fitting parts, they are the best solution.

Look, no glue. To tighten joints without glue, use toothed metal strips that are bent around the end of the rung before it is inserted in the hole. These metal strips, available in hardware stores and woodworking outlets, have the additional benefit of needing no clamping.

Hide-bound. If you have a complicated assembly that involves arranging several clamps, consider using old-fashioned hide glue. It dries hard and strong, and it takes 3 to 4 hours to set, versus 15 minutes to 1 hour for yellow glue.

Gluing wood

WHAT YOU'LL NEED

Scraper, wood rasp, or sandpaper

Aliphatic resin glue (yellow or "carpenter's" glue)

Waterproof aliphatic glue (for outdoor furniture)

Small paintbrush or notched spreader

Nail and string (if needed)

Tape, clamps, or weights for pressure

Wet cloth

1 Scrape, file, or sand old glue from joints. Wrapping a dowel with sandpaper is a good way to get into dowel holes. Leaving the old glue in the joints could prevent the new glue from penetrating the wood fibers.

2 For a narrow surface, apply a bead of glue and spread it with a brush. To spread glue over a larger surface, use a notched spreader or an old hacksaw blade. The teeth will spread the glue easily and to an even depth.

 Apply glue to both surfaces and let it soak in for 1 minute to increase bond strength.

An ounce of prevention.
Before regluing an inside corner joint, run some masking tape along the joint line. Peel off the tape—and the excess glue—after the glue dries. This will save you a lot of work trying to remove the glue from the corner.

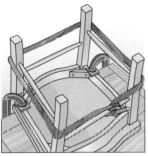

Get a leg up on clamping.
When you need a web or tourniquet-type clamp to pull furniture pieces together, use an old pair of pantyhose. The stretchy material can be pulled tight with no risk of damaging the wood or the finish.

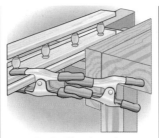

Handle it. If a clamp's not tight enough, slip another clamp inside the handle to squeeze the first clamp shut.

Born-again brush. An old inexpensive paintbrush can easily be transformed into a great glue brush. Just trim the bristles short—they'll be stiff enough to spread the glue quickly and evenly.

New life for old handles.
Don't trash your old disposable foam brush before detaching the handle from the foam. The stiffener at the end of the handle makes a great paddle or mixing tool for small cans of putty or epoxy. If you want, you can even customize the shape of the stiffener with a quick pass of a belt sander.

Reusable brush. Thread a piece of clothesline through a snug hole drilled in a piece of dowel, and you have a renewable glue brush. Lop off the end of the clothesline when you're done gluing to expose a fresh surface.

Great glue scrapers. Use the small plastic squares that fasten the tops of bread bags to scrape off hardened glue beads from flat surfaces.

Straw scoop. Scrape up hardened glue that has squeezed out of corners with a plastic drinking straw. The straw's flexibility makes it easy to scrape the glue from even tight areas.

Loosening up the joints.
If a joint won't come apart for regluing, squirt in a little white vinegar from a clean oil can, wait a few minutes, repeat, and pull it apart.

3 To repair split wood, hold the split open with a nail, inject glue into the gap, and draw a piece of string back and forth inside the gap to spread the glue. Remove the nail and apply clamping pressure.

4 Always bind a glued joint with clamps, tape, small finishing nails, or brads. Or apply weight for a minimum of 15 min. To bind a chair leg, use a web clamp or string-and-stick (tourniquet-style) clamp.

 Too much clamping pressure can force glue out of a joint.

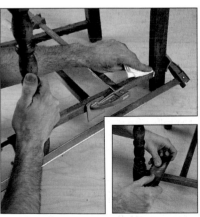

5 Glue should ooze from a joint, but the excess must be removed. If the piece is to be painted, one wiping with a wet cloth will do. If clear finish or stain is to be applied, rinse the cloth again thoroughly and wipe to remove all glue residue.

Smooth operator. For easy, soundless movement of wood drawers in a wood frame, install self-adhesive vinyl wall-corner molding on the bottom edge of each drawer. The molding is a snap to install—just cut to length and press in place.

In a jam? To unstick an overstuffed drawer, first remove the drawer below it. Then press upward on the bottom of the jammed drawer while sliding it forward to release it.

A dry run. A wood drawer often sticks because humidity has temporarily swelled wood fibers. Before making any repairs, take out the drawer and dry it in a warm place for several days. You may be surprised to find that the drawer works like new when you place it back in the track.

Battle of the bulge. Sometimes a drawer will jam because the bottom is warped out of shape and the convexity catches in the cabinet frame. An easy solution is to disassemble the drawer and flip the bottom. If the drawer bottom is in really bad shape, consider replacing it.

Stay on track. Straighten out a bowed metal drawer track by gluing a small wood block to the cabinet side. This will prevent the drawer roller from slipping out of the track.

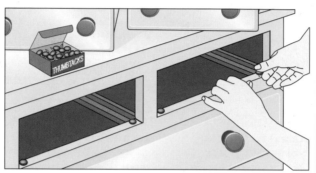

No more droopy drawers. If a drawer sticks or scrapes when pulling it out, try raising the drawer to the proper height within its frame. Then tack a pair of large-headed thumbtacks to the front of the frame just under the drawer's edge on each side to correct it.

Pack the gap. To fill small cracks or nicks, paint on some yellow glue, let it dry until tacky, then sand. The sanding dust will combine with the glue for an invisible repair. After the glue dries, resand. Or mix glue with sawdust to make the repair.

Repairing a cabinet drawer

WHAT YOU'LL NEED

Pry bar

End-cutting pliers, nail puller, or nail punch and hammer

Nails

Lumber

Tape measure

Wooden mallet or hammer

Glue and clamps

Block plane or jack plane

Screwdriver and screws (if needed)

Wooden matchsticks (optional)

Coarse sandpaper and wood block

Wood sealer or paint

Paraffin wax or butcher's wax

1 To replace a drawer bottom, pry back edge from drawer with pry bar and pull out nails with end-cutting pliers or nail puller (or drive nails through with nail punch and hammer). Take out old bottom and slide new bottom into place. Rack drawer, applying pressure on opposite corners, until diagonal measurements are equal; then nail it. If bottom sets into groove on back, remove back to replace bottom.

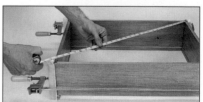

2 To repair unsquare joints, disassemble the drawer by carefully knocking it apart. Use a hammer or mallet with a block of wood to soften the blows. Remove all old glue residue; then reglue and reassemble the drawer. Clamp in place for at least 1 hr., checking the diagonal measure during and after clamping to make sure it is square. Measure corner-to-corner; if measurements are not equal, adjust clamping.

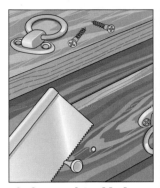

Fix for a stripped hole.
It's easy to rejuvenate a stripped screw hole with a wooden golf tee. Sand off the paint, dab on a little glue, tap the tee into the screw hole, then saw it flush with the surface. When you drive the screw, it will bite into good wood.

Cover the point. Before nailing into fine wood, try running the nail points in and out of a candle bottom. The wax will help the nail go in easier.

Soap surrogate. Fill up a small 35mm film container with butcher's wax to lubricate screws. Wax isn't as messy as soap and won't encourage rusting. And a film container is air-tight and highly portable.

Damaged nail? If you can't get a grip on a nail with a hammer claw, secure locking pliers to the nail shank, then lever up the nail by sliding the hammer claw under the plier jaws.

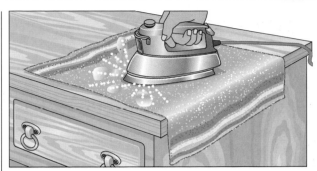

Steamy scheme. Dents in wood can often be raised with steam, which swells the compressed fibers back to their normal size. With a pin, prick the dented area repeatedly; then cover it with a wet towel. Give the dent several shots of steam from a hot iron—checking frequently to make sure you're not scorching the wood.

Pounding pint-size nails? Tiny nails are a pain to hold for hammering. Make the job a lot easier by using a magnet to hold the nail upright before you start driving it home.

Hand cushions. A simple bicycling glove is a good defense against blisters and cramps when using a hammer or screwdriver for any length of time. The fingerless style allows complete mobility while the padded palm cushions your hand.

3 If the bottom edges of the drawer's sides are worn, locate the damage. Often, the back part is more worn than the front. Use a block or jack plane to create a straight surface. Glue new strips of wood that are slightly larger than needed to each edge, and clamp. After the glue has dried, plane the pieces until level with the old edge.

4 Tighten a loose wooden handle or knob with a screwdriver. If the hole is stripped, replace the screw(s) with the next-larger-diameter screw. Or insert a glue-coated wooden matchstick into the hole before driving the screw. Break off the matchstick so it is flush with the drawer front.

5 To fix a sticking drawer, locate the parts that are binding and sand with coarse sandpaper until they move freely. Apply a wood sealer (or paint) to prevent future swelling. Lubricate runners and guides with paraffin wax or butcher's wax.

A tack in time. Substitute flat-headed upholstery tacks for staples, especially if the new covering is heavy fabric or plastic. Although stapling is easier, the tacks will hold more securely.

Give yourself a hand. Tape the fabric edges to the bottom of the chair seat with masking tape if you're having trouble adjusting the fabric with the single-center-tack method (below). Once the fabric is positioned to your satisfaction and you begin tacking it, you can remove the tape as you go.

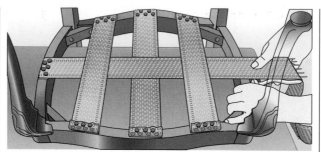

Webbed feat. To reweb the base of a chair seat, start at the center of the rear rail. Fold webbing under 1 inch and fasten with five tacks in a zigzag pattern, tacking first the middle, then corners, then midpoints. Pull webbing taut across seat frame with a webbing stretcher, and anchor with four tacks along the front edge. Cut the strip, leaving 1½ inches extra; then fold it over the top and tack it down with three tacks. Attach other back-to-front strips in same way. Starting again with the center strip, interweave and attach side strips.

Glue solution. When using a slippery fabric, it helps to glue the foam padding to the seat to keep it from moving around or bunching up when you're tacking down the fabric. Use regular white household glue.

Let it be. Save time by reupholstering right over old fabric that is smooth and in good condition. Torn fabric or lumpy padding, however, should be removed.

A good example. If the old seat covering has to be removed, do so carefully; it can make a handy pattern for cutting the new one. Iron the old fabric flat, pin it to the new fabric, then cut around the pattern for a precise fit.

Just like butter. When using high-density sheet foam padding for your reupholstering project, cut it with an electric carving knife. The knife will slice quickly and cleanly through the foam. A band saw—if you happen to have one—will also do a great job.

Reupholstering a slip seat

WHAT YOU'LL NEED

Screwdriver

Tack puller

Foam or fiberfill

Upholstery fabric

Muslin (if needed)

Pencil

Tape measure or ruler

Sharp pointed scissors

Upholstery tacks

Tack hammer or small hammer

Dust-cover fabric

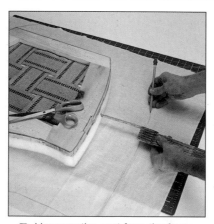

1 Unscrew the seat from the frame; pull out all staples or tacks with a tack puller. Check the webbing or other seat support to see how stable it is. Also inspect the foam or fiberfill and the webbing to make sure it is in good condition. If you need to replace the muslin, follow the sequence for changing upholstery fabric (steps 2 through 5).

2 Cut the new fabric cover. First, lay the fabric upside down and place the foam or fiberfill and seat bottom on top, also upside down. Allow several inches extra on each side when cutting. Fold the fabric over onto the bottom and tack the center point on one side. Pull the cover just taut, and tack the opposite center point. Working from these points, tack outward on all sides to within 3 in. of the ends.

Note for a novice. For a first-time reupholstery project, select a solid-colored fabric or one with a small overall print. Cutting and positioning materials with stripes or repeating or central patterns can be difficult—and frustrating.

No-hassle patterns. If your heart is set on a fabric with a centered pattern, you can get guaranteed results with a fabric designed specifically for chair seats. These materials, available at many fabric stores, have precentered medallions or other motifs and are easy to position.

For built-in endurance, choose cottons or synthetics that have the pattern woven throughout the fabric for your upholstery projects. Polished cottons with surface-printed patterns are pretty but far less rugged.

Go electric. If you will be using staples to cover a number of seats, invest in an electric stapler. These tools are reasonably priced, and they are easier to use—and do a better job of fastening—than manual models.

The last step. Newly reupholstered dining chairs will be on the firing line, susceptible to potential stains at every meal. Although it seems obvious, don't neglect to spray new seats with one of the many available fabric protectants.

Plan ahead. Stash any leftovers from the job—fabric scraps, decorative tacks, etc.—in a large manila envelope, and staple it to the bottom of the furniture piece. If you need a patch, just reach down under for matching materials.

Froth away many stains with this simple cleanser. Add 1 part mild detergent to 4 parts warm water and whip with an electric beater. Brush just the foam on the spots. When the fabric is clean, blot it dry with a clean white cloth.

A litter help. If your upholstery has a musty odor, try sprinkling it with cat litter, then vacuuming up the litter after an hour or two. If the odor remains, repeat the application.

Plagued by pet hair? Quickly remove it from upholstered surfaces—old or new—with a few passes of a damp chamois cloth.

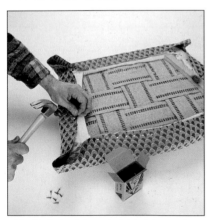

3 Tack the left and right sides, using the same method as in step 2. Place the tacks 1–1½ in. apart, working to within 2–3 in. of the ends. As before, pull the fabric taut, but not so much that it distorts the weave or wrinkles the fabric. The fabric weave should be square to the seat.

4 To make a neat corner, pull the cover fabric from the side of the frame toward the front, smoothing the fabric as you proceed. Fold the fabric and pull it back tight. Cut away the excess fabric. When you have a neat, tight fold, tack it down, starting at the outside edge and working in. Place tacks about 1 in. apart. Be sure to keep the fabric pulled tight as you work.

5 Finish by tacking a dust cover on the bottom of the chair seat. Make a paper template in the exact shape of the seat bottom. Cut the dust cover and tack it in place, placing the tacks about 1 in. apart. Fold the edges of the dust cover under about ½ in., and make sure the tacks go through both layers. Fold the corners under neatly.

Shower power. A twice-yearly moisturizing will do wonders to keep wicker furniture resilient. Pick a breezy day (the furniture will dry more quickly), move the furniture into the shade, and spray it lightly with a garden hose. Allow the wicker to dry thoroughly before moving it into a sunny spot.

Know your fiber. Wicker is a loose term that encompasses a variety of straight-grained fibers, including reed, rattan, and willow, as well as twisted fibers made from sea grass or paper. Care varies depending on the material. For example, twisted fibers should never be stripped or hosed down.

Give dirt the brushoff. Use a soft brush when washing down wicker. An old toothbrush is handy for getting hard-to-reach areas deep-down clean.

To soak or not to soak? Soaking replacement reed in warm water will make the material pliable, but it can also swell the fibers, making the reed hard to handle in tight spots. Oversoaking (for more than 20 minutes, depending on the thickness) can also cause the fibers to split or fray. The compromise? Try working replacement reeds dry first.

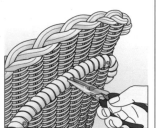

Nail-napping. It can be hard to remove nails from wicker furniture. Make the job easier by digging just enough material away from the nailhead, then removing the nail with pliers.

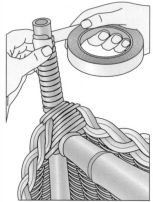

Tape to the rescue. After installing fresh binding cane, wrap the assembly with masking tape. This will keep the binding in place until the glue dries.

A better bond. Before repainting wicker, brush it with liquid sanding fluid to remove grease and grime. The sanding fluid will also soften old paint, allowing good adhesion between the old and new coats.

Repairing a wicker chair

WHAT YOU'LL NEED

Scissors or pruning shears

New wicker strand, presoaked

Waterproof aliphatic (yellow) glue

Diagonal-cutting pliers or aviation snips

New wicker spoke, dry

Needle-nose pliers

Utility knife

Cane strip, presoaked

Small-head nails or brads (not tacks)

1 To reweave a wicker strand, turn over the chair and use scissors or pruning shears to snip out the damaged strand. Cut the ends at an angle over the nearest spokes or cross-strands. Then cut a new presoaked strand a few inches longer than the space to be filled.

2 Working on the chair's underside or back, weave in the new strand, following the original pattern. Pull the wicker taut as you proceed. When finished, trim the new strand to fit so the ends butt against the old one; apply glue between the ends.

 For an extra-secure hold while the glue dries, clamp the ends with a spring clamp.

Brush-on brightener. If all your cleaning efforts won't lighten moldy or mildewy wicker, revitalize it with a solution made from ¼ cup of household bleach mixed with a quart of water. Wearing rubber gloves, brush on the solution with a paintbrush. Let the wicker air-dry in the shade, then rinse off.

By the sea. In coastal areas, protect wicker and other outdoor furniture from salt damage by spraying it with flexible rubber paint. The weather-resistant coating is available in both spray and liquid formulations.

A different angle. A sprayed-on finish will be finer and more even if you hold the spray can at about a 45° angle above the wicker. Spray the furniture first from one side and then the other, to make sure that the paint penetrates all the crevices in the wicker weave.

Clog buster. Does your aerosol paint can have a clogged nozzle? To clear it, take off the nozzle, pop it on the end of a spray tube attached to a can of penetrating lubricant, and blast out the clog.

Collect substitutes. If you do a lot of aerosol spraying, remove the old nozzles from the empty cans and toss them in a small container of solvent. When a nozzle clogs, you'll always have a quick replacement at hand.

SAFE AND SMART

➤ Work outdoors if at all possible when using aerosol finishes. The fumes are potentially explosive. Always pick a still day so the finish doesn't spray where you don't want it.

➤ Since spray finishes can pass through the weave of wicker right onto a wall, screen an indoor work area with large pieces of cardboard to confine the spray.

Two-tone effect. Give your painted wicker furniture an extra dimension by adding a second color. First, spray on the undercoat. When it has completely dried, apply the second color and, while it is still wet, wipe the paint with rags until you have the effect you want.

3 To replace a spoke, use diagonal-cutting pliers to snip off the damaged spoke a few strands into the horizontal weave at each end. Remove the spoke and cut a new (dry) spoke to the same length as the piece removed.

4 Grasp the new spoke with needle-nose pliers and feed it into place, following the original pattern. If you have difficulty working with the dry spoke, soak it to make it more pliable. With the new spoke in place, apply yellow glue to all four ends to anchor them in place.

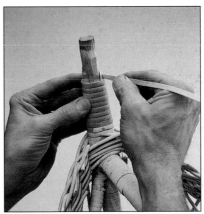

5 To fix unraveled binder cane, cut off the old piece with a utility knife. Then glue and tack down the end of a new presoaked cane strip over the end of the old one. (If the binding is brittle, predrill before tacking to avoid splitting.) Wind the strip tightly and evenly around the frame. At ½ in. from the end of the chair leg, apply glue, tack the strand, and cut off the excess.

Step one, step two. If a furniture piece needs refinishing as well as recaning, always do the refinishing first. The project will be easier and take less time if you don't have to work around brand-new caning.

The circle game. When recaning a circular seat, you'll need a pattern to cut the cane. To make one, tape a piece of paper over the seat and run a pencil along the inside wall of the groove. Cut the cane about an inch larger than the pattern.

'Buy-buy. When purchasing prewoven cane, order a piece that's about 2 inches larger than the area to be caned, to allow for at-home trimming. The spline should be a few inches longer than the length of the groove.

To cane or not to cane? Before recaning a piece of antique furniture, first make sure that it was originally designed to have a woven seat or back. A groove all around the seat indicates a prewoven cane seat. Evenly spaced holes all around the seat tell you that the piece was originally hand-caned.

Take it to the tub. Don't roll prewoven cane webbing to get it to fit into the soaking container—the cane should be kept flat. Instead, let it soak in the bathtub.

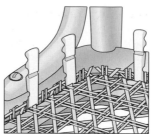

In the groove. Pull apart spring-type clothespins and use the pieces as wedges to firmly hold prewoven cane in the seat groove.

Salty cleanser. Scrub grubby canework with a soft brush and a solution of 1 tablespoon salt mixed with a quart of hot water. (The salt helps prevent stickiness and keeps the cane from darkening.) Wipe the cane with a clean cloth, then dry it with a hair dryer set on medium.

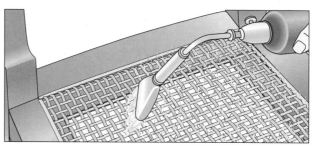

Hot tip. Instead of sanding freshly installed cane to remove loose fibers, singe them off with a propane torch while the cane is still wet. To be safe, work outside and keep the torch in constant motion, using only the very tip of the flame.

Recaning a spline-cane seat

WHAT YOU'LL NEED

Utility knife

Awl

Vinegar and water (if needed)

Prewoven cane webbing

Mallet

Wooden wedges

Chisel (well sharpened)

Spline

Pencil

Aliphatic glue (yellow or carpenter's glue)

Sandpaper

Tung-oil sealant or lacquer and brush

1 To remove the old cane, first take out the spline. Break the bond formed by the glue or finish by carefully scoring on both sides of the spline with a utility knife. Pry out the spline with an awl. If needed, cut a notch into the spline and apply a 50-50 solution of vinegar and water to soften the glue. Remove the cane. Scrape out glue or finish residue from the groove.

2 Soak the new cane material in water to soften it; then lay it over the opening, glossy side up. Align the pattern so it is parallel to either the front or the back edge of the frame. Tap a wooden wedge into the center of the back rail groove; then lightly stretch the cane toward the front rail, wedging it at the center of that rail. Repeat this process with the left and right sides.

When dirt is ingrained.
Ordinary baking powder makes a good cleanser for dirty, dusty canework. After wetting the cane with warm water, apply the powder with a paintbrush. When it dries, brush off the powder, rinse with cold water, and let it air-dry.

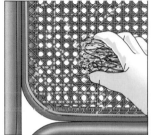

Flaky finish. The canework of old furniture pieces, often coated with varnish for extra protection, can develop scaly spots over time as the varnish peels off in patches. To remove the flakes, whisk them off gingerly with fine steel wool.

Finishing touches. If left in its natural state, cane will darken in color and develop an attractive patina. You can also darken the cane with a diluted stain or give it a gloss by applying shellac, varnish, or lacquer. Or you can simply help preserve it with a coat of tung oil or boiled linseed oil.

Avoid a sag ending. Cane seats often stretch out as they conform to the user's body, but a little preventive maintenance can help you bag the sag. Every month, turn the chair over and cover the bottom of the cane seat with a damp towel for about 30 minutes. As the water evaporates, the cane will shrink and tighten. Don't sit on it for 12 hours.

Mind the spline. When moisturizing a cane seat to tighten it up, try to keep water off the spline. Wet spline could wind up loosening in its groove.

Maintenance matters.
Avoid the following, and your cane furniture will last longer: carrying a cane chair by the seat instead of the frame; using the seat as a stepstool; or exposing the cane to dry air or direct sunlight for long periods.

For a modern look, try out some of these novel ideas on your cane furniture. Paint the frame a vibrant color and pair it with new prewoven cane in a light finish. You can also use paint to stencil or apply a pattern to the cane itself, although be aware that painting too much of the cane surface can cause it to become more brittle over time.

Get creative. Some other home projects that incorporate prewoven cane include room dividers and kitchen cabinet fronts. In both cases, you can use the spline-and-glue method or, to make the job easier, attach the cane to the wood with staples. Finish up by covering the staples with decorative molding.

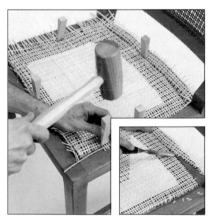

3 Using a mallet and a wedge with a blunted tip, tap the cane into the groove. To maintain a uniform tension and avoid distorting the pattern, alternate from side to side and from back to front. Then remove the wedges and use a sharp chisel to cut off the protruding cane just below the top of the outer edge of the groove (see inset). Be careful not to pull out the cane or to damage the wood.

4 Use a separate piece of dry spline for each side. Measure the spline against the groove and mark the ends with pencil. Use a chisel to cut the ends at a 45° angle. On rounded seats, use one length of spline; soak it if necessary to make it pliable, but do not oversoak. Place a bead of yellow carpenter's glue in the groove and gently press the spline into place.

5 Tap the spline, using a wedge and mallet, until it is flush with the surface of the frame. Take care not to crush the spline or to damage the chair frame. Allow 24 hr. drying time. Lightly sand the cane as needed to remove any loose fibers. Starting with the underside, seal both sides of the seat with tung-oil sealant or lacquer (see inset). Allow it to dry completely before using it.

Strong bonding. Don't forget to add a small washer when you are attaching new webbing to an aluminum lawn chair with screws. This fortifies the new connection.

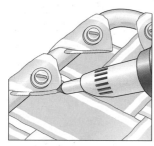

Preventing split ends. After installation, carefully make a pass along the ends of the replacement webbing with a hot soldering iron. The heat will fuse the plastic fibers together, preventing them from unraveling.

Protect your patio. Missing or broken rubber or plastic end caps on the legs of metal furniture puts a patio surface at high risk for scratching. Increase cap life by inserting a metal washer inside each one so that the leg won't cut into the cap.

More patio protection. Pieces of old garden hose slit down the center make good cushions for furnishings that rest on runners rather than legs. Not only will the hose deaden the sound when you drag the furniture around, but it will protect the patio from scratches and rust stains.

Wash 'n' wax. Soapy scouring pads do a great job of cleaning up unpainted aluminum chairs. For extra luster—and protection against scratches—treat the chairs to a coat of car wax when the metal dries.

Unseat rust. Drill drainage holes in the contoured seats of metal lawn chairs to prevent water from pooling and rusting the metal. Deburr the holes; then paint the chair and the edges of the holes with rust-preventive paint.

Rust doesn't sleep, but you can slow its return. When removing rust, try to work down to bare metal; but if you can't, use a direct-to-rust primer. This not only primes the metal but also encapsulates the rust and prevents it from spreading.

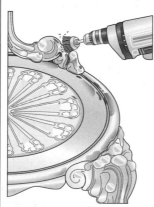

Rust-busting brush. A wire brush chucked in an electric drill can whisk rust off all the twists and curves of intricate metal furniture—quickly. The brushes come in fine, medium, and heavy grades to match the size of your rust-removal job.

Rewebbing an aluminum chair

WHAT YOU'LL NEED

Screwdriver, nut driver, or socket driver

New polypropylene webbing

Scissors

Hammer and awl

Wood block

New matching screws and washers

Pliers

1 To take out the old webbing, remove the screws with a screwdriver or nut driver. It is possible to remove webbing secured with rivets (by drilling out the rivets or cutting them with end-cutting pliers), but it's generally more work than it's worth.

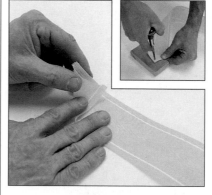

2 Cut a new polypropylene strap, using the old strap as a template. Fold the ends to make triangles by first folding over one edge, then the other. Then, using an awl, hammer, and wood block, make a hole in the center of each triangle.

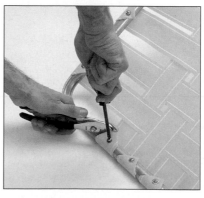

3 Install the new horizontal webbing. Insert a screw and washer into the hole in the webbing and screw into the hole on the chair frame. Pull each piece tight and hold it with pliers before screwing in the opposite end. Install and weave vertical webbing.

Stop the bleeding. Before freshening up stained redwood furniture with paint, be sure to seal in the stain with a spray coat of fast-drying oil-base primer. Otherwise, the stain will bleed through the new paint job.

Cheap chic. It's easy to jazz up old wooden chairs with paper appliqués. Attach the appliqués to the wood with vinyl-over-vinyl wallcovering paste; then coat them with two coats of exterior polyurethane containing ultraviolet inhibitors, allowing drying time in between.

Fun finish. For an unusual crackled look, sand and prime the wood, then basecoat it with latex paint. Paint the area to be crackled with a mix of 2 parts hide glue to 1 part water, and let the glue dry overnight. Then coat it with a different-color latex—the paint should crackle in about 30 seconds.

Unwanted stain can be a pain. After you bring home a new piece of redwood furniture, give it a good rinsing on the lawn before placing it on the patio. This will get rid of any excess stain that could run off the furniture—and discolor the patio—during the first rain.

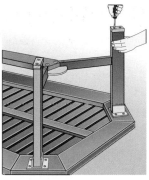

End guards. Keep the end grain of leg bottoms from wicking up moisture—and prevent untimely deterioration of your furniture—by screwing a small wood block to each leg. Since face grain is less absorbent than end grain, make sure to cut the blocks so the face grain is against the ground.

Which glue for you? Don't use yellow glue for repairs to outdoor furniture, because it isn't waterproof. Choose resorcinol, epoxy, or a plastic resin adhesive instead.

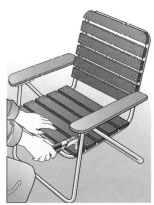

Redwood revival. Make a durable lawn chair by converting the torn covering to ½-inch-thick redwood or cedar slats. Fasten them to the frame with blind rivets—you'll have to predrill holes in the slats, and possibly the chair, to accept the rivets.

Restoring redwood and other wood furniture

WHAT YOU'LL NEED

Penetrating oil	Household bleach
Masking tape	Pressure washer
Open-end or socket wrench	Sandpaper
Hacksaw blade	Wood restorer
Nut splitter (automotive tool)	
Bucket and scrub brush	
Mild (non-ammonia) detergent	

1 To remove corroded bolts, apply penetrating oil to the nut, letting it soak in for 24 hr. Apply masking tape to the wood around the bolt to prevent staining. If this fails and you can't cut the bolt with a hacksaw, split the nut with a nut splitter.

2 To remove mildew from redwood and other wood furniture, scrub the wood with a mild detergent, then wipe on diluted household bleach and rinse. If necessary, use a stronger concentration of bleach for stubborn mildew stains.

3 To remove stains and restore the wood's original color, pressure washing is easiest. Sand wood lightly when dry. Another option is to apply a wood-restoring chemical to the wood, following the manufacturer's directions.

PLUMBING REPAIRS AND IMPROVEMENTS

Job ratings: Easy   Medium   Complex

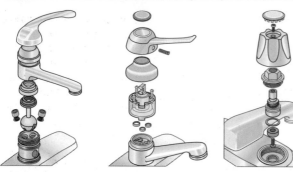

ID-ing the faucet. Single-handle faucets don't have washers, but that doesn't mean they are dripless or leakless: O-rings and valve seats can wear out. Types include ball (left), disc (center), and cartridge faucets (see "Replacing a Worn Faucet Cartridge," below). Compression faucets (right) do operate with washers. If you're unsure which you have, bring the faucet to the plumbing store when replacing parts.

Remove stubborn O-rings by cutting them with a utility knife or by prying them off with the tip of an awl or ice pick. To install an O-ring, roll it into place over the stem cartridge.

Tool time. Plumbing repair is a lot less daunting when you have the right equipment. Low-priced items like adjustable handle pullers, basin wrenches, and miniature pipe cutters can save you time and energy.

Turnover. In an emergency, turn over a worn seat washer in a compression faucet and reinstall it. The washer will usually last for a few days, long enough for you to buy a replacement.

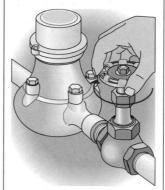

Where's the valve? Older homes may not have shutoff valves beneath the faucets. You'll have to turn off the main water supply instead. The valve is usually near the water meter where the water pipes enter the house. Turn the valve clockwise.

Shutoff valves may leak if they haven't been used in a long time. Before turning one to shut off the water, squirt a few drops of oil onto the valve stem so it runs beneath the packing nut. Wait for it to soak in; then loosen the nut a quarter turn before closing the valve.

Loosen up, part one. To loosen a corroded seat washer screw, apply several drops of penetrating oil to the screw. Tap the screw with a hammer to set up vibrations that will allow the oil to penetrate. Let the oil soak in for 10 minutes, and the screw should be ready to be removed.

Loosen up, part two. To loosen a stuck faucet handle, apply a cola soft drink to the stem, then strike it gently with the handle of a hammer.

Replacing a worn faucet cartridge

WHAT YOU'LL NEED

New identical faucet cartridge

New identical O-rings (if old ones are damaged)

Phillips screwdriver

Groove-joint or locking pliers

Needle-nose pliers

Small flat screwdriver

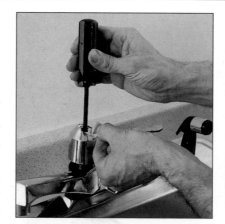

1 A worn cartridge is the main cause of drips in cartridge faucets. However, damaged O-rings are the most likely culprit if the leak is at the base of the faucet. First, shut off the water from underneath the sink or at the main water supply. To expose the cartridge and O-rings, remove the access cover on top of the faucet. Then take out the screw securing the handle.

2 Unscrew the retainer pivot nut. Instead of a nut, there may be a retainer ring that you will need to lift off, depending on the faucet model.

Spouting off. To determine which side of a double-handled faucet is causing the spout to leak, close one of the valves while leaving the other one open. If the leak persists, reopen the valve and close the other. (Hint: the left side of a faucet, supplying hot water, fails more often.)

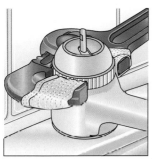

Don't scratch. Wrap plier jaws with thick duct tape or utility tape to prevent scratching a chrome or brass faucet. Or use fingertips cut from an old pair of leather gloves.

Who's on first? Line up faucet parts and those of other plumbing fixtures in the order that you remove them. When it's time to reassemble, pick up the parts in reverse order.

Drip, drip, drip. Valves on basement plumbing pipes usually work like compression faucets. If one leaks, shut off the main water supply and open all the faucets in the house to drain the plumbing. Then disassemble the leaky valve and replace the seat washer or the packing material.

Use plumber's grease to lubricate O-rings. Heat-proof grease won't dissolve in hot water or soften some types of rubber, as petroleum jelly can.

If a leaky faucet keeps you awake at night, stuff a piece of rag in the spout to carry water silently to the drain. Fix the leak in the morning.

If a faucet's seat washer is so squashed you can't tell its shape, look into the top of the faucet. If the base of the opening is angled, you need a beveled washer; otherwise, buy a flat washer.

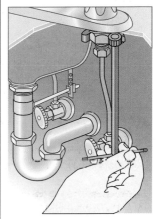

Wobbly faucet? Check for a loose locknut beneath the sink, and tighten it with an inexpensive basin wrench, available in hardware stores.

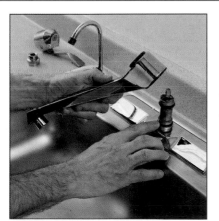

3 Lift off the spout sleeve and inspect the O-rings for pitted, worn, or damaged areas. If you see signs of damage, replace the O-rings with identical ones.

4 Using needle-nose pliers and a small flat screwdriver, pry off the retainer clip that holds the faucet cartridge in place.

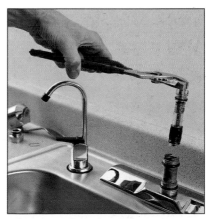

5 Lift out the old cartridge with groove-joint pliers. Install the new cartridge, following manufacturer's instructions. Reassemble the faucet.

Is it the aerator? If water runs slowly from a faucet, try this test to figure out if the aerator is the guilty party: Unscrew it from the nozzle and turn on the water. If the flow is strong, the aerator is probably clogged. Clean or replace it.

Wrap it up overnight. If you can't remove your faucet's aerator, there's still a way to clean it. Pour white vinegar into a sandwich bag; then use a rubber band to secure the bag around the spout. Make sure the aerator is fully immersed, and keep the bag there overnight. You can use this trick for a clogged shower head as well.

Getting the point. Use a pencil point to guide the tiny springs of some faucets into their holes during repair. Force the spring gently onto the pencil, insert the point in the hole, and then slide the spring off and into place with another pointed object or your finger.

Water streaming from an air gap—the mysterious dome on some kitchen sinks—means it is clogged with debris from the dishwasher or garbage disposal. Pry off the metal cover, and unscrew the assembly underneath. Fish out the blockage with long-nose pliers or a length of coat hanger wire.

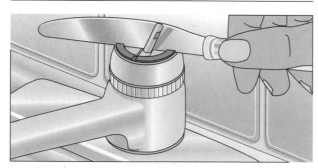

If a ball-type kitchen faucet leaks from beneath the handle, shut off the water to the faucet and remove the setscrew holding the handle. Pull off the handle to expose the slotted adjusting ring underneath; then use the back of a kitchen knife to tighten the ring by turning it clockwise. Reattach the handle and test the faucet. This simple fix usually cures the leak.

Cleaning a faucet aerator

WHAT YOU'LL NEED

Groove-joint pliers wrapped with tape (if needed)

Old toothbrush

Vinegar

Phillips screwdriver

Replacement parts as needed

1 Low water pressure at a kitchen spout can often be remedied by removing the aerator and cleaning it. Unscrew the aerator by hand. If it's too tight, use groove-joint pliers.

2 Disassemble carefully, laying out the parts in the proper sequence and orientation. Typically, there are two or three screens, a perforated nylon disc, and an O-ring. Some newer aerators aren't designed to be taken apart; replace the entire assembly.

3 Use an old toothbrush to remove any sediment. Soak the screens in vinegar to remove minor corrosion. If a screen is too corroded or damaged, replace it or the entire aerator. Reverse the procedure to reinstall.

One-stop shopping. If you need to buy a replacement hose for your kitchen sprayer, consider purchasing a new spray head at the same time. You'll find that it doesn't cost that much more and that it's also much easier to install them both in the same stroke.

A place for everything. After using the kitchen sprayer, be sure to retract the hose and return the head to its proper place beside the faucet. If it is left to soak in dirty sink water, the head will quickly clog with debris and bacteria.

Just say no to repairing an old faucet if you can't easily find replacement parts. You'll save time and usually gain a better faucet if you replace an obsolete model with a brand-new one.

Saucer savvy. Avoid an untimely disappearing act when taking apart a faucet or fixture with lots of small parts by first placing a saucer upside down over the drain opening or plugging up the hole with a thick dish towel.

To remove deposits from a sprayer, hold the sprayer handle open with a rubber band; then soak the sprayer head in a cup of warm white vinegar for 30 minutes. Run the sprayer under full pressure to dislodge any mineral deposits. Dunk the sprayer again if needed.

Sprayer not spraying? A sluggish sink sprayer may be kinked. Check under the sink to be sure the hose is straight and not twisted or pinched. If it is, you may have to disconnect the hose to straighten it.

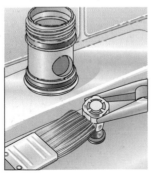

If water flows from the faucet even when you squeeze the sprayer handle, chances are the diverter is clogged. Shut off the water to the faucet, remove the handle and spout, then pull out the diverter from the faucet body with long-nose pliers. Clean it with a brush dipped in vinegar.

Repairing a sink sprayer

WHAT YOU'LL NEED

Screwdriver

Old toothbrush

Straight pin

Groove-joint pliers

Replacement washer

Basin wrench

1 To unclog a spray nozzle, remove the screw cover and retaining screw. Remove the perforated disc; brush it clean, and open any clogged holes with a pin; reassemble. If the screw cover isn't detachable, consider replacing the spray head.

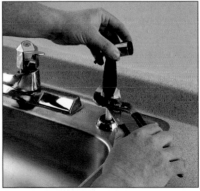

2 If the spray head leaks at the handle, try tightening the coupling. Be careful not to overtighten, as you could break the coupling.

3 If tightening the coupling does not stop the leak at the handle, unscrew the spray head from the handle mount and replace the washer. If the hose leaks at the other end, tighten that coupling with a basin wrench.

FILE IT

Water filters: Sifting through the claims

Different types of water filters remove different pollutants and no one filter works for everything, so make sure you know what you need before you buy.

	What it does	Downside
Carbon filter	Removes odor and bad taste. Also removes lead, pesticides, and herbicides.	Doesn't remove bacteria. Change the carbon filter often, or you could make your water worse.
Distillation filter	Reduces lead, pesticides, herbicides, bacteria, bad taste, odor, and sodium.	Uses a lot of energy and needs regular cleaning.
Reverse osmosis filter	Greatly reduces metals such as lead and copper, as well as bad taste, odor, pesticides, and herbicides.	Works slowly, producing only a few gallons of water per day. For each gallon of filtered water, 3 are wasted.
Ultraviolet light system	Kills bacteria and other organisms.	No protection against metals. Can be expensive to operate.

Testing 1, 2, 3. Testing your water can be costly, and no single test will detect all the contaminants. Call your department of health to find out about the likely contaminants in your area, and buy a water filter that specifically targets them.

Filter care. Don't take water filters for granted. Change or backflush a filter according to the manufacturer's instructions; otherwise filters can become a breeding ground for disease-causing bacteria and other microorganisms. Some filters require flushing when water has been standing longer than 72 hours.

Make the change. Write down the date that your water filter needs to be changed. An oversaturated filter will make drinking water drastically worse.

Rust in your water? Installing a whole-house water filter in the main water line, downstream from the main shutoff, may help the problem.

An automatic change. A water filter with a metered flow valve lets you know when it needs to be changed. After 1,500 gallons of water (roughly 1 year's use) have passed through it, the valve shuts off the water until you replace the filter.

Installing an under-the-sink water filter

WHAT YOU'LL NEED

Water filter system (housing, filter, tubing, faucet, saddle valve)

Safety goggles

Center punch

Variable-speed drill or step drill

Oil (if needed)

Hole saw (for laminate top)

Adjustable or open-end wrench

Groove-joint pliers

Screwdriver

1 Wearing goggles, drill a hole for the faucet. For a stainless-steel sink, use a step drill, lubricated with oil, at a low speed. For a laminate countertop, use a hole saw. With an adjustable wrench, mount the faucet according to the directions. Be careful: the sink hole will be very sharp.

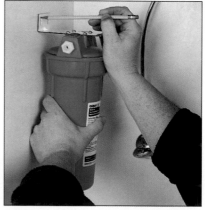

2 Choose a convenient place for the filter system: in the sink cabinet, for instance, or in the basement below. Mount the unit on a solid surface with screws through mounting holes, or for some models, with mounting brackets. Be sure to allow enough room to install and change the filter or filters.

Low-sodium plumbing. Softened water is higher in sodium than plain tap water and can be harmful for anyone on a sodium-restricted diet. Try installing the water softener only on the hot-water supply, or installing a separate tap for drinking and cooking water.

Coming to a boil. Boiling your water might seem like a logical way to purify it, but you can end up making the water worse. Boiling will kill off bacteria, but as the water evaporates, the concentration of other contaminants will increase.

Think "backward" when installing a water softener. Bags of softening chemicals can weigh as much as 50 pounds, so choose a site near an entry. Also, install a sturdy shelf next to the brine tank to rest the bag on while pouring out the chemical.

FILE IT

The hard truth about drinking water

"Hard" water contains high amounts of magnesium and calcium. Although a water softener is usually the answer to the problem, call an EPA-approved independent testing lab to test your water first—not a company that sells or rents water softeners.

Hardness	Grains per gallon	Parts per million
Soft	Less than 1.0	Less than 17.1
Slightly hard	1.0 to 3.5	17.1 to 60
Moderately hard	3.5 to 7.0	60 to 120
Hard	7.0 to 10.5	120 to 180
Very hard	10.5 and higher	180 and higher

Get the lead out. Plumbing installed before 1988 may contain harmful lead. Call your local health department for advice on testing. Meanwhile, use only cold water for drinking and cooking (hot water dissolves more lead from pipes). Let the water run for a minute or two before using it.

Living in an apartment? In many cases, local codes permit only professional plumbers to repair and install apartment plumbing, especially in cities. Check with a building inspector before installing an under-the-sink water filter system or making any other plumbing repair.

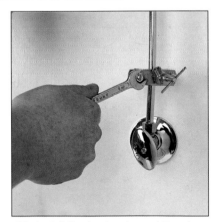

3 Install the feed-water saddle valve. Locate a nearby cold-water pipe, and shut off the water to it (and the main supply, if necessary). If you have rigid pipe, install a self-piercing saddle valve according to package directions.

! **If the local code prohibits saddle valves, have a professional cut a T into the supply line as an alternative.**

4 Connect tubing to the saddle valve and to the *In* fitting on the filter unit; install another tube between the *Out* fitting on the filter unit and the faucet. (Be careful not to reverse the connections.) Compression fittings are the most common.

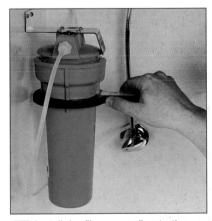

5 Install the filter according to the manufacturer's instructions. Shut the saddle valve and release pressure by activating the faucet. (Some systems have an additional release button on the filter.) Remove the filter housing and insert the filter into it; then reinstall the housing until it is tight. Open the saddle valve, and run water through the filter faucet for 5 min.

Beginner's luck. Even if you've never attempted home repairs, don't be afraid to tackle pop-up stoppers and other drain problems. You don't even have to shut off the water beforehand.

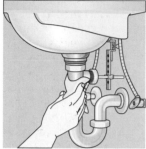

The drip test. Water dripping from around the retaining nut on a pop-up stopper may be condensation. Wipe all metal parts dry with a towel and see if the dripping recurs. If it does, remove the nut, pivot ball, and horizontal rod, replace any washers inside the pop-up assembly, and reinstall.

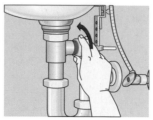

If the lift rod of a pop-up stopper won't stay raised, causing the stopper to open even when there is water in the sink, reach underneath the sink and tighten the round pivot ball retaining nut at the rear of the pop-up assembly. Turn the nut clockwise with your hand. Don't overtighten, or the rod will be hard to operate.

Fits like a glove. Wear disposable latex gloves—the kind doctors use—when doing plumbing repairs. Nowadays you can find them in many home repair stores; even professional plumbers wear them.

Quick fix, part one. If a sink's pop-up stopper doesn't lift high enough to let water drain freely, first try loosening the setscrew with a wrench or pliers, pressing the stopper down, and then retightening the screw.

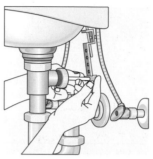

Quick fix, part two. If that doesn't work, reposition the pivot rod in a different hole by squeezing the spring clip, freeing the rod, and reinserting it one or two holes higher up. When the drain is closed, the pivot rod should slope slightly uphill from the drainpipe.

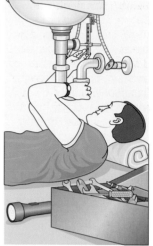

All the comforts of home. Working under a sink is no bed of roses, but you needn't make it more awkward than it has to be. Before scrunching down on your back, take time to clear the area, arrange a rolled-up towel for padding and support, and place all your tools, including a flashlight, on the floor within reach.

Adjusting a pop-up sink stopper

WHAT YOU'LL NEED

Locking pliers or groove-joint pliers

Old toothbrush and cleanser

New stopper or seal as needed

Stubby screwdriver or wrench

Flashlight

1 Most sink stoppers just lift out. Some stoppers, however, require a quarter turn counterclockwise, while others require that you remove the pivot rod. To take out the pivot rod, first loosen the retaining nut with locking pliers. Then pull out the rod ball assembly and remove the stopper.

2 Clean the stopper. Inspect the rubber seal, and remove or replace it if it's dry or cracked. Reinstall the stopper or a replacement.

Sealing the deal. When a pop-up stopper won't seal, check for any debris that is preventing the stopper from dropping far enough into the drain opening. If this doesn't fix the problem, remove the stopper and replace the O-rings, the washer, or the stopper itself.

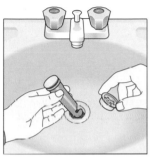

Make a switch. If your sink or tub is constantly backing up, consider removing the pop-up stopper and replacing it with a fine strainer.

Mystery leak. If your bathroom sink empties while the stopper is seated firmly in the drain opening, the problem may be faulty putty beneath the drain flange in the bottom of the sink Try loosening the locknut beneath the sink and then pushing up on the pipe to raise the flange. Unscrew the flange and remove it. Clean away all the old putty; then apply a ½-inch ribbon of fresh plumber's putty and reinstall the flange.

Avoid pop-up problems by getting in the habit of cleaning the pop-up stoppers in your bathroom sink and tub once a week. You'll be surprised at how much hair and grime can accumulate in that time.

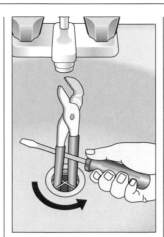

To replace an old-style strainer drain with a pop-up stopper, you'll first need to remove the strainer from the sink. Try inserting the handle ends of a pair of pliers into the strainer and then rotating the tool counterclockwise, using a longer screwdriver for leverage. If that doesn't work, use a strainer wrench, available at plumbing supply stores.

Tub tip. When removing the stopper in your bathtub, lay down a towel first. This will give you a place to set your tools without scratching the tub's surface.

Down the drain. Does water leak down the drain when you're taking a bath? Or not drain quickly enough afterward? Remove the overflow plate (usually held on by two screws) and clean the linkage behind it. There you'll find the adjusting nut, which lets you control the length of the striker rod; lengthen it to make water drain faster or shorten it to stop leaking.

Down the drain II. Or control the flow by removing the stopper and adjusting the nut to change the stopper's height. Elevating it helps water drain; lowering it stops water from exiting.

3 To ensure that the stopper will close snugly, the pivot rod must be set properly. The pivot rod may need to go in a different hole in the clevis rod, which is a perforated metal strap. To disconnect the pivot rod from the clevis rod, squeeze the spring clip while sliding the pivot rod out.

4 Reverse the removal procedure to reinstall the stopper. For the type that required removal of the pivot rod, have a helper lower the stopper while you look through the opening in the tailpiece. With the stopper held at the right level, insert and resecure the pivot rod. Test for leaks.

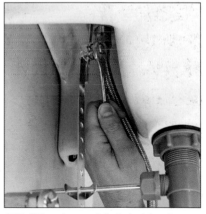

5 If the stopper fails to hold water in the sink, use pliers, a stubby screwdriver, or a wrench to loosen the setscrew from the lift rod. Press down on the stopper and retighten the screw. Instead of a setscrew, some units have a spring clip that you squeeze to free the lift rod.

Wrap it up. If a trap suddenly sprouts a leak, wrap the pipe with several layers of the plastic tape used for repairing garden hose until you can replace the trap. Place a bucket under the trap—just in case.

Sewer smells. Eliminate odor when replacing a sink trap by stuffing a rag in the pipe opening leading into the wall. Doing so prevents sewer gas in the drainage system from spilling out of the open pipe into the room.

Don't laugh; it happens. If you've removed a trap or stopper linkage to clear a drain, place a rag over the faucet handles to remind you not to run the water.

A tight fit. Tighten a leaking slip nut on a trap with two pipe wrenches, or with a wrench and groove-joint pliers. Wrap the jaws of both tools with duct tape to prevent marring the chrome pipe surfaces. Grip the lower pipe with one wrench to hold it stationary while turning the nut with the other.

Chemical drain cleaners are especially caustic on sink, tub, and shower traps. The heat generated by the cleaners can eat through the thin chromed brass, corroding it before its time. Use them as a last resort.

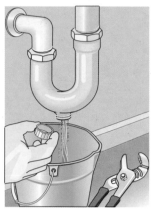

Trapping a clog. If a clogged drain doesn't respond to plunging, cleaning out the trap is your next best bet. Bail out the water from the sink, place a bucket under the trap, and remove the cleanout plug by unscrewing it with a wrench or groove-joint pliers. If a little water runs out, stick the end of a wire coat hanger into the opening to snag the blockage. If water flows freely, the blockage is probably in the wall.

Digging a little deeper. If the blockage is in the wall, try to dislodge it with coat hanger wire or a drain auger. If you can't snag anything, call a plumber.

Casting for clogs. If a drain clog isn't too deep, you can often pull it out with a fish hook tied to a string. Be sure to wear safety goggles and work gloves.

Replacing a sink trap

WHAT YOU'LL NEED

Plastic or metal sink trap

Container to catch water

Locking pliers or spud wrench

Replacement parts as needed

Hacksaw and felt-tip pen (if needed)

Compression (slip nut) washer

1 The procedure for replacing a corroded metal sink trap—whether in a simple P-trap system, as here, or a more complicated one—is the same. Remove the cleanout plug if there is one, and drain out water. Loosen couplings with pliers or a spud wrench (left).

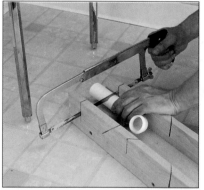

2 Use the existing compression washers and couplings and either PVC plastic or brass pipe. Purchase replacement parts, including adapters if needed. If necessary, use a hacksaw to cut the new tailpiece to length (see p. 176).

3 Slip the couplings over the ends of the pipe; then press on a compression washer, with the bevel side facing the end of the pipe. Slip the pipe into the appropriate fitting, and secure the nut until it's just snug. Test and tighten the fitting as needed.

A quick leak check.
Use your water meter to help you detect a leak. Turn off all the faucets and write down the reading on the meter. Keep everything off for at least an hour, making sure not to flush the toilets. Take another reading and compare the two; if the numbers have changed, chances are there is a leak.

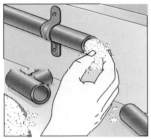

White or whole wheat?
Plug a pipe with bread to stop it from dripping while you solder it. The bread will dissolve when you turn the water back on after completing the repair.

Those who wait.
If the electricity is off and the pipes have frozen, your best option is usually to shut off the water supply and simply wait for the electricity to be restored. Chances are, when the power comes back on and the heat returns, the frozen pipes will thaw all by themselves.

Two ways to a tight fit.
Prevent leaks in threaded pipe connections by first applying plumber's thread-sealing tape or pipe joint compound to male threads. To use tape, simply wrap two or three turns clockwise around the threads before screwing the pipe into the fitting. To apply compound, brush it thoroughly around the outside of the threads before inserting the pipe.

A new ice age.
Don't panic if your pipes freeze! First shut off the water supply and open the nearest faucet. Then warm the pipes with a hair dryer, starting near the faucet and advancing the dryer along the pipe about a foot per minute. Hold the hair dryer about 6 inches from the pipe and wave it back and forth to heat the pipe evenly. You can use this method to heat pipes even if they are behind walls.

Trickle-down effect.
Let water trickle from faucets near vulnerable pipes to keep them from freezing during a cold snap. The movement of running water prevents ice from forming.

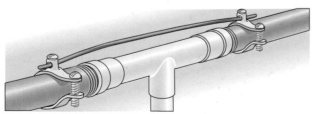

Stay grounded. If an electrical system is grounded by a wire attached to the metal water supply pipes, don't break the ground connection when installing a plastic patch. Attach ground clamps to the metal pipes on each side of the repair, and connect the clamps with a copper jumper wire.

Stopping a leak in a pipe

WHAT YOU'LL NEED

Sleeve clamp or adjustable hose clamp

Thin sheet rubber

Screwdriver

Solder or solvent cement

Two-part epoxy cement

Rubber gloves

Plastic electrical tape or plumbing rubber wrap

1 To temporarily fix a small leak, place a sleeve clamp and a sheet of rubber over the pipe, and tighten the clamp screws. Or bind a sheet of rubber over the leak with an adjustable hose clamp. The best solution, however, is to replace the pipe.

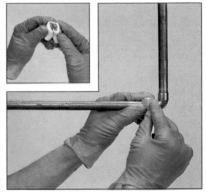

2 Use moldable two-part epoxy to temporarily fix a leaky joint. Wearing rubber gloves, mix and apply the epoxy to the leak. The joint should eventually be disassembled and repaired, using solder for copper pipe or solvent cement for plastic.

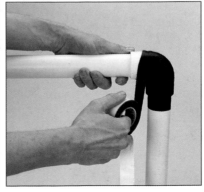

3 Leaks in non-pressurized drainpipe, including those at joints, can be temporarily fixed with electrical tape or plumbing rubber wrap. But permanent repairs are inexpensive and easy to do unless access to the pipe is restricted.

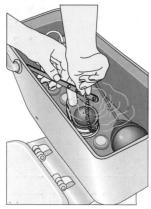

A common problem.
If your toilet won't flush, lift the cover and look inside. Chances are the chain that connects to the trip lever has come loose. If so, reconnect it.

Whistler's toilet. Eliminate whistling flushes, fairly common on older toilets with metal float arms and flush assemblies, by replacing the ballcock washers.

Above the rim. If your toilet runs noisily or water leaks from the handle opening, check inside to see whether the water level is above the rim of the overflow tube—the vertical pipe near the middle of the tank. If it is, grip the float arm with both hands and bend it so the ball at the end is slightly lower than before. The toilet should shut off sooner. Most toilets have a waterline etched into the tank wall. Use it as a guide.

Get a handle on it. Fix a floppy flush handle by holding it firmly with one hand and tightening the large nut surrounding it on the inside of the tank. Tighten the nut to the left or right, depending on the handle. Don't overtighten.

"Flushometer" toilets, often installed in urban apartments, have an adjusting screw to control the amount of water released with each flush. Look for the screw near the handle (it may be hidden under a decorative cover). To adjust it, hold the locknut steady with a wrench while turning the screw clockwise to decrease flow or counterclockwise to increase it.

Sluggish flushes? The siphon hole near the center of the bowl may be blocked with waste. Wearing gloves, twist a wire around in the hole to remove any clogs.

Ghostly flushes that occur when the bathroom is unoccupied are usually caused by a leaking flush valve. Water seeping from the tank into the bowl lowers the tank's water level, activating the toilet's fill valve. Exorcise the problem by cleaning the flush valve and/or replacing the flapper.

Is your toilet leaking?
Test it by pouring enough food dye into the toilet tank to change the color of the water. If the water in the bowl turns color, the flush valve at the base of the tank is leaking. If colored water collects outside the toilet, the tank itself is leaking.

Replacing a ballcock

WHAT YOU'LL NEED

Large sponge or old towel

Adjustable wrench or groove-joint pliers

Bucket or rags

Floating-cup ballcock

1 Close the shut-off valve beneath the tank, and flush the toilet. Remove the tank lid; sponge out the remaining water. Disconnect the water supply line, using an adjustable wrench or groove-joint pliers to loosen the nut that secures it to the tank.

2 Remove the locknut that secures the ballcock inlet to the bottom of the tank. Place a bucket or rags below to catch any water. Then carefully lift the ballcock-and-float assembly out of the tank.

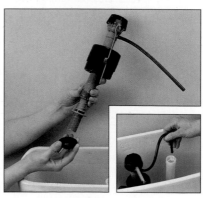

3 Install a new floating-cup ballcock. Follow instructions for placement of rubber seals. Secure the nut a quarter turn past hand-tight. Clip refill tube so it leads into overflow tube. Reconnect the water supply, open the valve, and check for leaks.

If a toilet leaks beneath the bowl, try tightening the bolts on both sides of the toilet. Don't overtighten them. If the bolts aren't loose, remove the toilet and replace the wax sealing ring underneath it (see "Reseating a Toilet," right).

Royal flush. Try replacing an old toilet with a new low-flow model. A family of four can save over 20,000 gallons of water each year. Ask your plumber about the models that work best.

No goldbricking. Don't put a brick in your toilet tank to save water by taking up space; it will eventually disintegrate, causing the toilet to leak. Instead, use a water-filled plastic bottle.

Bathroom condensation. A toilet tank may "sweat" in warm, humid weather for the same reasons that drinking glasses form beads of moisture. One cure is to install rigid foam insulation panels, available at plumbing supply stores, inside the tank. Or have your plumber install a tempering valve, which will admit a small amount of hot water into the tank.

Easy does it. Use special care with tools; toilets are porcelain and can be easily chipped or cracked.

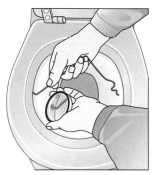

Get a close-up of clogs. Does the water in your toilet swirl but flush slowly? Wearing gloves, hold a mirror in the bowl and shine a flashlight against it to check the small holes under the rim. Clear out any clogged holes with a coat hanger wire.

Plunging like a pro. To unblock a clogged toilet, use a plunger with a funnel cup. Place the tool so it seals completely over the drain opening; make sure the cup is covered with water. Then pump up and down as hard as you can about 10 times. Remove the plunger. If the water is gone, draw a bucket of water from the bathtub and pour it into the bowl to clear the pipes.

Heavy hitter. Use a closet auger to unblock a toilet when a plunger won't work. The auger has a long shaft with a bend at one end. Insert the tool so the bend rests inside the drain opening. Hold the shaft and crank the handle clockwise to feed the auger into the toilet. When you feel pressure at the auger's tip, withdraw the auger by cranking it back toward the shaft.

Reseating a toilet

WHAT YOU'LL NEED

Large sponge or old towel

Pliers

Large screwdriver

Adjustable wrench

Drop cloth

Wax ring with sleeve

Waterproof white caulk

1 If a toilet base leaks, shut off the water, drain the tank, disconnect the supply lines (see "Replacing a Ballcock," step 1, facing page), and sponge water out of the bowl. Grasping them with pliers, unscrew the tank bolts. Then lift off the tank.

2 Take off the toilet seat. Then remove the floor bolt caps and unscrew the nuts with an adjustable wrench. Straddling the toilet, rock it from side to side and lift it off the bolts.

3 Lay toilet upside down on a protected surface. Remove old wax, and press a new wax ring over opening. Work caulk onto perimeter of toilet base. Position toilet over closet bolts and press it into place. Tighten nuts. Reinstall tank and seat.

A trickle-down shower.
Rejuvenate a clogged shower head by removing it (see step 1, right), disassembling the parts, and soaking them in warm vinegar. Unclog any blocked holes with a thin rigid wire; rinse off the vinegar and reassemble the head.

Switching arms. When you're installing a new shower head, you may find a ball shape at the end of the shower arm. If so, you will need to remove the arm by turning it counterclockwise. Replace it with an arm that has ½-inch threads.

Bathtub chips and nicks?
Repair them by cleaning the area with rubbing alcohol and covering with thin coats of epoxy touch-up paint.

Careful cleaning. Clean dirty fiberglass bathtubs and showers with either a gentle scratch-resistant cleanser or a commercial bathroom cleaner that contains EDTA (ethylene diamine tetraacetate).

The perfect shower.
If you have a single-lever faucet in the shower, press a self-sticking color dot or a piece of waterproof tape on the tile to mark your ideal water temperature.

Stain zappers. Rust stains on porcelain often come clean with a paste of cream of tartar (available in the spice department and also found in some baking powders) and hydrogen peroxide. Scrub the paste on gently with a brush. Let the paste dry, and then rinse. Repeat if necessary.

Installing a new shower head

WHAT YOU'LL NEED

Large adjustable wrench

Strap wrench (if needed)

New shower arm (optional)

Teflon tape or pipe dope

New shower head

Rag

1 To remove the old shower head, turn it counterclockwise with an adjustable wrench while holding the shower arm in place with a strap wrench, if necessary. Most heads have flat, smooth surfaces that will accept a large wrench.

2 Apply Teflon tape (3 to 5 rounds) or pipe dope on the male threads of the shower arm. If supplied, place a gasket in the new shower head, and screw it on. Tighten it with the adjustable wrench. Wipe off the excess pipe dope with a rag.

3 For units with a hand shower attachment, screw the hose onto the shower arm, and the shower head onto the hose, making sure to use the required gaskets.

A weighty solution. Fill the bathtub with water when applying new caulk around the tub/wall joint. The weight of the water will open the gap between the tub and wall as wide as possible, preventing cracking later.

Down the drain. Many shower clogs are easy to clear. Simply unscrew the strainer (the technique is described on page 169) and remove the clog with a plumber's auger.

If that didn't work...

Push a garden hose into the drainpipe as far as possible. Pack rags around the opening and hold them firmly while a helper turns the water on full force and then off again. Repeat several times until the clog separates; then flush the drain with water for 15 seconds.

SAFE AND SMART

➤ Mixing two different brands of drain cleaner could result in a violent chemical reaction.

➤ Pouring chemical drain openers through a plastic funnel will protect chrome or brass hardware on a sink or tub.

➤ For an extra-tight seal, run a ring of petroleum jelly around the lip of the rubber plunger.

The wrong tool. Forget about using an expansion nozzle to clear a clog. Although it is supposed to unblock drains with a high-pressure stream of water, it can cause a leak or rupture the pipe.

Don't take the plunge. Never use a plunger after you have added chemical cleaner to the drainpipes. Splashing water can cause skin burns and severe eye injuries, even blindness.

Taming the snake. A plumber's snake usually eliminates clogs, but it may emerge from the drain an ugly mess. Contain the mess and the snake by coiling it into a plastic trash bag, a big bucket, or a small garbage can.

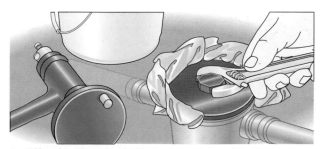

A different drum trap. Bathtubs in some older houses are linked to a drum trap, identified by a round plate in the floor nearby. To unclog these, squirt penetrating oil under the plate and then unscrew it with a large wrench. Have rags nearby, ready to soak up any overflow. Scoop out the debris in the trap; then use an auger to check for a blockage in the pipe leading to the tub or the pipe leading to the drain.

Snaking a drain

WHAT YOU'LL NEED

Rubber gloves

Groove-joint pliers

Auger

Screwdriver

Plumber's helper (toilet plunger)

Closet auger

1 To snake a sink drain, remove trap (p. 170) and clean it. Crank handle as you feed an auger into the drainpipe to break up any blockage. Reassemble trap, and test. If still clogged, try chemical drain treatments or consult a professional.

2 For a clogged tub, feed an auger through the strainer or the overflow-stopper assembly. Older tubs may have a trap located in the floor (see "A Different Drum Trap," left) or behind a special access panel.

3 If a plunger doesn't clear a toilet blockage, insert a closet auger until it hits the clog and rotate the handle clockwise. If this is difficult, back it out until it turns freely, and try again. When the auger hits the clog, move it back and forth until the clog breaks up.

The right fitting. To find the length of replacement pipe needed for a repair, measure between the bottoms of the sockets of each fitting. That way you will include the length of new pipe that will be inserted into the fitting at each end.

It's a snap. Use a pipe cutter to cut copper and plastic pipe cleanly. Open the tool and place it around the pipe. Then tighten until the wheel lightly scores the pipe's surface. Rotate the cutter around the pipe, tightening it after every two rotations. Continue until the pipe snaps.

Dynamic duo. Use pipe wrenches in pairs to separate pipes and fittings. With the two sets of jaws facing each other, place one wrench on a part of the plumbing that is to remain stationary and place the other on the part you wish to turn. Arrange both wrenches so the twisting force is directed toward the jaws, which tightens them against the pipe.

The right angle. If you must cut a length of pipe to remove it from between two fittings, saw through the pipe at an angle so you can swing each section free of the other to unscrew it.

Over your knee. Bend flexible copper pipe with a bending spring. Slide the tool over the pipe and then press it against your knee until it reaches the correct angle (just don't try to bend it more than 90°).

Run water through new plastic supply pipes for 30 seconds to flush out solvent fumes before using water.

Safer soldering. If you are soldering pipes near a combustible surface, prevent a fire by placing a barrier of fireproof cloth or a double thickness of 24-gauge sheet metal between the pipes and the surface.

A perfect union. You can replace metal pipe with plastic if the local building code allows, but be sure to use an adapter made for joining the two types of pipe. When joining pipes of different metals, use dielectric unions, which prevent the metals from touching. If you don't, both pipes will corrode at the joint.

Connecting rigid plastic pipe

WHAT YOU'LL NEED

Utility knife

Pipe and fittings

Felt-tip pen

Primer (for PVC and CPVC pipe)

Solvent cement

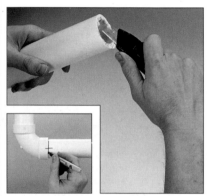

1 Deburr the cut ends of a plastic pipe, and using a knife, bevel the outside edge slightly. (This prevents the sharp edge of the pipe from scraping the wall of the fitting.) Test the fit in place, and mark both pipe and fitting at the joint with a felt-tip pen (inset).

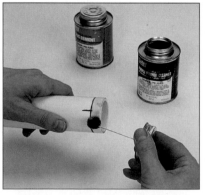

2 Apply primer to CPVC or PVC pipe, wait 15 sec., and then apply solvent cement to the mating surfaces of pipe and fitting. Primer is not required for ABS plastic pipe. Never cement two different types of plastic pipe together.

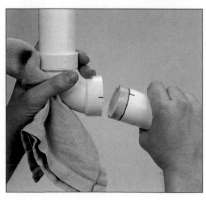

3 Press pipe forcefully into fitting a quarter turn off position. Twist to spread cement and align pen marks. Work quickly: cement sets in 60 sec. Hold pieces together for 30 sec. Wait 3 min. before starting next joint and 12 hr. before running water.

Grease, seal, or putty?

Plumbing is riddled with lingo. Here's a quick lesson on some common terms: plumber's grease lubricates faucets without affecting the water quality. Plumber's seal is a moldable two-part epoxy putty used to seal leaky pipe joints. Plumber's putty creates a watertight surface seal under a faucet or a sink or tub drain.

Before soldering

fittings and pipes, dry-fit the assembly on a workbench to make sure all the pieces fit. If it is a complex assembly, use a nail to scratch a line across each joint to make it a breeze to align when soldering the pipes in place.

Making a point.

You can temporarily plug a small pipe leak by breaking off a pencil point in the hole. Then cover the area with three layers of plastic electrical tape, extending the tape 3 inches on either side of the leak.

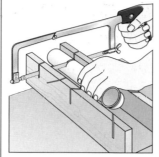

A smooth cut. For a straight, clean cut, use a trusty miter box. Hold the pipe securely against the side of the box with your hand and place a hacksaw in the 90° slot; keep the blade vertical as you cut.

If solder turns mushy, the pipe is too cool. Remove the solder and apply more heat to the fitting. If the solder sputters and forms tiny balls, the metal is too hot and should be allowed to cool. Solder should melt and flow instantly into the joint.

Solder sense. When soldering a joint near a previously soldered one, wrap a damp rag around the first joint to keep its solder from melting.

FILE IT

Making the connection

Sooner or later, every water pipe has to turn left, right, or head up to a second floor. This is where caps, elbows, and unions come in.

Type	Purpose
Cap	Seals the end of an open pipe
Coupling	Joins two same- or different-diameter pipes
Elbow	Joins with two rigid pipes of the same material to create a curve
Plug	Screws into a pipe or fitting to seal it
Reducer	Joins pipes of different sizes
T-fitting	Joins three pipes of the same material
Union	Joins same-size metal pipes in a straight line (joints made with a union can be taken apart)

Joining pipes with a compression joint

WHAT YOU'LL NEED

Pipe reamer
Pair of compression nuts and rings
Threaded union fitting
Pipe joint compound
Adjustable wrench and open-end wrench

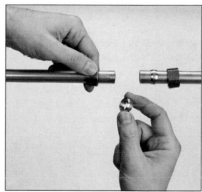

1 Turn off water and let the pipes drain. Deburr the cut ends of copper pipe by rotating a pipe reamer in the lip of the pipe. Slide a compression nut over both of the copper pipes you will be joining. Then slide on the compression rings.

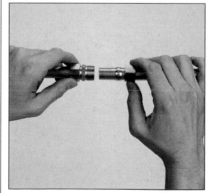

2 Hold the threaded union fitting against one pipe end. Apply pipe joint compound to the pipe's compression ring. Slide the compression nut over the ring, and screw it on the union. Repeat the procedure with the other pipe.

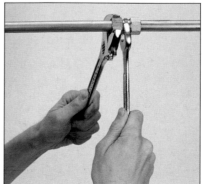

3 Place an open-end wrench on the union fitting and an adjustable wrench on a compression nut. Now tighten the nut one full turn. Repeat with the other nut. Turn the water back on. In case of a leak, tighten the nuts gently.

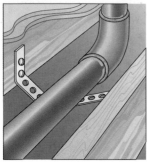

Hold those pipes. Brace pipes that run parallel to the joists by cradling them with metal plumber's tape and fastening the ends to the sides of the joists. Use two fasteners at each end, and be sure the heads of the fasteners are larger than the holes in the tape.

Brace sagging pipes with a copper clamp and screws (if the pipes are copper), a plastic hanger, or a 2 x 2 wood brace fastened between the joists.

Pipe inspection. Exposed pipes are often easy to silence. Take a look at the pipes in your basement when water is running through them at full force, checking for any that vibrate or knock against either studs or joists.

Shhhh! Quiet pipes that are rubbing against joists or floorboards by wedging a piece of foam-rubber pad between metal and wood.

Behind the walls. If your pipes make a thudding noise (called water hammer) when you shut off the faucets, it's probably because air chambers in the plumbing are full of water. To drain, shut off the water supply and open all the faucets. Wait an hour; then turn on the water and shut off the faucets one by one.

Try it again... If the thudding noise persists after you've tried the previous tip, install water-hammer arresters. See step 3, below.

No shortcuts. Don't try to make air chambers from pipes and caps to silence faucet problems; they'll just become waterlogged. Water-hammer arresters are better.

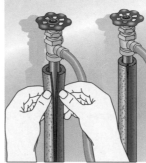

Water pipes should be at least 6 inches apart so they can be reached easily, and covered with foam pipe insulation to save energy.

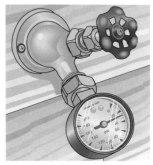

Under pressure. Whistling faucets or water spurting from fixtures can be a clue that the water pressure is too high. Call a plumber or the water company to test the incoming pressure.

Relieving the pressure. If your water pressure is higher than 80 pounds per square inch, you may need to install a pressure-reducing valve. (In some areas, the water company must supply one for free if it is needed. Check with your local building inspector.)

Silencing a noisy pipe

WHAT YOU'LL NEED

Screwdriver
Pipe straps or hangers
Foam pipe insulation or soft rubber
Pipe cutter
Pipe reamer
T-fitting, short nipple, and female adapter
Wire brush or emery cloth
Paste flux and applicator
Propane torch
Solder
Teflon tape
Water-hammer arrester
Locking or groove-joint pliers

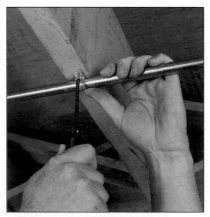

1 If pipes bang when the water is turned on, look for loose pipe straps or pipe hangers, and resecure or tighten them. Or add a strap or hanger, if needed. The minimum distance between pipe supports depends on the type of pipe being used (metal or plastic) and its orientation (vertical or horizontal). In general, however, there should be one strap or hanger for each 3–4 ft. of pipe.

2 If you hear a clinking or ticking sound when you turn on the hot water, the pipe is clamped too tight. A pipe should be just loose enough to slide in its strap. Either loosen the clamp or add a piece of rubber or foam between the pipe and the clamp or hanger to cushion it.

Keeping water clean.
Beware of cross-connections, where water that should go down the drain siphons into the drinking water system. Offenders include faucets or hand-held shower sprayers that are submerged when a bathtub or sink fills up, or a garden hose left submerged in a swimming pool.

Peace and quiet.
If you're building a new home or an addition, you can specify that you want cast-iron soil pipes. They will reduce the noise from flushing toilets.

Peace and quiet II.
Also specify that your cast-iron soil pipes should be located away from often-occupied areas like living rooms, dining rooms, and dens.

Knock-knock. Silence the knocking in a steam radiator by tilting it toward the inlet valve, located at one end of the unit. Turn off the heat, let the radiator cool, and disconnect the inlet pipe from the radiator. Then place shims under the far legs, and reconnect the inlet pipe. Open the inlet valve fully.

SAFE AND SMART

➤ Before closing up a vacation house for the winter, drain the plumbing to prevent freeze-ups. Tell the water company to turn off the supply to the house. Then close the main supply valve and open all the faucets, starting on the top floor. Be sure to open the outside faucets, too.

➤ When you're ready to leave a vacation home, flush all the toilets and pour plumbing-fixture antifreeze into each bowl and sink trap. Follow directions on the package.

➤ When restoring the plumbing system to your vacation house the following year, fill the water heater before turning on the power to it or lighting the pilot flame.

Open and shut. A radiator will knock if the inlet valve is open only partway. Close it entirely if you're not using the radiator. Make sure it's fully opened if you are.

Changing time. Replace a bleed valve with a new one if it leaks or is clogged. Shut off the boiler and drain the heating system first.

Letting off hot air. If the radiator isn't heating up, you may need to release air trapped inside (called "bleeding the radiator"). Turn the valve at the top of the radiator, or release the bleed screw if there is one, until all the air has escaped and water spits out. Have a rag ready!

3 If a pipe bangs when the water is shut off, install a water-hammer arrester as close to the appliance or fixture as possible. Turn off the water and drain the system. Cut the pipe with a pipe cutter, and deburr the cut ends with a pipe reamer. Assemble the T-fitting, short nipple, and female adapter. Clean the pipe ends and the inside of the T-fitting with a wire brush or emery cloth; the metal should shine.

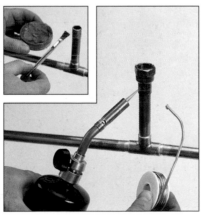

4 Immediately apply a thin coat of paste flux to the pipe ends and the inside of the fitting. Insert the pipe ends into the fitting, and twist the fitting to spread the flux; then wipe off the excess. Using a propane torch set for a soft flame, heat one joint until it's hot enough to melt solder. Apply the solder so that a thin bead forms around the entire joint rim. Wipe off the excess, and solder the other joints.

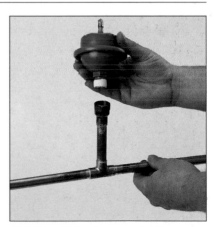

5 Wrap Teflon tape around the threads of the water-hammer arrester, and screw it into the female adapter with locking pliers.

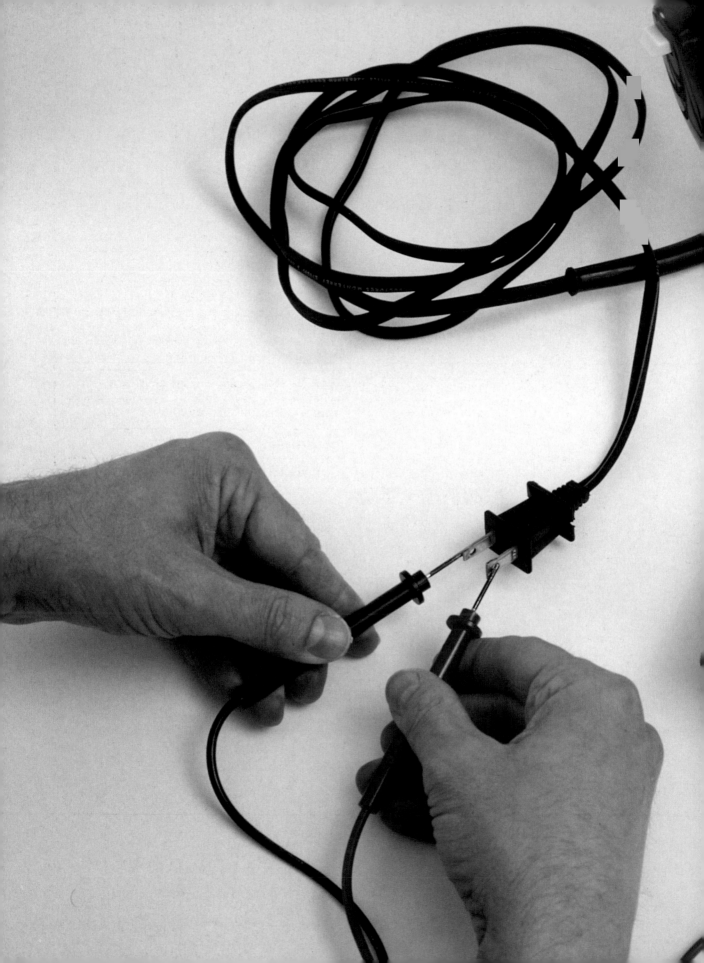

ELECTRICAL REPAIRS AND IMPROVEMENTS

Job ratings:　🔌 Easy　🔌🔌 Medium　🔌🔌🔌 Complex

A digital multimeter is easier to read and more accurate than an analog model. A display window shows the resistance or voltage, depending on the test; a beeping sound indicates continuity. An autoranging feature on some models automatically calibrates the meter to the proper range.

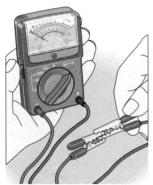

"Zero" an analog multimeter to eliminate needle error in resistance tests. Set the meter to the scale needed for the test you wish to make. Then turn the meter on, touch the probes together, and turn the adjustment dial until the needle rests over zero.

A free hand. An alligator clip attached to a multimeter probe allows you to adjust the meter or move the wires with a free hand during tests. Clips also reduce the shock hazard by keeping your fingers away from live connections.

Ensure accurate readings by laying a multimeter on a nonmetal surface. Use a range setting that keeps the needle in the upper third of the meter scale. If the scale has a mirror, look at the needle from an angle that causes it to merge with its mirrored reflection.

The right tool. Doorbells, security alarms, and thermostats all run on voltage that is too low for circuit testers to detect. Only a multimeter works on such low-voltage circuits.

Prolong the battery life of seldom-used multimeters and continuity testers (or any electronic gadget) by removing the batteries from their compartment before storing. It prevents the gradual draining of the batteries when the items are turned off.

A shocking experience. If you experience even a slight shock from a tool or appliance, "extend" one VOM lead to a cold-water line with an alligator clip and length of wire. Touch the cabinet of the appliance with the other probe. If any voltage is present, unplug the equipment and don't use it until you have located the source of the problem.

How to use a multimeter

WHAT YOU'LL NEED

Multimeter (multitester, volt-ohm meter)

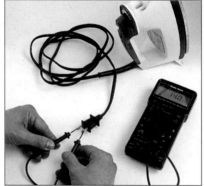

1 To check if a circuit is complete, unplug the appliance and turn it on. With the meter set to its lowest range (usually RX1), touch probes to the plug's prongs. Twenty to 100 ohms is usually good. Zero may show a short circuit; a high reading, an open circuit.

2 To check if a heating element is faulty, remove it from the stove. With the meter set to its lowest range (usually RX1), touch probes to both terminals. Twenty to 100 ohms is good.

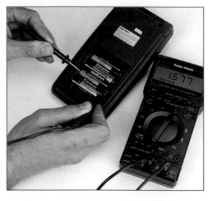

3 Test a battery while it is in the device. With the meter at a DC voltage range slightly higher than the battery rating, touch probes to the battery's terminals (red to +, black to –). If the reading is more than 20% lower than the battery rating, replace it.

Plug it in. An outlet analyzer is safer than a voltage tester when checking for current at receptacles. Plug in the device, and if the proper lights glow (the colors and pattern change, depending on the model), current is present. Be sure to check both pairs of slots.

A "chopsticks grip" is safest when using a voltage tester to check live connections (see step 2, right). Using both hands could cause you to become a channel for electricity.

SAFE AND SMART

➤ Seasoned electricians follow a safety ritual before making any repairs on circuits, wires, or receptacles. You should, too, when tackling an electrical job.

1. Always shut off the power by either tripping the circuit breaker or removing the fuse at the main service panel.

2. Then use an inductive voltage detector to make sure the power is off. Hold the detector close to each wire and press the clip; it shouldn't beep or light up.

Testing the tester. Before using any voltage tester, test it on an outlet that is working (plug a lamp into the outlet to make sure the circuit is live). Then try out the tester. If it works properly, the tester is good.

In an older house, check for old-fashioned knob-and-tube wiring in the basement. Hold an inductive voltage detector near the wires and press the clip. If the tester lights up, the wires are hot. Call an electrician to remove them.

Handle "quick connect" terminals by pushing against the socket portion with the tip of a screwdriver. Don't pull the wire, which could break it, or use pliers, which could crush the fragile connectors.

Faulty extension cord? Find out for sure with a continuity tester. Clip the end to the wide prong of the plug, turn on the tester, and insert the probe in the wide slot of the cord's receptacle. Bend and twist the cord. The tester's bulb should light. Then attach the clip to the narrow prong and insert the probe in the narrow slot. Again, the bulb should light. If the cord fails both tests, replace it.

How to use voltage testers

WHAT YOU'LL NEED

Inductive voltage detector

Neon test light

Screwdriver

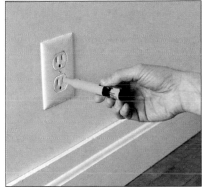

1 To test for power in an electrical outlet, insert the tip of an inductive voltage detector into each of the outlet's short vertical slots, and press the clip on the detector. If the voltage tester beeps or lights up at either slot, the outlet has power.

2 Use a neon test light to check if a 3-pronged outlet is grounded. Holding the probes only by their insulated parts in one hand, insert one probe into the grounding slot and the other into each slot. A bright light at one slot indicates a good ground.

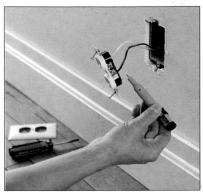

3 To find a hot wire in an outlet box, turn off power to the circuit. Remove the fixture with a screwdriver, separate the wires slightly, and restore the power. Hold an inductive voltage detector close to each wire, and press the clip; it will light at a hot wire.

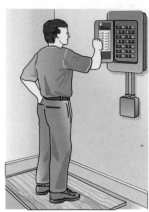

Don't be shocked. When opening the main service panel, stand on a dry surface, such as a rubber mat or a piece of plywood. Before touching the panel, examine it for signs of moisture, including rust; if you see any, call an electrician. Open the panel with one hand, to prevent conducting electricity through your body if you do receive a shock. Don't touch any other metal surface with your body.

Working alone? Plug a radio or vacuum cleaner into the circuit you want to shut off; when you trip the breaker in the cellar, you'll hear the silence.

Inspect a blown fuse to determine the cause of failure. If the window is cloudy or discolored, the cause probably was a short circuit. If the window is clear and the metal ribbon inside the fuse is parted cleanly, the cause was a borderline circuit overload.

Dangerous aluminum. Homes built during the late 1960s and early 1970s may contain aluminum wiring, which is a fire hazard if improperly installed or upgraded. Examine the cables entering the service panel: If they are marked "AL," they're aluminum. Call an electrician.

Stripping with heat. There is a foolproof way to remove the insulation from the end of an electrical wire without cutting or nicking the wire. Heat the insulation with a match at the point where you want it to break away. You'll then be able to pull off the softened plastic covering in a snap with a pair of pliers.

Crimp the connection. To join two wires with a crimp-on cap, twist the bare wire ends together, cap the wires, and crimp the cap with a multipurpose tool.

When stapling cable to wood framing, here's a trick to keep you from crushing the staple. Hammer lightly against the longer end of the staple to start it; then strike both ends, alternating, so the staple enters the wood evenly. Don't drive in staples so far that they crush the cable's sheathing.

Working with wire

WHAT YOU'LL NEED

Cable stripper

Wire stripper

Utility knife or scissors (optional)

Hacksaw

Tin snips (optional)

Multipurpose tool

Wire connectors

Long-nose pliers

Screwdriver

1 To strip nonmetallic-sheathed, or Romex, cable, slide a cable stripper onto the cable and squeeze the jaws closed so that the tooth pierces the sheathing 8–10 in. from the cable end. Slit the sheathing lengthwise, and trim off loose sheathing and paper wrapping with a wire stripper, a utility knife, or scissors.

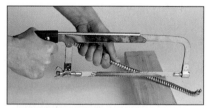

2 To strip steel-armored, or BX, cable, cut through the width of one coil with a hacksaw, 6–8 in. from the end, being careful not to cut through the insulated wires inside. Flex the cable several times to complete the break (or use tin snips, if necessary), and pull off the sheathing. Then, using a wire stripper, strip the paper off the inside wires as needed.

Use a metal tape rule to run wire short distances behind walls. Tape rules remain rigid for up to 5 feet when extended, and the hole in the end hook makes it easy to attach a wire.

What color is your wire? Wires sheathed with black or red insulation are live (hot); wires sheathed with white insulation are neutral. (Two exceptions: In 3-way switches, the white wire in the electrical box will be a hot wire, as is a white wire marked with black paint or tape.) Green or bare copper wires are grounds.

Electrically incorrect. Extension cords are marked with their capacities in amperes and watts. If there are no marks, assume the capacity is 9 amperes or 110 watts. Add up the wattage before plugging anything in.

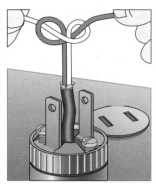

Tying the knot. When rewiring a lamp or replacing a flat-cord or round-cord plug, tie an Underwriters knot (above) to anchor the wires firmly in place.

To nail an electrical box to a stud where there's no room to swing a hammer, use a C-clamp to sink the nail. Just squeeze short nails into the holes in the sides of the box and into the stud by tightening the clamp. Better yet, use screws.

A good tape job ensures that an electrical connection will be waterproof and permanent. Use vinyl tape directly off the roll, and wrap it around the wires in tight spirals. Make sure not to touch the sticky side with your fingers. The shape of the connection should be visible through the first layer of tape.

Improve connections to audio speakers and other electronic equipment by upgrading bare-wire connections with Y-shaped spade lugs. Cut off about ¼ inch of wire to expose a fresh end. Use a wire stripper to remove about an inch of insulation; then twist the bared strands so they can't separate. Fit the lug over the bared wire end and crimp it with pliers.

Make soldering simple with a cordless butane-powered soldering pen that lets you control the heat. Rosin-core solder will protect against wire corrosion when used on electrical connections or components.

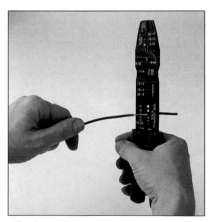

3 A multipurpose tool has several different gauges for stripping wires as well as a clamp for crimping wire connectors. To strip wire, select the proper gauge and feed in the wire. Cut the insulation by closing and rotating the tool; then squeeze the handle and pull the tool to remove the insulation.

4 When joining wires, strip ½ in. of insulation from the wire ends. For solid wires, hold the stripped wires together and twist the connector on clockwise until no bare wire is visible (top). Make sure not to overtighten. For stranded wires, first twist each wire clockwise; then twist them together clockwise before screwing on the connector clockwise (bottom).

5 To connect a wire to a screw terminal, first strip ¾ in. of insulation from the wire end. Using long-nose pliers, bend the bare wire into a loop; then hook it clockwise around the screw shaft and tighten the screw.

A permit may be required in your area for installing surface wiring. Check with your local building inspector's office before you install wiring. Inspection may also be required.

Straight and narrow.

Use a chalk line to mark long layout lines for surface-wired circuits. Measure the desired height of the raceway above the floor in two places at least a foot apart. Hold one end of the chalk line against the starting point, and have a helper stretch the line along the wall so the line touches both marks. While holding the line taut, pluck and release it gently near the middle so it snaps against the wall, leaving a line of chalk that is perfectly straight.

Circuit check. To determine if you can add more receptacles to a branch circuit in your home, figure 1½ amps per receptacle as a rule of thumb for a general-purpose circuit. This means a maximum of 13 receptacles for a 20-amp (12-gauge wire) circuit and 10 for a 15-amp (14-gauge wire) circuit. If you're unsure of the circuit's amperage, shut off the power and look for markings on exposed cable leading to the circuit.

No convenient outlet

for surface wiring? If you're installing it on the ground floor, head to the basement. You can run a new cable and circuit beneath the floor from the main service panel to the point where you wish to connect the wiring. Use a special starter box containing a clamp to secure the cable.

A good gauge. When installing a surface-wired circuit, always use the same gauge wire as the wires of the household circuit to which it is connected. Although markings on the wire and cable are often visible, you can double-check a wire's gauge size with a simple multipurpose tool: gently close the jaws around the wire and note the smallest hole through which the wire can pass.

Don't overload outlet boxes or raceways. Local building codes specify proper box and raceway sizes for all combinations of wires, wire connectors, and switches and receptacles. If in doubt, use extra-deep boxes and limit raceway wires to three. Call your local building inspector to find out about the requirements in your area.

The right height. Install receptacles and switches at consistent heights for convenience and to meet code specifications. The normal height for wall switches is 48 inches from the floor (36 inches in a child's room); the normal height for receptacles is 12 to 15 inches from the floor (24 inches is a convenient height for elderly persons as well as wheelchair occupants).

Installing surface wiring

WHAT YOU'LL NEED

Fixtures (receptacles, switches)

Measuring and marking tools (chalk line, level, combination square, pencil)

Surface wiring kit (two-piece channel raceways, connectors, covers, mounting hardware, fixture boxes, instructions)

Inductive voltage detector

Fine-tooth hacksaw

Electric drill and bits

Screws or hollow-wall anchors

Standard and Phillips screwdrivers

Approved electrical wire

Wire-stripping pliers

Long-nose pliers

Twist-on connectors

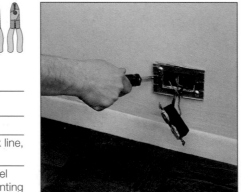

1 Choose a grounded receptacle to supply power to the surface wiring. Mark the location of the raceways and fixtures on the wall with chalk or pencil. Shut off the power to the receptacle, and use an inductive voltage detector to make sure the power is off (see p. 183). Remove the receptacle's cover plate, pull the receptacle from the outlet box, and attach the baseplate from the surface wiring kit to the box.

2 With a hacksaw, cut the raceway sections to the desired lengths. Using at least one backstrap per 5 ft. of raceway, screw the backstraps to the wall. If possible, screw into studs; otherwise, use hollow-wall anchors. Snap a section of raceway into place; attach the switchplate to the wall.

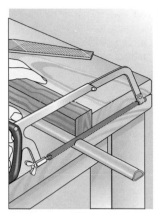

Choice cut. When cutting metallic raceway, use a fine-tooth hacksaw and remove burrs with a file. A support block screwed to the work surface will secure the raceway while you're cutting.

Choose one-piece metal raceway instead of plastic for durability and added protection in heavily used areas like workshops. It is comparably priced.

Corner work. Push wires through one-piece raceway by starting at a corner. This allows you to thread the wires in two directions without forcing the wires around corners.

In older homes, hide surface wiring by attaching raceways to the top of baseboard molding and painting the raceway the same color.

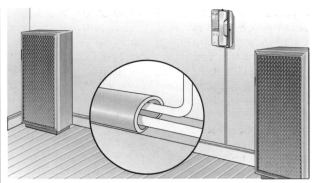

Conceal unsightly speaker wires, telephone extension lines, television cables, and other low-voltage wiring by covering them with decorative half-round raceway. Adhesive strips attached to the edges simplify installation; low-voltage raceway comes in brass and other finishes.

More juice. Add outlets for small kitchen appliances by attaching surface-wired receptacle strips to the undersides of the kitchen cabinets. The strips are out of sight for a neat appearance, and shorter appliance cords are safer and more convenient.

Use surface wiring as a design element if hiding it is too difficult. Select colored raceway to harmonize or contrast with paint or wallpaper, and install it like molding to divide large wall areas or to set off wallpaper from painted surfaces.

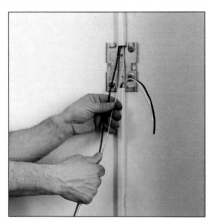

3 Thread enough new electrical wire into the raceway to reach from the receptacle to the switch plate, leaving a 6-in. tail at either end. Use black-insulated wires for hot connections, white for neutral connections, and green for grounding wires. Continue installing backstraps, raceway, and fixtures according to your plan.

4 Run electrical wires through each additional segment (see "Corner Work," above). For corner plates, push the wires against the baseplate and press the cover into position. Connect the wires to the fixtures, but not to the original receptacle.

5 To install a light fixture, connect the wires as in any ceiling box (see p. 190). Snap the fixture box against the baseplate. Finally, connect the wires to the original receptacle. Restore the power and test the fixtures. If the fixtures work, shut off the power again and attach the outlet cover plate. Restore the power.

On track. Install track fixtures close to the walls they're meant to light—2 to 4 feet away usually works well.

Don't stress the system. If you're using an existing outlet for a power source for track lighting, make sure it won't be overloaded when tying into it: Check all the lights or outlets that go dead when you shut off the circuit at the fuse or circuit breaker box. If there are major appliances or heavy-use outlets on this circuit, try another.

Vary lighting patterns by installing multicircuit tracks, which allow you to operate two or more groups of fixtures independently. Also choose between spot and flood beams, and spread them out for maximum effectiveness.

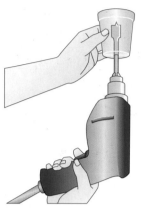

Knowing the drill. When drilling overhead to install the tracks, position a paper or Styrofoam cup on the drill bit to keep shavings from falling into your eyes. Wear safety glasses just in case.

Eliminate glare by illuminating objects indirectly. Light reflects off an object at the same angle the light rays strike it, so make sure reflected light does not shine upward at eye level.

Let there be light. If the beams of light cast by track lighting don't overlap, the track fixtures aren't spaced closely enough. Install additional fixtures.

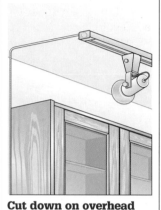

Cut down on overhead wiring chores with plug-in track lighting. Position the track so the end containing the cord is near a wall with an outlet. Hide the cord behind molding, furniture, or decorative raceway.

Install a dimmer switch to control track lighting intensity and to conserve energy when maximum illumination is not needed. If you plan to mix halogen lights and ordinary incandescent lights in the same system, first check with an electrical salesperson for compatibility. Don't use a dimmer with low-voltage track lights.

Enlarge a room and also increase illumination by washing the walls with light. The effect seems to push the walls outward, and the light is reflected toward the center of the room.

Mood lighting. Install colored filters over lighting fixtures to create the right mood. Use filters intended only for the purpose, and install them properly so the fixtures will not overheat.

Installing track lighting

WHAT YOU'LL NEED

Inductive voltage detector

Track lighting kit (track adapter, mounting plate, fixture cover, lighting tracks, track connectors, lights, bulbs)

Twist-on connectors

Wire-stripping pliers

Long-nose pliers

Measuring and marking tools (tape measure, straightedge, pencil)

Electric drill and bits

Screws or hollow-wall anchors

Standard and Phillips screwdrivers

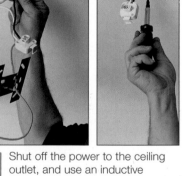

1 Shut off the power to the ceiling outlet, and use an inductive voltage detector to make sure the power is off (see p. 183). Using twist-on connectors, join the wires of the track adapter to the existing wires, connecting like-colored wires. Tuck the joined wires into the ceiling box, and attach the track's mounting plate to cover them.

2 Temporarily attach the first lighting track to the mounting plate with screws. Use a straightedge to make sure the track is parallel to the wall. Holding the track in place, pencil marks on the ceiling through the screw holes in the lighting track.

Damaged ceilings? Hide the imperfections by aiming track lighting fixtures downward toward the walls or by installing pendant fixtures instead of spotlights. Downlighting places the ceiling in shadow, discouraging occupants from looking up.

Cathedral ceilings? Show them off with track lights attached to the sloping surfaces or to beams spanning the open space between the walls. Aim the track lights upward to bathe the ceiling; the reflected light will add ambient illumination to the whole room.

In recess. If you opt for recessed lighting, try versatile eyeball fixtures, which rotate to a 45° angle and can be cleaned more easily than lights in cans.

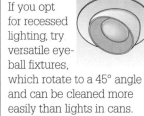

Get a grip on track or recessed bulbs with a duct tape "handle." Wrap your thumb and first two fingers in tape, sticky side out; then grip the bulb and turn it counterclockwise.

SAFE AND SMART

➤ Use the right bulbs in track lighting fixtures. A higher-wattage bulb may overheat, creating a fire hazard. Bulb ratings are usually printed inside the fixture or on the back of the bulb.

➤ Remove the lighting fixture from the track when replacing or cleaning a bulb. It makes the job easier and minimizes the chance of falling.

Neighborhood museum. Create an art gallery in your home with mini track lights, called framing projectors. Hang paintings, photos, or family treasures along one wall of a hallway, and install a lighting track so the projectors can be angled downward at a 30° angle.

Widen a narrow room by running track lighting across the shorter sides; lights placed along the longer walls will draw attention to the room's narrow dimension.

3 Remove the track, drill the screw holes, and then fasten the track to the ceiling with either screws or hollow-wall anchors.

! **When used with a power driver, "Zip-It"-type hollow-wall anchors drill their own hole and then seat themselves.**

4 Attach the track connectors and additional track sections, if desired. Insert the track adapter into the track, and rotate it to lock it. Attach the cover over the connector and ceiling box.

5 Attach the lights by inserting and rotating them in the track. Install the bulbs, and restore the power. Turn on the lights to check them.

Don't skimp. A good general rule is to provide at least 1 watt of incandescent light for each square foot in a living room or bedroom, and twice that amount for a kitchen or workshop. With fluorescent lights, figure about ⅓ watt per square foot in living rooms; ½ watt per square foot in kitchens.

Fixture won't operate? First check the circuit breaker or fuse protecting it before replacing the bulb. Not only is a blown fuse or tripped breaker often the cause of the problem, but a bulb that blows often trips the fuse or breaker during the process.

Broken bulb stuck? Shut off the power, place needle-nose pliers into the socket, open the handles to expand the jaws, and twist left to loosen the bulb.

Broken bulb II. Shut off the power, force a wad of newspaper into the broken socket, and twist counter-clockwise. Wear thick work gloves and safety goggles, especially when the fixture is overhead.

Check for overheating in the socket or the wiring when servicing ceiling fixtures, and replace if necessary. Never install bulbs that have more wattage than the rating printed on the fixture.

Replace taped splices, often found on older ceiling fixtures, with wire connectors. Shut off the power, snip off the taped splice, bare the fresh wire ends with wire-stripping pliers, and join the wires with an appropriate-size connector.

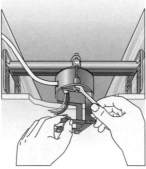

A fan's notes. When replacing a ceiling light with a fan, upgrade the junction box with one that is UL-listed for fans. Also install an adjustable hanger (rated for fan use) between the joists.

Many old ceiling fixtures were never grounded properly. Correct the omission by installing a new mounting strap and securing the ground wire to the green screw. Or attach the ground to one of the mounting screws (use a washer also) of the old strap.

Use long-life bulbs in hard-to-reach fixtures. Long-life bulbs produce slightly less light than ordinary bulbs of the same wattage, but they last up to 4 times as long.

Replacing a ceiling light

WHAT YOU'LL NEED

Screwdriver and screws

Inductive voltage detector

Metal mounting strap

Ceiling fixture

Wire connectors

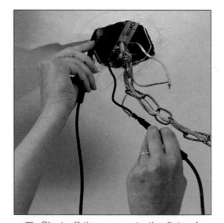

1 Shut off the power to the fixture's circuit. Remove the screws that hold the fixture to the ceiling. Use an inductive voltage detector to make sure the power is off (see p. 183). Disconnect the fixture wires and remove the old fixture and mounting strap.

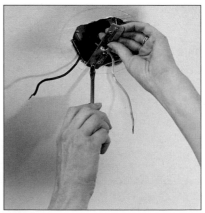

2 Attach the new metal mounting strap across the outlet box with the screws provided. If there is a ground wire in the box, attach it to the grounding screw on the strap.

With pull-chain fixtures, wrap metallic duct tape around the part of the string that touches the bulb to prevent it from burning.

Short-lived bulbs, especially near entry doors, may be victims of excessive vibration from slamming doors, which can break the bulb's delicate filaments. Install, instead, so-called "rough-service" bulbs, available from most electrical supply stores.

The right choice. Choose recessed fixtures carefully, to avoid creating a fire hazard. Unless the fixtures are marked IC (for "insulated ceiling"), they must be installed with at least 3 inches of clear space on all sides and on top to prevent heat buildup. Fixtures marked IC may come in direct contact with insulating materials.

No ceiling outlet? You can substitute a hanging swag light for a permanent ceiling fixture. Hang the light from a sturdy hook installed in a ceiling joist, and plug the light into a nearby wall outlet. When suspending a swag light over a dining table, make sure it's about 30 inches above the table to prevent glare.

Deeply recessed lights can reduce glare from overhead fixtures in rooms with low ceilings. Black interior finishes, baffles, louvers, and special nonreflecting lenses for recessed lights are also helpful features.

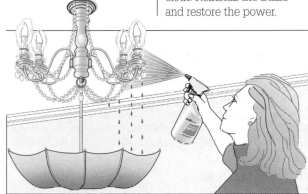

Flickering bulbs may simply need a quick cleaning. Shut off the power, remove each bulb, and sand its tip with fine sandpaper or steel wool until it shines. Blow away the sanding dust and wipe all surfaces with a soft cloth. Reinstall the bulbs and restore the power.

Clean a crystal chandelier without taking it apart by using a few spritzes of cleaning solution and an umbrella. Mix 2 teaspoons of rubbing alcohol in a pint of warm water. Hang an opened umbrella upside down, attaching the handle to the bottom of the chandelier. Cover the bulbs and sockets with sandwich bags secured with twist ties. Spray on the cleaner and catch the dirty drips with the umbrella.

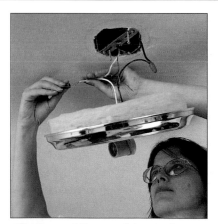

3 Connect the new fixture to the wires by wrapping the ends of the wires clockwise beneath the terminal screws (black wire to brass-colored screw, white wire to silver-colored screw), or by joining them to the leads of the new fixture with wire connectors.

 Enlist a helper to hold the fixture near the box while you connect the wires.

4 Fold the wires into the outlet box, and fasten the new fixture to the mounting strap with the screws.

5 Install the bulb and attach the globe; then restore the power, and test the light by operating it.

Wait it out. Don't rush to replace a bulb if a fluorescent light suddenly stops operating. Fluorescent tubes last longer than ordinary incandescent bulbs and often aren't the problem. Check "Troubleshooting Fluorescent Lights," facing page, for fluorescent fixes.

The inner tube. Remove a double-pin fluorescent tube by rotating it a quarter turn so the pins are lined up with the slots in the bulb holders; then gently pull the tube free. To remove a single-pin tube, press it toward the spring-loaded holder and pull the opposite end free.

Obtain natural lighting with fluorescents by choosing bulbs according to color temperature, measured in degrees Kelvin (K). High-temperature bulbs (4000K and above) contain a large proportion of blue light, which is harsh and cool. Lower-temperature bulbs contain more red light and are considered soft or warm. A 3500K bulb will provide the most accurate color.

If you need more color in a room, use a rare-earth phosphor bulb. It tends to make spaces look more colorful because the phosphors compress all colors into the blue, green, and red-orange bands of the light spectrum, increasing color contrast.

Winterize it. Most fluorescent lights are not designed to work in temperatures below 50°F. If you need a fluorescent fixture in an unheated room or garage, buy one that is rated for use in low temperatures, or replace the ballast with a low-temperature model.

Light up a workshop, and other areas where fluorescent bulbs are vulnerable to breakage, with shatterproof tubes coated with plastic. The coating keeps glass fragments inside if the tube is broken. Protective sleeves can also be installed over individual tubes.

If a tube breaks, clean it up carefully without touching any of the debris with bare hands. The mercury inside fluorescent tubes is poisonous, and the glass can cause cuts and splinters.

FILE IT

Fluorescent facts
Here are the three most common kinds of fluorescent fixtures and the types of tubes that go with them.

Rapid-start fluorescent
Two pins at each end

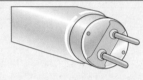

Preheat fluorescent
Two pins at each end; separate starter

Instant-start fluorescent
Single pin at each end

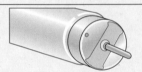

Replacing a fluorescent light fixture

WHAT YOU'LL NEED

Inductive voltage detector

Fluorescent fixture (including inner cover, lamp, and diffuser)

Nonmetallic sheathed cable

Wire-stripping tool and twist-on connectors

Level and pencil

Drill with bits and anchors (for mounting onto wallboard)

Screwdriver and screws

Cable clamp and locknut

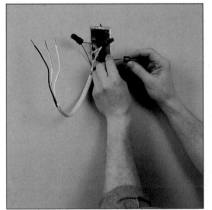

1 Shut off the power to the fixture's circuit. Remove the old diffuser, lamp, and inner cover. Use an inductive voltage detector to make sure the power is off (see p. 183). Remove the fixture (this may involve unscrewing wire connectors and removing a cable clamp). Attach a pigtail to the corresponding circuit wires with connectors (see "In Praise of Pigtails," p. 201).

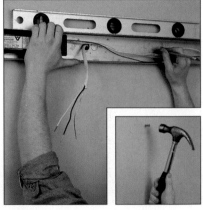

2 Punch out a knockout from the back of the new fixture for the circuit wires, and several small knockouts for screws. Hold the fixture against the wall, check for level, and mark the screw locations on the wall. If mounting onto wallboard, predrill the holes and install anchors.

FILE IT

Troubleshooting fluorescent lights

Problem	Cause	Cure
Light blinks on and off	Tube is wearing out	Shut off power; rotate tube to clean terminals; check for loose wires. It this doesn't work, replace tube.
Tube hard to start	Defective starter in older fixture; faulty ballast in rapid- or instant-start fixture	Replace starter with one of equal rating (twist starter to remove it); replace ballast with duplicate. To remove ballast, shut off power, disconnect wires, and remove mounting screw.
Light flickers or swirls	New tube or cold temperature	Leave new tube lighted for several hours to stabilize it. Install low-temperature ballast in cold areas.
Blackened tube ends	Tube is wearing out	Replace tube.
Fixture hums or vibrates	Loose parts or mounting screws; ballast short-circuiting	Tighten all screws. Replace faulty ballast.

Light longevity. Turning fluorescent lights on and off frequently wastes power and shortens bulb life. When leaving a room for less than half an hour, leave fluorescent fixtures on.

Avoid false economy when repairing a fluorescent fixture with a faulty ballast. It may be cheaper to replace the entire fixture, especially if it is an older model equipped with a starter, than to replace just the ballast.

Replacing a ballast? Choose an electronic model over an electromagnetic type. It is more efficient and will result in both brighter lighting and less flicker.

Create indirect lighting and hide fluorescent tubes from view by installing them behind coves, cornices, or wall brackets. Coves direct light upward onto the ceiling; cornices direct light downward (below). Wall brackets aim light in both directions. You can construct all three using plywood, wide molding, or wallboard supported by 1 x 3 furring strips.

3 Insert a cable clamp in the large knockout, and thread the circuit wires through it. Mount the fixture to the wall with screws. Twist the locknut onto the cable clamp.

! **Make sure the fixture is secure: a loose fixture may vibrate during operation and may eventually fall.**

4 Connect the wires, black to black and white to white, with twist-on connectors. Fold them into the fixture, keeping the black and white wires separate. If the fixture has a ground pigtail, connect it to the ground wire with a connector. Otherwise, connect the ground wire to the green screw or the screw marked GRD, using a pigtail if needed to reach the screw.

5 After joining the wires, tug them gently to make sure the connections are tight. Attach the inner cover, lamp, and diffuser. Restore the power, and operate the fixture to test it. Flickering can be expected in new fluorescent bulbs; blinking indicates a loose wiring connection or a loose lamp.

The right slot. Receptacles are usually identified by their slot pattern. Two-slot receptacles, found in older houses, are ungrounded; three-slot models (two slots and the U-shaped ground) incorporate a grounding slot that connects them to a continuous grounding system in the household wiring; T-slot receptacles have a 20-amp capacity for use in appliance circuits.

Reduce shock hazard from faulty receptacles by replacing metal faceplates with plastic ones. Plastic is nonconductive, so touching the plate won't deliver a shock if loose wiring contacts it. (If a receptacle doesn't work, shut off the power and remove the plate to inspect it.)

Cutting the cord. If a heavy-duty extension cord becomes damaged, cut out the damaged section and wire the good ends into a spare plastic receptacle box. Not only have you fixed the cord, but you've also added an extra power source.

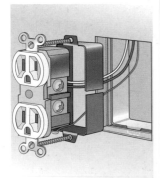

When remodeling walls, install extender rings in the outlet boxes to keep the old receptacles flush with the new wall surface.

Loose plugs are a fire hazard and usually mean the receptacle is worn out from heavy use. Replace such outlets with "specification-grade" receptacles designed for rugged service.

Don't replace a two-slot receptacle with a three-slot model unless you know the wiring system is grounded. Three-slot types in an ungrounded system don't provide adequate grounding protection and can mislead future occupants and electricians performing repairs. If you are not sure whether your system is grounded, check with an electrician.

The hot zone. If an appliance makes a crackling noise, smells hot, or emits a spark when you turn it on, don't unplug it or touch the outlet. Go to the main service box and turn off the breaker or unscrew the fuse controlling the circuit. Then, with dry hands, cover the appliance plug with a thick dry towel and pull it out. If the problem is in the switch, turn it off using a clean dry stick or wooden spoon, not your hands.

Terminal choice. The terminal screws of a switch or receptacle may provide a better connection than the push-in slots at the back.

Replacing a receptacle

WHAT YOU'LL NEED

Inductive voltage detector

Screwdriver

Long-nose pliers

Receptacle (with same slot pattern as original receptacle)

1 Shut off power to the receptacle's circuit, and double-check with an inductive voltage detector (p. 183). Remove the cover-plate screw and the plate; then loosen the receptacle's mounting screws, and pull the receptacle from the outlet box.

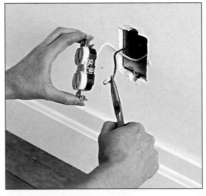

2 Connect wires to new receptacle following same configuration as old wiring. With pliers, bend wires in advance; wrap wires clockwise around contact screws. Connect white wires to silver contacts, black to brass contacts, bare or green to green screw.

3 Insert the receptacle into the outlet box, folding the wires carefully, and tighten the mounting screws. Reinstall the cover plate, restore the power, and test the receptacle with a voltage tester.

Light longevity. Extend bulb life with a dimmer. Incandescent bulbs will last longer if they're operated at the below-normal voltages that dimmer switches supply. Dimmers also "start" bulbs more gently, reducing the blowouts that can occur when turning on a standard light switch.

Current concerns. Dimmer switches are sold in different wattages. To calculate what you'll need, just add up the bulb wattage of the lamps you want to dim—100 watts for the table lamp, 200 for the wall sconces. In general, knob-controlled dimmers handle 600 watts; toggle dimmers, 300 watts. Don't overload the dimmer beyond these limits.

Digital dimming. Don't want to dim every light uniformly? New wireless or computer-controlled dimming systems can turn the lights down 50 percent in most of the room, 80 percent near the TV, and keep them on high in a reading corner. Some systems can control the lighting in the whole house by remote.

Brilliant idea. Halogen bulbs hooked up to a dimmer switch tend to darken over time. To keep halogens burning brightly, turn up the bulbs to full capacity at least 20 percent of the time.

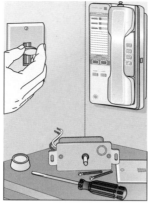

Static on the line? Older dimmer switches may interfere with nearby AM radios, audio equipment, and cordless telephones. Static or humming usually results. To cure the problem, replace old dimmer switches with new ones having either an RF or an RFI filter.

Using light colors for rugs walls, draperies, and upholstery will save on energy costs. The lighter the color of the decor, the more light is reflected—and the less light you need to provide.

SAFE AND SMART

➤ Standard fluorescent lights can't be hooked up to a dimmer. You have to buy a fixture with a special ballast to mute them.

➤ Because halogens burn much hotter than incandescent bulbs, buy bulbs that are 300 watts or less.

➤ Position halogen lights away from windows, where a strong wind could knock over the light or curtains could accidentally drape over a white-hot bulb.

Installing a dimmer switch

WHAT YOU'LL NEED

Screwdriver

Inductive voltage detector

Long-nose pliers and wire-stripping pliers (optional)

Wire connectors

Dimmer switch (single-pole type if original switch has two terminal screws; three-way type if original switch has three terminal screws)

1 Shut off the power to the switch, remove the cover plate and the switch, and then use an inductive voltage detector to make sure the wires aren't hot (p. 183). *183* If a second switch occupies the same box, you may have to loosen it.

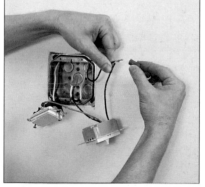

2 Remove all the wires and straighten the wire ends with pliers, or strip the insulation to create 1/2-in. wire ends. Join the dimmer-switch wires to the circuit wires with wire connectors, and attach the ground wire.

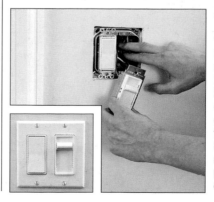

3 Insert switch, folding wires carefully into box, and tighten mounting screws. Be sure top and bottom are aligned correctly. Reinstall cover plate, and then press switch knob onto shaft, if necessary. Restore power, and test dimmer switch.

Keep the tags. Try the lamp at home first before making it a keeper. A "pharmacy" lamp, whose bulb hangs below the shade, may glare uncomfortably when you are sitting on the sofa. If a lamp is too low, the top of the room will remain dark, and if the shade is narrow, you may not get enough light for your needs.

The right height. Table lamps should be placed so the bottom of the shade is just below eye level.

If a bulb flickers but works fine in another lamp, try cleaning the socket. Unplug the lamp, wipe the socket interior with fine sandpaper or scrape it with a screwdriver tip until it shines, and then bend up the metal tab at the bottom to improve contact with the bulb.

Touch halogen bulbs only by their base. They become extremely hot during use, and oil deposited on cool bulbs from your fingers can weaken the glass and cause it to break.

Let there be more light. Go for bulbs with higher lumens numbers. Manufacturers are often optimistic about the lumens and wattage ratings they print on the packages. The real numbers can be 5 to 30 percent lower. Factor that into your lighting layout.

Clean light. Dust lamps, lighting fixtures, and bulbs frequently. Dirt and grime can impede up to 50 percent of the illumination coming from a bulb.

If a compact fluorescent bulb doesn't fit your standard table lamp—they are often shaped differently than incandescent types—buy a harp extender or a larger harp (the metal frame that flanks the bulb) to accommodate it.

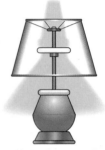

More light for your lamp. A ring-shaped fluorescent bulb allows more light to pass through a lampshade, which can otherwise absorb around 80 percent of the light generated by a conventional incandescent or compact fluorescent bulb.

Rewiring a table lamp

WHAT YOU'LL NEED

Screwdriver

Utility knife

Long-nose pliers

Wire-stripping pliers

Electrician's tape

New lamp cord with plug

New lamp socket (optional)

1 Unplug the lamp, and remove the shade, bulb, and harp. Remove the shell and insulating sleeve from the socket by depressing the sides marked *Press* and pulling upward. Tighten any loose wire connections on the socket terminals, reassemble the lamp, and test it to make sure it's the cord that's faulty.

2 Free the socket by loosening the terminal screws. Cut off the Underwriters knot or remove the strain relief; then remove the harp holder and any other hardware. Remove the felt covering from the lamp base and cut off the plug from the end of the old cord.

Don't spend extra for a new shell, insulating shield, and base when replacing a lamp socket. Unless these parts are damaged, buy only the socket portion containing the switch and threaded bulb holder. Polish and reuse the other parts.

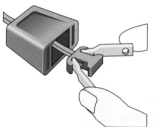

Cut down on cord.
Shorten a meandering lamp cord by cutting it and pushing the cut portion into a replacement flat-wire plug. Tiny internal prongs within the plug penetrate the insulation and complete the circuit. Be certain that the cord is inserted fully.

Avoid entanglements.
Tape long lamp cords to the baseboard with duct tape, or snap decorative plastic raceway over them.

Add versatility to a table lamp by replacing its single-switch socket with a three-way one. There's no trick to it, the wiring connections are the same for both types (see "Rewiring a table lamp," below). Three-way bulbs provide economical ambient lighting at low wattage levels.

Replace a faulty switch in a lamp base by unscrewing the retaining ring on top, removing the cover from the base, and pulling the switch out from below. Sketch the wiring pattern before disconnecting the wires, and install a new switch following the sketch. Test the lamp before replacing the base cover.

Rub a true parchment shade with either castor or neat's-foot oil once a year to keep it from drying out.

Hands off. Oils from fingers can discolor shades made of translucent material. Rub spots from paper shades with a clean art-gum eraser, or use wallpaper-cleaning dough. Take cotton, linen, or silk shades to a dry cleaner.

A scorched lampshade is a telltale sign that the bulb is too powerful and could be a potential fire hazard. Always switch to a lower-wattage bulb rather than a larger shade.

3 Splice the new cord onto the old cord and wrap with tape. Thread the new cord through the lamp by pulling upward on the old cord while pushing on the new cord. Cut the new cord just below the tape and remove the old cord.

4 Split the top 3 in. of the new cord, and strip ¾ in. of insulation from the wire ends. Replace the harp holder and socket cap, and tie an Underwriters knot.

5 Fasten the wire ends to the socket. The wire with ribbed insulation or silver wire is neutral and should be connected to the silver screw. Reinstall the socket shell and insulating sleeve by snapping them back into the socket base. Install the strain relief where the cord passes through the base; then glue the felt back.

Working the phone.
The small voltages that run through phone lines won't shock most people, but they can upset a pacemaker's operation. Before doing any phone work, remove the handsets from all the extension phones to prevent them from ringing, which can deliver enough voltage to give anyone a shock.

New phone, old jack?
Install a modular jack converter, available at telephone or electronics supply stores. Remove the cover from the old jack and carefully snip off the wires leading to the old telephone, making sure you don't cut incoming phone-service wires. Press the color-coded caps of the converter onto the appropriate screw terminals of the old jack's baseplate. Attach the jack converter's cover; then plug in the new phone.

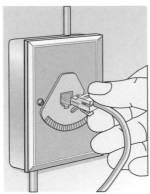

Got a problem? To determine whether a phone problem is your responsibility or the phone company's, plug a working telephone into the jack on the network interface—the junction box where the phone company wires enter the house. If the phone works there but not at the inside jacks, the problem is in the house wiring and is your responsibility. If the phone doesn't work at the interface, ask the telephone company to fix it.

Hearing voices? If you hear voices on the line during a phone call, it could mean that the wires of your phone cable are touching other cable wires somewhere in the system. Notify the telephone company; this is not a problem you can fix.

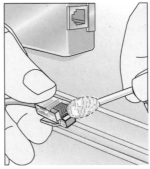

Clean modular plugs
if static or intermittent connections plague phone conversations. Simply wipe the plugs with a foam swab dipped in denatured alcohol. Cotton swabs can clog the plug's connection slots.

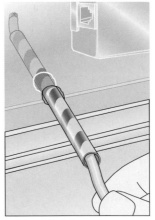

Use a drinking straw
to feed phone wire through a wall horizontally. Select a straw through which the telephone wire slides easily. Drill a hole through the wall, slightly larger in diameter than the straw; then insert the straw in the hole and thread the wire through it. Remove the straw before installing the plug on the wire.

Adding a phone extension

WHAT YOU'LL NEED

Modular telephone jack base, cover, and mounting screws
Long-nose pliers
Wire-cutting pliers
Wire-stripping tool
Standard and Phillips screwdrivers
Pencil
Electric drill and bits
Staples and staple gun or hammer
Telephone and cord
Telephone extension cord (if needed)
Telephone junction box base, cover, and mounting screws (if needed)
Telephone cable (if needed)

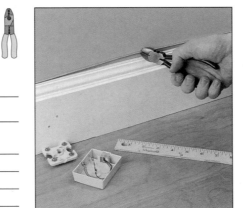

1 Find exposed telephone cable near the desired location of the new phone. Free up about 1 ft. of cable by removing staples and rerouting. Don't tug on the cable; the thin wires inside break easily. Now cut the cable. If you can't free up 1 ft. of cable, or if the new phone will be more than 25 ft. from the exposed cable, see step 4. Twist knock-outs from the jack base as needed, using long-nose pliers.

2 Strip 4 in. of sheathing from both the incoming and the outgoing telephone cable, and ½ in. of insulation from all wire ends. Holding the wires together, wrap them once around the back of the jack base as a strain relief. Then attach each pair of same-color wire ends and the corresponding wire from the jack cover to their color-coded terminal on the jack base. Tighten the terminal screws.

To feed telephone wire

vertically, drill entry and exit holes for the wire directly in line with each other. Splice the wire securely to a length of strong string, and tie a washer or nut to the string's other end. Then drop the string through the upper hole and fish it through the lower hole by snaring it with a bent wire. Pull the string through the holes, drawing the telephone wire with it.

Phone plug broken?

Simply buy a new plug and a multipurpose tool at a telephone or electronics supply store. Cut off the old plug about an inch from the end of the cord, and strip ½ inch of insulation from each wire, using the tool. Place the new plug in the tool, lay the wires on top, and then squeeze the tool's handles to join the plug to the cord.

Not hearing bells? If your phone has a dial tone but doesn't ring, or if you find that messages were left on your answering machine when you were at home, check the phone's volume control; it may have been turned down by accident.

Sticky telephone keys?

Remove the phone housing, blow away accumulated dust between the keys with a can of compressed air, and then mop up any remaining gunk with a foam swab dipped in denatured alcohol.

Getting a charge. If the battery on a cordless phone doesn't hold a charge, leave the phone turned on until the battery runs down completely, and then recharge the battery fully. Repeating the procedure at least three times should solve the problem.

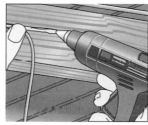

If you're all thumbs when it comes to hammering in staples, here are two options for securing telephone cable that will be hidden from view. Apply a track of hot glue to the wall or joist, and then quickly press the cable into the glue. Or use cable clips with adhesive backing.

Fax and modem notes. If you're operating either of these devices on a single-line telephone, disable call-waiting and other features beforehand by dialing a two- or three-digit code. Call your local telephone company for the code in your area.

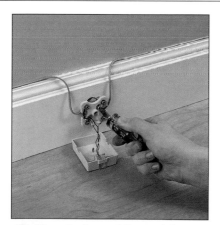

3 Place the base of the modular jack against the wall or baseboard. Mark the locations of the mounting screws; then remove the base and drill starter holes on the marks. Fasten the base to the wall, and then the cover to the base, with the mounting screws. Restaple incoming and outgoing cable to the wall. Plug the new phone cord into the jack. If an extension cord is needed, run it along the wall.

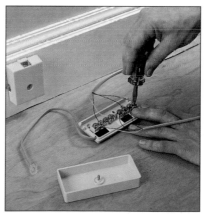

4 Install a telephone junction box in addition to the jack if you can't free up enough existing cable to attach both cut ends to a single jack, if the new phone will be more than 25 ft. from the new jack, or if you are installing more than one new phone. Follow step 2, but attach only the incoming cable to the jack, and attach the original outgoing cable and the new cable for the additional phone lines to the box.

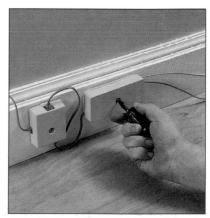

5 Mount the junction box base and cover to the wall, and plug the junction box cord into the jack. Then reattach the original outgoing cable to the wall and route the new telephone cable to the new phone locations, installing a new jack for each new phone (see step 2). An alternative: Tap off an existing jack by wiring new cable to it; then run the cable to the new phone location and install a new jack.

Why a GFCI? A GFCI receptacle protects against electrical shock—but not circuit overloads—caused by a faulty appliance, extension cord, or plug. The GFCI detects small changes in current flow and and can shut off power in 1/40 second. *Note:* The more receptacles a GFCI protects, the more susceptible it is to "phantom tripping"—shutting off power because of tiny, normal fluctuations in current flow.

FILE IT

Current events: GFCI options

The National Electrical Code requires GFCI's in all new bathrooms, kitchens, and laundries, as well as for outdoor receptacles. The safest, smartest choice is to install a GFCI at the main service panel.

A GFCI breaker will protect every receptacle on a circuit when it is substituted for a standard breaker in the main service panel. Call a professional to install it.

A GFCI receptacle can be substituted for a standard receptacle and, depending on how it's wired, can protect all downstream receptacles.

A portable GFCI will protect just one receptacle. Plug it into a three-slot receptacle that isn't outfitted with ground-fault protection.

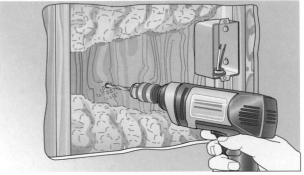

Scouting the outlet. In order to determine a safe location for a new outdoor outlet, you may have to make an opening in the wall. First shut off the power (see "Safe and Smart," p. 183), and remove the indoor receptacle you plan to tap off (p. 194). Then remove a section of wallboard that's larger than the hole for the outlet and that spans the studs on either side of the hole (p. 84). Choose a spot that's at least 6 inches from the indoor receptacle and that's free of wiring and other obstacles; drill a hole to the outside.

Weathertight wiring. When installing a recessed outlet in wood siding, always caulk between the gasket and the siding to seal out the elements.

Get permission. Always obtain a permit to install an outdoor outlet. Check with your inspector on any special restrictions or requirements in your area.

Installing a GFCI outdoor outlet

WHAT YOU'LL NEED

Inductive voltage detector

Electric drill and bits

Approved electrical cable

Surface-mount outdoor outlet box, outlet cover, GFCI, and provided screws and clamps

Cable stripper

Utility knife

Long-nose pliers

Screwdriver

Conduit (if needed)

Wrench (if needed)

Twist-on connectors

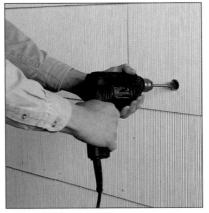

1 Choose an existing outlet with adequate amperage on the inside of an exterior wall. Turn off the power to the circuit at the main service panel, and make sure the power is off with an inductive voltage detector (see p. 183). Now determine the exact spot for the outdoor outlet (see "Scouting the Outlet," above, and "Inside, Outside," next page). Drill a pilot hole from the inside of the house, and then complete the hole from the outside.

2 Cut a piece of electrical cable that's 18 in. longer than the distance between the indoor receptacle and the hole for the outdoor outlet. Fasten the cable to the inside of the outdoor outlet box with an internal cable clamp, allowing about 9 in. of cable to emerge from the box. Strip 8 in. of sheathing from the cable and 1/2 in. from the wire ends. Mount the box to the wall.

Planning for the future.
Position outdoor fixtures and receptacles so that they are easily accessible when maintenance is required and close to the appliances they will be powering.

Make a sketch of the wiring before you disconnect any wires, and you'll have an easier time reconnecting them.

Circuit correction. Make sure you aren't overloading the circuit from which you intend to branch out. Here's how to figure it out. No more than 10 outlets and lights should be powered from one 15-amp circuit (13 from a 20-amp). A 15-amp circuit can support 1,800 watts; so estimate the load already on the circuit, then determine whether it can handle the extra load.

Inside, outside. Measure the distance from the indoor outlet to a reference point, such as a windowsill, that can be seen from the outside. Then mark the location of the indoor outlet on the exterior wall to make sure you've chosen a good site.

Cushioning the cable.
When burying UF cable outdoors, lay a pressure-treated or redwood board on top of it before covering it with dirt. This will prevent anyone digging in the area from cutting through the cable.

Waterproof current.
The National Electrical Manufacturers Association now requires exterior electrical boxes to be waterproof while in use. If yours isn't, install a watertight cover to protect the receptacle from precipitation. Some covers can be retrofitted to an existing box.

Light for all seasons.
For outdoor fixtures, use weatherproof light bulbs that will resist shattering in severe weather.

Give a test. Make sure the GFCI passes muster by testing it monthly. Pressing the *Test* button should cut power to the receptacle or circuit. Pressing the *Reset* button should restore it. Replace the GFCI if it fails.

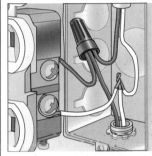

In praise of pigtails.
Lengthen too-short circuit wires with a pigtail. A pigtail connects to a fixture's screw terminal at one end and to the circuit wires, using a wire connector, at the other. Always make sure all the wires have the same electrical capacity.

3 If you will be using the outdoor receptacle to power additional outlets, thread electrical cable through metal conduit and into the outlet box. Fasten the cable to the outlet box with an internal cable clamp; strip the sheathing and wire ends. Use a compression fitting to attach the conduit to the box; fasten the nut with a wrench.

4 Attach the wires, including the ground wire, to the corresponding screws on the outdoor GFCI. If you are tapping off this outlet, as in step 3, you will need to attach both sets of wires. Then screw the receptacle into the outlet box.

5 Place gasket, if supplied, over outlet box and install outlet cover. Indoors, strip new cable sheathing and wire ends. Disconnect indoor receptacle's wires, if you haven't already. Using twist-on connectors, connect indoor and outdoor wires to pigtails (see "In Praise of Pigtails," above), and attach pigtails to indoor receptacle. Turn on power and test. If outlet works, replace wallboard (see pp. 84–85).

Call ahead. Before digging a trench for laying underground wiring, consult the front pages of your phone book under "Call Before You Dig." One call should verify the location of all current utility lines. Call your local building inspector's office, too; installing new electrical circuits indoors or out usually requires inspection.

Go short. Divide a long lighting circuit into short segments to ensure adequate power to each bulb. Voltage falls as it travels.

Location, location. Use an electronic stud sensor to pinpoint a good location for a receptacle cutout. It gauges wall density and indicates the exact location of wall studs. This allows you to cut a receptacle opening right next to a stud for maximum support.

Flattering hues. Use colored lenses on outdoor lights to achieve dramatic effects. Green lenses brighten evergreens and tropical foliage; red lenses heighten autumn colors. Use blue lenses to accent blue and green colors, and amber to enrich yellow, orange, and brown.

A clock timer can turn outdoor lights on and off at preset times; changing the time frequently will fool burglars. An override switch allows you to operate the lights independently of the timer.

Protect outdoor wiring above ground level with rigid metal or plastic conduit and waterproof fittings. Attach plastic bushings to the ends of metal conduit to prevent damaging the cable inside. For outdoor use, most electrical codes specify Type UF cable, which is buried directly in the ground.

Basement bonus. Extending power from the cellar is a quick way to create an outdoor circuit. Run cable from the service panel along an overhead joist. Drill a hole through the header joist, located above the foundation. Install a section of conduit in the hole; then thread the cable through it to the outside. Call an electrician to connect the cable at the main service panel.

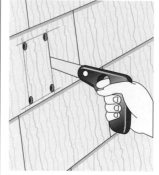

To cut a square hole for an outdoor receptacle, draw an outline of the hole on the house siding and drill holes ½ inch in diameter at each corner. Then cut along the lines between the holes with a saber or keyhole saw.

Two-slot receptacles and even three-slot models are unsafe outdoors. Replace them with GFCI types (see "Installing an Outdoor GFCI Outlet," p. 200), which protect against shocks caused by damp conditions.

Installing low-voltage lighting

WHAT YOU'LL NEED

Low-voltage lighting kit (contains light fixtures, low-voltage cable, transformer, hardware, instructions)

GFCI (if necessary)

Screwdriver

Electric drill and bits (optional)

Shovel (optional)

Mulch (optional)

1 Before installing low-voltage lights, spend time planning the layout. Also, make sure you have a ground-fault circuit interrupter (GFCI) near the intended location of the light transformer. Now place the cable over the contacts in the channel, located at the base of the fixture, and press the cable to hold it in place. Then slide the closed ground stake over the cable and lock it in place.

2 Spread the stake legs. Press the cable together at the fixture base and fold it into one leg of the ground stake. Line up the cable with the notches on both sides of the stake. Snap the legs together to close them.

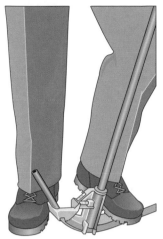

To bend metal conduit, use a conduit bender, which can be rented at most electrical supply stores. Simply insert the conduit in the tool, place it on a hard surface, then stand on the tool's footstep and pull upward on the handle. The tool's spirit levels and gauge indicate when you've achieved the desired bend.

Sidewalk strategy. Lay a cable beneath slabs without removing them by flattening the end of a length of a metal conduit with a hammer and driving it through the soil under the walk. Once it's through, saw off the ends of the conduit and install compression fittings and bushings to cover the sharp ends. Thread the cable through the conduit.

Sticking with it. Use a hot-melt glue gun when securing low-voltage wiring to walls and ceilings. Make a line of glue 1 inch long and ⅛ inch wide, press the wire into the line, and hold it there for a few seconds until the glue sets. Repeat the process every 2 feet.

Protect grass beside trenches when installing outdoor cable by spreading plastic sheeting on both sides. When digging, place sod on one side of the trench, loose dirt on the other. Or rent a trencher: You need only a one-inch slot.

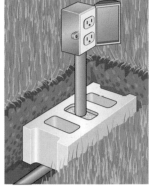

Secure a freestanding outlet by embedding it in concrete. Use a cinder block or a plastic bucket as a form, cutting a hole in the bottom of the bucket for the cable and conduit. Slip the block or bucket over the conduit, and set it in place below the frost line. Install the outlet, bracing it so it won't tip, and fill the block hole or bucket with concrete. When it has cured, cover the block with soil and plant sod if desired.

3 Dig a hole about 8 in. deep for the ground stake, so you won't break the light or the stake when installing it. Then push the ground stake and fixture into the ground and fill the hole with dirt.

4 Now cover the cable with mulch or dirt, or bury it in a shallow trench. To protect it from a lawn mower or other power tool, bury the cable in a 1-ft.-deep trench.

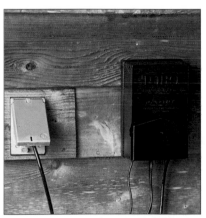

5 Mount the transformer near the GFCI outlet. (If the unit is equipped with a photoelectric eye, you will have to mount it outdoors.) If the transformer isn't prewired, connect the cable to the low-voltage terminals on the transformer. Now plug the power cord into the GFCI. Set the timer and adjust the photo-eye sensitivity.

HOME HEATING AND COOLING

Job ratings: ▌Easy ▌▌▌Medium ▌▌▌▌Complex

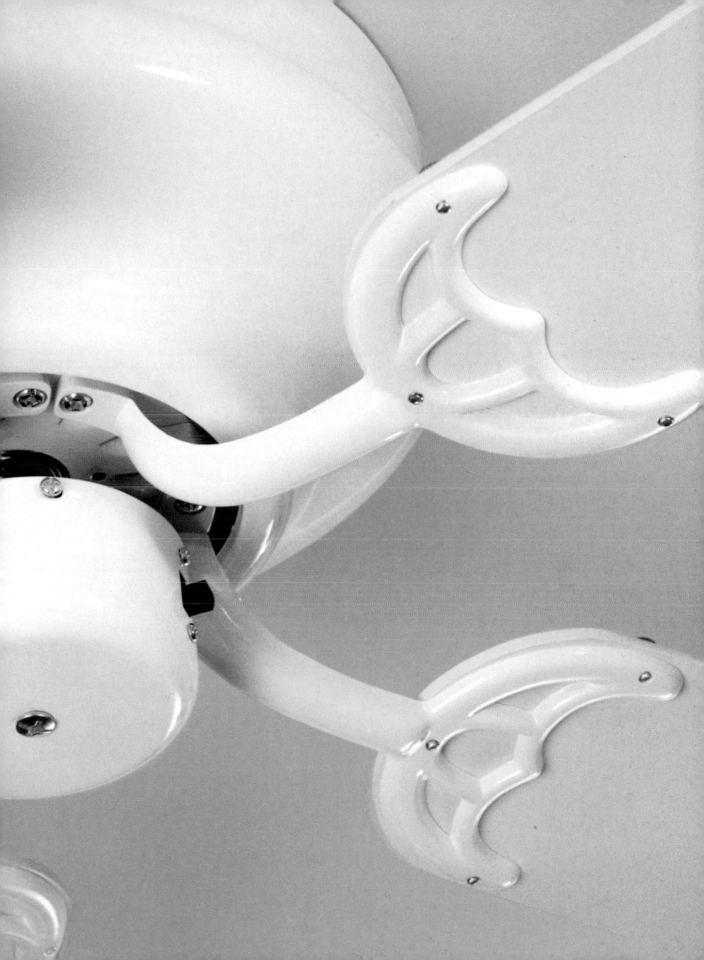

Get a good one. Choose a reliable contractor to install a central air-conditioning system; otherwise, shoddy welding or faulty seals may require costly repairs later on. Get references with the bids, and check them carefully before hiring anyone.

Bigger isn't better. Avoid buying an air conditioner with a larger capacity than the space in your home requires. It will turn on more often and run for shorter periods; those brief operating cycles cannot effectively remove the humidity from the air.

Don't fence it in. Enclosing an outside air-conditioner condenser to shade it from the sun can restrict airflow and lower the condenser's efficiency. Shade from distant trees is more desirable.

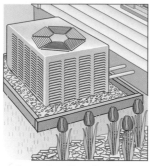

A freewheeling fan. To cut down on the dust sucked into an air conditioner's fan, cover the ground around the outside condenser unit with gravel and add a layer of mulch to nearby flower beds.

Thermostat strategy. To run an air conditioner most efficiently, set the thermostat to the highest temperature you can live with, and avoid readjusting it. When you plan to be away for more than a few hours, raise the setting to 80°.

Fan facts. In very hot weather, switch the fan to the *On* position. Continuously circulating air makes you feel cooler and prevents stratification of temperature levels. During normal temperatures, the *Auto* setting cycles the fan on only when the compressor is on.

Focus the airflow from the air ducts by installing plastic deflectors on lower wall registers. Held in place by magnets, they can be positioned to direct the cooling air upward.

Tough to change the filter on a central air conditioner because it's hard to reach? Try removing it; then filter the air at a different point in the system by replacing the grilles on return-air vents with filter grilles. They will also quiet the airflow.

Super filter. Replace a standard air-conditioner filter with an electrostatic filter. They're more expensive ($25 to $250), but they're far more effective at cleansing the air.

Improving central air-conditioning performance

WHAT YOU'LL NEED

Pruning shears (if needed)

Small adjustable wrench or sockets

Standard and Phillips screwdrivers

Oil in telescoping oil bottle or flex-spout oiler

Fin straightener tool

Coil cleaner solution

Pressure washer or garden hose

Vacuum cleaner

Replacement filters

1 Turn off the power. Cut away any shrubbery or grass growing within 2 ft. of the condenser unit to prevent blockage of airflow. The unit should be on a concrete pad that elevates it well above any potential water intrusion.

2 Remove the top cover. In some cases, the fan and motor will be attached to the cover. If the fan motor has oil ports, remove the plastic plugs, and oil with the specified lubricant. You can use SAE 20 non-detergent motor oil if the specified lubricant is unavailable.

Reduce humidity inside the house by turning the blower speed to a lower setting (check with the manufacturer first). As the air moves more slowly over the evaporator coil, more moisture will be extracted. Don't drop the blower speed too far, or the coils could ice up.

If water leaks around the evaporator or inside the blower compartment, look to see if algae may have clogged the condenser drain. Flush out the algae with water, then pour 2 tablespoons of household bleach into the line to kill any remaining spores.

Pass up home cooking. Kitchen stoves generate a lot of heat and make an air conditioner work harder. Give your system an occasional break by cooking in the microwave or outside on the grill. Take-out food is another convenient option.

During a power outage, turn the air conditioner off, and allow it to remain off for at least 6 minutes. If the unit had been running for a while before the power went out, restarting it right away would seriously damage the compressor. (The same is true if you switch off the unit accidentally.) Also, if the thermostat is electronic and has no battery backup, be sure to reprogram it before turning it on again.

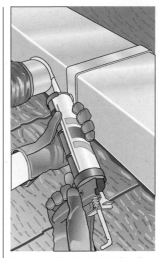

Inspect ducts periodically for escaping hot or cold air, especially around their seams. Seal small leaks with a caulking tube of special duct sealant. For larger gaps, wrap fiberglass mesh tape (the kind used for wallboard) around the crack and spread liquid duct sealant over the tape with a putty knife.

Sunblock. Covering windows inside with blinds or shades, or outside with awnings, can help to trim electric bills during the cooling season. For maximum effect, shade 70 percent of a window's height if it faces east or west. Shade 50 percent if it faces north or south.

3 If any of the fins of the condenser coil are bent, straighten them with a fin straightener tool. Next coat the fins of the condenser coil with coil cleaner solution. Use a strong spray from a pressure washer or garden hose to flush residue from the coil.

4 Turn off the power to the blower compartment. If the blower unit has a belt drive, tighten the belt so it deflects about 1/2 in. with moderate pressure between pulleys; check for tight retaining screws on direct-drive versions. Remove oil port plugs, and oil with specified lubricant or SAE 20 non-detergent motor oil. Carefully dust and vacuum the area surrounding the motor and any openings in the motor housing.

5 Finally, give the air supply system a tune-up. Filters should be cleaned or replaced regularly. Balance the airflow by adjusting manual dampers in the branch runs or at registers, closing down the airflow to rooms that are too cold and opening the flow to those that are too hot. Allow 24 hr. between adjustments before evaluating their effectiveness.

Size-wise. Buy a window air conditioner with a capacity suited to the room where it will be installed. Never get a bigger unit, hoping to cool an adjoining room, unless there is a very large opening between the two rooms. Cool air cannot turn corners without the help of a huge ventilating fan. It's better to cool any adjoining room with a small unit of its own.

Spring checkup. Every spring, inspect the seals and gaskets around a window air conditioner to see that they don't leak air. Repair those that have deteriorated.

Fall follow-up. Unplug the unit, remove the metal shroud, and clean out any leaves or debris from the condenser. Check to see that the drain pan holes and tubes are clear. Unclog them with a length of wire.

Higher is better. Most air conditioners are installed at window level or below, but the best place to install a unit is higher up, near the ceiling—where the hot air accumulates. (Through-the-wall installation is recommended near the ceiling, since a window's structure is not strong enough to hold up the weight of a unit in the top of the window.)

Too cold to function. Never run a window air conditioner when the temperature dips below 60°—it could damage the compressor.

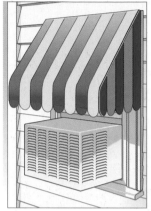

Keep it cool. Window air conditioners are less efficient when operating in direct sunlight. If possible, install a window unit in a shady wall, or put an awning over it.

Be cool when you walk through the front door by plugging your air conditioner into a heavy-duty timer set for an hour before you leave work. Note: A timer used for lamps can't handle an AC's amp load.

Fan speed. When the weather is humid, set the air conditioner fan on *Low*. You will get less of a cooldown but more moisture will be removed from the air. Otherwise, keep the fan on *High*.

Installing an air conditioner in a window

WHAT YOU'LL NEED

Air conditioner cabinet, chassis, and provided hardware

Tape measure and pencil

Spirit level

Standard and Phillips screwdrivers

Electric drill with bits and screwdriver tips

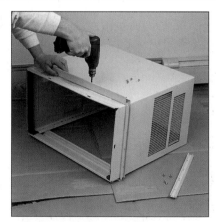

1 Remove the air conditioner from the cabinet. Attach foam gaskets to the top rail and the side retainers. Using the screws provided, attach the top rail and side retainers to the cabinet.

 Installing an air conditioner, especially a heavy one, is easier and safer when you have someone to help.

2 Slide the window filler panel into the panel retainer on the side of the cabinet, following the manufacturer's instructions. Do the same on the other side.

 When installing the cabinet in the window, make sure it is level side to side and pitched slightly (about ¼ bubble on a spirit level) to the outside.

Save on AC bills by replacing an incandescent bulb, which converts 90 percent of its energy to heat, with a fluorescent bulb where possible; you'll eliminate excess heat and save energy.

The air conditioner filter is the key to keeping an AC operating efficiently. Be sure to clean it every 30 days. First vacuum the filter, then wash it with soapy water, rinse it thoroughly, and let it dry. Spray a household disinfectant on the filter to reduce mildew and keep incoming air smelling fresh.

An extra fan placed near the AC will spread the cool air farther without a major bump in your energy bill.

Jalousie windows are seldom airtight, so they allow air-conditioned air to escape. Replace them with sash windows wherever possible, or install interior storm windows over them.

The color of your house affects how hard an air conditioner has to work. Dark colors—particularly on a roof—absorb 70 to 90 percent of the sun's radiant heat. Shield the house from the heat by installing a radiant heat barrier. Aluminum-faced foam sheeting, available at home centers, can block 95 percent of the heat absorbed by the roof. Staple it between the rafters in the attic. If the aluminum facing is on only one side, fasten it with the shiny side facing the roof.

Film it. Reflective window film allows light to enter a room while reflecting the heat from the outside. Apply the film on windows that face east and west.

Close it off. To save energy, tour the house and shut doors to areas that do not need to be cooled. Make sure the doors are weather-stripped properly.

3 Open the window and mark the center of the window stool. Place the cabinet in the window so that it is properly positioned and centered on the mark. Lower the window temporarily behind the top rail to hold the cabinet in place. Fasten the cabinet to the window stool with the provided screws. You may want to predrill the screw holes.

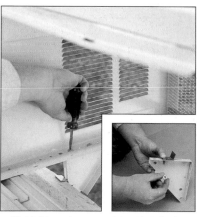

4 Hold each support bracket flush against the outside of the sill and tight to the bottom of the cabinet. Mark the brackets at the top level of the sill and remove. Attach the sill angle brackets to the support brackets at the points you have marked. Then attach the support brackets (with the sill angle brackets attached) to the appropriate hole in the bottom of the cabinet. Make sure all the bolts are attached securely.

5 Make sure the window is securely closed behind the top rail, and attach the rail to the sash with the provided screws. Trim the sash seal to the proper width and insert it into the gap between the upper and lower sashes. Secure the sashes with the provided hardware. Seal the bottom rail to prevent air from coming in. Carefully slide the air conditioner chassis into the cabinet. Install the cover and the knobs.

Hiding the hole. If the opening in your ceiling or the unpainted area under the old fixture is too wide for a ceiling fan canopy to cover, don't despair. A decorative medallion can be mounted above the canopy. But plan ahead; it must be positioned before the fan's wiring is connected.

What size fan do you need to cool a room? Install a 32-inch fan for a room up to 64 square feet in area; a 42-inch fan for a room up to 144 square feet; and a 52-inch fan for a room up to 400 square feet.

Four blades or five? It seems that five-bladed fans ought to be more efficient than four-bladed models, but the reverse is true. A four-bladed fan moves more air because of the additional space between the blades.

A material choice. Are wooden fan blades more efficient than plastic ones? Studies show that blade material does not affect performance.

A good angle. The greater the angle of a ceiling fan's blades, the more air they move. The optimum pitch is between 13° and 15°.

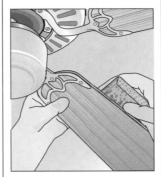

Clean the blades on your ceiling fan regularly with a dry lint-free cloth. Dirt can upset blade balance and cause the fan to wobble.

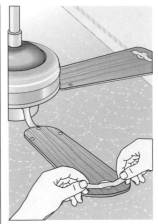

Cut the wobble. If the fan blades continue to wobble after they are cleaned, rebalance them by attaching small weights, such as washers or pennies, to the top of the blades with masking tape. Test one blade after another, repositioning the weights until the blades cease to wobble; then glue the weights in place.

Installing a ceiling fan

WHAT YOU'LL NEED

Ladder

Inductive voltage detector

Wire-cutting pliers

Standard and Phillips screwdrivers

Fan installation kit (including washers, nuts, and screws)

Replacement electrical box and hanger (if needed)

Twist-on connectors

Fan light kit (optional)

1 Turn off the power and check that it's off with an inductive voltage detector (see p. 183). Remove the existing light fixture.

To install separate switches for the fan and the light, you will need a third wire (switch leg) to the switch box. Remote-control fan kits require only two wires to the switch box.

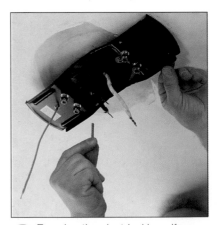

2 Examine the electrical box; if it is mounted to a secure 2 x 4 between joists, the fan mounting plate can probably be attached directly to it. If it is not, replace it with an electrical box and hanger to hold the weight of your fan. The mounting plate shown here attaches to the box with ¼-in. screws and flat and spring washers.

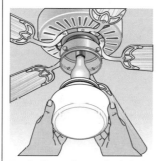

Assuming control. Want to change the settings on your ceiling fan from your favorite easy chair? Conversion kits that will allow you to operate most fans by wireless remote control are available at home centers.

Dimmer damage. Don't use a standard dimmer switch to control a ceiling fan's speed; it could damage the fan motor. Shop for a variable-speed control designed for ceiling fans.

Hushing the humming. It's common for a ceiling fan motor to emit a humming noise if the wall switch and the fan aren't the same brand. Eliminate the noise by replacing the wall switch with a no-hum fan control, available where ceiling fans are sold.

Bad vibes. Stop a fan's light fixture from vibrating by fitting a large rubber band around the neck of the fixture's glass globe. The band will act as a noise buffer between the globe and the screws that hold it in place.

It's in the bag. After oiling a fan motor, cut a plastic bag at the bottom, slip it loosely around the motor housing, and tie it at both ends. Then turn the fan on high for 2 or 3 minutes to catch any excess oil.

People fans. Fans cool people, not rooms. Running a ceiling fan (or any other fan) in an unoccupied room only wastes energy.

Cool trick. The air moved by a ceiling fan makes your body feel cooler even when the temperature is relatively high. Save energy by raising the air conditioner's thermostat 6° above your normal setting and running the ceiling fan along with it.

Which way to turn. The blades of a ceiling fan should turn counterclockwise during the summer and clockwise (the fan's reverse mode) during the winter. The winter direction helps distribute heat more evenly around the room by forcing warm ceiling air downward. Put the fan on its lowest speed to avoid causing a draft.

Getting clearance. Fan blades must be at least 7 feet above the floor and 1 foot below the ceiling.

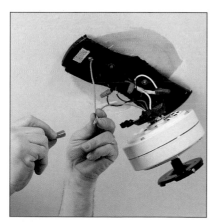

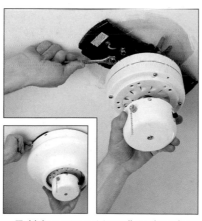

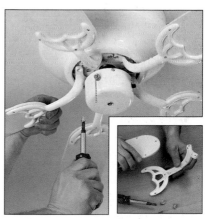

3 Hang the motor on the hook on the mounting plate, and wire according to the instructions for your fan. Connect like-colored wires; the ground wire should be connected to the screw or ground wire provided on the fan. It's best to connect white wires first; when disconnecting, leave white wires for last.

4 Using care not to pull on the wire connections, position the motor against the mounting plate. Match the holes at both ends of the motor's mounting bracket with the threaded studs of the mounting plate. Secure the motor to the mounting plate with flat washers and self-locking nuts. Put on the fan body, lining up its mounting holes with the threaded holes in the mounting plate. Firmly tighten screws.

5 Mount the blades on the blade holders, using screws and washers. Attach the blade holders and blades to the motor with screws, making sure the screws are tightened securely. If a light kit is used, connect like-colored wires. Many newer fans have plug-in connections for lights.

If it burns, vent it.
Combustion, whether in a furnace, fireplace, or appliance, needs adequate air intake; otherwise dangerous oxygen depletion can result. Vents or even an intake duct may be needed. A rule of thumb with heating equipment is to allow 1 square inch of combustion air intake for every 1,000 BTU's of rated furnace capacity.

Warning signs. How do you know if the ventilation in your house is inadequate? Telltale signs during winter months are frequent allergy problems among family members, and lingering odors and musty scents. Consider installing vents and fans to improve ventilation and correct the in-house problems.

A two-way street. Proper ventilation requires both a vent allowing air to flow in and one to let air flow out. Plan the placement of vent intakes and exhausts to "wash" the largest possible surface area.

Clean vent fans often to keep them operating efficiently. Remove the grille and wipe off the fan blades with an ammoniated liquid cleaner. Also use a vacuum to suck out dirt from the grille and the motor.

Use the bad air. To get fresh-air ventilation in a tightly sealed home, consider installing an air-to-air heat exchanger (also known as Energy Recover Ventilation or ERV) to your furnace. It provides a constant supply of filtered preheated fresh air in winter and pre-cooled fresh air in summer.

Back-draft test. Perform this test periodically to see if exhaust gases are backing up into your home. Shut down the furnace, and close all exterior doors and windows. Turn on all exhaust fans and the clothes dryer. Start up the furnace; then hold a candle near the draft hood on top of the furnace. If the candle flame blows away from the hood, gases are coming back into the house.

Back-draft cures. The easiest way to prevent furnace exhaust gases from back-drafting is to crack open a basement window. A better, more permanent solution is to vent the furnace directly to the outside.

Weeping windows. Storm windows have small vents called weep holes near the bottom of the frame that allow moisture to escape. Clean the holes periodically with a pipe cleaner so condensation won't build up between the windows.

Installing a roof vent

WHAT YOU'LL NEED

Hammer and nail
Roof vent and template
Saber saw
Shingle knife
Pry bar (if needed)
Roofing nails
Caulk gun and roofing cement

1 From the attic, pick a spot between roof rafters close to the ridge, taking into account the location of any eave and gable vents. Drive a nail through the roof sheathing from the underside to mark the center of the vent. On the roof, position the template to mark the vent opening and cut away the shingles as well as a pilot hole in the roof's sheathing.

2 Again using the template as a guide, cut additional shingles as required with a hooked shingle knife to allow the upper flashing of the vent to slide under the two upper courses of shingles.

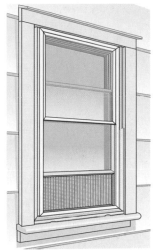

Filtered air. If you enjoy opening a window during spring and fall but don't enjoy the dust and pollen that invade the living area, measure the window and install a panel filter between the lower sash and the sill. If you can't find the exact size, a heating-cooling shop can usually cut one to fit.

Cure a cold basement by installing small vents in the forced-air ducts running from the furnace through the basement. Install one or two in the hot-air duct to circulate the air and eliminate the clammy chill.

Moisture and mildew can be eliminated by installing an exhaust fan. Match the fan's capacity to the size of the room. When installing it, remember to exhaust the fan to the outside, not into the attic.

Smart fan. Bathroom and kitchen exhaust fans are effective if they are left running long enough to evacuate all the moisture from the room. Humidity-activated fans that detect ambient moisture are also available. These units shut down when the moisture drops to an acceptable level.

A baffling problem. If insulation between the joists in the attic has been installed so that it blocks the air spaces around soffit vents in the eaves, rake it back and install baffles to allow room for air to flow through the vents.

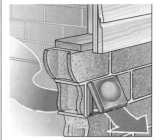

Ventilate a crawl space with a powered vent, which exhausts air with a fan when the temperature rises. Or install a thermostatically controlled vent, which opens in warm weather and closes in cold. Use a GFCI-protected receptacle for a powered vent.

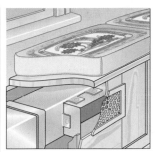

Have a seat. Disguise metal ductwork in a finished attic by boxing it into a built-in banquette or window seat. Frame it with construction-grade lumber and finish with paneling. (Attach metal sleeves to the registers to bring them to the front of the frame.)

Defective ducts. Leaking or broken ducts can suck up attic dust or insulation and blow it throughout the house. Have a qualified HVAC contractor perform a flow-hood test on your ductwork to pinpoint leaks.

3 Mark the outline of the vent; then carefully pull out any nails that might block the flashing from being inserted under the shingles. Enlarge the hole to the size of the vent.

4 Carefully slide the flashing under the top courses of shingles and over the bottom courses; then press the vent down to seat it directly over the opening. Nail the vent in place with roofing nails.

5 Spread roofing cement over the nails and along the edges of the vent. This applies to most types of roof vents; power vents require an electrical line.

Plug the leaks. Before laying down insulation, look for open spaces around wires, pipes, and air ducts that may allow air currents under the insulation. Inject caulk or foam sealant into the cavities to plug them.

Check the chimney for gaps where warm air may be escaping. Close any gaps between joists and chimney with sheet metal. First butt the edge of the sheet metal against the chimney and tack the other edge to a rafter. Then seal the edges with high-temperature silicone caulk.

The value of air. Remember, it is the air trapped in minute spaces within the insulating material that provides insulation. Packing and compressing insulating material only degrades the insulation's effectiveness.

No vapor barrier on the underside of the insulation in your attic? Check at paint stores for a "roll-on" barrier. It can be painted like a primer coat on the ceilings of rooms below the attic. If it isn't available in your area, apply a heavy coat of paint to the ceiling.

Stairs in a box. Make a box from rigid polystyrene insulation and install it over folding attic stairs and whole-house fans. This will keep warm air from escaping through the openings into the attic.

Crisscross installation. If you are adding an extra layer of fiberglass on top of previously laid batts, place the new batts perpendicular to the old to block unwanted airflow. Use batts with no facing for the second layer to avoid trapping moisture between the two vapor barriers. Excess moisture could make the insulation ineffective.

Allergic to insulation? Installing fiberglass insulation can be a nightmare for people with allergies. Shop for cellulose fiber insulation or Miraflex encapsulated insulation instead; neither will aggravate allergies. And wear a dust mask when handling any insulation.

Wild things. Field mice and squirrels find loose-fill insulation ideal for nesting. Inspect your attic during the winter months to make sure that outdoor rodents haven't infested the insulation. If you find any, contact a pest control expert.

Insulating an attic

WHAT YOU'LL NEED

Respirator or dust mask
Goggles
Gloves
Walk plank (2 x 8-ft. piece of plywood)
Tape measure and pencil
Insulation batts
Straightedge and utility knife
Soffit vents
Drill
Saber saw
Screwdriver
Stainless-steel tapping screws

1 Measure the distance between the joists to determine the width of the batts to purchase. Cut the batts to the proper length by compressing them between a straightedge and the walk plank; then pull a utility knife across the compressed area. This technique will result in a neat, clean cut.

2 Press the insulation into the cavity between the joists, making sure the vapor barrier is facing down toward the room. Place the insulation so that the vapor barrier lies completely against the ceiling and the insulation is not compressed. You may need to thread the insulation under running boards or other obstructions.

Kitchen power tool. Cut rigid foam insulation with an electric carving knife if no power saw is available. If you have a power saw, use a fine-tooth blade.

Not the roof. There's no need to insulate the roof of an attic if you are not finishing the attic or forming a cathedral ceiling in the room below. Attic floor insulation is sufficient. In fact, insulation between the rafters may deter proper attic ventilation and damage roof shingles and rafters.

Canned heat. A well-insulated attic can cause the warm air in a house to collect in upstairs rooms. Keep them from overheating by closing dampers on warm-air systems and turning off upstairs radiators.

Placing insulation over a recessed light can create a fire hazard. Make a three-sided box out of fiberglass duct board (with 6 inches of clearance) to house the light, leaving the top off to let heat escape.

Find the leak. Use a smoking incense stick to track airflow patterns under the roof. Ideally, air should flow in through the gable or soffit vents (see "When Insulating a Roof," right), across the underside of the roof, and out the ridge or roof vents near the top. Plug unwanted openings or place wooden boards as baffles to direct the airflow so it "washes" up the maximum surface of the roof.

A clean sweep. Use a broom to push fiberglass batts under the eaves where headroom is limited. Don't tear the insulation or place it over soffit vents.

When insulating a roof for a finished attic space, install baffles to create air channels between the roof and the insulation. Installed between the rafters, baffles should help form a channel from the soffit vent to the ridge vent to prevent moisture buildup.

3 Exterior soffit vents help dissipate unwanted attic moisture during the winter and hot air during the summer. To install one, first position the vent on the soffit. Trace around it; then measure 1 inch in on all sides and draw that outline. Drill out the four corner holes.

4 Using a saber saw, cut along the lines you have drawn to make the opening for the vent.

5 Place the vent in the opening and screw it into the wood with stainless-steel self-tapping screws. Make sure the vent is placed so that air flows into the attic, up the underside of the roof, and out the ridge vent (see "When Insulating a Roof," above).

Night moves. Lowering a thermostat at night may not save energy if the furnace has to work harder to heat the house in the morning. Limit night setbacks to no more than 10 degrees. Do not lower the thermostat when the outside temperature is close to zero.

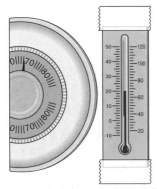

Temp test. Check the accuracy of your thermostat with this simple test. Tape a small thermometer to the wall next to the thermostat, wait about 15 minutes for the thermometer to adjust to the room temperature, and then compare it to the thermometer on the thermostat. If it's more than 5 degrees off, have the thermostat recalibrated.

Level solution. A thermostat with a mercury switch will malfunction if its alignment is accidentally disturbed. Check the level by placing a small spirit level across the "ears" on the base. Realign it if necessary.

Too much hot air? Reset the fan switch (located on the blower cabinet near the furnace) from 135° and 100° to 110° and 90°. But be prepared for "short-cycling"; the warm heat exchanger may turn the fan on 2 or 3 times after each cycle.

Hot appliances. Position a TV or any large heat-producing appliance away from a thermostat. The extra warmth can throw off the thermostat's heat sensor.

Caught in the draft. Strong drafts can affect a thermostat. Check for leaks around windows and exterior doors by moving a lighted candle around them. A flickering flame indicates that the weatherstripping is inadequate. Note: Remove any curtains from windows or doors before doing this.

Body heat. Remember to lower the thermostat a couple of degrees when having a large group of people over. Their body heat will make up the difference, and you'll conserve energy.

Wire worries? If you're replacing an old (heat-only) thermostat with a new one, you may wonder where to connect the third wire (the red one). Don't be concerned; new thermostats need only a two-wire hook-up. Tape the end of the extra wire and push it to the side.

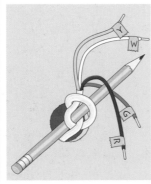

Wrap it up. When replacing a thermostat, prevent the hook-up wires from falling back into the wall by wrapping them around a pencil.

Installing an energy-efficient thermostat

WHAT YOU'LL NEED

Standard and Phillips screwdrivers	Drill
Pencil and masking tape	Long-nose pliers
Thermostat	Wire cutter or knife
Awl	Backup batteries
Level (for nonelectronic models)	
Anchors (for hollow walls)	

1 Turn off power. Remove the cover or ring from the old thermostat. Take off the thermostat body. Loosen the terminal screws and remove the wires, marking the terminal color code (R, W, G, Y) on each wire. Then take the subbase-plate off the wall.

2 With a pencil, mark the mounting screw locations for the new subbase; then make the holes with an awl. If it is a nonelectronic thermostat, you will need to make sure it is level. If the wall is hollow, install anchors in the mounting holes.

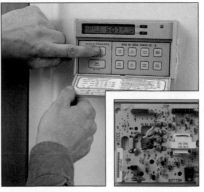

3 Connect the wires to the corresponding terminals on the subbase. Then install the new thermostat body on the subbase. Make sure the backup batteries are in place, and program the thermostat according to the instructions.

Change with the season.
Reposition dampers according to the season to maximize the benefits of the hot or cold air produced by the central system. Since warmed air tends to rise, in winter close the dampers (either partially or fully) in the ducts leading to upstairs rooms and open those going downstairs. Reverse the procedure for the summertime.

Closed doors can decrease the efficiency of a forced-air system by limiting air circulation. Trim an inch off the bottom of interior doors, or install pass-through grilles near the bottom of the doors to allow air circulation even when the door is closed.

A clean-air act. Clean registers weekly, with a vacuum's brush attachment, to keep dust out of the air. Stop dust at the source by spritzing the air filter in your furnace with a filter adhesive. The sticky coating acts as a dust magnet.

Slow balance. When balancing an airflow system, change the dampers, located in the ducts or registers, in small increments. Give the system 24 hours to adjust to each change before trying another setting.

Temper the cold. Deflectors can channel the air coming out of the registers to produce a more consistent temperature within each room. Even the most efficient glass cannot stop some radiation of cold air from a window; a deflector placed on the heating register under the window can direct warm air toward the glass and temper the cold air before it can form a draft.

In hot water. A forced hot-water system can be balanced like a hot-air system, except that adjustments are made at the flow valves on the branch lines or at the inlet valves at the convectors or radiators. For more efficient control, install thermostatic valves. With baseboard hot-water heating, adjusting the louvers is the simplest solution.

Even up. Certain rooms in the house may be colder or warmer, depending on their size, the number of windows, the direction they face, and how well they are shielded from the elements (such as by shade trees or adjoining buildings). To make the temperature in the house more uniform, adjust the dampers in the duct system room by room, directing airflow where it is needed.

Adjusting dampers and deflectors

WHAT YOU'LL NEED

Indelible marker

1 The ideal position for dampers is in supply ducts near the plenum. Close the dampers in ducts for rooms that are too hot; open them for rooms that are too cool (in heating mode). The handle should be parallel to the damper inside the duct.

2 For future reference, clearly mark the settings for each zone damper—for example, "B" for basement. You may need to change the settings when you shift between heating and cooling modes. Perhaps use "S" for summer and "W" for winter.

3 Registers with self-contained dampers are not as effective as in-line types, but they can work quite well. Deflectors also improve efficiency and comfort: Direct air up for cooling and down for heating to take advantage of natural convective airflow.

Filter facts. If a filter has been in place for 3 months without showing any signs of dirt, it may not fit properly. Check for gaps between the filter and the duct frame, and seal them with RTV sealant or duct tape so that dirty air cannot bypass the filter and get into the house.

Sealing heating ducts?
Use the shiny metallic duct tape rather than the fabric tape. It's fire-resistant and forms a tighter seal.

Extend an air filter's life by cleaning it periodically with the brush or crevice attachment of a vacuum cleaner. Then hold up the filter to a bright light. If it is opaque, it needs more vacuuming or replacement.

Installing a new furnace?
Make sure that there is sufficient space around it to allow you to change the filter without difficulty.

Venting the right way.
When you're putting a forced-air system into a newly constructed house, make sure the vents are built into the walls. Vents installed on the floor can send up dirt along the walls and are likely to catch anything that spills.

Dusty hobbies. Woodworking, painting, model making, and pottery are hobbies that create airborne dust, which can get sucked up into the air system. Install an exhaust fan in the hobby workroom to keep these pollutants from being pumped into the rest of the house.

Whistling ducts?
Ducts that are too small can restrict airflow and cause an audible whistle when air passes through them. Consider replacing noisy ones with ducts that have a larger diameter (at least 6 inches).

A sick motor. If a fan motor hums but doesn't turn, try turning it by hand (with the power off) to see if it's free of obstructions. Next check to see if it's been properly lubricated according to the owner's manual. Then check the belt tension, and finally look for loose mounting bolts.

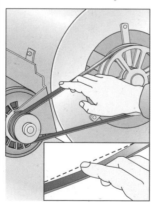

Belt-tension test. Check the belt tension on a fan motor by gently pressing on the belt at its midpoint: if it deflects more than ½ inch, it's too loose. Turning the adjustment bolt often tightens the belt, but check the owner's manual first.

Installing a high-efficiency air filter

WHAT YOU'LL NEED

Cordless drill with nut driver adapter	Sheet-metal snips
Screwdriver, wrenches, and pliers (if needed)	Sheet-metal adapter (if needed)
Leather safety gloves	Filter housing and media
Marker	Sheet-metal screws
Tape measure	Duct tape

1 Using a cordless drill with a nut driver adapter, remove the sheet-metal screws that hold the return-air plenum to the furnace. Loosen the return ducts if necessary, and separate the plenum from the furnace.

2 If the gap is too small for the filter housing, try to move the ductwork (wearing gloves). If it can't be moved, mark and cut the duct with sheet-metal snips. If the housing does not fit the furnace openings, a sheet-metal adapter may be needed.

3 Secure the filter housing with sheet-metal screws, and seal openings with duct tape. Insert the filter media into the housing with the arrow indicating airflow facing the fan. Most filters need to be cleaned or have their media replaced twice per season.

Humidify and save.
Adding humidity to the air in winter makes people feel comfortable at lower temperatures. If the air is dry, most people are comfortable with an air temperature between 75° and 80°F. If the air has 50 percent relative humidity, the same people will be comfortable at 70°F.

When shopping for a small one-room humidifier, look for these handy features: (1) A see-through detachable tank to make refilling easy. If the tank is opaque, make sure there's a water-level indicator. (2) An on-off button separate from the humidistat, so you don't have to reset the humidity level every time you turn on the machine. (3) A nozzle that swivels 360°, so you can direct the air where you want it.

Safety first. Dirty humidifiers can spew bacteria, mold, and mineral dust into the air. One of the safest types is a wicking-filter evaporative unit. It comes with a disposable filter that traps minerals and discourages microbial growth.

Scale solutions. Using tap water in the humidifier can cause mineral scale deposits. If your household water is hard, use distilled water instead.

To kill bacteria in the reservoir of a portable humidifier, clean it once a week, using a solution of 1 tablespoon bleach per pint of water. Or add a special bacteriostatic treatment to the water.

Catch a whiff. For special occasions or to purge a chlorine smell, add a few drops of rose water, orange-flower water, or a light cologne or aftershave to the reservoir water.

Humidifier always on?
Check your house for open windows or an open fireplace damper that may be pulling out the humidified air. Otherwise, it's likely that either the on-off switch or the humidistat (the humidity sensor) is broken.

Shut down dry. If you have to shut off a humidifier for any length of time, be sure to empty the water reservoir to keep bacteria from breeding in the standing water.

SAFE AND SMART

➤ If you are an allergy sufferer, read the manual very carefully before cleaning a humidifier.

➤ Unplug a humidifier and empty any water before repairing it.

Installing a humidifier in ductwork

WHAT YOU'LL NEED

Humidifier kit (includes tubing and saddle valve)	Insulation tape (optional)
Marker	Screwdriver
Cordless drill with nut driver adapter	Wrenches or pliers
Leather safety gloves	Duct tape
Sheet-metal snips	Wire connectors
Sheet-metal screws	

1 Turn off the main power to the furnace. Using the templates supplied with the kit, mark the ductwork and drill pilot holes. Cut openings for the humidifier and humidistat in the supply and return air plenums, following manufacturer's instructions.

2 Install mounting plate and humidifier on supply plenum, using sheet-metal screws. To ensure a tight seal, you may want to put insulation tape on back of mounting plate. You will also want to be sure unit is located near power and water lines.

3 Locate humidistat in the return air plenum so it samples air coming from living spaces first. Install humidistat and connect wires in accordance with instructions and local codes. Connect humidifier to water line with tubing and saddle valve.

Cool down the heater.
A water heater thermostat set to 150° or higher costs more to operate. Lower the thermostat temperature to 130° for safer, more economical operation.

Button up. Wrap a heater with an insulation blanket to keep the water's heat from dissipating. On gas models, don't cover the top of the tank or block the airflow to the burner at the bottom. On electric models, cut the insulation away at the power connection and at the element access panels.

Hot water on the spot.
If your water heater doesn't supply enough hot water, consider adding a small point-of-use heater. These have 5-gallon tanks that can supply water directly to a dishwasher or shower.

Signs of corrosion. A small puddle underneath a water heater may signal a corroding tank. But before you replace the heater, check the valves and fittings; if they're leaking, tightening them could remedy the problem.

Checking corrosion.
Make an annual inspection of the sacrificial anode— a magnesium or aluminum rod submerged in the tank to absorb the chemical action that causes tank corrosion. Shut off the water and power to the heater and remove the rod by loosening the anode bolt at the top of the heater. If the rod has corroded away, replace it.

Place a hand mirror on the floor under the heater to help you light or check the pilot light.

Cold water only? On a gas heater, the pilot light is probably out; relight it. On an electric heater, check both pairs of thermostat terminals with a multitester according to the manual.

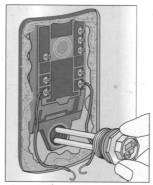

Still have cold water?
The top heating element is usually the culprit. (If hot water runs out too soon, it's usually the lower element.) Shut off the power and test the element with a volt-ohm meter set to RX1. Replace it if the meter reads infinity. Turn off the water supply and drain the tank; remove the element's cover. Loosen the mounting screws, disconnect the wires, and remove the element. Reverse to install the new one.

Cleaning a water heater

WHAT YOU'LL NEED

Pliers

Short hose, such as a washing machine hose (optional)

Bucket

1 Turn off the power or gas valve. Turn the handle on the drain near the bottom of the water heater, and let the water flow into a bucket. You may use a short hose. Examine the sediment; if there is considerable buildup, do this more frequently.

2 The pressure relief valve is a crucial safety device. Flush it after draining the tank by lifting the lever and allowing it to flow until water clears. If it does not reset, turn off the water supply and call a professional.

3 Inspect the flue pipe for signs of deterioration or separation. This is important because the flue pipe takes harmful gases out of the home. Be careful when doing your inspection; the flue pipe can be hot if the water burner is running.

Breaking an old rule.

A long-standing guideline for stoves or fireplaces has been to burn only hardwood, because burning softwoods contributes to creosote buildup. This rule doesn't apply to the newer high-tech clean-burning catalytic stoves. They burn hotter, so creosote buildup is unlikely.

Spotting problems.

Once a fire is into a normal burn cycle, go outside and look at the chimney. If you see lots of smoke exiting the flue, you're either burning the stove too cool or using poor firewood.

Enameled stove touch-up.

To clean an enameled stove, wash off dirt or soot with a solution of equal parts vinegar and warm water. Repair chips and scratches with a touch-up kit sold by the manufacturer.

Cast-iron care. After painting a nonenameled stove, light the first fire on a day when you can open the windows. The stove will smoke as the paint cures.

Suck it up. Clean the interior of a stove at the end of the heating season to prevent internal rusting. Use a shop vacuum fitted with a crevice tool to remove soot and ash, and spray a light coat of silicone lubricant inside the stove and flue to protect against humidity.

Beware of backpuffs.

Because the air is warmer, chimney drafts are weaker in the spring and fall than in winter. Consequently, backpuffs (when smoke collects and ignites in the firebox) are more likely. During those seasons light smaller fires, using less wood, to let more air into the firebox.

Check the door gasket once a month during heating season. When the stove is cold, hold a dollar bill in the door and close the door on it. Tug on the bill. If you can easily pull it out, adjust or replace the door gasket (see right). If the bill won't budge, the gasket is good. Check for loose spots all around the stove's door gasket.

Replacing a door gasket on a wood stove

WHAT YOU'LL NEED

Screwdriver, chisel, or knife

High-temperature RTV sealant

New gasket

Utility knife

1 Starting at the seam or a break in the old gasket, gently pull it away from the door, following with a screwdriver, chisel, or knife to clear away old sealant and gasket remains from the mounting surface or channel.

2 When the channel is completely clean, apply a liberal amount of high-temperature RTV sealant—or other sealant specified by the manufacturer completely around the door channel surface.

3 Press the new gasket firmly into place, seating it completely in the bed of sealant. If trimming is necessary, cut carefully to ensure a tight fit at the butt joint. Close door, and wait 24 hr. to maintain pressure on the seal until it is completely cured.

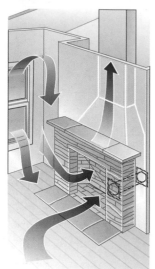

Carbon monoxide can be a problem in a room with a fireplace, especially if it is a gas model. Install a carbon monoxide detector to alert you to a buildup of carbon monoxide that might be caused by a downdraft or a plugged-up chimney.

Raise the fire. Smoke continuously entering a room from a fireplace may indicate that the chimney opening is too high. Place a layer of firebricks on the fireplace floor to raise the fire high enough for the smoke to be pulled up the chimney.

A fireplace can often cool a room rather than warming it. That's because a roaring fire draws air from the room (including the heated air) up the chimney. One way to avoid this is by making smaller fires. A more permanent solution is to install an exterior air vent at the side of the fireplace opening.

From the ashes. A ½-inch bed of ash left in the fireplace after cleaning is an excellent insulator that will prevent heat from being absorbed into the hearth. Instead, the heat will be reflected upward, giving you a better-burning fire.

Hardwood hints. It's best to burn hardwood rather than softwood in a fireplace, but all hardwoods are not alike. Poplar, for instance, is a softer hardwood that burns fast and throws off little heat. If possible, choose hardwoods such as oak, elm, and maple for a fireplace.

Free firewood. Save money on firewood by visiting construction sites. Often there are newly cut trees that are ideal for firewood. Contractors will usually allow you to cart off all the wood you can carry free of charge, but be sure to obtain permission first.

Installing a gas fireplace insert

WHAT YOU'LL NEED

Goggles and work gloves

Gas fireplace insert that fits the size of your fireplace, and all required materials

Vacuum

Brushes for cleaning bricks and chimney

Hammer and cold chisel for fixing cracks

Fire-rated cement

High-temperature gasket cement

Electric drill and bits

Self-tapping sheet-metal screws

Cardboard or another protective surface

Screwdriver

Logs, burner, and "glowing embers"

1 Vacuum and clean the fireplace, and repair any cracks with fire-rated cement. Make sure the chimney is in good repair. First, the vents and chimney cap need to be installed and the damper must be removed; you may want to have a professional do this. Once the flexible vents are installed, apply high-temperature gasket cement to the vents on the fireplace insert; then attach the flexible vents to them.

2 Secure the vents with a drill and self-tapping sheet-metal screws. Slide the fireplace insert into place.

 Before sliding the insert into place, rest it on a sheet of cardboard or another protective surface so that it doesn't scratch the floor or hearth.

Raccoon remover. Chase nesting raccoons from a chimney with a drop light and a portable radio. First, close the damper; then turn on the light and radio and lower them down the chimney. Raccoons hate music (especially heavy-metal rock), so after a few minutes they will evacuate.

Fireplace cleaner. Make an ideal cleaning solution for a brick or stone fireplace by shaving 2 bars of naphtha soap into 3 quarts of hot water. Add 1½ pounds of powdered pumice and 1½ cups of household ammonia. Brush the solution on the fireplace walls and let it stand for an hour. Then scrub the walls with a stiff-bristle brush and rinse them with clear water. For a tile or slate fireplace, use an all-purpose household cleanser.

Soot eraser. Another way to remove fireplace soot is with a special commercial sponge, available at home centers. Made of natural tree rubber, it removes soot like a giant eraser.

Making the final cut. Well-seasoned firewood generally has darkened ends with cracks or splits visible, is relatively lightweight, and makes a "clunk" sound when you bang two pieces together. Always have firewood cut to length and split 6 months before you use it so the wind and sun can dry it out properly.

Cap the chimney. Keep squirrels, birds, and raccoons from nesting in a chimney by installing a cap on it. It will also keep airborne sparks and embers from igniting nearby trees.

SAFE AND SMART

➤ Keep a chemical fire extinguisher designed to put out chimney fires near the fireplace.

➤ Don't burn painted, stained, or pressure-treated wood in a wood stove or fireplace. It will introduce harmful chemicals into the air.

➤ Check with the local building inspector before installing a fireplace insert. Special requirements for installation vary in different areas.

3 Connect the gas line to the insert. It is best to have a licensed plumber make the connection (this may be mandated by local code). If the fireplace insert has a fan or a remote control, you will need to connect it to an electrical source. Once the connections have been made, check the fireplace insert for level, and adjust the leveling screws on the bottom of the insert as needed.

4 Attach the decorative surround to the fireplace insert, using a screwdriver and the supplied screws. Then put on the other trim pieces as specified in the instructions.

5 Install the logs, burner, and "glowing embers" as recommended by the manufacturer. Put on the glass door, and make sure it is tightly sealed; this is important to ensure proper combustion and venting.

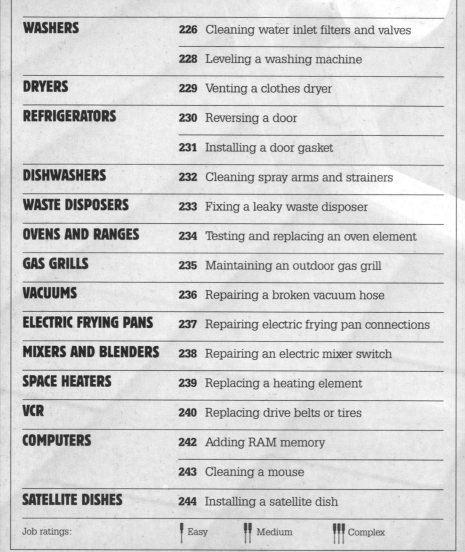

APPLIANCE REPAIRS AND ELECTRONICS

Job ratings: ┃ Easy   ┃┃ Medium   ┃┃┃ Complex

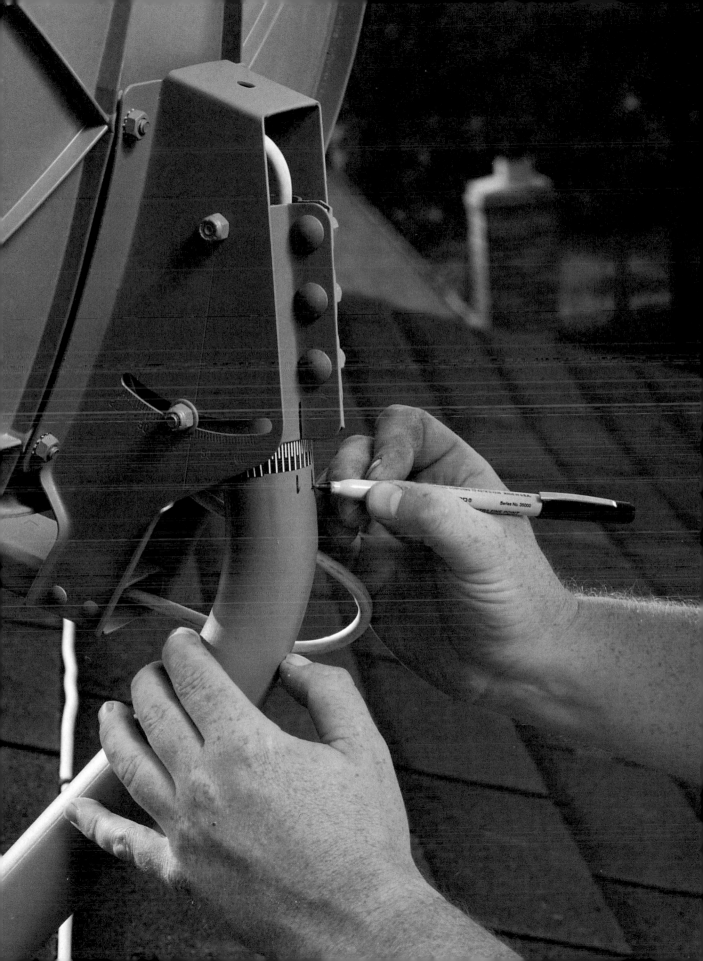

The right connections.
Locate a new washer as close as possible to the hot-water source. Also make sure there is at least 4 inches of clearance between the back of the appliance and the wall. Finally, hook up the washer to its own electrical circuit, 115 volts, 60 Hz. Do not use an extension cord.

The book of knowledge.
What seems like a malfunction can often be a variation in a particular wash cycle. In fact, in more than one-third of all service calls, the technician refers the customer to the service manual to help correct a problem. Save time and money by carefully reading the manual before dialing for help.

Get some traction. When moving a washer or any slick-surfaced appliance, wear rubber gloves for a grip that won't let you down.

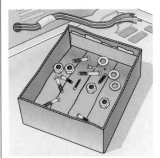

Hold on. When taking apart a washer, screws, nuts, bolts, and other small parts can roll out of reach and sight forever. Keep them together with a "holding box." Line a small plastic or cardboard box with duct tape, sticky side up. As you drop each part into the box, the tape will capture and hold it until you're ready to reassemble them.

A chipped tub inside the washer can eventually rust. To keep clothes free of nasty rust marks, cover any chips or gouges immediately with clear nail polish, silicone sealant, or an epoxy touch-up made for the purpose. To get a perfect touch-up every time, tear out a match from a matchbook, dip the torn end in the paint, and apply it to the chip.

Locating the snag.
If clothes are coming out of the washer torn, place old pantyhose over your hand and feel around the tub until you locate the rough spot. Touch it up with epoxy.

Muffling banging pipes.
When the washing machine inlet valve shuts suddenly, water rushing through the supply pipes comes to a slamming halt. The result is a loud banging noise. Quiet things down quickly by installing a water-hammer shock absorber at the cold and hot hose connections.

Cleaning water inlet filters and valves

WHAT YOU'LL NEED

Groove-joint pliers

Small screwdriver or awl

Toothbrush

Replacement screens and/or washers

Nut driver or socket driver

Masking tape

Volt-ohm meter (VOM) or digital multi-meter (DMM)

Replacement water inlet valve

Wrench

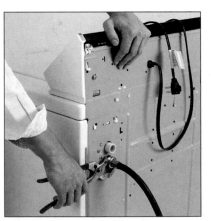

1 Shut off the hot- and cold-water valves, and run the washer momentarily to relieve the water pressure. Unplug the machine; then loosen all hose couplings with groove-joint pliers; remove the couplings.

2 Using a small screwdriver or awl, carefully pry the edges of the filter screens from the ports and hoses. Rinse them under running water, using an old toothbrush to remove debris; then reinstall. Replace any damaged screens and damaged or dry washers. Using a screwdriver that fits just inside the ports, press the screens until they are fully seated. Reinstall the hoses carefully to avoid damaging the threads.

When time stops. When a washing machine fails to advance from one cycle to the next, the timer is usually at fault. Before replacing a costly timer, check out the timer motor for continuity with a multitester. A faulty motor can cause timer malfunction, and usually costs about two-thirds less than the entire timer assembly.

Save on water bills by presoaking heavily soiled clothes instead of washing them twice.

Material results. Some fabrics leave lint; others capture it. Terry cloth, flannel, and soft cottons shed lint while corduroy, permanent press, and velveteen fabrics hold it. Avoid washing lint givers with lint holders, but if you forget, use a fabric softener in the rinse to help alleviate the problem.

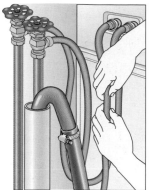

Damaged inlet or drain hoses can cause the washing machine to malfunction or, if one bursts, fill your cellar or house with water Inspect them closely every 6 months for cracks or deterioration; replace those that are worn or weak. (Make sure the drain hose is cut to the exact length needed to reach the standpipe.) As a further safeguard, check for kinks or large bulges in the hoses while the washing machine is operating.

A real drain. The drainpipe for the washer should be approximately 34 inches off the floor to prevent siphoning the wash water from the machine. If you must hook up to a lower drain, such as a floor drain, install a siphon break, inserting it in the drain hose on the back of the washer. It should be 4 inches above the machine's maximum water level.

Don't get snagged. Button buttons, zip zippers, and hook hooks on clothes before washing to avoid damaging other clothes or the fasteners themselves.

Detergent buildup can affect washer performance. Run the machine through a full wash cycle with a cup of vinegar to remove soap scum; then wash again with a cup of baking soda to neutralize any sour residue.

Deterring detergent. Too many suds can cause a washing machine to work even harder. Follow the manufacturer's directions; more is definitely not better.

Motor maintenance. Dust and dirt can accumulate on the motor windings, restricting airflow and causing burnout. Once a year, unplug the machine, pull it away from the wall, and gently vacuum the motor windings with a plastic crevice tool.

3 Check the machine's manual to find out how to remove the back panel. Unbolt the inlet valve from the cabinet, and disconnect the wire terminals, using masking tape to identify them for reinstallation. With a multimeter set to its lowest ohm rating, probe each pair of terminals on the solenoids. Look for a resistance of between 100 and 1000 ohms.

4 If either test fails, replace the water inlet valve. First, using a wrench, unclamp and disconnect the hose connected to the water inlet valve; then connect the wires to the replacement unit. Attach the replacement to the mounting plate and cabinet.

 Individual replacement solenoids are available for valves.

5 If the solenoids pass the resistance test, unscrew them from the valve. Disassemble the valve and clean it thoroughly with a toothbrush under running water. Then reassemble and install it. Replace the washer's back panel, reattach the hoses, and plug the machine in to test its operation.

Spin doctoring. If there's too much vibration during the spin cycle, open the top and rearrange the load in the tub. When washing heavy items, do several at one time to create a balanced load.

Wash and wear. Overloading the tub increases wear on the machine and results in poor washing and damage to clothes. To determine if your washer is overloaded, observe the wash cycle closely: the clothes should be circulating freely with the water, not bunched around the top of the agitator.

Snubbing noise. If a washer produces a cacophony of squeaks, slick snubbers may be the culprits. Tape the machine's lid down, insert a putty knife under the front corners, and lift up the top of the machine. Remove the springs from the snubbers, and roughen the snubbers' underside with medium-grade sandpaper.

Machine overflowing? Turn the dial to the end of the cycle to empty the machine. Then recheck the directions on the laundry detergent box.

Get an earful. Pinpoint strange sounds during the washing cycle with a mechanic's stethoscope, available at auto supply stores, or improvise with an ordinary screwdriver: Hold the handle near your ear and place the blade on the machine housing near the suspect sound to tune in to what's ailing the washer.

Washer rattling? Silence the beast by laying a scrap of flame-retardant carpet underneath the machine.

Leveling a washing machine

WHAT YOU'LL NEED

Carpenter's level

2 x 4 lumber scrap

Adjustable wrench

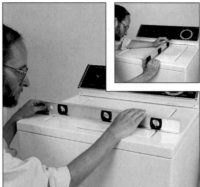

1 Place a carpenter's level on the washing machine—first side to side, then front to back—to find out how much the legs must be adjusted. On most models, you can adjust only the front legs; the rear legs are self-adjusting.

2 Tilt the washer back, and prop it up with a piece of 2 x 4 on edge. With an adjustable wrench, loosen the jam nuts on the front two legs. Then raise or lower the feet as needed by turning the legs clockwise or counterclockwise by hand.

3 Remove the wood scrap, and check to see if the washing machine is level. If it is, use the wrench to tighten the jam nuts. If it isn't level, repeat step 2. If the rear legs won't adjust, tilt the machine forward about an inch and let it drop.

An outside chance. Install an outside vent hood that has tight-closing louvers or flaps to seal out wildlife. Field mice find the clothes dryer an ideal nesting place in the winter. They'll make their way through the vent and into the house.

Avoiding great lengths.

The maximum length for a dryer vent duct is 22 feet for a straight run. One elbow in the duct reduces the length to 17 feet; two elbows will shorten it to 12 feet. If you're using flexible duct, cut these distances in half and use only UL-listed fireproof vent duct.

SAFE AND SMART

➤ Dry laundry in consecutive loads to save on electric or gas bills. Warming up the dryer after it has cooled requires more energy.

➤ Be sure the dryer vent has an outlet flap to keep cold air out of the house in winter.

➤ Don't vent a dryer indoors. It can add enough moisture to the house to warp paneling, flake ceilings, and wreak havoc on interior paint.

Fuzz busting. Unplug the dryer, attach a vacuum hose to the blower end, and move the nozzle around the drum to blow loitering lint into the air-intake opening. Then reverse the hose and suck up the lint from the opening.

Dryers need fresh air

to work properly. If the dryer is installed in a utility closet or other tight area, keep the door open during dryer operation or the appliance will overheat. Or install a louvered door, which allows air to circulate even when it is closed.

Fabric softener buildup

or residue from antistatic sheets can coat the inside of the dryer drum and prevent electronic sensors from shutting off the appliance when clothes are already dry. Correct the problem by washing the inside of the drum with hot water and a mild detergent (do not use an abrasive cleanser).

Button up. If the dryer doesn't start after closing the door, the button switch that activates the motor might have worn down. Taping thick cardboard to the inside of the door will fill the gap and activate the button until you can replace the switch.

Venting a clothes dryer

WHAT YOU'LL NEED

Hammer	Exterior caulk and caulking gun
Drill and ⅜-in. bit	Screwdriver and nut driver
Jigsaw with wood-cutting blade or large (4¼-in.) hole saw	Flame-retardant flexible or metallic duct kit
Keyhole saw	Duct tape
Wall cap	Tin snips or utility knife

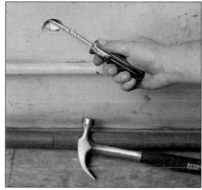

1 Determine the shortest and most direct route from the clothes dryer to an outside wall. Punch or hammer a small hole through the interior wall to probe for wires, pipes, or ductwork. If the path is clear, drill a ⅜-in. pilot hole to the outside.

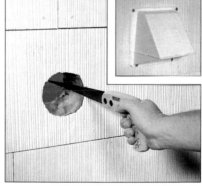

2 Cut a 4¼-in.-dia. hole in the siding with a jigsaw (call a mason if you have brick walls). Cut a corresponding hole through the wallboard with a keyhole saw. Install the wall cap, caulk under the flange, and then screw it to the siding.

3 Cut the vent pipe 2–3 in. from the inside wall and seal the edges with duct tape. Cut the ductwork as needed. (Note: many areas don't allow flexible duct; check local codes first.) Attach the duct to the dryer port and wall cap with clamps.

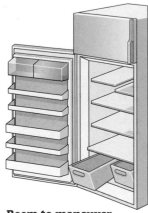

Room to maneuver.

When planning a location for a new refrigerator, factor in enough space for a full door swing. The door must open wider than 90° to allow the fruit and vegetable drawers to slide out, so plan several inches of clearance between the hinge side of the door and the adjacent wall. If you're remodeling a kitchen, buy the appliances and have them delivered before installing new cabinets so you can anticipate installation snafus.

Case closed.

Make a self-closing refrigerator door by inserting small squares of ¼-inch plywood under both front legs. This will tilt the refrigerator slightly backward so gravity pulls the door shut every time. Tilting the fridge too far back may interfere with the icemaker.

A moving experience.

Refrigerators manufactured within the last 5 years can be transported more easily on their side or back. Once the refrigerator is installed in its new home, allow it to stand upright for at least 24 hours before turning it on. This allows the compressor oil to drain back to its proper position.

Your muscles thank you.

Moving a large refrigerator can be hard labor. Make the job easier by slipping a section of carpet, pile side down, under the appliance. It will slide across the floor with a firm push.

Clean dusty fridge coils

every 3 months. Unplug the refrigerator and pull it away from the wall, or on many models just snap off the front grille, to get at the coils. Then suck up the dust with a nonconductive plastic vacuum attachment.

Dip the chip. Use a simple epoxy repair kit to cover up scratches and chips. First scrub the damaged area with soapy water, let it dry, and sand it lightly with medium-grit sandpaper. Then mix equal parts of the hardener and color, and brush it on. The kits, available in appliance repair stores, come in a wide range of colors ranging from basic white to baby blue.

Rub out stains and light rust on the exterior of the refrigerator with light-duty rubbing compound, available in auto supply stores. Its mild abrasive will scrub away the stain without damaging the paint.

Reversing a refrigerator door

WHAT YOU'LL NEED

Nut driver or socket driver

Screwdriver

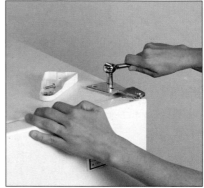

1 Unplug the refrigerator, empty the shelves, and remove the base grille. Then remove the upper door's top hinges with the nut driver. Take off the door by opening it slightly while lifting up and out. Don't loosen any of the washers or shims.

2 Take off the lower door by lifting the handle while loosening the middle hinge pin. Remove the handle and hinge hardware from cabinet and doors, and reinstall them on the opposite side. The handle-mounting screws may be hidden under caps.

3 Reinstall the doors, tightening the hinges until they are snug. Align the doors, and tighten the top hinge screws at least a half turn more. There may be a plastic filler on the grille that needs to be removed and reversed before the grille is reinstalled.

Don't blow a gasket.
Fix it instead with silicone caulk. Open the door and tape a sheet of wax paper to the refrigerator opposite the damaged door gasket section. Then close the door and draw a bead of caulk over the broken gasket. Wipe off the excess caulk with a wet paper towel, and let the patch cure overnight.

Dampening moisture.
Keep door openings to a minimum to reduce condensation buildup on the interior walls. Covering all liquids and allowing hot liquids to cool before placing them in the refrigerator will also help.

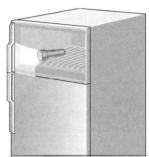

Light work. Check a refrigerator door seal by placing a lit flashlight in the refrigerator and aiming it toward the seal. Now shut the door. If light shines through, adjust or replace the seal.

Dusting down under.
Wrap a dust cloth around a yardstick, secure it with rubber bands, and spray it lightly with a dusting spray. Then slide it under the fridge in circular motions to pull out the dust.

Clean the drains in the refrigerator and freezer compartments periodically. Poke a piece of flexible wire into the hole to clear any clogs; then use a baster to flush the system with hot water. Follow with a teaspoon of bleach to kill any algae spores, and re-flush.

Winter thaw. Winter is a great time to defrost a freezer. Wait until it is almost empty; then pack any food in a cardboard box, and place it on a cool back porch while the ice thaws.

Installing a door gasket

WHAT YOU'LL NEED

Screwdriver, nut driver, or socket driver

Replacement gasket

1 Using a nut, socket, or screwdriver, loosen the screws in the metal retainer found under the gasket until the lip of the gasket can be removed (no need to take the screws or retainer out). Gently pull the lip of the old gasket from under the retainer.

2 Carefully press the lip of the new gasket under the rim of the metal retainer on the top of the door. Continue doing this along the perimeter of the door liner.

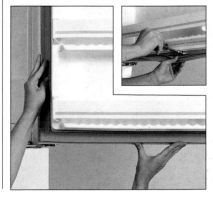

3 Smooth the gasket around the door, making sure it's not too tight or too loose. Tighten the middle screws on each side; then tighten the remaining screws just enough to hold the gasket in place. Finish by firmly tightening all the screws.

Strong-arm tactics.

A cracked washer arm can produce a powerful, erratic spray that will knock over glassware and dishes and cause water to leak past the door seal. Mend the crack with a little household epoxy cement. If the cement doesn't hold, replace the entire washer arm.

A lake in the kitchen?

A flood under the dishwasher may be due to a loose connection at the inlet line. To check, shut off the power at the service panel and the water at the hot-water shutoff valve beneath the sink. Then remove the lower front panel to access the valve, and tighten the nut. A flood under the sink may be due to a loose packing nut at the hot-water shutoff valve. Tighten it with a wrench, if necessary.

No water when you turn

on the dishwasher? First make sure the float, located on the floor of the appliance, springs up and down (free it if it sticks). Second, look under the sink to inspect the inlet hose, if there is one. Be sure that it isn't kinked or squashed by an object pressing against it.

Washing the dishwasher.

Freshen up a dirty or foul-smelling dishwasher by pouring a bowlful of vinegar in the bottom of an empty machine after it has filled with water. Then run the wash and rinse cycles.

The shining. To clean appliance chrome dirtied with food or dried-on soap, try rubbing it with baby oil, club soda, or a piece of lemon. Wash the surface with a damp cloth; then rub with a clean dry cloth.

Energy management.

A typical wash cycle uses up to 16 gallons of water, so save energy and water by loading up a dishwasher to the max before turning it on. Then use a kitchen timer to shut off the machine before the drying cycle starts. Open the door slightly to let the dishes air-dry. Newer dishwashers have an air-dry cycle built right in.

Going on vacation?

Dishwashers retain some water near the seals and O-rings to keep them from drying out and deteriorating. If you'll be away for more than 2 weeks, pour a little mineral oil into the bottom of the dishwasher to slow evaporation of the water. Run the washer empty before using it again to get rid of the oil.

Cleaning a dishwasher's spray arms and strainers

WHAT YOU'LL NEED

Screwdriver, nut driver, or socket driver

Toothpick or pipe cleaner

1 Some dishwashers have screws or a clip that must be unscrewed before the lower spray arm can be removed. On others, it simply lifts off or the screw can be removed by hand. Once the arm is removed, clean any filter or screen that is now visible.

2 To remove the upper spray arm, unscrew the retaining clip, then disconnect the arm from the water channel by removing the center screw. On other models, you'll need to remove the tray and unclip a protective grid, then remove the center screw.

3 Clean any clogged openings in the spray arms with a toothpick or pipe cleaner. Flush water through the arms while tilting them back and forth to wash out foreign objects. Reverse the removal procedure to reinstall the arms.

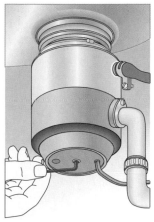

Buyer's guide. Look for a model with a large motor. A ¾-horsepower disposer may last as much as 3 to 4 times longer than a ½-horsepower model. Stainless-steel parts will also last longer than parts made of carbon steel or aluminum, which may rust or corrode. To cut down on service calls, look for a disposer that comes with a special wrench that will turn the shaft when the machine is jammed.

Quiet, please. Although no disposer is noiseless, limit the decibel level by installing a cushioned mounting bracket.

In a jam? If a disposer quits under a heavy load or won't start after you have unjammed it, wait 15 minutes for the motor to cool and then press the restart button below the motor. After unjamming the machine, drop in a handful of ice cubes and run the disposer to help remove any remaining residue.

Chemical dependency. Unclogging a disposer with a chemical drain cleaner may damage the unit.

Boning up. According to the Plumbing-Heating-Cooling Information Bureau, it's OK to grind up poultry, beef, and lamb bones in a disposer. The bones actually help clear out the residue and acid deposits left from vegetable and meat scraps. Don't put oyster or clam shells in, however; they don't pulverize easily.

Cold-water flush. Use cold, not hot, water when running the disposer. Hot water will melt any grease in the dishwater, and the grease will then cool and congeal in the plumbing. Cold water lets the grease stay solid so the disposer can break it up.

A twist of lemon. For a clean and fresh-smelling disposer, dump in a tray of ice cubes with a few lemon rinds, turn on the water, and run the disposer. Or pour in ½ cup of baking soda and rinse with hot water.

Cleaning cubes. Ice cubes made of water and vinegar are also effective disposer fresheners. Make up a tray and keep it on hand for periodic cleanings.

Fixing a leaky waste disposer

WHAT YOU'LL NEED

Nut driver, socket driver, or screwdriver

Replacement gaskets as needed

Wrench, hex wrench, or offset screwdriver

Special hex wrench, broom handle, or wooden spoon

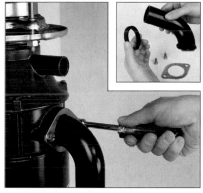

1 Stop a waste disposer leak at the drain-pipe by shutting off the power to the unit at the service panel and tightening the drain gasket screw with a nut, socket, or screwdriver. Or remove the trap and drain-pipe (p. 170), and replace the gasket.

2 Stop a leak at the sink by tightening mounting screws with wrench, hex wrench, or offset screwdriver. Or remove trap, rotate lower mounting ring a quarter turn to remove disposer, and remove upper ring. Replace sink gaskets and reinstall.

3 Free a jammed rotor by using a special hex wrench (supplied with the disposer) or by inserting a broom handle or wooden spoon into the mouth of the disposer. Never use your hand.

Lasting connections.
When replacing the heating element on a range top, attach heat-resistant solderless terminals to the ends of the connecting wires to prevent future burnout. Clean the connections before making any hookups.

Electric oven acid test.
Quickly determine if a heating element or thermostat is at fault by placing an oven thermometer in the middle of the oven and turning the oven to *Bake* at 450°F. The bottom element should glow to an even red. Now turn it to *Broil* with the temperature at its highest position; the upper element should glow. If neither heats or if the temperature is off by more than 35 degrees, the thermostat or the selector switch is faulty.

Catch a buzz. When an electric oven's buzzer fails to alert you at the end of a baking cycle, chances are the contact arms are clogged with cooking grease. Unplug the appliance and wipe the contacts with a cotton swab dipped in mineral spirits. If the buzz still doesn't sound, the alarm itself is defective.

Beating burnout.
Using the oven to heat the house on a cold day can damage the thermostat and cause premature burnout of the heating element. Lining the floor of the oven with foil for easy cleanup can damage both element and liner.

Save energy by starting an oven's self-clean cycle right after baking or roasting. The already hot oven will require less energy to fuel the cycle.

Grease guard. Catch spatters before they hit the wall with a piece of metal splash shield. Drill two small holes, and suspend it from cup hooks inserted into the wall. When grease builds up, remove the guard and clean it with soap or ammonia.

To clean dried spatters inside a microwave, place a cup of water in the oven, turn on the microwave to bring the water to a boil, then wipe off the softened stains with a damp cloth.

Less of a mess. Puncture tomatoes, potatoes, and other tight-skinned fruits and vegetables before cooking them in a microwave to prevent a messy explosion all over the interior.

Got a match? If you can't quite reach the pilot light of an oven or gas grill with a match, light one end of a piece of dry spaghetti to instantly extend your reach.

Testing and replacing an oven element

WHAT YOU'LL NEED

Screwdriver or nut driver

Masking tape and marker

Volt-ohm meter (VOM) or digital multimeter (DMM)

Replacement element

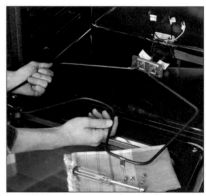

1 Shut off power to the oven at the service panel. Remove the element's bracket screws and pull it out. Label the wires with tape; then unscrew them from the terminals. Broilers have support brackets that must also be removed.

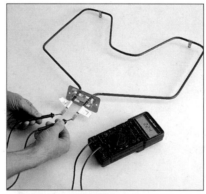

2 To test the element, set a volt-ohm meter or multimeter to its lowest range (RX1 on some models), and probe the two terminals. Look for a reading of between 15 and 30 ohms. If there's no reading, replace the unit.

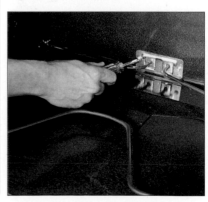

3 To reinstall the element or to install a new one, attach the wiring and reattach the bracket. For broilers, reattach the support brackets. Once everything is connected, restore the power at the service panel.

Barbecue bites. Food that is cooked on a gas or electric grill tastes just as flavorful as food cooked over charcoal. Barbecue flavor comes from the smoke produced by juices and fats dripping on a hot surface.

Buyer's guide. Grills with multiple burners provide more even heating and greater cooking options. You can sear meat on the left side of the grill and cook vegetables on the right. Or turn off the burner directly under the food and slow-cook with indirect heat.

Lighting it up. Open the grill hood before lighting it to avoid an explosion that could blow off the lid and seriously injure you. If the burners don't ignite in 5 seconds, shut them off to allow the gas to dissipate. It's better not to wear a long-sleeved shirt or loose clothes when barbecuing.

Clean a grill like an oven by spraying it with oven cleaner, letting it sit, then rinsing it off with a hose.

SAFE AND SMART

➤ Marinate meats in the refrigerator—not at room temperature—to keep bacteria from growing.

➤ To prevent food from sticking to a grill's wire racks, brush them with vegetable oil or spray on some nonstick cooking oil before cooking.

➤ Barbecue sauce burns easily, so wait until the food is almost cooked before brushing it on.

To clean up briquets, turn them over, grease-side down. Then light the grill and turn the heat to *High* to burn the grease away.

A natural painkiller. Keep a potted aloe plant near the gas grill. In the event of a minor burn, break off a leaf and rub the soothing gel onto the wound.

Fire extinguishers. Smother a fire flare-up caused by grease dripping on hot coals with a wet lettuce leaf. The greens will char and blacken but won't burn. Keep a bucket of sand nearby for larger fires.

Running out of gas? Some propane grills have tanks that warn you when the gas is low. If your grill doesn't have one, buy a stick-on gauge, available at most propane-refill stations. Activate the gauge by pouring hot water on it; then monitor its color. An orange gauge is empty; a yellow one is full.

Maintaining an outdoor gas grill

WHAT YOU'LL NEED

Venturi brush
Wire brush
Soapy water
Hose with nozzle
Toothpicks or pipe cleaners
Paintbrush
Wrench

1 To clean blocked venturi tubes, remove the burners and tubes from the gas valves. Then push a venturi brush into each tube until it hits the end. Clean the outside of the burners and tubes with a wire brush and soapy water.

2 Using a hose with a nozzle, flush water through the venturi tubes to determine if any burner ports are blocked. If so, unclog them by gently inserting a toothpick or pipe cleaner into them.

3 Finally, inspect all gas connections by brushing the hose fittings and valves with a soapy water solution. Watch for bubbles, which indicate leaks. Tighten with a wrench and retest loose areas, replacing any faulty fittings or valves.

Vacuum losing suction?
The most likely culprit is a full vacuum bag, followed by a clogged hose or secondary filter, or a blocked exhaust port, which can inhibit airflow as much as an obstructed hose.

Pins and needles jamming the vacuum? Attach a magnetic strip near the intake. Presto! No more clogged brushes or stuck pins.

A vacuum is worthless if the drive belt breaks. Replacing it, though, is easy. Unplug the vacuum and remove the bottom plate, sliding the brush out of the housing. Slip a new belt in place on the brush and in the housing, using a screwdriver to pull the belt over the drive pin. Reinstall the plate and plug in the unit.

Seeing sparks. Sparks and arcing from the on-off switch of a canister vacuum frequently go unnoticed because the switch is covered by the operator's foot. Bend down and inspect the switch by hand. The problem can often be corrected by cleaning and tightening the switch's terminals.

Slow it down. One leisurely stroke of the vacuum beats four quick strokes. A vacuum needs time for the beater bar to loosen the dirt and for the airflow to suck it up.

Slippery connections.
Lubricate hard-to-separate hose connections by rubbing the ends with wax paper. Or spray them lightly with silicone spray or nonstick food spray.

Sucking up. If vacuuming inside a drawer or on top of a bureau, cover the nozzle with cheesecloth secured by a rubber band so that valuables aren't sucked up into the hose. It's also a good way to find a lost contact lens or other small object.

Grooming the vacuum.
A dog's stiff-bristle grooming brush is a perfect tool to remove lint, string, and hair from the beater brush.

Repairing a broken vacuum hose

WHAT YOU'LL NEED

Garden hose

Duct tape or vinyl electrical tape

Utility knife

Wire cutters

Pliers

Rubber cement

Glue brush or applicator

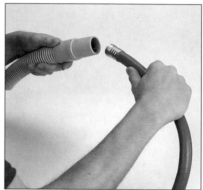

1 If the hose is clogged, try to blow out the obstruction by attaching the hose to the exhaust port. If the clog is near the end of the hose, push it out with a stiff garden hose.

2 For a quick fix, wrap the damaged area with duct tape or vinyl electrical tape. For a lasting repair, cut away the damaged section with a utility knife. For an older hose with reinforcing wire, cut the wire and pull out remaining wire with pliers.

3 Next, lift off or slide away the collar and scrape old glue from the fitting. Apply rubber cement to the outside portion of the hose that will be covered by the collar; then thread or push the new hose onto the fitting and under the collar.

Heat control burned out?

Before tossing the frying pan, try using a heat control from an electric wok, waffle iron, or slow cooker. If the terminals and the sensing element match exactly, you're ready to cook.

Jiggle it.

When the heat control flips on and off, there's an easy way to isolate the malfunction. With the unit turned on, hold the cord and jiggle the control. If the light flickers, the control is defective. If it doesn't, repeat the test, holding the control and jiggling the cord. To further isolate the malfunction, run a continuity check on the cord, being sure to flex the cord to reveal any hidden line breaks.

Use a heavy-duty plug,

not a lamp cord plug, when replacing a faulty plug on frying pans or any heating appliance. Wrap the cord wires clockwise around the screws on the prongs, and tighten the strain relief on the cord. If the cord is damaged, check the part number and order a new one.

Taking the temperature.
How do you know the heat control unit is accurate? Pour some cooking oil into a clean pan, turn the thermostat to 350°F, and wait for the control to turn off. Now insert a deep-fat thermometer into the oil. If the readings vary by more than 25 degrees, adjust the thermostat: Unplug the unit, lift off the dial cap, and turn the adjustment screw clockwise to raise the heat or counterclockwise to lower it.

Stay indoors. Never use electric frying pans outdoors or warm them over a gas or electric burner.

Rust relief. Use a cork sprinkled with scouring powder to remove rust spots from a non-stainless-steel wok or frying pan. Finish up by washing with warm soapy water. Dry the pan and then season it, with a thin coat of mineral oil.

Repairing electric frying pan connections

WHAT YOU'LL NEED

Steel wool
Very fine sandpaper
Screwdriver
Electrical contact cleaner
Point file (available at auto parts stores)
Bond paper

1 Take out the control and polish the heat control probe with steel wool. Clean female terminals in control by inserting and rotating a thin roll of sandpaper. With steel wool, clean pins on frying pan; you may have to remove the unit that houses them.

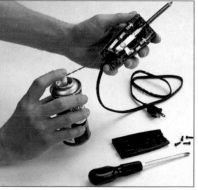

2 Plug the control back into the frying pan to check its operation. If further repair or cleaning is necessary, disassemble the control with a screwdriver and spray all components with contact cleaner.

3 Clean burned or pitted contacts in the control using a point file. Finish by gently polishing the contacts with a strip of bond paper. Reassemble the control, and plug it back into the frying pan to check its operation.

SAFE AND SMART

➤ Before cleaning, check the owner's manual: Some appliances can't be immersed in water even if they have detachable heat controls.

➤ Never move a pan that contains hot oil or hot water.

➤ Recondition nonstick coatings with cooking oil; check the owner's manual for frequency.

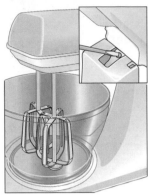

In for a dime. The proper clearance between mixer beaters and the bottom of the mixing bowl should be about 1/16 inch. Check it by placing a dime in the center of the bowl. If the beaters just barely clear the dime, the clearance is acceptable. If not, raise or lower the beaters by turning the adjustment screw under the motor housing.

Blocked air vents reduce air circulation and cause a small appliance's motor to overheat. Use a pipe cleaner to break up the clogs of food in the vents; then vacuum up the loosened debris.

Buyer's guide. Look for a blender that has a glass container (plastic scratches) and blades that unscrew from the bottom.

Misaligned blades on a blender not only won't make the cut but will also tax the appliance's motor. Periodically check the blade alignment by placing the blade assembly upside-down on a flat surface to see if the blades and assembly are parallel to it. If the blades are bent or dull replace the entire assembly.

Self-cleaning blender. Instead of arm wrestling to clean the recesses of a blender, fill it partially with hot water, add a drop of detergent, and turn it on for about 10 seconds. Rinse it with clean water and let dry.

Blender blahs. If a blender no longer revs to its full rpm's, sediment may be obstructing the blade. Fill the container with warm water and some liquid detergent, and let it sit overnight. If that doesn't restore full power, take apart the blade assembly and clean and lubricate it. Food residue often seeps past the seal into the motor's bearings and can cause the lubricant to congeal.

Gaining entry. The housing screws for a blender or processor are often hidden near or under the feet of the appliance. On some models, they may be located under the small rubber pads on the base of the unit; on others, inside the foot column itself. In most cases, you'll need a long-shank screwdriver to remove the screws from their hiding place.

Volume control. If a food processor's decibel level is giving you a headache, lower the volume by placing the machine on a place mat.

Repairing an electric mixer switch

WHAT YOU'LL NEED

| Screwdriver |
| Electrical contact cleaner |
| Bond paper |
| Diagonal-cutting pliers |
| Wire stripper/crimper |
| Replacement switch |
| Wire connectors (optional) |

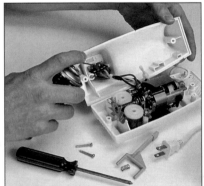

1 Pull the plug, and using a screwdriver, disassemble the appliance as needed to access the mixer switch. Spray electrical contact cleaner into any cracks or openings; then allow the parts to drain and dry. Reassemble the mixer and test it.

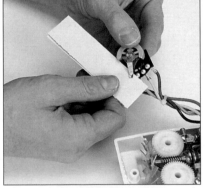

2 Inspect the contacts on the rotary slide switch. If they are dirty, spray with contact cleaner and then polish with bond paper. Slide the paper beneath the contact arm to polish the contact on the underside as well. Test the mixer.

3 If cleaning fails, replace the switch. Using diagonal-cutting pliers, cut the wires as close to the switch as possible. Strip 1/2 in. of insulation from the wire ends; then attach them to the new switch. If necessary, use wire connectors.

SPACE HEATERS

In good position. Set up a space heater where you'll need it most, but keep it away from furniture and draperies. Avoid using an extension cord—most don't have adequate capacity.

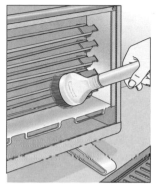

A clean sweep. At the start of the heating season, vacuum the heating element and reflector surface with a brush attachment before turning the heater on; this will remove any dust and debris that could ignite.

Speed up the heat by maintaining the house's relative humidity at 50 percent. A heater has to work longer to heat up a dry atmosphere. Low humidity also causes skin moisture to evaporate, making you feel cooler.

Just the reverse. Set a ceiling fan on reverse to return hot air that rises to the rafters. Always use a slower speed to avoid creating a draft.

The right element. If you can't find a replacement element for an older heater, note the wattage listed on the name plate and take a section from the burnt-out element to an appliance parts store. They can make up the element from stock.

Taking apart a heater? Manufacturers frequently hide the housing bolts or screws behind decorative name plates and chrome trim, which are held in place by spring clips. Remove them with a gentle tug to get at the bolts.

Keep the heat on. Lubricate the motor shaft periodically with a few drops of 20-weight nondetergent motor oil, manually turning the fan blades to work the oil into the bearings. Unplug the unit before performing the lube job.

It's shocking. A heating element that touches the reflector will cause shocks. Unplug the heater and gently draw the element away from the reflector with a handy "hook" made from a paper clip.

Replacing a heating element

WHAT YOU'LL NEED

Screwdriver

Long-nose pliers

Replacement heating element

1 Unplug the heater, and undo the screws to remove the cover. Then remove the screws that secure the heating element housing. Inspect the wires for discoloration, and note their positions for when you install the new element.

2 Remove the wire terminals with long-nose pliers, and separate the heating element from its support base. Either remove the retaining screws or turn the heating element terminal 90° so that it fits through the larger slot in the insulator.

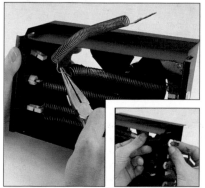

3 Next, unhook the element from the insulators with pliers. Install the new element by lifting it over the insulators and locking it into place. Don't stretch the heating coils any more than is necessary. Reconnect all wires, and reassemble the housing.

Void if prohibited. Before attempting any VCR repairs, read the warranty closely. Do-it-yourself fixes can void many of them.

When repairing a VCR, place the machine on a large plastic tray with a slight lip to prevent small parts from rolling off the table and disappearing forever. Working in a room with hard floors is better than one with deep pile carpeting.

Model-specific glitches. Don't trash a VCR if it or any of its accessories up and die on you—from a clock that goes dark to defective parts just falling off. Many models can be resurrected at small expense with special kits or a simple fix. Check with your VCR manufacturer to find out about model-specific problems or recalls.

Can't eject a tape?
Turn it off or pull the plug and wait a full minute or two. Sometimes the VCR gets into a confused state, and depowering it allows the microcontroller to reset itself. If this doesn't do the trick, you will need to open up the VCR to help cycle the cassette-loading mechanism by hand.

The right connections.
Hooking up a TV, cable box, and VCR all at once makes it hard to isolate a problem or glitch. Start by attaching the incoming lead to the VCR, connecting the "out" on the VCR to the "in" on the TV. If everything works, connect the cable box between the incoming lead and the VCR.

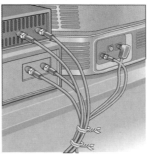

Use twist ties to rein in a gaggle of wires behind the TV, VCR, cable box, and stereo. Or cut a slit down the side of a short length of vinyl tubing and clamp it around the unruly cables.

A cool perch. Keep a VCR cool by placing spacer blocks under it before positioning it on top of a television. Cut four 2-inch squares from ½-inch-thick plywood, and place them under the VCR's legs to allow air to circulate. Paint the blocks the same color as the TV console to disguise them.

Store tapes upright with the fully wound spool on the bottom to prevent warping. Play the tapes at least once a year to keep the magnetic particles and binders from sticking together.

Replacing drive belts or tires

WHAT YOU'LL NEED

Screwdriver and small containers
Tweezers
Magnifying glass
Lint-free cloths or cotton swabs
95%-pure isopropyl or denatured alcohol
Replacement belts or tires
Dental pick (optional)

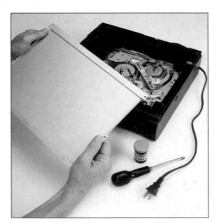

1 If the VCR is running slow or won't advance or rewind a good tape, you may need to replace the drive belt. Unplug the VCR; then remove the bottom panel (or top cover) with a screwdriver to access the drive belts and tires. Keep all removed screws organized and identified in small containers, such as film canisters.

2 Lift off a tire or belt with tweezers, or simply use your fingers. Depending on the VCR, additional disassembly may be required to reach the belts. Inspect each with a magnifying glass for fine cracks across the surface or wear lines along the perimeter.

 Wrap tape around the tweezer's jaws to avoid damaging the belt.

Tape quality affects not only the sound and image of a video but also the performance of the VCR. Low-quality or old tape sheds metal particles or bits of tape that can damage VCR heads and ruin other tapes. Quality, not price, should be the guide. Opt for a standard-grade tape from an established manufacturer over a high-grade tape manufactured by a bargain-basement company.

A clear head. White streaks, snow, or no picture at all is usually a telltale sign that the VCR heads are dirty or bad. Clean the VCR heads after every 20 hours of use—more frequently if you rent a lot of tapes. Remember: Taping a 1-hour show and playing it back equals 2 hours of use. Professional cleanings, which cost $20 to $40, are also recommended after 300 hours of operation.

When timing tapings, set the VCR clock a few minutes early so you won't miss the beginning of a program and a few minutes late to allow for long commercials. When recording a program on public television, be aware of fundraising drives and set the VCR timer accordingly.

Dry, wet, or magnetic? There are three types of cassette-style head cleaners. The dry technique is the most abrasive, literally sanding off particles from the VCR heads. The wet technique is better because the heads are swabbed with a gentle cleaning solution. Magnetic-base cleaning systems are considered the most effective and least damaging to the VCR. If you choose a cassette-style cleaner, make sure it comes with a warranty.

Manual rewind. When a VCR pulls the tape out of the cassette, rewind it by hand if it isn't damaged. Press the door release on the side of the cassette and prop it open. Then insert a finger into the take-up spool and turn it to wind the tape back. If the reel doesn't turn, insert a pencil into the brake release hole to disengage the spring clip.

SAFE AND SMART

➤ Wear lint-free gloves when respooling videotape. The oils from bare fingers can degrade the tape.

➤ Lubricating the drive belts and other soft rubber parts in a VCR can damage them.

➤ Cover the VCR when it's not in use and turned off; airborne dust is attracted to the magnetic heads.

➤ Always replace a videotape if the sound or picture drops out periodically.

3 If belts or tires are stretched or damaged, replace them all, rather than just one. Replacement kits for each model of VCR are available. If necessary, use a belt gauge, as printed in a parts catalog, to determine the proper replacement belt size. To allow for the stretching of the old belt, choose a replacement that is 3% to 5% smaller than the old one.

4 If the belts or tires are not over-stretched or worn out, clean them with lint-free cloths or cotton swabs dampened with isopropyl or denatured alcohol. Don't touch belts or tires with your fingers. Use tweezers or handle them with a lint-free cloth.

5 Reinstall the belt, using tweezers. A dental pick or similar tool may also be handy to pull the belt over a difficult-to-access pulley. Reassemble the VCR completely before plugging it in to test its operation.

Additional memory will make a computer quicker and more responsive. Eight megabytes of random access memory (RAM) is considered the minimum these days; 12 megabytes has become the the standard. If you have a CD-ROM drive, 16 megabytes is ideal.

Don't remove labels from memory chips. In addition to identifying the item, the label protects the chip from ultraviolet light.

Selective memory. When adding memory to a computer, make sure the new RAM's speed matches that of the old. IBM-compatibles, in particular, don't like to mix speeds. Buying faster memory is a waste of money, anyhow; it won't speed up computing time.

Powerful protection. Hook up the computer, printer, disk drives, and other peripherals to the same power strip to eliminate electrical differences in the ground circuit. Just make sure the power strip has surge protection.

Floppy disk stuck? You can eject it from a disk drive (in a Macintosh) with a straightened paper clip. Insert the clip in the small hole under the disk slot to release the spring holder and free the disk.

A turn-on? The more times you turn on a computer, the quicker you'll wear it out. The expansion and contraction of connections and components can result in broken solder joints and even short circuits. If you're going to be away from the machine for more than a couple of hours, turn it off. Otherwise, leave it on as you come and go, and turn it off at the end of the workday.

Ground control. It is essential to unplug an appliance before doing any maintenance or repairs. With computers, it may be better to leave the unit plugged in and turn off the power switch. A grounded power cord helps dissipate static electricity buildup that could damage sensitive circuitry. Ground yourself with an antistatic wrist guard (available at electronics stores).

Safe storage. Store disks away from the floor, where a vacuum cleaner's electric motor can create a data-deleting magnetic field.

Adding RAM memory to a computer

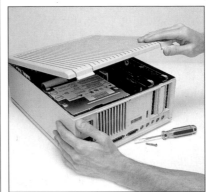

1 Unplug the computer, and disconnect all external cables. Remove screws or catches to remove the housing. To increase the RAM, you must add or replace existing chips; the supplier or maker can tell you which.

2 Put on an antistatic wrist guard before removing any chips. For most computers, you must press the retaining clip aside and tilt the chip outward. If there's no retaining clip, grasp the chip by the edges and gently pull it out.

3 To install a new chip, carefully align the notched end with the socket. Then align the other end and press the chip firmly into place. When handling chips, touch only the edges. Reinstall the housing and reconnect the computer.

Keyboard keys. Clean the keyboard with cotton swabs dipped in commercially prepared computer cleaner, working into the crevices between keys. Then keep the keyboard dust-free by installing a plastic seal over the keys that allows you to type while it's in place.

Screen saver. Commercial window cleaners can leave a static film on a monitor that is a magnet for dust. Instead use a monitor cleaner, available in pads or spray. If using a spray, don't squirt it directly on the screen; the liquid can seep into the circuitry. Spray the cleaner on a lint-free cloth, then wipe the screen

Printer pointers. When changing the printer's ribbon or cartridge, clean the rubber roller, or printer platen, with commercially prepared platen cleaner. Cover the printer when it's not in use; printer components are more susceptible to damage from dust than are those of the computer.

Paper chase. Buy some spare printer trays to save time when you need to change paper size. Load the trays, and slip in the appropriate size when needed.

Laptop logic. Checking a laptop at an airline baggage counter can result in damaged circuitry caused by jolts on its way to the plane. Always carry it with you.

Toner tip. Save the box after installing a new toner cartridge in a printer. If you have to remove the cartridge to work on the printer, you'll have a perfect package in which to store it.

Cleaning a computer mouse

WHAT YOU'LL NEED

Clean lint-free cloth

Isopropyl alcohol

Dishwashing detergent (optional)

Plastic cap from a pen

Canned air

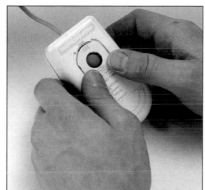

1 Shut off the computer, or unplug the mouse. Turn the mouse upside down and press on the ball-cage housing cover while pushing it forward or, with some models, by rotating the ball-cage housing counterclockwise.

2 Remove the ball, and clean it with a lint-free cloth dampened with isopropyl alcohol. Or let the ball soak in a solution of warm water and dishwashing detergent. Make sure it's completely dry before you reinstall it.

3 Scrape plaque from the rollers with a plastic cap from a pen; then swab them with isopropyl alcohol. Blow additional dust out of the cage with canned air, and reassemble.

FILE IT

Stress-free computing

A long day in front of the computer can leave you feeling tired and achy. Skip the strain with these workstation tips.

The right light. Indirect light from nonfluorescent sources eliminates glare and harsh reflections that can tire the eyes. The primary light source should be above and to the rear of the screen.

The right view. Place the monitor 18 to 20 inches from your eyes, with the top line of the screen display slightly lower than eye level, to reduce eyestrain. And don't forget to give your eyes a rest from time to time.

The right height. To avoid carpal tunnel syndrome, position the keyboard so that when your hands are placed on the keys, your forearms are parallel to the floor and your elbows form a 90° angle. A rolled-up hand towel placed under the wrists can provide added comfort.

Dish speak. First-time consumers can be confused by dish jargon. Don't be. *Dish temperature* refers to the amount of interfering ground noise the dish may pick up. *Efficiency* is the percentage of the signal the dish can collect. *Low-noise block* (LNB) is the pickup in the center of the dish. *Reflector weight* is simply the total weight of the dish.

Future growth. When mounting a satellite dish, factor in how your garden grows. Tree growth can weaken the satellite signal, which doesn't pass through leaves and branches.

FILE IT

Are you satellite-ready?
When you dish out all that money for a dish, you want it to deliver on its promises. Here is a checklist to determine if your house is correctly configured for a satellite setup.

Location. You need a clear line of sight to the satellite. There should be no trees, leaves, or buildings between the dish and the satellite.

Mounting method. Plan on a site that allows you to clear off snow and ice from the dish without endangering your safety. The safest mounts are often on the side of the house, on a deck or patio, or on a pole in the yard.

Equipment. If you're looking for the best picture and sound quality, you'll need a TV equipped with separate RF, audio-video, and S-video inputs and a VCR that comes with RF and audio/video inputs, coaxial audio/video, and S-video cables.

Cleaner connections. Satellite signals are minute compared to conventional broadcast signals. To prevent signal loss and degradation over time, coat each connector and connection with dielectric compound (available from electronic parts suppliers) before you tighten it.

Lost and found. Satellite dishes can give you 170 channels, but they won't provide local or network programming. To receive those channels, either hook up an antenna or rabbit ears, or subscribe to your cable operator's basic service.

Installing a satellite dish

WHAT YOU'LL NEED

Digital satellite dish and receiver

Installation kit and/or assorted brackets, cables, lag screws, bolts, washers, line and telephone surge protectors, and other hardware as needed

Compass, screwdrivers (straight and Phillips), hammer, pliers, wire cutters, and other tools as needed

Drill and bits

Roofing cement

Level

Ratchet or open-end wrench

Telephone modular jack or splitter

Ladder (optional)

1 Use compass and instructions to determine the best site for the dish (for example, the side of the house, roof, or chimney). If you are mounting on the roof, locate a rafter by tapping on the roof or by using a stud detector. Position the foot of the mounting hardware, and drill holes for screws that will secure foot to the rafter. Apply roofing cement to bottom of the foot and the drill holes; install with lag bolts.

2 Raise the mast to a near-upright position, and check with a level in one direction, then by turning the level in a perpendicular direction. Use the adjustment screw to level the mast, taking into account the pitch of the roof. Horizontal leveling, if needed, will require placing several 5/16-in. washers beneath the foot for shimming and then resealing around it with roofing cement.

Advance warning. You can hook up more than one TV to the satellite receiver, but all the sets will be tuned to the same channel. Multi-channel setups usually require buying another expensive receiver.

Snow job. A snow or ice storm can interfere with a dish's incoming signal and also damage the actuator. Installing a dish cover, made of lightweight mesh, will shield the equipment from the white stuff (but not rain interference) without weakening the signal.

Designer dishes. A large satellite dish sitting in the backyard can be an eyesore. Designer covers can disguise or camouflage the equipment, transforming a dish into a patio umbrella or even a large rock.

Close tabs. To keep a satellite or TV remote within easy reach, attach a Velcro strip to the TV and a corresponding strip to the back of the remote.

Cleaning the screen. For a dust-free TV screen that matches crystal-clear satellite reception, wipe it with a fabric-softener sheet dabbed in rubbing alcohol. Spraying the screen or wooden casing with glass cleaner or oil could foul up the innards of the television.

ANTENNAS

To the point. Since antennas are directional pickup devices, they have to be pointed at the transmitted signal to be effective. Most antennas have a V configuration; the twin points of the V should point toward the transmitter.

A shock to the system. An antenna that comes in contact with an electrical power line could deliver a lethal electrical charge to the entire home. Set up the antenna so that the distance between it and the nearest power line is at least twice the length of the antenna.

TV reception weak? Isolate the problem by hooking up an indoor antenna to the TV. If the picture quality improves, the roof antenna is the problem.

Great reception. The most desirable configuration would be a large antenna on a tall mast, but if this isn't feasible, then a large antenna mounted on a short mast is best.

SAFE AND SMART

➤ Cable companies can charge a steep service fee to change subscription packages. In some cases, it may be more economical to start with a higher-priced service rather than upgrade a few months later.

➤ Not all communities welcome satellite dishes in the neighborhood. Be sure to check all local laws and codes before buying or installing an expensive dish.

Power boost. If you have a good antenna but still have weak reception, boost the signal with a 2-component preamp. The preamp is attached to the antenna mast and the power supply is placed inside the home, away from the elements.

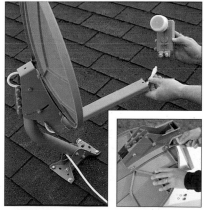

3 On the ground, bolt the satellite dish to the bracket on the LNB arm. On the roof, slide the clamp on the arm over the mast, but do not tighten it yet. Route the cable through the mast and arm; then tighten the connector. (Some models come with more than one connector.) Finally, slide the LNB into the opening and secure it with a bolt.

4 Route the cable to the receiver, using clamps to secure it to the wall and overhangs. Installing a grounding block helps prevent lightning damage, while drip loops prevent water from entering connections or the inside of the house. The ground wire attaches to the ground rod. Other connections include the receiver to the TV and the receiver to the telephone jack.

5 Use audio and video display from the receiver to zero in on the strongest satellite signal; on rooftop installations, this usually requires a helper. Make azimuth (side-to-side) and elevation (up-and-down) adjustments using very slight movements. Center the adjustments in the middle of the strongest signal area, marking the placement on the mast.

STONE, BRICK, AND CONCRETE

Job ratings: Easy   Medium   Complex

Room to move. Allow at least 25 square feet of patio per house occupant. A dining table and chairs require at least a 6 x 6-foot area. Add in extra footage for a grill, lounge chairs, and any other outdoor amenities.

Flour power. Flour is cheaper to use than limestone or spray paint for marking out excavations for patios or pool enclosures. Dispense it from a coffee-can sifter jammed into a saw cut on the end of a piece of 2 x 2 and screwed in place. Tap the handle with a mallet to release the flour.

Feeling low? Fill low spots in the excavation with the same crushed stone you'll be using for the job, and tamp down. Dirt will eventually settle, causing a depression in the pavement.

Pile dug-up dirt and sod on a tarp, where it will be easy to haul away. Leaving the dirt on the lawn for more than a few days could damage or kill the grass.

Sand sense. When paving is delayed because of bad weather, cover the sand bed with plastic sheeting to protect it from the elements. Or spread the sand in 10-square-foot sections just before laying the pavers. And throw a tarp over that sand pile to protect it from kids, wind, and animals.

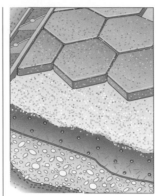

Keep paver joints clear of weeds and grass by covering the layer of aggregate beneath the sand with a layer of solid membrane. A good choice is 15-pound builder's felt. Lap the felt 6 inches at the seams, and cut small holes for drainage.

Brick trick. When laying bricks or pavers, drop them directly in place. Sliding them on the sand will create high or low spots that you'll have to level—again.

Pavers over concrete? Most types of pavers can be placed on top of concrete slab work with a coat of thinset adhesive—check with the paver manufacturer. Be sure the concrete is in good shape and level, applying a concrete leveling compound if needed.

Shapely curves. Plastic or aluminum paver edging secured by steel spikes is the best edging for curves. Plastic (shown here) is easier to install, but aluminum is sturdier. With both types, use a single uncut piece when rounding a curve.

Installing a walk with bricks or pavers

WHAT YOU'LL NEED

Goggles, gloves, and knee-pads

Stakes and mason's twine

Line level or spirit level

Garden hose or rope

Shovel and wheelbarrow

½-in. crushed stone and coarse sand

Rented plate vibrator and wet saw

Aluminum, plastic, or plywood edging

Wood to make a screed and a tamp

Pavers or bricks

Rubber mallet

Stiff broom

1 Use stakes and twine to lay out the walk and a line level to adjust the proper height. Consider the paver dimension (leave an extra ⅛ in. for length and width) and the bond (pattern) to determine the walk's width. For curves, use two lengths of rope or garden hose. Then excavate the area at least 8 in. Allow for gravel (compacted with a plate vibrator to 4 in. minimum), a 2-in. sand bed, and the paver thickness.

2 Place, level, and compact the gravel bed; then pitch the walk ¼ in. per ft. Install the edging with the top at the desired walk surface. For curved walks, use edging made of flexible aluminum or plastic or two layers of ¼-in. luan plywood (one at a time). For straight walks, use wood edging set against the stakes. Check the pitch with a spirit level.

Seal the deal. A water sealer enhances the color of pavers and protects them from stains. Clean pavers before sealing, if necessary, with an acid-base product recommended for that purpose, and reapply the sealer every 2 to 5 years.

Paver pullers. Use a pair of pullers made from coat hanger wire to remove individual pavers for releveling. Slip the pullers down each side of the paver, rotate a quarter turn, then pull up the load.

A critical turnover. When patio blocks become pitted or grooved from water runoff, just dig them out, flip them over and, if necessary, level each block with sand. The new surface will last as long as the side you just buried in the sand.

On the level. Because they fit tightly together, pavers can be a pain to reset. To ease the task, wiggle the last few as close to position as possible, cover them with a short piece of 2 x 4, and tap each paver level with a 3-pound maul.

Go to boardwalk. If you're building only a small pathway, consider a wooden boardwalk. Make each section from ten 14-inch pieces of 2 x 6 redwood or cedar held together on the bottom with plumber's tape tacked with roofing nails.

FILE IT

Picking a pattern

Here are some of the more popular configurations for constructing a walkway or patio from bricks or pavers.

Brick patterns

Running bond

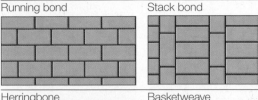

Stack bond

Herringbone

Basketweave

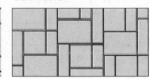

Paver patterns

Cobblestone

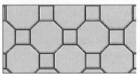

Geometric

3 Place, tamp, and level a 2-in. sand bed. To level, use a notched screed equal to the thickness of the pavers. If edging with bricks, place them against the edging first. If using soldiers (standing pavers or bricks), install them in a trench against the edging.

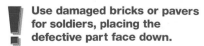 **Use damaged bricks or pavers for soldiers, placing the defective part face down.**

4 Working a section at a time, lay the pavers or bricks in the desired pattern, spacing them ⅛ in. apart. Use a rubber mallet to tamp them level with the edging and with each other. Use a diamond-blade wet saw to cut the pavers or bricks as required. It is best to wait until the entire walkway is laid before you do your cutting. This allows you to make final adjustments.

5 Spread coarse sand over the finished walk, and brush it at a 45° angle to force it into the joints. If the edging is temporary, remove it and backfill with soil and sod. Water the walk daily, brushing more sand between the cracks as needed.

Be conservative when ordering flagstone; most dealers won't take back the excess. As a guideline, a ton of 1½-inch-thick flagstone covers approximately 100 square feet.

Take time to outline. Lay out the stones for a stepping-stone walkway right on the grass; then dust them with flour. Pick up the stones and you'll have a map for your shovel to follow.

The three-step pattern. If you want a patio that looks less formal than one made of identical-size stones but more formal than a random pattern, work to the design shown above. It uses three sizes of precut stone, but you can also design a surface using 1-foot square and 2 x 3-foot rectangular stones.

From the outside in. When laying flagstone in a random pattern, position the largest stones around the perimeter of the job first. This configuration will help prevent the interior pieces from shifting.

Foiled flagstone. A piece of aluminum foil makes a handy template for missing pieces of irregular flagstone. Lay the foil over the spot to be filled, scrunch the edges to the desired shape, then trace around the template with a nail to mark the pattern on the flagstone.

Score! Remove large segments from flagstones with ease by scoring the cut with a brick set or stonemason's chisel and a heavy hammer before breaking them off. Score along the sides and bottom as well as the top.

Trimming tip. If a bricklayer's or stonemason's chisel won't cut a stone, undercut it first. Flip the stone over, and chip off bits of stone on the waste side of the cut line.

Installing a flagstone patio

WHAT YOU'LL NEED

Goggles, gloves, and ear plugs

Stakes and twine

Shovel and wheelbarrow

½-in. crushed stone and stone dust

Rented plate vibrator

Wood for edging and screed

Portland cement and sand

Mason's trowel

Flagstones

Long straightedge and spirit level

Small sledgehammer or rubber mallet

Brick trowel and jointing tool

Dry mix

Stiff broom

1 Lay out, excavate, and place the bed (see pp. 248–249). Measuring by the shovelful, mix 1 part portland cement and 5–6 parts mason's sand. Spread a 3-in. layer on top of the gravel in a manageable 3-ft. row.

 Break the installation work into walk-size dimensions, moving temporary edging as you go.

2 Bend at the knees to lift stones, or "walk" them, first one corner, then the next. Drop them into place about ½ in. apart. The layout string should be positioned at the desired finished height (about 1 in. above the ground) and at the proper pitch (¼ in. per ft. away from the house).

Cutting a pile of stones?
Make a sandbox table to ease the load. Nail a 1 x 2 to each side of a piece of 1-inch plywood to hold the sand, and support the box with 2 x 4 legs or a pair of sawhorses. The sand will cushion the cuts, and the height of the table will spare your back.

Save the stones. Tilt up a large piece of flagstone on its edge before you lift it, even if you have a helper. Lifting up the stone flat may cause it to break in the middle under its own weight.

The right way to pry.
When you need to remove flagstones to repair a sand paving bed, use a piece of wood as a fulcrum for the pry bar. The wood will not only make lifting easier, but also protect neighboring stones from damage.

Faux flagstone. Avoid backbreaking stone-work by making a walkway or patio from poured concrete and carving "joints" into the smoothed concrete with a brick jointing tool. Work from a predrawn pattern so the concrete won't set up before you're done. Include control joints in the design.

SAFE AND SMART

➤ Don't stamp or jump on hard flagging to level it. You may crack the stone and also injure your knees.

➤ Wear safety goggles and gloves when scoring or breaking flagstones.

➤ To lift a heavy flagstone, bend at the knees first or "walk" the stone corner by corner.

Are stains a pain?
Remove food stains on flagstone with a solution of dishwashing liquid and water. Swab the solution on the stain and work it in with a stiff scrub brush; then rinse with clean water. If this doesn't do the trick, mix ammonia into the solution.

3 As each stone is placed, lay a 2 x 4 straightedge and a spirit level across the stone, and extend it to the layout string. Place a wood scrap on the stone and tap it with a small sledgehammer until it is level in one direction and aligned with the layout string.

4 When you have completed a row, stretch a string across the stones to make sure they are level with each other. Relocate the layout string and repeat the procedure until the patio is complete. Backfill and repair plantings at the patio's edges.

5 Use a brick trowel to spread dry mix over the joints and a jointing tool to press it in place. Sweep off any excess mortar, and gently hose down the patio once a day for a few days. Avoid heavy traffic for several days until the mortar has set.

Flex time. Use a mason's trowel with a flexible blade to spread mortar like a pro. The blade should bend about an inch when the point is pressed against a flat hard surface.

Winterize your brick. Outdoor work demands exterior brick that can stand up to the weather. If you're unsure whether the bricks you bought can take the cold, soak a couple of them in water, freeze overnight, let them thaw, then repeat the freeze-thaw cycle several more times. If the brick doesn't crack, it will probably endure the worst that winter has to dish out.

Dry facts. Dry bricks will suck the moisture out of the mortar as you set them, resulting in a weak bond. If your mortar is drying out too fast, dip each brick in a bucket of water, let the surface dry, then lay it in place.

Ready-mix mortar is easy to use, but you pay for the convenience. If you'll be laying ⅜-inch joints, buy an 80-pound bag of mix for every 65 bricks. Wider joints will eat up the mortar faster, so you'll be able to set fewer bricks per bag.

To avoid waste, mix up only enough mortar to carry you through about 1½ hours of labor. If the mortar starts to dry out, you can retemper it by thoroughly stirring in a little water. You can retemper only once, however.

Bad temper. Don't retemper colored mortar if it dries out. Doing so will alter its shade, and it won't match the rest of the project. Throw out the mortar and mix a new batch.

The match game. To match new mortar to old, blend a batch of test samples using various colors of cement and sand. Tool the samples the same way you'll finish the brickwork, let them set, and compare. If necessary, combine two or more colors of sand to produce a closer match.

SAFE AND SMART

➤ The lime in mortar can dehydrate your skin, leaving it cracked and sore. Protect your hands by wearing waterproof gloves or, for a less cumbersome fit, disposable latex surgical gloves.

➤ If you use that old standby—muriatic acid—to clean off dried mortar, prepare it in a weak solution (1 part acid to 10 parts water) in a nonmetal pail. Pour the acid into the water, not the other way around, and wear goggles, a long-sleeved shirt, and rubber gloves. Also use a respirator designed to protect against acid fumes.

Mixing and handling mortar

WHAT YOU'LL NEED

Mortar (3 parts sand, 1 part masonry cement or packaged mortar mix)

Garden hose or water in a bucket

Hoe and shovel

Wheelbarrow, large sheet of old plywood, or other mixing container

Mortarboard (24-in.-sq. plywood)

Pointed mason's trowel

Stone or unit masonry (brick, concrete block, etc.)

Jointing tool

Stiff-bristle brush (for cleaning tools)

1 Mix mortar to a smooth consistency until the sides of a furrow hold their shape. Shovel a mound onto a mortarboard. To load a trowel, separate a slice of mortar from the mound; then use the back of the blade to shape the mortar into a lump about the length and width of the blade.

2 Place the trowel flat on the board behind the slice. With a swift forward motion, slip it under the mortar. Lift, and with a down-and-back snap of your forearm, seat the mortar on the trowel.

No second chances. Don't reposition a brick once you place it or you'll break the bond between the brick and mortar.

Do it over. Rather than repositioning a misaligned brick, pop it out completely, clean it, scrape all the mortar out of the joint, then replace the brick with some fresh mortar.

Thumbs up. Pressing your thumb into mortar will tell you when it's time to tool the joints. If you leave a thumbprint without gunking up your glove, the mortar is ready to smooth.

Accelerated aging. Mist new exterior brickwork with water-soluble plant fertilizer to create an aged look fast. The fertilizer will encourage the growth of mold, which produces the characteristic mottled look of old brick.

Fast patina. Give the soft luster of age to new interior brick by swabbing on a coat of boiled linseed oil after the mortar has dried. Let the oil soak in for 2 to 3 hours; then rub off the excess with clean lint-free rags.

FILE IT

Mortar joints and shapes

Concave. Most common joint; sheds water well. Use a convex forming tool.

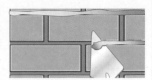

Flush. Fairly water-resistant; best under plaster or stucco. Just scrape off extra mortar.

V-joint. Looks dramatic and sheds water well. Form with V-jointing tool or trowel tip.

Raked. Good-looking but not water resistant; best for indoors. Use a raking tool.

Weathered. Sheds water well. To form, press trowel tip up and in.

Struck. Sheds water poorly. To form, press trowel tip down and in at an angle.

3 Position the point of the trowel over the spot where the line is to begin. Rotate the trowel 180° as you raise it, and with a downward snap of the wrist and forearm, throw down the line, centered on the masonry unit. With the trowel at a low angle, run the tip down the center to evenly furrow the mortar.

4 Butter the abutting edges of masonry units before setting them in the mortar bed. Pick up an appropriate amount of mortar on the top of the trowel and spread it on the unit. Then press the mortar down on all four edges to bond it. The mortar will take the shape of a truncated pyramid.

5 Place the unit with its buttered end pushed against the adjoining unit until the head and bed joints are a little thicker than the desired finished joint. Tap the unit with the heel of the trowel until it is level, aligned, and has the proper joint thickness. Cut off excess mortar with the trowel's edge.

Pretty harmful. Some lovely vines are murder on mortar joints, causing them to crumble. Grow vines on trellises, or try a mortar-friendly species like climbing hydrangea.

Take it all off. When removing vines from brickwork, get off every little bit or the leftover vegetation will oxidize, leaving ugly marks. After pulling off as much of the vine as you can, wait a week or two for the remainder to dry; then scrub the brick with strong detergent and a stiff brush.

A shady situation? Mold and mildew thrive in shaded areas. They may not hurt the brickwork, but they do cause discoloration. Remove mold with a spritz of a 50-50 solution of household bleach and water, a stiff-bristle brush, and plenty of elbow grease. Rinse with clean water after an hour.

Gather no moss. A dose of weed killer, sprayed on according to the manufacturer's directions, will remove even stubborn moss from brick walls.

If you rent scaffolding to repair brickwork on the upper stories, work from the top to the bottom. This way, you can get the scaffolding back to the rental shop quicker, cutting down on rental fees.

Hearing test. When replacing damaged bricks with salvaged ones, use your ears to determine if they can withstand the weather. Holding the brick in one hand, tap it lightly with a hammer—a dull thud often indicates a soft brick; a metallic ring, a hard brick.

A soft edge. Before restoring brickwork that is more than a century old, consult an experienced repair mason to make sure the mortar you use is softer than the brick. Standard modern mortar mixes, usually harder than old bricks, can cause the brick edges to spall.

SAFE AND SMART

➤ Gear up for brick-and-mortar work. Protective goggles are a must when repointing mortar or replacing bricks, as are sturdy work gloves and old clothes. In fact, it's a good idea to wear a shirt and pants that are on their last legs so that you can throw them out once the job is finished.

Repointing bricks

WHAT YOU'LL NEED

Safety glasses

Old screwdriver

Mason's hammer

Mason's chisel or narrow cold chisel

Stiff-bristle brush

Mixing container or wheelbarrow

Mortar mix (or masonry cement and sand)

Water

Trowel

Pointing tool

Rake with wheels

Brush

1 Wearing safety glasses, remove loose, soft mortar to a depth of ¾ in., scraping it out with an old screwdriver. Use a mason's hammer and mason's chisel for more solid mortar, being careful not to chip brick edges. Clear all chips and dust from the joints with a stiff brush.

2 Dry-mix 3 parts cement with 1 part sand to make the mortar. Add water to make a stiff, but not crumbly, paste. If the mortar is too wet, it will slop onto the bricks and have to be cleaned off later.

 Ask the concrete supplier to help you match the new mortar to the old, so the repair isn't noticeable.

Putting the squeeze on.
For big repointing jobs, cut your work time substantially by using a grout bag instead of a pointing trowel to fill mortar joints. Just add a little more liquid than usual to the mortar to make it flow more easily, and control the flow by twisting the bag.

Tooling along. To tool repointed mortar joints to a concave profile, use a piece of metal tubing or the end of a spoon handle. Or buy a convex joint tool specially made for this purpose.

Brick scrubber. A broken piece of same-colored brick will "erase" excess mortar or paint specks. Testing first in an inconspicuous place, rub spots with the softer interior surface of the brick—the harder outside could scratch.

Hard truth. Large clumps of mortar stuck to brick-work are easily removed when they are allowed to completely harden. Just strike them off with a sharp blow of a trowel. Wiping off still-soft mortar will smear the surface of the bricks.

FILE IT
Brushing up on brickwork
A guide to diagnosing and handicapping brick troubles.

Symptom	What it means	Difficulty
Loose, crumbly, cracked mortar	Bricks need repointing	Fairly easy
Chipping or flaking bricks	Bricks are softer inside than outside, and they deteriorate as they weather. Badly weathered bricks should be replaced.	Fairly easy
Cracks in walls	Hairline cracks are usually harmless. Diagonal cracks along joints may indicate settling.	Easy to difficult, depending on the cause
Window and door openings out of square	Structural members above wall openings deteriorate faster than the rest of the masonry, forcing windows and doors out of position.	Difficult
Bulges in walls	Walls bulge as water, which enters through cracked mortar joints, freezes and thaws.	Difficult

3 Place the mortar on the trowel and stuff it into the joints with a pointing tool, making sure that the joint is completely filled.

4 Run a rake with wheels over the joints to level and flatten the still-wet mortar so that it matches the shape of the old joints.

5 Sweep the joints with a brush after the mortar begins to stiffen in order to remove loose material and to match textures.

A dry run. Stack concrete blocks on a wood pallet and cover them with plastic sheeting as soon as they're delivered. Wet blocks expand—and then shrink when they dry out, possibly cracking mortar joints.

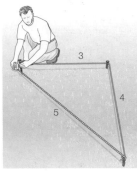

Square up. A triangulation test can tell you whether the layout lines of the wall form a square corner. Measure 3 feet down one line and 4 feet down the other, and measure across the end points—if the distance is 5 feet, the corner is square.

A simple story stick can keep your block wall honest, preventing small mistakes in spacing from multiplying into major ones. To make a story stick, mark the dimensions of the blocks and the mortar joints for each course on a length of 1 x 2. As you progress, compare your work against the markings on the stick.

Stringing in the rain. To keep chalk lines from washing away, spray them with a quick-drying aerosol lacquer. Not only will the lines survive inclement weather, they'll also stand up to frequent sweeping.

Strike and save. Use a brick trowel to cut and catch excess mortar that squeezes from the joint. Flip it back onto the mortarboard, give it a quick mix, and use again.

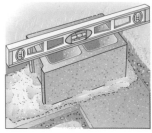

Room to maneuver. Lay the level right down the center of a block so you can tap the block's edges to adjust its placement without disturbing the level itself.

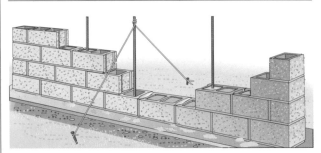

Steady as it goes. Keep rebars from wobbling in the first courses of a block wall by bracing them with stakes positioned in the ground on both sides of the wall.

Building a unit masonry wall

WHAT YOU'LL NEED

Spirit level, line level, and water level

Chalk line

Mason's string line

Mortar mix

Concrete block (or other unit masonry)

Mixing container or wheelbarrow

Garden hoe

Mason's trowel

Reinforcing wire and rods

U-shaped line blocks

Pointing tool

1 Transfer wall position from layout lines to footing with a spirit level. Mark outside corners and snap a chalk line between marks on the footing. Use a line level stretched on taut twine to see if one end of footing is higher.

 If the wall is to be faced with stone or brick, place metal ties in the joints every few feet for each course. Bend the ties up.

2 Place and furrow a 1-in.-thick, 4-ft.-long mortar bed at the high end. Set a corner block in the mortar. Make sure it is in line with the layout twine, is level in all directions, and forms a ³⁄₈-in. joint with the footing.

 Lay blocks with the flared web side up to provide a larger area for the mortar bed. This also makes blocks easier to grip.

Neat trick. A homemade funnel will deliver the mortar where it belongs—in the cavities of concrete blocks, not down the sides or on the ground. Make the funnel from a piece of ½-inch plywood. Saw cutouts in the sides to support the bucket rim during the pour.

Cut concrete blocks with a brick chisel and a 3-pound stone hammer, scoring along the cut line with firm taps. When the sound of the chisel drops in pitch, lighten up—the block has fractured and will soon split.

Cushion the cut. Support the block to be cut on a slightly resilient surface, such as a bed of sand or a scrap of wood. You'll get a cleaner, easier cut than if you work on concrete or another ungiving surface.

Set rocks like blocks. Lay up a stone wall the same way you would a brick or block wall—by placing the stones one over two and two over one. The overlap makes the wall more durable.

Why dry? Not only is a dry-laid stone wall easier to build, but it will last longer than a mortared one. A dry wall can roll with the punches from freeze-thaw cycles better than a mortared wall, which will eventually crack under the seasonal stress.

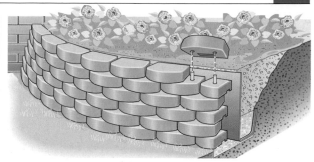

A quick retaining wall. Interlocking concrete blocks cost more than common blocks, but you'll save on installation time—you don't need footings or mortar for walls up to 3 feet high. The interlocking wall above uses fiberglass pins, which fit into holes in the block.

SAFE AND SMART

➤ When cutting concrete blocks, wear safety goggles and use a hammer that's designed to strike other tools, not a regular carpenter's hammer. The flying metal shards that can break off the hammerhead are as dangerous as shrapnel.

➤ Before starting work on a wall, check with your local building department about building codes and foundation requirements for your area. All block walls must rest on concrete footings that extend below the frost line.

3 Stand some blocks on end to butter their flanges. Lay two stretcher blocks in the first course, pressing the buttered flanges against the adjacent block to form a ⅜-in. joint. Similarly, lay the beginnings of the second course and third course as shown. Repeat at the other end; use a water level to verify that the first course at the two ends is dead level.

4 Stretch a mason's string line taut between line blocks at the ends so it sits at the outside upper edge of the first course. Complete each course in alignment with the string line, constantly checking the level. If vertical ½-in. reinforcing rods are required, overlap the rods about 15 in. and bind them together with No. 8 iron wire; then grout (fill) those cavities with mortar.

5 Press a web of reinforcing wire into the setting bed of every other course. Install bond beam (U-shaped line blocks) on the top course. Half-fill it with mortar and lay in two lengths of reinforcing bar (overlapped and bound together); fill to the top. If desired, lay cap blocks. Strike off excess mortar as you work, and tool the joints when thumbprint-hard.

Ligten the load. Your back will thank you every time you pass on picking up a heavy bag of cement or sand. Instead, slip a rectangular snow shovel under the load and slide it along.

Portable cement mixer. Prop up each corner of a 4 x 8 sheet of plywood on a couple of bricks or wood scraps to create a shallow "tub" just right for mixing small batches of concrete. Clean off the plywood as soon as you're done, and you can use it again with the other face up.

From the outside in. Start pouring concrete in the farthest corner of the form. Pack each load up against the preceding one. Don't dump concrete in widely spaced piles and spread it to both sides because the concrete can separate.

Quick fixes. Set the poles for swing sets in quick-setting concrete, and the kids will be able to "test" the equipment within a few hours (check the bag for curing time). Fence, mailbox, and sign posts are also good candidates, since the fast drying time eliminates the need for bracing.

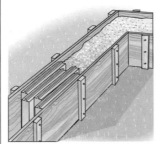

Easy pour. When you need to stop a pour before completion, force pieces of rigid insulation between the form walls to hold back the concrete. Offsetting the pieces creates a keyway that reinforces the joint between new and old concrete.

Salt in the earth. Here's a decorative technique well suited to warmer climates: To create a textured look and give more traction during wet weather, sprinkle rock salt on freshly poured concrete, then embed the grains with a float so they're flush. When the salt dissolves, it will leave behind a unique pitted surface.

Tools encrusted with hardened concrete? A propane torch is a sure-fire way to remove it. Because the metal heats and expands more quickly than the concrete, the hard stuff should slip off after just a few passes.

Mixing and pouring concrete

WHAT YOU'LL NEED

Square shovel and tarp	Hoe and mixing container or wheelbarrow
Concrete mixer	Tall juice can
½-in. crushed stone, sand, and portland cement	Board
Concrete mix	Rod for stirring
Water	Ruler

1 To power-mix, turn on the mixer and add the aggregate and half the water. Then shovel in the sand and cement, adding as little water as needed for a cohesive mixture. Wash out the drum after every batch.

2 To hand-mix, blend the dry ingredients well. Add water to a shallow depression, pulling the dry materials into the water with a hoe. Draw sections toward you until all the mix is at one end. Now pull it to the other end, adding water as needed.

3 To test the consistency, cut off the lids of a metal can. Set it on a board and fill it with concrete. Stir concrete 25 times with a rod to eliminate air pockets, then lift can straight up. If the concrete settles more than 3 in., add sand to the mix and retest.

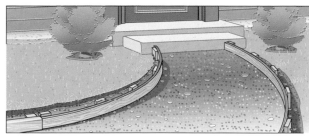

Form long curves with pieces of 4-inch lap siding instead of the usual ¼-inch kerfed plywood, and you'll save yourself the time it would take to rip the material and cut the saw kerfs. Support the siding by screwing in 1 x 4 stakes about every 3 feet. Make sure the tops of the siding forms are flush with the top of any other formwork.

Forms and footings

WHAT YOU'LL NEED

Tape measure	Tamp
Metal stakes and twine	Concrete
Square shovel	No. 8 iron wire
Level	Screed
Lumber form sides and wooden stakes	
Screw gun with galvanized wood screws	
Metal reinforcing bars	

Free formwork. Instead of buying special tubes for pier footings, ask a local carpet installer for the cardboard tubing left behind from rolls of broadloom. Oil the inside face of the tube so that it strips off easily once the concrete has cured.

The root of the problem. When digging a trench for a footing, use a reciprocating saw with a pruning blade to get a clean cut through tough tree roots. Be careful not to cut through roots thicker than your arm, or you could kill the tree.

When ordering concrete to be delivered to the site, overestimate by about 15 percent and tell the company you'll call in the specific yardage the day of the pour. This way, you'll be able to measure the formwork as built—which should result in a more precise order.

Keep forms clean. If concrete spills onto the outside of the formwork during screeding, remove it with a shovel or other tool before it has a chance to harden, or the forms will be extremely difficult to dislodge.

Leftover concrete? Mold it into stepping stones using garbage-can lids as forms. Brush a coat of motor oil on the inside of the lids so the cured concrete will slide out.

1 Lay out the footing (wall width plus 4 in. min.) with twine attached to metal stakes. Excavate to the desired depth; then level and tamp the soil. Drive in the form stakes, allowing for the thickness of the forms.

2 Using a screw gun, attach the form to a stake at one end, level it, and secure it to another. Repeat for the other forms. Half-fill with concrete, tamping with a shovel to remove air pockets. Lay in 2 lines of reinforcing bar. Bind overlaps with No. 8 iron wire.

3 Finish filling with concrete. Use a 2 x 4 screed, sliding it back and forth across the tops of the form sides, to strike off excess material. If vertical reinforcing rods are required, press them to the bottom of the footings at measured locations.

Clean sweep. Sprinkle some moistened coffee grounds on a concrete floor or patio before sweeping it. The grounds will keep down the dust while helping to trap the dirt.

An absorbing job. Even if you don't have a cat, store some kitty litter in the garage to absorb motor-oil stains on concrete floors. Toss the litter down, grind it lightly with a brick to reduce it to a fine powder, and sweep it up the next day.

Root causes. To prevent buckling and cracking of concrete slabs, sever tree and plant roots along the slab's edges at least once each summer. Sink a spade 6 to 8 inches below the slab, withdraw it, then sink it again, making sure to overlap the previous cut.

Making it stick. Increase the adhesion of new paint on an old concrete floor by washing down the floor with straight white vinegar and letting it dry completely (no need to rinse). Then paint.

All wet. A patching mix is too wet if water squeezes out of the hole when you pack it in.

Save money on sealer. Reseal heavily trafficked garage floors annually to prevent spalling. A home-made sealer of equal parts boiled linseed oil and turpentine works well and costs a lot less than commercial products. To boost protection, apply a second coat 24 hours after the first.

Scan the can. Take time to read product labels. They often include helpful tips and tricks to make the work go quicker and easier.

Add an acrylic fortifier to concrete and sand for a stronger bond to old concrete. It's not always necessary—just good insurance.

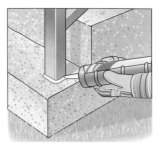

Stall spalling. Metal railings and fasteners expand as they rust, causing the concrete surrounding them to chip or flake off. Keep it together by periodically caulking where the metal meets the concrete.

Maintaining and repairing concrete

WHAT YOU'LL NEED

Goggles, dust mask, and gloves

Cement-base caulk

Mason's hammer and cold chisel

Latex patching concrete

Steel trowel

Wood float

Large brush for concrete sealer

Wire brush, scrub brush, power washer or vacuum

Chemical sealer for concrete

Small sledgehammer

Wooden brace

Latex bonding agent

Stiff broom

1 Fill cracks up to ⅛ in. deep with any cement-base caulk. For larger cracks, chip out loose edges with a narrow cold chisel. Trowel in latex patching concrete, and smooth with a steel trowel or a wood float.

2 Eliminate dusting by applying a chemical sealer. First clean the slab with a wire brush, scrub brush, power washer, or vacuum, and possibly a degreaser, and allow it to dry completely. Be sure to wear goggles, a dust mask, and gloves. If cleaning the slab doesn't work, grind off the weak layer of concrete at the surface. Apply the chemical sealer with a large brush.

Filling fine cracks.
Hairline cracks can be repaired with auto-body filler. Dip a rubber-gloved finger into the compound, then press it into the crack.

Soften the blows. Equip a chisel with a shock absorber before cleaning out a crack. A simple sponge ball placed around the chisel's shaft will cushion the blows and prevent tendon-damaging vibrations from running up your arm.

The chips are down.
When cleaning out or under-cutting repairs, punch the chisel through a square of window screening to pre-vent sharp concrete chips from flying up in your face.

Homemade patch. Filling a bunch of large holes with commercial patch material can get expensive. To cut costs, fill large holes to within ¼ inch of the surface with a compound made from 1 part portland cement, 2½ parts sand, and enough water to make a stiff paste. Top off the repair with commercial patch.

A tough patch. When using latex patching material to fix a deep hole, construct the patch from several thin layers of the material, allowing drying time in between. The patch will be much stronger.

Watch the edges. Look for a latex patch to begin to lighten around the edges, then mist it with water from a plant sprayer. Do this for the duration of the curing time, which is specified on the product label.

Long vertical cracks are easily fixed by applying duct tape to the bottom 3 feet of the crack. Insert a funnel at the top of the tape, and pour in a mixture of 1 part portland cement and 2 parts masonry sand blended with water to a paintlike consistency. Wait 4 hours; repeat with the next section.

Tools of the trade. Use a steel trowel to create a very smooth finish on a patched surface. Use a wood float to create a rougher surface that will provide better traction.

3 To repair spalled concrete, use light swings with a small sledge to break up all the weakened con-crete. (It sounds hollow when pounded.) Scrub the surface with a wire brush and rinse with water. When it is dry, apply latex patching concrete and smooth it with a steel trowel or a wood float.

4 To repair a step, use a mason's chisel and a small sledge to break away loose concrete and to square up tapered edges. To contain the patch, brace lumber against the step, making sure the form is level with the step. Dampen the area and brush on a latex bonding agent. Fill the form with latex patching concrete, and smooth it with a wood float. Roughen the surface with a stiff broom before it sets.

5 Secure a loose railing that is set in or anchored to concrete by first chipping out 1 in. of concrete (about 2 in. deep) from around the post with a cold chisel and small sledge. Vacuum and then dampen the surface. Fill the hole with patching concrete, and smooth it with a trowel or wood float.

Too slick. Select only unglazed varieties of tiles—or textured nonskid types—for exterior projects. The slick, shiny surface of glazed tiles looks great, but it can become treacherously slippery when damp.

On the edge. When storing slate tiles in preparation for resurfacing, stack them on edge to minimize damage. Laying slate tiles on top of one another in a pile could cause them to break under the accumulated weight.

Check that concrete is level before resurfacing by rolling a long piece of pipe over the slab. As you roll, look for light peeking under the pipe; mark low spots (deeper than ¼ inch) with chalk so they can be filled.

Bump or glide. Factor in convenience when planning a patio. It's easier to pull in and push away chairs from the patio table on quarry tiles than on pavers. The right-angle edges of the quarry tiles encourage smooth travel, while the rounded edges of the pavers make for a bumpy ride.

Care for seconds? For a unique look—and significant cost savings—shop around for tile "seconds." Although the tiles are sold at greatly reduced cost, the defects are usually cosmetic and the slight irregularities will give your new patio a one-of-a-kind look.

When fixing low spots with self-leveling latex-modified mortar compound, fill the hole from the center out. The compound will level itself, but you can smooth the edges with a trowel if you like.

Stain fighting. Hide ugly stains on concrete with a decorative spatter-painted finish. Select a paint that is formulated for masonry, load up the paintbrush, then smack it against a stick to send the paint drops flying over the offending spots.

Resurfacing a concrete patio

WHAT YOU'LL NEED

Safety goggles and work gloves

Power washer and degreaser (optional)

Cement-base caulk and cold chisel

Trowel and latex patching cement

Sponge float

Tape measure, string, and chalk line

Tile or other surfacing material

Latex additive or water

Container and hoe for mixing mortar

Dry-set mortar for freeze-thaw conditions

Notched trowel (¼-in.-wide by ⅜-in.-deep notches)

Rubber mallet and long straightedge

Wet saw

Sanded grout and foam float

Large specialty sponge and water bucket

1 Power-wash a structurally sound patio slab to blast away all dirt, mildew, moss, or dust. Remove any oil or grease stains with a degreaser. Fill small cracks with cement-base caulk; chisel out wide cracks, and patch them with a trowel and latex patching cement. Smooth with a sponge float.

2 Locate the center of the slab by measuring out from an abutting structure and/or by stretching two strings between the corners and marking the intersection. Next, snap a chalk line through the center point and parallel to the house and a second line perpendicular to the first. Then test the pattern by laying out tiles along both lines to the edges of the slab, making sure to allow for ⅜- to ½-in. joints.

Sort the slate. Before laying out irregular pieces of slate for a new patio, sort them into same-size piles. Position the largest pieces evenly over the area first; then lay down progressively smaller pieces until the surface is covered. This way, you'll ensure an even distribution of sizes.

Space program. To create even grout joints between pieces of exterior flooring material, use spacers made from strips of wood the size of the joints. Remove the spacers as you finish setting each flooring piece, and use them with the next piece.

Grouted out. To remove old or stained grout, use a simple jig made by driving a 10d nail through a piece of dowel. Draw the point of the nail along the grout line. Hammer in a new nail if the old one bends.

Growing in concrete. If you have a few concrete blocks lying about, press them into service as quick and easy patio planters. Position them so that the openings face up, add soil, and plant flowers.

Night lights. Pop small votive candles into clay pots to create an easy, inexpensive lighting system for a patio. You can light up an adjacent walkway the same way. Just don't leave the lights unattended.

SAFE AND SMART

➤ If you are renting a wet saw to cut stones, do all the cutting at one time, then promptly return the equipment to the store to save on rental fees.

➤ If you're putting railings on the patio, place a small glass jar where you plan to install each post. After the cement has cured, break the glass and bolt in the hardware where the glass was positioned.

➤ Before power washing, seal off nearby electrical outlets with plastic sheeting and duct tape. Shroud shrubbery and plantings as well to protect them from the force of the spray.

➤ When power washing, wear goggles and rain gear. Be sure to aim only at the surface to be cleaned—the spray can break window glass or injure bystanders. Keep the wand moving as you work.

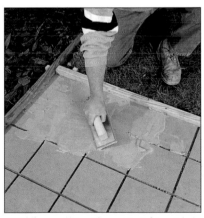

3 Mix water or latex additive into a flexible dry-set (thinset) mortar that is specified for exterior use and freeze-thaw conditions. Working on one segment at a time, spread mortar onto the slab just up to the lines. Draw a toothed trowel across the mortar to create an even ridged setting bed.

4 Press the tiles (or pavers, stone, or similar exterior flooring) into the mortar, tapping each one lightly with a rubber mallet. Lay a long straightedge across the tiles to make sure they are level. Remove excess mortar from joints as you work out to the edges. Mark tiles for cutting with a wet saw.

5 Keep off the tiles while laying them and for at least 48 hr. after. Using diagonal strokes and holding a foam float at an angle, press sanded grout into the joints. As it sets, wipe the surface with a damp sponge to remove grout from the tiles without disturbing the delicate joints.

 For stain resistance, use epoxy grout or an additive (consult your supplier).

Play detective. A close look through a strong magnifying glass can clue you in to the cause behind cracked or flaked stucco. Salt crystals in the body of the stucco indicate that moisture on the inside of the house is migrating outward. Crystal-free stucco suggests that the damage has resulted from frost damage—and moisture penetration—on the outside.

Just say no. Ignore hairline cracks in stucco. They are usually harmless and the repair is often uglier than the hard-to-notice blemish.

A long crack can mean that the foundation supporting the wall is settling. Epoxy some duct tape across the crack, and inspect it every 2 months. If the tape splits or twists, the masonry is moving. Call in a home inspection expert to evaluate the problem.

Bye-bye birdie. Repair major cracks in stucco as soon as you notice them to avoid damage from feathered friends. Insects will often call a crack home, and when dinnertime comes around, a woodpecker won't discriminate between your house and the trees.

Quick fix. Narrow cracks can be easily fixed by filling them with premixed stucco compound or specialty stucco caulk, which maintains a flexible bond within a crack. Clean out the crack, chisel an undercut along the edges of the crack for good adhesion, then pack it with either compound or caulk. If using compound, smooth the repair with a putty knife for a neat finish.

No-smudge caulk. To keep caulk from smearing when filling cracks in stucco, cover the crack with a wide strip of masking tape. Then slice the tape with a utility knife, and inject caulk through the slit. Strip off the tape before the caulk hardens.

What color's your stucco? If the finish coat of stucco is to be tinted with dry pigments, use white cement in the stucco mix. If the wall will be painted, use regular gray cement. Pigment should be mixed in "dry" before water is added.

Repairing a stucco wall

WHAT YOU'LL NEED

Work gloves and safety goggles

Mason's chisel and hammer

Wire lath and tin snips

Broom or shop vacuum

Wire brush

Garden hose with nozzle

Premixed stucco

Mixing container or wheelbarrow

Steel trowel

Scarifier or similar tool

Lumber (for screed)

Wood or sponge float

Masonry cement, sand, and water

Dry pigments and brush

Stiff long-bristle brush

1 Chisel away loose stucco with a hammer and mason's chisel, being sure you wear goggles. If there is a wire lath base, replace any that is damaged. Vacuum or blow the repair area clean, and dampen it to prepare for the scratch coat. If the base is masonry, scrub it clean with a wire brush and dampen it to prepare for a brown coat.

2 Apply the scratch coat with a steel trowel (top), pressing it into the lath and to within 1/2 in. of the surface. Wait about 30 min., and scratch the surface with a scarifier (bottom), home-made scratching rake, or the edge of the trowel to a depth of 1/8 in. Wait 24 hr. for the scratch coat to set, spraying with a mister every 4-6 hr.

Problems with pigments. When matching the new stucco to the old, let the test sample dry thoroughly before evaluating it. Colors can fade up to 70 percent during the course of drying.

Watch the clock. Don't mix more stucco than you figure you can spread in an hour. To increase the working time, stir the stucco every 10 minutes. Once it begins to set up in the pail, it's time to toss it.

Lime is the key. When making stucco for the finish coat, add about 4 cups of hydrated lime to every 4 gallons of mix. The lime will make the stucco more plastic and easier to spread and texture.

Strong finish. When painting stucco, use acrylic latex or a paint formulated for exterior masonry surfaces, priming the surface first if the product label recommends it. Always wait 4 weeks before painting over new stucco.

Be square. It's easier to make a square corner when you have a form against which to press the stucco. To make one, nail a 1 x 2 to the wall perpendicular to the one being stuccoed; reverse the 1 x 2 when working on the opposite wall.

Make a rake. Roughening up the scratch coat encourages bonding between it and the subsequent coat. A scratching rake, made by pounding a few 3d nails through a 1-foot piece of 1 x 2, is cheaper than renting or buying a commercial tool, called a scarifier, and much faster to use than the edge of a trowel.

Let stucco breathe. Brushing on a sealer will trap moisture in the material, preventing it from evaporating. This not only will cause stucco to crumble but also makes repairing the finish more difficult.

Leftover stucco wire? If you're using 2 x 2 square wire as lath, roll it into a cylinder to create a storage basket for blueprints, posters, or children's artwork. Cap it with a trash-can lid to cover sharp edges and to add stability.

3 Trowel on the brown coat, and level the surrounding area with a screed, sliding the board back and forth while drawing it upward across the patch. Smooth with a wood float. Be sure to mist the patch to keep the base coat damp for 2 days, and protect it from direct sun.

4 For the final coat, mix 2½ parts masonry cement, 3½ parts sand, and enough water to yield a soft, buttery texture. Match the color to the dampened old stucco by adding dry pigments, making sure you test it first. Dampen the surface and brush on a ⅛-in.-thick coat.

5 Texture the new patch by flicking stucco mix from a stiff long-bristle brush. Practice on a piece of scrap board first. Then draw a steel trowel lightly over the surface to flatten the peaks to match the old texture.

Look below the surface.
Before making a repair, make sure the driveway doesn't have poor drainage or a weakened subbase. If you don't correct the underlying problem, you'll wind up making the repair again and again.

Pick your day. Choose a dry day without a threat of rain to seal a driveway. The weather should be warm but not hot, preferably above 10°C/50°F day and night. High temperatures will dry out the sealer too quickly.

Speed-clean a driveway prior to sealing it by washing as you sweep. Tape a garden hose to the handle of a broom, and the nozzle will direct water in front of the bristles as you whisk them over the blacktop.

Oil be gone. To erase stubborn oil stains, sprinkle on strong granular detergent and hot water. Scrub with a stiff brush, walk away for an hour, then rinse off the solution, and stain, with water.

A second coat of sealer isn't necessarily better than a single coat—too much can make a driveway slick.

Save your soles. Most driveway sealers contain emulsified asphalt or coal tar, which is impossible to remove from footwear. If you don't want to toss your work boots after completing the job, wrap them in clear plastic grocery bags before starting to seal.

Save money with sand.
If a driveway crack is deeper than ½ inch, fill it three-quarters full with sand, tamping it as you work. Top off the repair with either liquid asphalt filler or asphalt patch material.

Take a deep breath.
Most paving contractors don't recommend annual sealing of the driveway. Too many layers of sealer will flake and peel.

Filling and sealing cracks

WHAT YOU'LL NEED

Broom	Caulking gun
Garden hose and nozzle	Pointed trowel
Rubber and work gloves	Acrylic asphalt sealant
Detergent and degreaser	Disposable squeegee
Bucket and scrub brush	
Asphalt spot primer	
Asphalt filler	

1 Sweep and hose off the driveway, or power-wash it. Wearing rubber gloves, scrub grease or oil stains with detergent and degreaser. When the area is dry, spot-prime to ensure that the sealer adheres.

2 Force in the asphalt filler with a caulking gun or a pointed trowel, being sure to overfill the cracks. Level and smooth with a trowel.

3 Spread pools of sealant with the applicator, brushing it into the surface one way, then smoothing it with the squeegee at a 90° angle. If needed, a second coat should be applied within 24–48 hr. Protect from traffic for 2 days.

Go to the tape. If a crack won't stay repaired, try a self-adhesive tape-type filler. Press the tape, made from asphalt-impregnated polypropylene fabric, onto clean blacktop like a big bandage. The patch can be driven over or walked on immediately.

How cold is cold? If a bag of cold-patch material is lumpy, it's too cold. Bring the bag in the house and let it warm up overnight before beginning repairs the next day. Just be sure to lay the bag on a piece of plastic or an old towel to protect the floor from any leaks.

Bubble zap. Air bubbles that get trapped in the cold-patch compound can weaken a repair. After tamping down each layer, poke the compound gently with the tip of the trowel to burst any bubbles.

Hot patches. For a stronger patch, after tamping it in place, warm each layer of cold-patch compound with a heat gun set to a low temperature. The oils in the mix will blend as it "melts," creating a firmer bond.

In a hole. If the hole is deeper than 4 inches, fill it to that level with gravel and tamp it firmly with a wooden post. Then shovel patching compound into the hole to create a 2-inch-thick layer when tamped again.

Get a handle on it. If you're using a 4 x 4 to tamp the patch material, screw large door handles to the post on opposite sides. You'll find that it's easier to pound down the patch.

Sprinkling sand over freshly applied filler will prevent it from sticking to car tires.

Mineral spirits will quickly clean tools, and warm soapy water will help rescue soiled gloves and clothing. Just start the cleanup right after finishing the job.

Chill out. Wait a year to seal a driveway after patching a pothole with cold-mix compound. The respite will give the material time to harden and settle.

Patching potholes

WHAT YOU'LL NEED

Work gloves and safety glasses
Mason's chisel and small sledge
Tamper
Cold-patch asphalt patching material (60-lb. bags)
Trowel or hand shovel
Sand or scrap of plywood
Car

1 Use a chisel and sledge-hammer to cut asphalt from the damaged area; undercut the edges so the patch won't be pushed out. Next, remove 2–3 in. of the base, and tamp it down.

2 Half-fill the hole with asphalt patch, and level it. Compact the asphalt well with the tamper. Add more asphalt, level it, and tamp again, until the the patch is about ½ in. above the surface.

3 Cover the patch with sand or a piece of plywood. Drive over it several times to compact the asphalt. Add more patching material as needed, and drive over it again until the patch is level or just above the surface.

YARD AND GARDEN

Job ratings: Easy   Medium   Complex

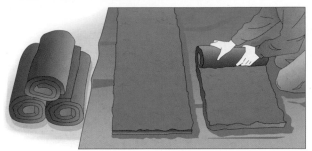

Storing sod. Sod is best installed within 24 hours of harvest. If storing it more than a day or two, unroll it as soon as you get it home and lay it out in the shade—grass side up—on either pavement or sheets of plastic. Water regularly, and it should keep for a few weeks.

Patching damaged lawn? To get a neat fit, use the damaged piece as a template for the new patch.

For even coverage, use a spreader when seeding or fertilizing the lawn. Work in a crisscross pattern: Set the spreader at half the recommended application rate and travel back and forth across the area, then up and down.

Air it out. Increase air and water circulation in the lawn by aerating it in spring. Walking over grass with spiked shoes is good exercise but not very effective. For deeper treatment, rent a mechanical core aerator that pulls out plugs of soil, which can just be left on the lawn to decompose.

Timely nutrition. Feed your lawn just twice a year with a fertilizer formulated for blade growth in spring and root development in fall. Use a slow-release fertilizer, which provides a steady supply of nutrients; over-feeding or using a quick-release high-nitrogen food stimulates top growth at the expense of deep roots.

When fertilizing, add flour to the spreader so you can easily touch up any spots you may have missed.

Limit lawn edging by laying a strip of bricks, flat paving stones, or landscape ties where grass meets garden bed. The mower will pass over the edging, eliminating the need for time-consuming hand trimming.

Sodding the lawn

WHAT YOU'LL NEED

Sod
Board
Flathead rake or lawn roller
Topdressing of sand and compost
Watering can or sprinkler
Peg and string with funnel and sand
Half-moon edger

1 Lay the first strip of sod against a straight edge. Butt the end of the next piece flush with the first. Set a board atop the first row and kneel on it when installing the next one. Always be sure that you stagger the sod joints.

2 When the whole area has been laid, tamp down the sod with the back of a rake or a light lawn roller. Spread the topdressing to fill in the gaps between the strips. Keep the sod moist until it is firmly rooted.

3 For a curved edge, mark the shape first. Set in a peg tied with a string, or if going around a tree, tie the string to the trunk. Attach a funnel to the string end and dribble sand as you pull the string taut over the sod in an arc. Cut with a sharp edger.

The right stuff. Select a grass seed suited to the growing conditions on site —including sun exposure and soil type—and to your regional climate. Garden centers often stock grass-seed mixtures custom-blended for local conditions. Kentucky bluegrass does well in most regions of Canada, but must be watered well in hot spells, especially if the soil is poor.

To keep lawn edges neat, use a strip of wooden molding as a guide while you first "saw" the sod with a sharp carving knife. Next, insert the blade, flat side up, under the grass to cut the roots from the soil. Flexible plastic molding, held in place with rocks, works well when trimming a curved edge.

Hit the spot when reseeding bare patches with a homemade shaker constructed from a coffee can and two plastic lids. In one lid, pierce holes large enough for the seed to pass through; store the second lid on the can bottom. When you're through reseeding, switch lids to seal in the unused seed.

Get to the root of it. To remove the taproot of a pesky dandelion, soak the soil around the plant, then push the leaves to one side and sink a trowel or weed digger vertically into the soil as close as possible to the stalk. Pop the tool handle downward to lever out the weed, root and all.

Water wise. Lawns need about 1 inch of water weekly, which penetrates up to 6 inches in clay and 12 inches in sand after 24 hours. To make sure you're delivering the full amount, mark off 1 inch inside some old drinking glasses and place them near the sprinkler.

Water when? Turn on the sprinkler early in the morning, so that the grass will dry by sunset; leaving grass damp overnight can invite diseases. Never water at midday—too much moisture will evaporate before it can penetrate the soil.

De-bugging the blades. To rid your lawn of Japanese beetle grubs, let the grass dry out between waterings during the summer and raise the pH of the soil by spreading lime in the fall or spring. This will make your lawn less hospitable to the larvae, which prefer moist acid soil.

Reseeding a bare patch

WHAT YOU'LL NEED

Cultivator

Lawn fertilizer

Flathead rake

Watering can

Grass seed

Topsoil

Straw or fine-mesh netting and pegs

1 Pull up and remove any dead grass, weeds, or debris from the patch until it is clean. Loosen the soil to a depth of 3 in., taking care not to damage the surrounding grass.

2 Broadcast fertilizer over the area lightly, and rake it in well. Level the soil and water until moist. Spread grass seed at the recommended rate and cover with a thin layer of topsoil. Gently firm the soil by tamping with the back of a rake.

3 Scatter a thin layer of straw over the seeds to protect them as they germinate. Or stretch a piece of netting over the patch and secure the edges with pegs. Keep the seeds evenly moist by watering lightly each day.

Read the weeds as a guide to soil type. Dandelions, chicory, and creeping buttercup prefer clay soil, while goldenrod, sheep sorrel, and bindweed like sand. Chickweed and lamb's-quarters grow best in loamy soil.

An easy texture test. Soil contains three components that determine texture—sand, silt, and clay. To analyze texture, place a cup of soil in a jar and fill with water. Let the mixture settle until layers form: sand at the bottom, silt in the middle, and clay on top. The thickness of the layers indicates the proportion of particles. Ideal "loam" soil contains about 50 percent sand, between 25 and 50 percent silt, and up to 25 percent clay.

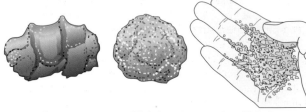

An easier texture test. Lightly squeeze a handful of moist soil. Clay soil will form a sticky mass, loam will form a spongy ball, and sandy soil will crumble apart.

A cure-all. Organic matter, such as compost, rotted manure, and dead leaves, works wonders in correcting soil texture: it loosens and lightens heavy clay and helps sand retain nutrients and moisture. Dig in generous amounts—up to 25 percent by volume—when preparing planting areas, and add 1 inch of it each year to garden beds.

Sweet or sour? Use a home test kit to check soil pH—a measure of acidity and alkalinity. If your soil is acidic, "sweeten" it with lime; if it's alkaline, add sulfur. Spread it at the manufacturer's recommended rate. Heavy soil needs more material than sandy soil.

A quicker acid test. If your hydrangeas bloom blue, the soil is acidic; if they're pink, it's alkaline.

Turn it over. Digging deeply loosens soil texture and incorporates oxygen, which helps beneficial microorganisms break down organic matter and release nutrients. Most plants prefer soil that has been turned to a depth of 6 to 12 inches.

Sifting the soil. A simple plastic milk crate from a supermarket makes a great soil sifter. Dirt will fall through the holes but roots and rocks will not.

Preparing a garden bed

WHAT YOU'LL NEED

Lengths of garden hose or stakes and string

Spade

Plastic tarp

Compost or other organic matter

Complete fertilizer

Spading fork

Shovel

Flathead rake

1 Mark the desired shape of the bed. Use a hose to outline a curved bed. For a bed with straight edges, drive in stakes and stretch strings between them.

! If the hose is too stiff to make a curve, let it lie in the sun until it softens up.

2 Cut the sod around the outline with a spade; then remove the hose or the string and stakes. To sever the grass roots from the soil, insert the spade horizontally under the sod edge, and slide it beneath the turf. Continue lifting the sod piece by piece until all the soil is exposed.

No worms? Fewer than 6 to 10 worms per square foot of soil may indicate the need for fertilizer. Have the soil tested at a lab and amend the deficiencies as indicated. Use a "simple" fertilizer, which has one primary nutrient, or a "complete" fertilizer, which has three primary nutrients: nitrogen (N), phosphorus (P), and potassium (K).

The right path. When planning a large bed, include some handy maintenance paths. Lay double rows of bricks lengthwise at 4-foot intervals for the entire length of the garden. This will allow you to weed or deadhead virtually any plant without stepping on smaller, delicate ones.

No wet feet. Most plants need well-drained soil so roots won't rot. To check drainage, dig several holes 1 foot deep by 2 feet wide in dry soil; fill with water and note drainage time. Between 30 and 60 minutes is ideal, although drainage times up to 4 hours are tolerated by many plants. To correct drainage problems, add organic matter to the soil or build a raised bed.

Natural herbicide. A kettleful of boiling water is an efficient weedkiller, especially in tight spots like cracks in concrete.

Containment policy. To lessen soil leakage from a flowerpot or container's drainage hole, place a piece of used screen over it before adding soil and planting.

Don't be rash. Is your soil overrun with poison ivy or other rash-inducing plants? Remove them safely by covering one hand and arm with a long plastic bag before pulling up the plant. With your other hand, slide the bag down your arm and over the plant, being careful not to touch any part of it. Seal the bag and toss it right in the trash.

Keep off. Never tread on or work wet soil, especially clay—it will just become more compacted. Lay down planks or stepping stones if you must walk through damp areas. To see if the soil is ready to work, dig down about 3 inches and grab a fistful of soil: it should crumble rather than clump.

3 Prepare the soil for planting by digging up the topsoil. Lay a tarp alongside the bed and place the soil on it. Add compost and fertilizer, and incorporate them into the topsoil.

4 Using a fork, loosen the soil remaining in the garden bed to the depth of the tines. Break up large clods, remove stones, and clean out any weeds or roots.

5 Spread several inches of compost over the soil and turn it in thoroughly with the fork. Shovel the amended topsoil on top of the bed, and rake the surface until smooth and level.

 Stand up straight when pressing the fork vertically into the ground with your foot; then step back and draw the handle toward you.

Let there be light. Snapdragons, impatiens, and scarlet sage are among the annuals whose seeds require light to germinate. After sowing, press them lightly into the soil, but don't cover them.

Poor travelers. Some annuals, such as larkspur and poppies, resent transplanting. Sow seeds of such plants outdoors, or sow them indoors in clean eggshell halves and then simply plant the eggshells in the flower bed.

When sowing tiny seeds, soak a cotton string in water and dip it into a tray or pan of seeds. Then plant the entire seeded string right in the ground.

Tiny seeds II. Mix very small seeds, like those of petunias and wax begonias, with a little clean sand when sowing. The sand will help you handle the tiny seeds and keep track of where you've placed them.

Seedling savvy. When buying annuals at the nursery, choose plants about 2 to 4 inches in height. Plants that are 6 inches tall are too leggy; those less than 2 are slow growers.

Buy annuals within 30 days of the plants' delivery to the nursery—which is usually in April or May. The longer you wait, the less healthy the plants may be.

Plants that reproduce. Select annuals that seed themselves, such as cosmos, California poppy, and blanket flower. Watch for "volunteers" the second year around the area where self-sowers had been planted. Let them grow in place or transplant them.

Speed-plant seedlings by digging holes with a bulb planter. Just twist the tool a few times to make a hole 2 inches deep, set in a plant, and shake the soil from the bulb planter around the stem. Firm the soil and move on to the next one.

No manure. Annuals don't like it, even if it's well rotted. The jolt of nitrogen that manure provides promotes lush green growth at the expense of blooms.

Planting annual seeds outdoors

WHAT YOU'LL NEED

Spading fork

Compost or other organic matter

Complete fertilizer

Rake

Lime or sand; or stakes and string

Seeds for annuals

Labels

Watering can or hose

1 Prepare a new garden bed (see p. 272) or refresh an existing bed by turning over the soil with a fork until it has a fine, crumbly texture. Also turn in compost or soil amendments at this time. Broadcast fertilizer at the recommended rate and rake the soil until smooth and level.

2 To create a colorful patterned garden, mark off planting areas. Sprinkle lime or sand in free-form shapes, or use stakes and string for angular beds. Sow a different type of seed within each section. Either follow the spacing indicated on the package or scatter the seeds at random.

Losing weight. When planting an arrangement of annuals in a large container, reduce the weight and amount of soil needed by adding a layer of foam packing "peanuts" or placing a plastic flowerpot upside-down over the drain hole.

Feed annuals with a complete low-nitrogen fertilizer, such as 5-10-10, at planting time. If performance flags at midseason, give them a boost with a diluted dose of a complete liquid fertilizer.

Treat them tender. Minimize transplant shock when setting out seedlings. Wait for an overcast day or until early evening so tender specimens aren't scorched in the sun. Water the plants 2 hours beforehand to make sure that the soil clings to the roots. Resoak the roots after planting.

Pinch an inch. After planting, pinch the growing tip of each stem back to a leaf or set of leaves. While pinching delays bloom, it forces energy into developing roots and stems, resulting in a healthier, bushier plant. Also pinch occasionally throughout the season to prevent excessive legginess.

Deadhead, or remove spent flowers, to prevent annuals from setting seed. This not only neatens up the garden but also stimulates more blooms. Let seeds form only if you want to save them.

Shake it up. Before throwing away plants at season's end, pull them up, place a plastic bag over the seed heads, turn upside-down, and shake. You'll catch a bunch of seeds for next spring. Or for a free-flowing wildflower look, shake the seed heads over an empty bed, cover with soil, and tamp lightly.

The party's over. Clean out annuals from the beds in fall and toss them in the compost pile to minimize disease and pest problems the following spring.

The cutting garden. Many annuals, including cornflowers, stocks, and zinnias, make ideal cut flowers. Cut the stems with a sharp knife in early morning or evening, and plunge them immediately into a pail of lukewarm water. Before arranging, hold the stem ends underwater and recut at an angle. Be sure to strip any foliage that will fall below the waterline of the container.

3 Gently firm the seeds into the soil so they make good contact. Next, cover them lightly by gently pulling the back of a rake across the surface of the soil. Many seeds need only 1/8 to 1/4 in. of soil cover, and some small ones should not be covered at all. If a planting depth is not given on the package, cover to a depth of twice the diameter of the seed.

4 Label the different areas with the names of the plants. This will help you distinguish plants from weeds as the seedlings emerge.

 For homemade labels, write plant names with an indelible marker on ice cream sticks.

5 Water the seeds after planting. To avoid dislodging the seeds, use a watering can with a fine-spray nose or mist the soil with a garden hose fitted with a nozzle adjusted to fine. Water whenever the soil becomes dry. If you scattered the seed, thin the plants to the recommended spacing.

Save money by splitting the cost of a high-priced perennial with a friend. Divide the plant once you get it home, and suddenly you have two beauties for the price of one.

Smart shopping. Beware of a perennial that looks too large for its container—it may be pot-bound, with roots so coiled that they won't spread successfully in the planting hole. Slide the plant out of the container carefully and inspect the roots closely before buying the plant.

Think small. Look for perennials in money-saving six-packs. The plants usually catch up to larger, more expensive specimens in 6 to 8 weeks.

Buying bare. Mail-order nurseries sometimes ship bare-root perennials, which are dormant specimens with their roots packed in damp sphagnum moss instead of soil. Unpack the plant immediately, moisten the roots, and plant as soon as possible. Bury only the roots, keeping the crown—where roots and stem meet—at soil level.

Provide a good home. Soil preparation is especially important with permanent garden members like perennials. Amend the soil for drainage, fertility, pH, and texture if necessary to provide the growing conditions the specimen requires.

Lime disease. Don't plant acid-loving perennials too close to stucco or cement foundation walls. They release alkaline lime into the soil, wreaking havoc on lime-hating plants.

Go for the bold. If you are planting perennials in a very sunny flower bed, stay away from pastel-colored flowers, which look washed out in bright light. Opt instead for reds, oranges, or yellows.

Easy-to-grow seed. Perennials can be grown from seed just like annuals. The easiest to sow are pinks, columbine, coneflower, coral bells, coreopsis, delphinium, foxglove, and primrose.

Blessing or bane? Yarrow, rose campion, and columbine are among the perennials that like to throw their seeds around. If you enjoy a naturalistic garden or free plants, let the seeds flourish wherever they fall. If you like a more formal look, send these volunteers to the compost pile; heat from the compost will kill the seeds.

Isolate invaders. Some perennials, such as bee balm and loosestrife, have particularly vigorous roots that will overrun their neighbors. Confine rampant root spread by planting a creeper in a large pot, then sinking the pot in the soil until the rim is just below grade level.

FILE IT

Made for the shade

Perennials can provide color in the darkest corners of a garden. Here is a sampler of some of the best performers. Check with your nursery about other shade-loving species that will thrive in your region.

Latin name	Common name
Aconitum spp.	Monkshood
Alchemilla mollis	Lady's mantle
Aquilegia spp.	Columbine
Aruncus dioicus	Goatsbeard
Astilbe	Astilbe or False Spirea
Bergenia cordifolia	Bergenia
Cimicifuga racemosa	Bugbane
Convallaria majalis	Lily-of-the-valley
Corydalis lutea	Corydalis
Dicentra spp.	Bleeding heart
Epimedium	Epimedium
Helleborus niger	Christmas rose
H. orientalis	Lenten rose
Hosta spp.	Hosta
Macleaya cordata	Plume poppy
Mertensia spp.	Bluebells
Primula spp.	Primrose

Design in drifts. Arrange perennials in odd-numbered groups, or drifts. Cluster large plants in threes and smaller ones in fives or sevens. Don't plant in straight rows—a triangular or round shape looks more natural.

Basic care. Feed your perennials in early spring and again in late fall with a complete fertilizer. Top-dress annually with compost or well-rotted manure, and keep the beds covered year-round with about 3 inches of shredded bark or another ornamental mulch. Water deeply but infrequently during prolonged dry spells.

Mark the spot. Large flat stones make handsome markers for plants. Write the name on the stone with a waterproof marker and surround it with soil.

Keep it cool. Don't use decorative pebbles or rocks around the roots of young perennials. The materials absorb and retain heat, causing undue stress on tender plants. Use an organic mulch instead.

Deadhead spent blooms to tidy up the garden and divert energy back to the stems and roots. While you're at it, also prune out any damaged or diseased stems and monitor for pests.

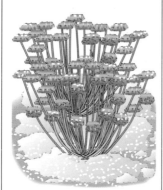

Stalking a winter garden. Leaving the stalks on spent perennials pays dividends in the off-season. The stalks are a natural magnet for falling leaves, holding them in place as winter mulch, and are also a beautiful contrast with a bed of snow.

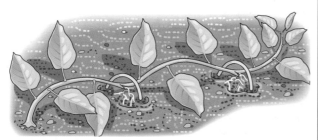

Propagate plants by "layering" them. Select a long pliable stem and bend it down to the ground. Cut a small nick in the bottom side and use galvanized wire to peg it into a 2-inch-deep hole. Cover with soil. After the stem sprouts roots, sever the new plant and move it to a desired location.

Dividing perennials

WHAT YOU'LL NEED

Spading fork

Sharp knife or spade

Pruning shears

Watering can

1 Carefully pry up the plant, inserting the fork at an angle several inches outside the perimeter of the top growth. Work all around the plant, lifting gently until the clump comes free from the soil.

2 Set the plant down on a flat surface, and slice through the crown with a knife; use a spade if the plant is woody. Divide the clump into as many smaller pieces as desired, making sure that each piece has vigorous shoots.

3 Prune back any dead or damaged foliage. Also trim some of the top if it is too lush to be supported by the new root ball. Then replant the divisions at the same depth as the original specimen, and water in.

Shop early. Save money by taking advantage of early-purchase discounts offered by many mail-order bulb catalogs in midsummer. Since the bulbs generally arrive in August, you'll need to store them: hang them in a net bag in a cool, dry place or refrigerate them until planting time.

Shop carefully. Look for firm, smooth, robust bulbs that seem heavy for their size; reject any that are soft, bruised, dried out, moldy, or sprouted.

Rich and dry. For best growth, bulbs need rich, very well drained soil. Loosen the soil to 1 foot and amend liberally with organic matter. Fertilize with bonemeal or a high-phosphorus complete fertilizer, such as 5-10-5.

Digging depths. The rule of thumb is to plant a bulb at a depth of 3 times its height. A 1-inch-tall bulb would be planted 3 inches deep. There are exceptions: the Madonna lily bulb, for instance, should be planted only 1 inch deep.

Weed by hand. If you dig out weeds with a hoe or hand cultivator, you always risk damaging shallowly planted bulbs.

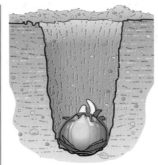

Noses up, feet down. Set in the bulb with its tip, or "nose," straight up and its base in firm contact with the soil so that roots can form.

Mass appeal. Arrange large bulbs of the same variety in clumps of at least five or seven for a spectacular splash of color. Group small bulbs, such as crocuses, in drifts of at least a dozen—2 dozen of these little charmers will occupy only a square foot of garden space.

It's only natural. A favorite way to plant narcissus is in informal clumps that will spread, or naturalize, into fields of bloom. Choose one variety, scatter the bulbs at random in an area where they won't be disturbed, and let them create colonies of color. Other good naturalizers include scilla, crocus, cyclamen, and grape hyacinth bulbs.

For fragrance, plant scented hyacinth, lilies, tuberose, and other perfumed bloomers near a sitting area—a patio or deck, for example—where you can not only enjoy their color but also their sweet smell while they bloom.

Planting bulbs individually

WHAT YOU'LL NEED

Spade	Bonemeal or fertilizer
Compost or other organic matter	Bulbs
Flathead rake	Watering can
Pail	Organic mulch
Trowel or bulb planter	Labels
Board for kneeling	

1 Spade up the soil in the planting area to a depth of 1 ft. Amend the soil well with compost or other organic matter to ensure good drainage. Rake the soil surface until it is smooth and level.

2 Arrange the bulbs in a row, or for a more natural look, toss them gently out of a pail and plant them where they fall, but at least 2 in. apart. Dig a hole for each bulb, using a board for kneeling to avoid crushing bulbs that are already planted.

3 Sprinkle a bit of bonemeal or fertilizer in the hole and cover with a thin layer of soil. Set in the bulb with the "nose," or tip, facing up. Cover with soil and tamp lightly; water. Then cover with mulch and label.

A bulb blueprint. To avoid damaging already planted tulip bulbs when putting in new ones in fall, plant gladiolus bulbs in late spring next to fading tulips. Then in the fall, dig up the gladiolus bulbs for winter storage and you have ready-made holes for new tulip bulbs.

Free bulbs. Daffodils and crocuses produce bulblets that can be carefully pulled off the parent and replanted in the soil. Look for them the next time you dig up daffodils or crocuses. In a year or so, they'll put on an equally flowery show.

Critter control. Toss some sharp gravel into the bulb hole, and squirrels and other munchers will decide to dine out elsewhere.

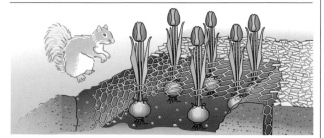

More critter control. Protect bulbs from hungry squirrels and chipmunks by covering the bed with a layer of chicken wire; be sure to tuck the edges deep into the soil and top with mulch. Or you can plant a group of bulbs in a wire cage. Narcissus bulbs are relatively rodent-proof, so you don't need to protect them.

After bulbs bloom, trim the spent flowers right away. But you must let the foliage die back naturally, so it can replenish the bulb with energy for next year's bloom. Snip off the top growth once it has withered completely, generally in 6 to 8 weeks.

Good neighbors. Because the fading foliage is unattractive, interplant bulbs with bushy annuals or perennials that will grow tall enough by summer to hide the yellowed tops. Tall bulb plants, such as gladiolus and some lilies, benefit from close companions that will help prop up spindly stems.

Winter care. Dig up tender bulbs before first frost, dry them for a week, then store in a box of peat moss or sawdust and keep in a cool, dark place.

Planting bulbs in groups

WHAT YOU'LL NEED

Shovel	Watering can
Plastic tarp	Organic mulch
Compost or other organic matter	Labels
Bonemeal or bulb fertilizer	
Bulbs	
Flathead rake	

1 Dig a hole for the planting area 1 ft. deep. Place the soil on a tarp and mix in compost or other organic matter. Also cover the bottom of the hole with a few inches of amended soil, depending on planting depth.

2 Sprinkle a bit of bonemeal into the hole, working it into the soil. Set in the bulbs with tips up, making sure to space them 2–6 in. apart.

3 Backfill the hole with the rest of the amended soil. Rake the soil surface until it is smooth and level. Tamp down lightly and water in. Cover with a few inches of mulch, and label the area.

The right site. Roses need at least 6 hours of sun each day. Morning sun is best, since it evaporates disease-causing dew from the foliage. In hot climates, roses will appreciate some light afternoon shade.

No fungus among us. Select a site with good air circulation to prevent fungal diseases, such as blackspot and rust. Space most roses at least 2 feet apart; some large shrub types require 6 feet of room. Also keep roses a good distance from other mildew-prone plants, such as bee balm and lilac.

Gorgeous ground cover. Use ground-hugging roses on slopes and other problem areas. Look for a vigorous variety, such as 'Red Cascade,' that will spread into dense mats.

Old salts. If you live at sea-side or areas exposed to deicing salts, look for rugosa roses (*Rosa rugosa*), which thrive in salty conditions.

Go for the old. Besides modern hybrids, seek out the so-called old garden roses, which were in cultivation before 1867. Bourbon, Damask, Alba, Gallica, and other classic rose types are fragrant and easy to grow. The downside: many bloom only once per season.

Drink deep. Roses, especially when young, need plenty of water. Give the roots a long, slow soaking of about 1 inch per week, but always be sure to keep water off the foliage.

Big eaters. Roses have hearty appetites—satisfy them by scratching in a specially formulated rose fertilizer around the base, then watering in. Feed young roses after they bloom, then once a month thereafter. Feed mature plants about a month before blooming in spring, then once a month thereafter. Stop fertilizing all roses 6 weeks before blooming ends.

Growth spurt. To stimulate growth, sprinkle a table-spoon of magnesium-rich Epsom salts around the base of each rosebush in May and June.

Sturdy support. Tall roses need strong support to keep them from toppling. To prevent damaging the roots, drive a rot-resistant wooden stake at the back of the planting hole before inserting the rose. Then fasten the stem loosely to the stake with plastic strap ties.

Handle with care. To plant a container-grown rose, cut out the bottom of the pot, then set pot and all in the hole. Slit the container's sides from top to bottom in several places with a sharp utility knife, remove the pot sections, and backfill the hole.

FILE IT

Roses for beginners
Agriculture Canada and the Canadian Rose Society say these are hardy, disease-resistant, and easy to grow.

Climbers	Color
'Compassion'	Apricot
'Isle Krohn Superior'	White
'Sympathy'	Red
Florabundas	
'Europeana'	Dark red
'Iceberg'	White
'Sunsprite'	Deep yellow
Hybrid Teas and Grandifloras	
'Double Delight'	Apricot or Pink blend
'Mister Lincoln'	Dark red
'Pristine'	White
'Touch of Class'	Pink blend
'Tournament of Roses'	Medium yellow
Miniatures	
'Pink Petticoat'	Medium pink
'Rise 'n' Shine'	Medium yellow
Shrubs	
'Explorer'	Yellow, Cream, and Pink White
'Heritage'	Light pink
'Parkland'	Red and White

Good drainage. Make sure your roses' roots won't be waterlogged by testing the planting site for drainage. Dig a hole 18 inches deep and fill with water; it should drain in 2 hours or less. If not, move the plant to a different spot, add mulch and compost to the soil, or build a raised bed.

Please don't squeeze.
When pruning roses, never use anvil shears—they can crush the canes. Instead use scissor-type pruning shears for a clean cut.

Prettify the patio with miniature and patio roses— dwarf types that average 1 foot in height and are ideal for containers. Keep potted plants well watered. Also, apply a balanced rose fertilizer in spring and a diluted liquid fertilizer during the growing season as needed.

Getting horizontal. Climbing roses flower most abundantly when the canes are trained to grow horizontally.

Night show. Roses make a perfect border for a deck or patio. And for a treat at night, plant white or light-colored varieties, which show up in the dark.

A thorny issue. For roses that last longer, look for varieties with prickers on the stem. Roses with prickers usually last 1 to 3 days longer than their thorn-shorn cousins.

Ban the beetles. Japanese beetles are voracious rose nibblers. Pick them off by hand and drop them in kerosene. Or spray roses with neem oil, which is extracted from an Asian tree and available through mail-order outfits.

Get hip. Although roses should be deadheaded to remove spent flowers and encourage new ones, leave some blooms on roses that develop colorful seed capsules, or hips, in fall. Harvest the hips to make some jelly or tea. Or let them be: they will attract birds and beautify the winter landscape.

Planting a bare-root rosebush

WHAT YOU'LL NEED

Bare-root rosebush	Pruning shears
Pail of water	Watering can
Shovel	
Plastic tarp	
Compost or other organic matter	
Bonemeal or fertilizer	

1 Soak the roots in a pail of water for 24 hr. before planting. Dig a hole 18 in. wide and deep. Shovel the soil onto a tarp and mix in compost and fertilizer. Make a mound in the hole with some of the soil.

2 Prune any damaged roots, and center the rose over the mound, spreading out the roots. Be sure that the bud union, where the top growth meets the rootstock, is at soil level in mild areas and 1–2 in. below in cold climates.

3 Water the hole and let drain. Fill with a third of the soil and water in. Repeat twice, until the backfill is at soil level. Mound more soil loosely around the canes to support them. You can remove the mounded soil when leaf growth reaches about 1 in.

Make your own. Use a chipper-shredder to turn brush and dry leaves into mulch. Or lay down 5 to 10 sheets of moistened newsprint and cover with soil. (Don't use colored newsprint; metals from the ink will eventually leach into the soil.)

Use what? Look around your area for sources of unusual but effective mulches. Take away spent hops from a brewery. Ask mushroom growers for the compost they've finished using as a growing medium. Haul away manure from farms, zoos, stables, or feedlots.

Free mulch. Tree-trimming companies and municipalities that have set up brush-collecting sites often have excess wood chips available at no cost.

From little acorns. Rather than hauling acorns to the recycling center each fall, run them through a chipper-shredder (always wear safety goggles). They make an attractive spring mulch for daffodils and daylilies.

If you are a newspaper mulcher, prepare papers throughout the winter by gluing them together, length to length. Keep gluing until your mulch "mat" is as long as the bed you want to use it in. Roll it up and store until spring.

Save money by limiting expensive ornamental mulches, including shredded bark, and bark nuggets, to permanent plantings and flower displays. In the vegetable garden, use less-expensive mulches that you can turn under at season's end to enrich the soil, such as straw, manure, or chopped leaves or corncobs.

Match your mulch to the plant. Use oak leaves and pine needles, which release acid as they decompose, around acid-loving plants like rhododendrons and blueberries. Use neutral materials, such as buckwheat hulls or corncobs, on plants that don't like acid.

Lighten up. Some mulching materials will cake up when put down and inhibit air and water circulation. Mix a denser mulch of grass clippings, coffee grounds, or peat moss with a lighter, more porous material, such as chopped leaves, before spreading it in a bed.

Food thieves. Fresh wood chips and sawdust rob nitrogen from the soil as they decay. Compost them for 6 months before using, and supplement the soil with a high-nitrogen fertilizer such as blood meal if needed.

If a wood-chip mulch smells like vinegar, ammonia, or sulfur, it may indicate that the wood is acidic and will form acids as it rots. Use the chips only on acid-loving plants.

A no-no. Never use plastic mulch in permanent plantings. It isn't permeable, prevents the circulation of water and air, heats the soil excessively in summer, and will suffocate the roots.

Mulching timetable. Mulch perennials, shrubs, and trees with a layer about 3 inches thick, and leave in place all year, refreshing the top as needed. Mulch vegetables and annuals in spring once the soil has warmed. Mulch overwintering bulbs and vegetables after the ground freezes.

Breathing room. Don't pile mulch too close to stems and trunks—it can shelter slugs, mice, and other pests and also suffocate roots. Always leave a ring of bare soil around each plant.

By hand only. Avoid using sharp tools to clear away winter mulch in the spring—you might damage the emerging shoots. A gloved hand will get the job done safely.

Roll out the carpet. Old pieces of wool or cotton carpet work well as a weed-suppressing mulch between rows in vegetable and cutting gardens or nursery beds. For camouflage, just cover it with a thin layer of soil.

A better way. Geotextile mulch—a fabric that allows water and air to pass through—is a good choice for trees, shrubs, and perennials. Spread a piece over prepared soil and cut holes for installing plants; make sure the holes are large enough to permit fertilizing around the roots. Top with an ornamental mulch to hide the fabric and slow its decay from sunlight.

More uses. Spread geotextiles when planting slopes—they prevent erosion and protect young plants from runoff. You can also fit the fabric behind a stone, block, or timber retaining wall to limit soil erosion.

Perfect for paths. To keep a new path weed-free, lay plastic or geotextile mulch over the soil, under the paving material. The mulch is also good for suppressing weeds under decks; cover with ornamental gravel.

SAFE AND SMART

➤ Use plastic mulch to create a bed in grass or a weedy patch. Laying a sheet over the proposed planting area will kill the vegetation beneath it.

➤ To get a head start on the growing season, use a piece of plastic mulch to warm up the soil, and pop in the plants once the threat of frost is past.

Laying black plastic mulch

WHAT YOU'LL NEED

Black plastic mulch

Rocks or bricks

Trowel

Sharp knife or scissors

Vegetable seedlings

Watering can

1 Lay a sheet of mulch over a prepared planting bed. Weight the edges with rocks or bricks. Dig a shallow trench around the sheet, and bury the edges in the soil to anchor them. Remove rocks or bricks. Be sure the sheet is flat but not too taut.

2 Cut crosses in the mulch to allow for planting. Space out these slits according to the mature size of the plant. Peel back each X and dig a planting hole with a trowel.

3 Set the seedlings in the soil directly through the mulch. Firm the soil around the plant. Water through the slits, and smooth the mulch around the stems to retain soil warmth and to suppress weed growth.

Blast from the past. The seeds available at most garden centers are modern hybrids bred for agriculture, not home gardens. Look in specialty catalogs for the seeds of vintage vegetables—nonhybrids in cultivation before 1940. You'll be rewarded with hardy, easy-to-grow, disease-resistant plants that produce fruits with superb flavor.

Cozy up. You can set out your tomato seedlings once nighttime temperatures are above 55°F/13°C. Keep them cozy by flanking them with flat stones or tiles that will retain the sun's heat in daytime and radiate it at night.

Shady neighbors. Always keep corn, tomatoes, and other tall vegetables at the north side of the garden, so they won't shade out their shorter companions.

Mixed salad. What to do with a variety of leftover lettuce seeds? Mix them all together in a bag, shake them up, and sow into the soil. At harvest time, you'll have a "pretossed" salad.

Cagey compost. Provide tomatoes with both food and support by planting them around a compost cage. Simply erect a wire cylinder about 2 feet tall and 3 feet wide and toss in compostables or rotted manure; water and turn as needed. Set six seedlings around the cage perimeter and tie in the stems as they grow. The tomatoes will feed at will.

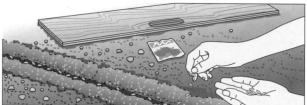

Fast furrows. To speed direct planting of small seeds, press a furrow into the soil with a 4-foot-long scrap of ½-inch plywood. Sow seed, then gently whisk the soil back in place. Cut a slot near the center of the board for a handy handhold.

Recycled seed pots. Save money—and minimize transplant shock—by sowing seeds in quart-size milk cartons trimmed to several inches tall and filled with potting soil. At planting time, cut away the carton with scissors and set the seedlings into the hole.

Making a raised bed

WHAT YOU'LL NEED

Stakes and string

Spade

Spading fork

Rototiller (optional)

Compost or other organic matter

Untreated boards (1 x 6 or 1 x 8) or landscape ties

Galvanized nails or rods

Hammer or electric drill

Level

Complete fertilizer

Flathead rake

Garden hose

1 Select a location that gets at least 6 hr. of direct sunlight daily. Outline a rectangular bed with stakes and string, making it no more than 4 ft. wide. If possible, orient the bed with the long sides running north and south; this ensures the most light and least shade.

 To make sure the bed is straight, measure the diagonals. They should be equal.

2 Strip the sod from the bed location if necessary, and turn over the soil to a depth of 12 in. to promote drainage. For large areas, use a rototiller instead of digging tools. Incorporate compost, rotted manure, or other organic matter into the soil.

Space race. When room is limited, make every inch count. Grow pole beans and other "vertical" crops. Raise dwarf varieties in beds or containers. After harvesting cool-weather crops, such as lettuce, replace with warm-weather plants like summer squash. Plant quick crops, like radishes, among slow ones, such as tomatoes; you can harvest the fast growers before the slow ones mature.

Stop grasshoppers and other vegetable pests with homemade sprays that are safe to squirt on edible plants. Thin blackstrap molasses with enough water to make a sprayable solution. Or mix 6 garlic cloves and 2 hot chilies with 2 cups water in a blender and strain. Or mix 2 ounces dishwashing liquid and 1 tablespoon vegetable oil in 1 gallon water. Reapply the spray after it has rained.

Tea for the tomatoes. Give growing veggies a boost at midseason with a drink of manure tea. Shovel some rotted manure into a pantyhose leg, tie the top, and steep the "tea bag" in a garbage can of water for a week. Sprinkle the brew on the soil around the plants with a watering can, but be careful that it doesn't splash on the foliage.

Until you plant again, store leftover seed in 35mm film canisters. The black plastic blocks out light, and the canisters are waterproof. If you're not a shutterbug, photo shops usually have extras on hand.

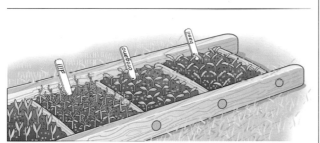

Instant herb garden. Have an old wooden ladder? It's the perfect start to an herb garden. Fill in the spaces between the rungs with soil and pop in the plants.

3 If the ground isn't level, dig a shallow trench around the perimeter of the bed, and set in the retaining walls. They should be 6–8 in. high and level. With boards, butt the ends and nail together; brace each corner with a cleat. Secure landscape ties with cleats. If the soil is poor and a deeper bed is desired, stack ties so the ends overlap. Drill through the ends and drive in a rod that reaches at least 6 in. into the soil.

4 Fill the bed with topsoil amended liberally with compost. Also work in fertilizer. Make the soil as rich as possible, since a raised bed is planted more intensively than the traditional vegetable plot. Keep the soil level 2 in. below the top of the enclosure to prevent the soil from washing away.

5 Rake the soil until smooth and level. Water the bed well and let the soil settle. Add more soil if needed and rake again. Seed the bed or plant out seedlings in rows or groups. Water frequently and watch for pests.

 Raised beds dry out quickly, so water as needed and spread mulch to inhibit moisture loss.

Roots of success. When buying shrubs, look for a profusion of young white roots. These absorb moisture and nutrients and boost the chances that the shrub will "take." To inspect, slip the plant gently from the pot or remove the burlap from the root ball.

Oh, deer! Discourage nibbling, whether by rabbits, birds, or deer, by surrounding shrubs loosely with plastic or wire mesh—it's unattractive but easy and effective. You can also use pieces of strong-scented soap: Make a pouch out of plastic mesh, tie off one end, fill it with soap bits, and hang the bag on the shrub. Sprinkling human hair in the bed or spraying the area with a special repellent will also help deter pests.

For maximum growth, nick the root ball with a cultivator or knife before placing the plant in the hole. The roots will send out new growth in response.

Chow time. Feed shrubs each spring and fall with a balanced complete fertilizer, such as 10-10-10. Acid-loving shrubs, such as azalea, camellia, holly, and hemlock, need an acid-forming fertilizer; just ask for it at any garden center.

Steep slope? Plant it with low, spreading shrubs such as cotoneaster, juniper, bearberry, or pyracantha. They fill in quickly, require little maintenance, and are an effective hedge against soil erosion.

Beware of burlap. If the burlap surrounding a root ball is natural, cut away as much as possible after setting the shrub in the hole; any fabric that sticks above the soil can draw moisture from the roots. If the burlap is synthetic, completely remove and discard it.

Weave a tapestry. Design a hedge with a mix of shrubs that create a living tapestry. Alternate plants that have complementary foliage colors, such as red- and green-leaved barberries, or variegated shrubs with plain ones—silver-splotched with blue hollies.

Planting a container-grown shrub

WHAT YOU'LL NEED

Spade or shovel

Plastic tarp

Compost or other organic matter

Complete fertilizer

Hand cultivator

Gypsum (optional)

Container-grown shrub

Scissors

Pruning shears

Stake or pole

Watering can

Organic mulch

1 Dig a hole twice the width of the shrub's root ball and a bit deeper than the container. Lay a tarp beside the hole and place the topsoil on it; discard the subsoil (add it to the compost pile). Mix enough compost into the topsoil to compensate for the subsoil that was removed. Add fertilizer.

2 Loosen the soil at the sides of the planting hole with a hand cultivator. Also lightly loosen the bottom of the hole. If the soil is heavy clay, scratch gypsum into the base of the hole at the recommended rate to aid drainage around the young roots.

Never buy a bare-root ever-green shrub. The roots can't provide enough moisture, which evaporates constantly from the leaves.

Use a shallow-rooted, shade-tolerant ground cover around your shrubs instead of mulch. A patch of periwinkle, pachysandra, or bugleweed will keep the soil around shrub roots cool as well as weed-free.

Snap those suckers. If your shrub sends out suckers—unwanted shoots that form on the roots or rootstock—get rid of them promptly, since they sap energy from the plant. Always pull—don't cut—them off carefully as close to the base as possible; then scrape away any nubs with a utility knife.

Spare the shears. Every shrub needs regular pruning for growth and health; the timing and technique depend on the plant. But the watchword is restraint: never alter the plant's profile radically. Remove any dead, diseased, or damaged stems, making sure to follow the plant's contours to maintain an attractive silhouette.

When transplanting, prepare the shrub for the move. Several weeks before moving day, sink a sharp spade in a circle around the perimeter of the roots to sever horizontal roots and stimulate growth of new feeder roots. After moving, keep the shrub watered until roots are established.

Spiny shrubs make good barriers. Plant them along paths to keep baby strollers in line and under first-floor windows to repel intruders.

Winter woes. Drying winds and heavy snow can harm evergreen shrubs. Soak the plants well before the ground freezes, and spray the foliage with an antides-iccant to retard moisture loss. Erect burlap screens around individual plants or the whole bed, but leave the top open for air circulation. Gently brush off snow from plant tops with a broom.

Give it shelter. For a shrub that takes a beating from heavy snowfall, construct a simple roof over its head. Attach a couple of hinges to two pieces of scrap plywood that are slightly larger than the shrub, and position the "tent" over the plant. When the snow falls, it will slip down the sides.

3 If possible, cut away the container. Otherwise gently slide the plant out by turning the pot over at an angle and supporting the trunk with one hand. Never pull the plant out by the stems. Place the shrub on the tarp and inspect the roots, teasing out any that are pot-bound. Prune any roots that are encircling the trunk, since they can strangle the plant.

4 Set the plant in the hole and direct any protruding roots into the soil. Lay a stake across the hole and make sure that the crown, where the trunk meets the root ball, is at soil level; adjust with soil as needed. Backfill the hole, tamping firmly to eliminate air pockets, and water.

5 Prune off any damaged, diseased, or weak shoots. Also trim back any stems that are crossing others or growing inward. Spread 2–3 in. of mulch, forming a shallow ring of the material around the edge of the hole to retain water. Level the ring once the plant is well established.

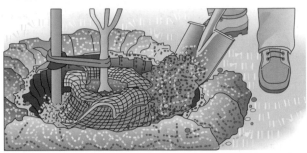

Helping hand. If you're planting a tree solo, give yourself a third "hand." Place the tree in the hole in the desired position, pound in a stake beside the root ball, and tie the tree trunk to it near the soil line—this will keep the tree stable while you backfill. When you're done, just remove the stake.

No improvement needed. Unlike other plants, trees should not be treated to amended soil—the roots soon outgrow the planting hole and may be "shocked" when they hit native soil. Simply set them in the desired site and let their roots adapt to existing conditions while still young.

Come to grips. To move a heavy balled-and-burlapped tree, thread rope handles through the twine securing the burlap to the root ball and pull the tree along gently. Or place the root ball on a spade or tarp and drag it to the planting hole.

Start small. Don't go for the biggest tree at the nursery unless you need to fill a spot quickly. A small or average-size tree will be easier to transport and plant and will adjust to its surroundings more readily.

Damage control. Gouged, split, or cracked bark is a doorway to disease. Look for trees with smooth, healthy, unbroken bark.

Clean trees. Never place trees that drop excessive amounts of leaves, twigs, petals, or seedpods near an outdoor living or high-traffic area. Tree debris not only is time-consuming to clean up but also can stain bricks and pavers or become slippery when wet.

Sleeping beauties. Plant trees when they are dormant—in early spring or fall for deciduous trees and in late summer for evergreens. This lets the trees establish their roots before the foliage starts demanding water and nutrients.

Spaced-out fruit trees. To spread out the branches of fruit trees when they are still young, clamp together the "mouths" of two spring-type clothespins. Then carefully wedge the forked ends between the trunk and limb.

Planting a balled-and-burlapped tree

WHAT YOU'LL NEED

Shovel

Gypsum (optional)

Hand cultivator

Tree

Hand pruners or scissors

Pliers

Complete fertilizer

Organic mulch

Garden hose

Sledgehammer

Stakes

Wire

8-in. lengths of old garden hose

Tree trunk bag (optional)

1 Dig a planting hole 2 to 3 times as wide as the tree's root spread but no deeper than the height of the root ball, placing the soil on a tarp. The juncture of the trunk and roots should be at grade level in most soils and raised a few inches in heavy soils. Also, in heavy soil, scratching gypsum into the base of the hole aids drainage. Once the hole is dug, loosen the soil at the sides with a shovel tip or hand cultivator.

2 Position the tree in the center of the hole. Be sure it is at the proper depth and is standing completely upright—not leaning. If necessary, rotate the tree in the hole to be sure that its branches will not interfere with any structures nearby and that the most attractive side is facing the direction from which the tree will be viewed.

A mulch margin. Spread 2 to 4 inches of organic mulch over the tree's root zone, starting 6 inches from the trunk. Don't use fresh manure, grass clippings, or sawdust—they're too "hot" with nitrogen—or gravel, which can get caught up in a mower.

No delays. Plant bare-root trees no later than 24 hours after purchase. Before setting the plant in the hole, soak the roots in a bucket of water for at least 12 hours, then trim off damaged or broken roots.

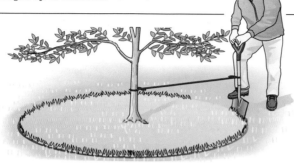

Get an edge. Want a professional finish around trees planted in the lawn? Loop a rope around the tree trunk and the shaft of a spade, adjusting the length so that the spade reaches to the dripline of the tree. Scribe the outline of a circle, then remove the rope and retrace the circle, sinking the spade in vertically to make a neat, clean edge. Strip the turf under the tree and cover the area with mulch. You'll need to neaten the edge every year or so.

Ironclad repellent. To keep deer from munching on young trees, wrap galvanized bailing wire loosely around the lower branches, extending it 1 inch beyond the branch. Deer will quickly move on rather than face the prospect of a metallic mouthful.

Foiling insects. Pests that climb the trunks of fruit trees can be turned back by wrapping the trunk with strips of aluminum foil. The invading bugs can't get a good toehold on the foil's slick surface.

Standing straight. Staking a young tree after planting helps keep it upright until the fibrous roots can take hold. But be sure to remove the staking after a year so that the trunk can develop.

Don't bother. Tree roots are greedy and sometimes shallow, and the leaf canopy can be dense. So don't expect grass to thrive under trees. If you must plant beneath a tree, use early spring bulbs or a shade-tolerant groundcover; install the plants while the tree roots are young.

Storm-resistant trees. According to the U.S. Forest Service, the sturdiest specimens are live oak, bald cypress, black gum, sweet gum, Southern red oak, magnolia, white oak, beech, sugar maple, and sycamore.

3 Using hand pruners, cut away as much natural burlap as possible; remove synthetic burlap and wire. Mix fertilizer in the soil and fill the hole three-quarters full; water and let drain. Fill the hole and tamp firmly. Build up a 3-in. soil mound around the hole's edge to create a basin. Spread 3 in. of mulch and water again.

4 With a sledgehammer, drive two stakes opposite each other 2–3 ft. from the trunk. Thread wire through the hose and loop wire around the tree—the ideal height is about a third of the way up the tree. Secure the wire ends to the stakes, leaving enough slack so that the tree can move.

 In a pinch, use an old lamp cord instead of wire and hose.

5 Surround the trunk with a "gator" bag, which is designed to hold water and release it slowly to the root ball. Insert a hose in the slit at the top of the bag, and fill it until water begins to come out the top. Refill when the root ball begins to dry out—perhaps a week later. Leave the bag on through the first growing season, until the tree is well established.

Smart cleanup. Spread a plastic or canvas drop cloth beneath the tree or shrub before you start pruning. When you're done, just drag the debris to the recycling or compost bin.

Stay low. Don't bother trying to prune a branch that you can't easily reach from ground level. If you need a ladder, then it's time to call a professional.

A girdling root wraps around the base of a tree, strangling it. Get rid of it by cutting the root with a handsaw, working as close to the trunk as possible.

Stop the bleeding. Some trees, including maples, birches, and cherries, will "bleed" if pruned in spring, when the sap is flowing. Prune them in midsummer.

Steady now. Before pruning tall tree branches with a pole pruner, don a carpenter's apron. Rest the tool base in a pocket to help control its lateral sway; then your hands will be free to guide the pole and pull the line.

Heading back means removing the growing tip to stimulate growth of side shoots and create a bushier plant. Use pruning shears or your fingers to nip off a branch or stem just above a single leaf, a set of leaves, or an outward-facing bud.

Thinning out means removing branches or stems down to their base—either at the ground or at a crotch. Use shears or a saw to thin out dead, diseased, or damaged stems, or over-crowded stems that block out too much light.

They don't stop rot. Wound dressing, tree paint, and tar won't stop decay around a pruning wound on a tree. Let the air and sun help the tree heal naturally.

Stamping out stumps. If a diseased tree must be cut down and only a pesky stump remains, try killing it yourself. Drape several unopened plastic trash bags over it, and anchor them with rocks and string. Remove the bags after a month, cut off any new growth, and then re-cover. In several months, the stump will die and can be removed more easily.

Pruning a tree branch

WHAT YOU'LL NEED

Pruning saw or bow saw

1 First reduce the length of the branch to ease handling. Then, starting 12 in. from the trunk, cut a third of the way through the under-side of the branch. This will prevent the bark from ripping if the branch snaps.

2 Make the second cut on top of the branch, placing the saw $1/2$ in. farther from the trunk than the first cut. As you saw through, the branch's weight will close the under-cut and make the cutting easier.

3 To remove the stub, make an undercut just beyond the "collar," where the branch and trunk join. Then saw from above to meet the undercut, angling the saw away from the trunk for a clean cut.

FERTILIZING

Organic vs. synthetic.
Both types of fertilizer
provide nutrients to plants
in the same way, but there
are differences. Organic
fertilizers are derived from
plants or animals, release
their nutrients slowly, and
feed the soil. Synthetic
fertilizers, on the other
hand, are manufactured
from chemical sources; their
nutrients are concentrated
and feed the roots directly.

Garden too green? You
may be applying too much
nitrogen, which stimulates
lush growth at the expense
of blooms. Water plants
often to wash it out of the
soil, and use a low-nitrogen
food such as 5-10-10.

Keep granular fertilizer
away from plant foliage; it
can do irreparable damage
to leaves and flowers.

More isn't better. Always
apply fertilizer at the manufacturer's recommended
rate. Using more food won't
speed growth—it's wasteful
and can harm plants.

Pot spots. Cut back on
feeding if white deposits
appear on clay pots. They
may mean an excess of
fertilizer salts has built up.

When to feed. Plants vary
in their feeding habits—
from light eaters like herbs
to heavy ones like roses.
As a general rule, feed
woody and hardy plants
in early spring and late fall;
feed annual plants at the
beginning and middle of the
growing season.

Fast and slow. A quick,
easy way to feed trees is
with slow-release fertilizer
spikes. Insert them into the
soil at the recommended
depth; they take about a
year to break down, letting
trees absorb nutrients
gradually over a long period.

Smart storage. Granular
fertilizers can absorb the
fumes of herbicides and
then damage plants when
applied. To be safe, store
bagged fertilizer away from
weed-killing chemicals.
If storage space is limited,
place the fertilizer in a
tightly sealed plastic bag
to prevent contamination.

Get to the roots. Phosphorus aids root growth, but
moves slowly through the
soil. Make sure you apply
it right around the roots, digging up the soil as needed.

Fertilizing a tree

WHAT YOU'LL NEED

Tape measure or ruler

Complete fertilizer

Auger or iron bar

Funnel

Sand or soil

Hose

1 The fertilizer
application
rate depends
on the trunk size.
Calculate the
diameter of the
tree with a tape
measure so that
you can apply the
amount specified
on the fertilizer
label. Measure out
and set aside.

2 Use an auger
or iron bar
to bore holes
3 in. around and
1 ft. deep in the
soil. Space the
holes 2 ft. apart
in rings around
the tree. Start 2 ft.
from the trunk and
extend 2 ft. beyond
the tree's drip line.

3 Funnel an
equal portion
of fertilizer into
each hole, and plug
the top with some
sand or soil. Water
well with a hose to
help dissolve the
fertilizer granules.

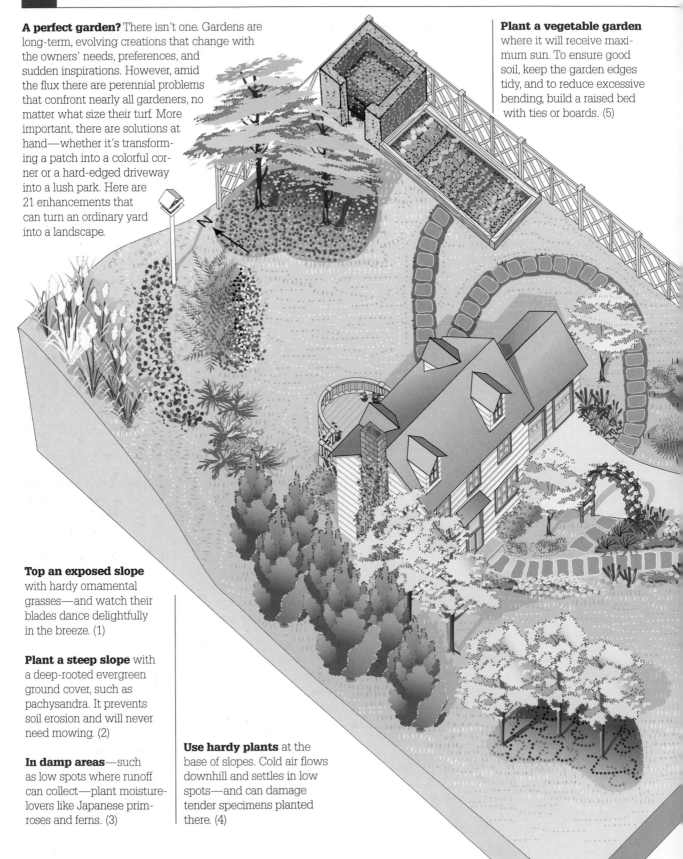

A perfect garden? There isn't one. Gardens are long-term, evolving creations that change with the owners' needs, preferences, and sudden inspirations. However, amid the flux there are perennial problems that confront nearly all gardeners, no matter what size their turf. More important, there are solutions at hand—whether it's transforming a patch into a colorful corner or a hard-edged driveway into a lush park. Here are 21 enhancements that can turn an ordinary yard into a landscape.

Plant a vegetable garden where it will receive maximum sun. To ensure good soil, keep the garden edges tidy, and to reduce excessive bending, build a raised bed with ties or boards. (5)

Top an exposed slope with hardy ornamental grasses—and watch their blades dance delightfully in the breeze. (1)

Plant a steep slope with a deep-rooted evergreen ground cover, such as pachysandra. It prevents soil erosion and will never need mowing. (2)

In damp areas—such as low spots where runoff can collect—plant moisture-lovers like Japanese primroses and ferns. (3)

Use hardy plants at the base of slopes. Cold air flows downhill and settles in low spots—and can damage tender specimens planted there. (4)

Screen the compost pile
with a section of fencing or an evergreen hedge shrub, like boxwood or inkberry. (6)

Leave the sight line open
to a pretty view, and draw attention with an eye-catching feature—perhaps a stone bench, a sculpture, or a birdhouse. (7)

Don't bother with grass
under a heavy leaf canopy. Plant the space with a shade-tolerant ground cover, such as ivy or periwinkle. Keep climbing specimens clipped back 6 inches from the trunks. (8)

Put year-round mulch
under ornamental lawn trees and underplant with spring-flowering bulbs. They'll bring early color to the front yard and receive enough sun before the trees leaf out. (9)

Use a tough turf grass
that can stand up to repeated wear in play or heavy-traffic areas. (10)

Perk up a deck or terrace
in summer with pots of annuals and herbs—try fragrant varieties like nicotiana. For eye-appeal in winter, plant dwarf conifers in containers. (11)

Plant evergreen trees
in staggered rows to screen prevailing winds. Note that a windbreak protects an area 10 times its height, so a stand of 5-foot-tall trees will reduce wind up to 50 feet away. (12)

Cover a brick chimney
with a self-clinging perennial vine, like climbing hydrangea or silver-vein creeper, neither of which will harm mortar. (13)

Place shade trees at least 20 feet from the southwest facade of the house. The shade will keep rooms cooler in summer, while bare branches in winter allow sun to penetrate. (14)

For a weed-free path, lay down a plastic or geotextile sheet and cover it with pebbles or shredded bark. If desired, lay stepping-stone slabs that are spaced at a striding pace. (15)

A fence provides privacy, but select a style, such as lattice, that lets air circulate while blocking the view. Dress it up with an apple tree or pyracantha trained in a decorative design on a wire grid. (16)

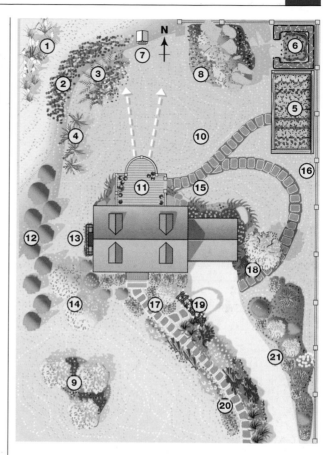

Mix in a small tree, like a dogwood, with foundation shrubs to provide both height and beauty without obscuring the view from indoors. (17)

Install foundation plants
in layers, planting the tallest in back. Anchor the house corner with a specimen tree whose mature size is in proportion to the house—and be sure to plant it far enough away to allow for growth. (18)

Mark the transition
between an entry path and the driveway with a flowering arch. Use a coated-steel or cedar structure and train a bright-blooming rose or clematis to climb up it. (19)

Make an entry path more inviting with a mass of colorful annuals. Select kinds that will spill over the path and blur the hard line. (20)

Line a driveway with a diverse shrub border. This low-maintenance garden reduces lawn area and softens the "hardscape." (21)

SAFE AND SMART

➤ Fences are cheaper than walls and need less skill to install.

➤ More than any other landscape feature, trees make a garden look established and give it depth and dimension.

Good neighbors. If your fence faces a neighbor's property, make sure their side is as attractive as yours. It's not only good manners but may be specified in local building codes. Also be sure that you erect the fence within your property boundary and that it conforms to any ordinances on height and design.

Consider the wind. Closed fences block gusts but also create powerful downdrafts on the leeward side. When you need to buffer wind, select a fence that allows some air to filter through— but at a much slower speed.

In for the long haul. Buy rot-resistant fencing of cypress, red or white cedar, or pressure-treated pine—it will last longer and require less maintenance.

The soft approach. Ground too hard for digging a fence-post hole? Dig a shallow hole, fill it up with water, and let it sit over- night. Then finish digging the hole the next day, when the ground is soft.

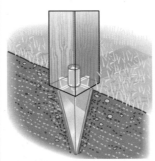

Easy anchor. Metal spear connectors make it easy to set fence posts. Pound the spears into the soil with a sledgehammer, leaving the tops several inches above the ground to aid drainage. Then top them with predrilled posts.

Rock-solid footing. Place a large flat rock in each post hole before setting the post and adding gravel. You'll use less gravel, get rid of a few rocks, and won't compromise either drainage or the decay resistance of the wooden posts.

Fencing flexibility. Attach prebuilt sections of picket fence to posts by fitting the rails into metal brackets instead of nailing them. You can lift off the fence when you need to paint it or when you need to move large objects in and out of the yard.

Prefinish fence parts with paint, stain, or preservative before you assemble them. It's much easier to cover every inch of the wood— and you'll make less mess.

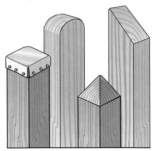

Shedding water. Trim fence posts to a point or a slant so they will shed rain, or cover them with metal caps. Protect the top of a board fence with domed or sloped coping.

Gripping gateposts. Help stabilize gateposts, which see a lot of action, by beefing them up with 10d common nails: drive nails in halfway in a stag- gered pattern all around the end that will sit in the hole. When you pour in concrete, the nails will provide a good grip.

Building a picket fence

WHAT YOU'LL NEED

Stakes and string
Tape measure
Posthole digger or auger
Tarp
Shovel
Crushed stone
Fence posts (4 in. x 4 in. x 5 ft.)
Level
Wheelbarrow with mixed concrete
Tamper and masonry pointing trowel
Fence rails (preferably 2 in. x 3 in.)
Electric screwdriver
Galvanized wood screws
Electric saw
Fence pickets (1 in. x 3 in. x 3 ft.)

1 Mark the position of the end posts with stakes. Run a taut string line about 2 in. off the ground along the proposed course of the fence. Measure the length of the line and divide it into equal intervals to determine the spacing of the intermediate posts (no more than 8 ft. apart). Use stakes to mark the location of each post center.

2 Dig a hole for the first end post 30 in. deep and 12 in. in diameter, placing soil and sod on a tarp. Shovel 2 in. of stone into the hole and insert the post; it should be 32 in. above ground. Pack 6 in. of stone around the post to stabilize it. Check for plumb with the level. Dig the hole for the second end post and set it in the same way, then continue with the other posts.

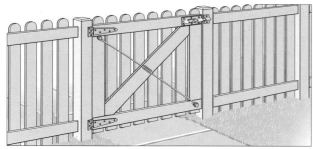

Stop sagging. If you're using a diagonal wooden brace to support a gate, attach the top end of the brace to the latch side and the bottom end to the hinge side to prevent the gate from sagging. To add a sag rod, or turnbuckle, run it in the opposite direction of the brace: install the top of the rod on the hinge side and the bottom on the latch side.

Even spacing. When positioning pickets, attach a cleat to the end of an extra picket and hang it on the rail to mark the distance between pickets. When installing a top rail, cut a piece of wood equal to the distance between the bottom and the proposed top rail and use it as a spacer.

Annual checkup. After the fence has been up for a year, caulk any spaces between the concrete footings and the posts to keep out water, which can cause rot. Also check for flaking paint or worn stain—and promptly repair the finish before the wood is exposed.

SAFE AND SMART

➤ Use a clamshell digger if you need only a few holes. For a big job, rent a power auger meant to be used by two people; the one-person model can be hard to handle. But be warned: neither tool works well in rocky soil.

➤ You need to see oncoming traffic as you exit a driveway, so never erect a tall fence near the end of a drive.

Outfox intruders that may sneak beneath a solid fence to feast on your garden. Dig a narrow trench about 12 inches deep beside the fence. Cut pieces of chicken wire long enough to run the length of the fence and wide enough to stretch from fence bottom to trench. Attach the top edge of the wire to the fence with staples, and sink the rest into the trench; then fill with dirt.

3 Put some concrete in the first hole and tamp it down. Add concrete in stages, tamping and checking the post for plumb. Overfill the hole by 1 in. to create a "collar." Using a trowel, slope the concrete away from the post to promote drainage away from the wood. Repeat with the other posts. Let the concrete cure for at least 2 days.

4 Cut top and bottom fence rails to the needed length. The rails should be flush with the end posts and meet at the center of the intermediate posts. The bottom rail should be about 3 in. off the ground. Stretch a level string line along the fence to mark the bottom rail position. Attach the rails to the posts with screws, checking for level. Next attach the top rails. Cut any posts that aren't flush with the top rail.

5 Position a picket flush on each end post and in the center of each intermediate post, with the bottom about 2 in. off the ground. Measure the distance between the pickets on two adjacent posts, and space the pickets evenly in between, making sure that the bottoms are 2 in. from the ground. Check for plumb before attaching pickets to both rails with wood screws.

Signs of stress. Plants need water when the foliage wilts, droops, or seems dull and when fruit and flower development is poor. But remember that many plants droop at mid-day as a natural reaction to overheating; water them only if they don't perk up by evening.

Good catch. Mound mulch or soil in a circle under the drip line of trees and plants to create a shallow basin. The depression will catch and retain rainfall.

Keep two watering cans handy at all times—one for regular watering and one for applying water-soluble chemicals, such as weed-killer or pesticides.

A big drip. An efficient way to water is with a soaker hose—a porous or pierced tube that lets water seep gradually into the soil. Snake it around your plants close to their root zones and then cover it with mulch, which will inhibit evaporation.

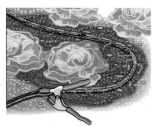

Shortcut. If the soaker hose is too long for the area you want to water, shorten it to the desired length with a spring clip or C-clamp.

FILE IT

Desert flowers
Reduce watering by planting drought-tolerant specimens, whose waxy, fuzzy, or pale-colored foliage helps them trap and conserve moisture.

Warm climates	Cool climates
African iris	Aster
Alyssum	Columbine
Aspidistra	Evening primrose
Autumn sage	Flax
California poppy	Snow-in-summer
Lantana	Yarrow
Primula spp.	Primrose

Repairing a leaky outdoor faucet

WHAT YOU'LL NEED

Large adjustable wrench
Screwdriver
Needle-nose pliers
Washer
Noncorroding screw (optional)
Lubricant

1 Before removing the faucet, turn off the main water supply. Next, unscrew the packing nut with a wrench and open the handle. The entire assembly should come free.

2 Remove the old washer and the screw that secures it. If the screw won't move, slice away the washer and remove the screw with the needle-nose pliers.

3 Replace the washer with an identical one. If the screw needs replacing, use a noncorroding variety. Lubricate the screw, insert it, and secure the washer. Then lubricate the assembly and reinstall it.

Let it roll. Make your own hose guides to prevent hoses from snagging on rocks, crushing plants, or getting nicked. Insert dowels in strategic places around the garden, and place lengths of PVC pipe over them.

Ready, aim, water. To avoid scattershot watering, turn your hose into a homemade watering wand by taping a 3- or 4-foot length of old broomstick to it with duct tape.

Maximize moisture. Since 25 percent of a sprinkler's moisture evaporates before hitting the soil, water when it's overcast and still. Make sure the spray is aimed at the soil—not the pavement.

Sprinkler savvy. To deliver water when plants need it, install a moisture sensor on your automatic sprinkler system. When the soil becomes dry, the sensor opens an electric valve to turn on the water.

The buddy system. Give a thirsty plant its own watering system. Pierce tiny holes in the sides of a clean 1-gallon plastic jug. Bury it next to the plant so that the spout is just above soil level. Fill the container with water, which will leak out around the root zone.

A snack for houseplants. The water left over from steaming vegetables or boiling eggs makes a mineral-rich treat for houseplants. Just let the water cool first.

Going away? Water your houseplants and wrap the pots in plastic wrap, folding it loosely over the soil so it touches the stem. Moisture will be slow to evaporate.

Replacing an automatic sprinkler head

WHAT YOU'LL NEED

Spade

Pipe tape

Flexible sprinkler head

1 Turn off the timer and close the shut-off valve. Cut into the grass around the sprinkler head with a spade, and set aside the sod. Lift out the dirt carefully to avoid damaging the sprinkler connection fitting and the pipe.

2 Gently lift out the old flexible sprinkler head and unscrew it from the nipple connector. Remove any residue of pipe tape from the threads of the nipple connector and replace with new pipe tape.

3 Turn on the water briefly to blow out any pebbles or dirt that may have gotten into the pipe. Turn the water off and screw on the new flexible sprinkler head. Backfill the hole, carefully tamp down the soil, and replace the sod.

Exhausting possibilities.
Before firing up your mower for the first time in spring, look for and clean out any debris from the muffler opening. Small rodents often warehouse their foodstuffs in the exhaust systems of power equipment during the winter months.

Wait when wet. Make sure the soil and grass are completely dry before you cut. A heavy mower or tractor could sink into the wet soil and create compacted ruts that are difficult to repair. Mowing wet grass will result in uneven cuts and clumps of clippings that not only smother the lawn but also clog the mower.

A makeshift mulcher.
If you own a mower with a side discharge chute, remove the grass-catching bag and let the nourishing clippings fall where they may. Just mow more frequently, slicing off no more than the top third of the grass blade each time.

Or fit your old mower with a new mulching blade, available for many models.

To remove clippings that have already hardened on the underdeck, soften the buildup with a blast from the hose, then scrape it off with a putty knife, old wood chisel, or other sturdy tool.

For the cleanest cut, always check the mower wheels. A wobbly wheel, often caused by a loose bolt, can result in a ragged cut.

A clean underdeck is a mulching-mower must. Spray the underside of a mower with cooking spray to prevent a buildup of clippings. To avoid messy oil spills, do it between draining the old engine oil and putting in a fresh supply.

Handy wipe. To prevent a mower deck from rusting, clean off grass clippings with an oily rag after you're done mowing.

Let it be. Use a mulching mower, which pulverizes grass clippings, to save time, energy, and money. No need to rake up tiny clippings—they will decompose and deposit nutrients back in the lawn, thus reducing the need for fertilizer.

Sharpening a mower blade

WHAT YOU'LL NEED

Work gloves

2 x 4

Wrench

Hammer

Vise

Medium-rough flat file

Spike-and-cone balancer

Screwdriver (optional)

1 To remove the blade, disconnect the spark plug cable and wedge the blade into a stationary position using a 2 x 4. Grasp the blade with your gloved hand and loosen the bolts with a wrench. If the bolts stick, tap the wrench with a hammer. Once the bolts are off, remove the blade.

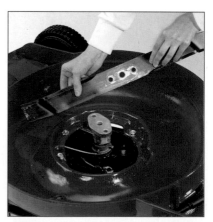

2 Inspect the blade (and the stiffener if the unit has one) for damage. Replace any damaged parts with new ones specified by the manufacturer. If the blade is bent, don't attempt to straighten it.

Not so inclined. Mow across a sloped lawn rather than up and down it. It's easier on your arms and much safer, since the mower can't run away from you when working downhill or roll back on you when working uphill.

Save the trees. Sharp mower edges can easily gouge delicate tree bark, leaving the tree vulnerable to insect attack and disease. To prevent damage, install a bumper made from plastic car-door guards on the sharp edges of your mower.

Change direction. Vary the mowing pattern each time you cut the grass. Otherwise the soil could compact or wear patterns could become etched in the lawn.

Coil colorful vinyl tape around your electric-mower cord to keep it visible.

Making the last cut. Lower the blades and clip the grass to no more than 2 inches in height at the end of the mowing season. Shorter grass is less susceptible to disease over the winter and makes for easier, quicker cleanup of garden debris come spring.

Before storing away a mower for winter, remove the spark plug and pour a tablespoon of motor oil into the hole, turning the mower upside down to distribute the oil evenly.

Run on empty. Suck out gas left in the mower tank at the end of the season with a turkey baster; then run the engine for a few minutes to burn off the rest. Or leave gas in the tank and add fuel stabilizer to prevent gasoline breakdown.

SAFE AND SMART

➤ To protect the mower blade and your eyes from damage, clear the lawn of rocks, branches, and other obstructions before mowing.

➤ Wrap an electric-mower cord over your shoulder or coil it around your elbow, and you'll be less likely to run over it as you mow.

➤ When tipping the mower on its side to make a repair, always be sure the oil fill hole is above the crankcase. This will prevent hard-to-clean oil spills on the driveway or garage floor.

3 Using a medium-rough flat file, sharpen the blade along the original angle of each cutting edge, on opposing ends of the blade. File in one direction only—toward the edge. Take equal amounts of metal off each edge.

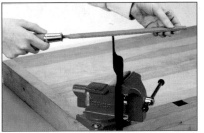

4 Check to be sure that the blade balances horizontally, using a spike-and-cone balancer (available from an auto parts store) or a screwdriver. Check the balance one way, then flip blade over and check again. If the blade does not balance, file metal from the heavy end. Avoid filing the newly sharpened cutting edge. Continue filing until the blade balances.

5 Once the blade is balanced, reinstall it, making sure that the lift wing on each end points toward the deck of the lawn mower. This will allow the blade to cut and discharge grass properly.

LEAF BLOWERS

Cool running. Because electric and gas-powered blowers are air-cooled, regularly remove debris from the cooling system vents. This easy cleanup can prevent the buildup of excessive heat, which could eventually burn out the engine.

Snug it up. Engine vibration from a power tool loosens the nuts on the exterior housing. Keep them nice and snug by dabbing clear nail polish or special thread-locking compound on the bolts before retightening the nuts.

One-step cleanup. How can you remove wet leaves that are stuck to paved areas? Attach a vegetable brush to the end of the leaf blower—you can scrub off and blow away debris in one easy step.

To advance a leaf pile to a collection tarp or wheelbarrow, blow the looser portions of leaves and clippings at the top of the pile first; then quickly follow with a blast to the denser base.

Before powering up a leaf blower, familiarize yourself with local laws governing noise. A too-loud blower could cost you a lot more than angry complaints from the neighbors.

CHIPPER/SHREDDERS

Fill 'er up. Periodically check the fuel level of a chipper/shredder. If you run out of gas, you'll have to unclog the hopper or the chipper chute and clean the discharge area before restarting the engine.

Stay sharp. When mulch chips become stringy or the chipper discharge slows down, it's a sure sign that the blades need to be sharpened right away.

The savvy shredder. Don't shred leaves or branches that are green or wet. They not only can clog or jam the machinery but also can yield moldy mulch.

Cooperate and save. If you don't have enough trees to make renting a chipper-shredder cost-effective, but you still want shredded leaves for mulch, ask several neighbors to split the expense. Everybody gets to use the equipment, and you get your leaves.

Replacing the starter cord on a leaf blower

WHAT YOU'LL NEED

Torx driver or hex wrench

Scissors

Screwdriver

Replacement cord or spring assembly

Work gloves

Safety goggles

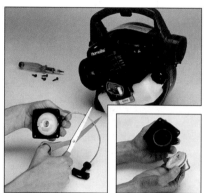

1 Remove the bolts that hold the housing in place. If necessary, cut the old cord and then loosen the bolt or screw that secures the pully-and-rope assembly in the housing. Remove the assembly, being extremely careful not to remove the spring.

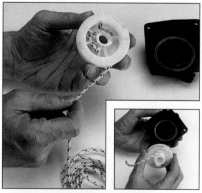

2 Take off the old cord. Wind the new one in the same direction, making sure the inner end is secured in the fastener or slot provided. Put the pulley in place over the spring.

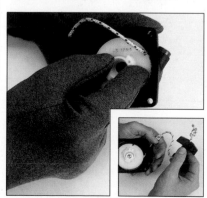

3 Wearing work gloves and goggles, rotate the pulley 2 or 3 times (check the owner's manual) in the same direction in which the cord pulls. Re-insert the center screw. Insert the cord's end through the handle opening and secure with a knot or clip.

CHAIN SAWS

Start your engine by pulling the starter cord straight up out of its housing. Repeatedly yanking it at an angle against the housing will eventually fray it.

Flip the bar. The guide bars of most chain saws are reversible. To even up wear, reverse the bar after every 5 hours of use.

From chips to dust. When your chain saw starts to produce sawdust, it's an indication that the blade is dull. Stop work immediately and resharpen the teeth.

Capping the teeth. Cover a chainsaw's sharp teeth with a split piece of garden hose when hanging it up.

SAFE AND SMART

➤ Dress defensively when using a chain saw: gloves, earplugs, boots with a solid tread, safety glasses, and a hard hat.

➤ Don't cut anything above shoulder height.

➤ Always shut off the saw when you are getting into position to cut.

STRING TRIMMERS

No scalping. When using a string trimmer, keep the cutting head level at all times. Tilting the head will give the grass an unsightly crewcut.

Back off. Don't trim right up to the base of shrubs and trees. The spinning line of the trimmer can easily scar tender bark.

If you must cut close to trees and shrubs, then attach a heavy plastic collar, available at garden centers, to the base of the trunk.

The right machine. Trimmers with automatic or semiautomatic string-feeding systems are a lot easier and faster to use. With manual systems, you have to turn off the trimmer, fool around with locks and housings, then pull out the fresh line by hand.

Quick release. When replacing the string on a trimmer, use your car's oil-filter wrench to loosen that stubborn head.

Clear the air. Never cut back poison ivy, oak, or sumac with a string trimmer. Toxic particles are released into the air and could cause a reaction if they come in contact with your skin.

Installing a monofilament line on a string trimmer

WHAT YOU'LL NEED

Brush

New spool or new line

1 Press the locking tab on the side of the spool while rotating the locking ring counterclockwise. Pull off the locking ring and inspect it; replace if damaged.

2 Pull off the automatic feed button (sometimes called a tap button). Inspect it for cracks and other damage; replace if needed. Brush away debris.

3 Press the spool down, turn it slightly to release the locking tabs, and slide it carefully from the hub. Replace the spool with a prewound model, or wind a new line onto the old spool. Reinstall the spool.

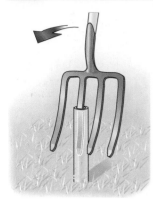

Good tines. Make a jig for straightening bent tool tines by inserting a 3-foot length of 1-inch-diameter galvanized pipe about 2 feet into the ground. Whenever you bend a tine on a fork, position it in the pipe and bend to straighten it out.

Flashy tools. Brushing tool handles with colorful paint will keep them within eye-shot even in long grass and messy beds.

Stow gardening tools and gloves in a mailbox hung on a fence post or shed wall. They'll be protected from the weather and always within reach.

No-bend gardening. If you have trouble bending or kneeling, you can still be a crackerjack gardener. Many nurseries and catalogs stock trowels, cultivators, and weeding tools with extra-long handles.

Rustproof tools by keeping a bucket of sand mixed with vegetable oil near the shed or garage. Before putting away your tools, simply dip the blades into the bucket. The sand will scour off dirt and sap while the oil will coat the metal, keeping it rust-free.

Step softly. To cushion your foot as you dig, slip a piece of old garden hose over the shoulder of the shovel blade.

Sowing machine. Build a time-saving planting tool from ¾-inch scrap plywood. Drill 2 dozen ½-inch-deep holes into one side of the plywood, insert 1½-inch-long wooden dowels, and secure with small sheet-metal screws. Press the dowels into a prepared garden bed, and you're ready to pop in 24 seeds at a time.

A grapefruit knife makes a nifty weeder. It's light-weight and comfortable to hold, and it allows you to work close to delicate plants. Plus, its serrated edges cut right through gritty soil.

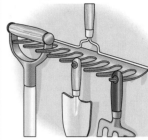

A handy hang-up. Saw off the broken handle of an old rake and nail the rake to a garden or shed wall, tines facing outward. The tines not only hold small tools, such as trowels, but also larger ones like shovels with D-shaped handles.

Replacing a shovel handle

WHAT YOU'LL NEED

Power drill with a grinding-wheel attachment

Center punch

Hammer

Wood screws

Screwdriver

Metal vise

Rubber mallet

Paper and pencil

New hardwood handle

Crosscut saw

Carbon paper

Wood rasp or Surform tool

Wooden block

1 Grind off the head of the retaining rivet with the grinding-wheel attachment on a power drill. Drive the rivet out of the toolhead socket with a center punch and hammer. Extract the stub of the old handle by screwing a long wood screw deep into the stub. Secure the screwhead in a vise, then hit the tool's head with a mallet.

2 Roll up a strip of paper into a tube and slip it inside the now-empty socket. Let the paper unroll until it fits the socket diameter, and secure it at that size with a piece of tape. Now slip the tube of paper over the tapered end of the new handle and mark the corresponding circumference.

Old rakes never die, they just turn into squeegees for patios, decks, and walkways. Slit one side of a length of old garden hose and pop it over the tines of the rake—you can whisk away a mini-flood before it becomes bigger trouble.

Sharp and clean. To keep shears, loppers, saws, and clippers in top shape, sharpen the blades after about 10 hours of use, clean off any sap or debris promptly, and disinfect tools used on diseased growth with diluted household bleach.

Preventing split ends. Rub boiled linseed oil into wooden tool handles every so often to seal areas where the varnish has worn away. Hardworking handles won't split and splinter if you seal the pores before moisture can get in.

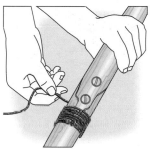

If a handle does split, squirt yellow glue into the crack, clamp the assembly together until the glue dries, then insert short wood screws across the break. For extra reinforcement, wrap the repair with epoxy-soaked heavy twine.

To quickly remove sap from a pruning saw's teeth, spray some oven cleaner on the sticky area and clean off with a toothbrush. Rinse with water, dry completely, and spray with a lubricant.

Tools to go. A carpenter's apron is a perfect tool belt for gardeners. Use the pouches to hold gardening shears, a trowel, seed packets, or twine and to bring back cuttings from beds.

Garden sled. Haul small tools and supplies out to your garden on a child's snow saucer. It will save you time and labor and won't damage the lawn.

SAFE AND SMART

➤ To extend the life of gardening gloves, place small duct-tape patches or iron-on patches on the fingertips.

➤ For blister-free gardening, slip a piece of foam pipe insulation over the handle of your trowel, shovel, or rake and secure it with a piece of tape.

➤ To prevent an aching back, use a cultivating hoe as you would a broom, gripping it with both thumbs facing up. Keeping your back straight, sweep just under the soil's surface, shaving off the weeds as you go.

3 Measure the socket depth; then measure the corresponding distance from the pencil marks toward the end of the taper. Secure the handle in the vise, and using a crosscut saw, cut the tapering end of the handle at the point you have marked.

4 Wrap carbon paper around the tapered end of the new handle, and insert the handle into the socket of the toolhead. Pull out the handle without twisting it. The paper will leave dark marks on the high spots of the handle. Remove the high spots with a wood rasp or Surform tool. Repeat this process until the carbon paper turns the handle uniformly dark.

5 When the taper is correct, the handle should fit snugly into the socket up to the pencil line. When the handle fits, strike it on a wooden block to drive it into the toolhead socket. To secure the new handle in the socket, drill pilot holes from both sides at slight angles. Then insert round-head wood screws that are slightly shorter than the diameter of the handle.

To bin or not to bin. You can make compost in an open pile—just cover it with a plastic tarp to prevent nutrients from leaching out in the rain. Or use any type of closable container, such as an old garbage can, with holes poked in it for air circulation. Even a corrugated plastic enclosure with wooden posts will do the trick.

No admission. Never add any oil, meat, or dairy products except eggshells to the pile. They decompose too slowly, emit odors, and can attract pests. Also dispose of diseased plants in the trash, not the composter.

Head start. The smaller the material, the faster it will decay. Cut up kitchen scraps or pulverize them in a blender. Shred leaves and garden debris with a shredder or lawn mower, or place them in a garbage can and chop with a string trimmer.

Making deposits. Toss any vegetal matter in the pile: fruit and vegetable scraps from the kitchen, grass clippings, leaves, plant prunings, sod, straw, nutshells, and spent flowers. You can also add such odds and ends as wine corks, laundry lint, pet hair, fireplace ashes, and fish bones.

Convenient compost. Locate the compost pile near the garden. Hauling debris to the bin and bringing finished compost to the flowerbeds will be easier.

Weed watch. Don't add weeds that have set seed to the pile. They may germinate and sprout once you spread the compost in the garden.

For a quick bin, set three wooden pallets in a box shape and wire the corners together; pallets are often available for free at lumberyards. Old refrigerator or oven racks work well, too. Add boards to the front as the heap grows higher.

Liquid refreshment. Keep the compost pile moist. Besides water, you can use leftover juice, coffee, tea, or vegetable cooking broth.

Making compost in a wire bin

WHAT YOU'LL NEED

Garden brush or cornstalks

Garden and kitchen debris

Watering can

Fresh farmyard manure or fertilizer

Soil

Sledgehammer

Stakes

Wire fencing or hardware cloth

Wire or twist ties

Plastic tarp

Cardboard (optional)

Fork

Broom

1 Spread some garden brush on the ground where you want to place the compost pile; this porous layer will permit drainage and air circulation. Top with 1 ft. of garden debris, such as dead leaves, grass clippings, and plant trimmings. Water until moist. Top with 1 in. each of manure or organic nitrogen fertilizer and soil.

2 With a sledgehammer, drive four stakes around the perimeter of the pile and encircle them with wire fencing. Fasten the fencing in place as needed with wire or sturdy twist ties. Cover the pile with a tarp.

 Line the bin with several sheets of cardboard in order to reduce moisture loss.

To help compost "cook," mix 1 part "green" materials, which supply needed nitrogen, with 3 parts carbon-based "brown" ones. Good sources of greens are grass clippings, clover, manure, and vegetable parings. Good choices of brown materials include straw, dead leaves, cornstalks, even sawdust.

Pests be gone. If raccoons, skunks, deer, or other pests are raiding your bin, spray it with a scent repellent or household ammonia. If flies and insects are a problem, add soil or shredded newspaper to dry the pile, limit the amount of manure, and keep the pile covered.

Spread compost whole, or pass it through a sifter made by stapling a piece of fine mesh to a frame of scrap lumber; custom-size the sifter so that it fits over your wheelbarrow.

A short stack. Compost that reaches more than 4 feet tall and wide is tough to manage and won't permit air to reach the center.

For better air circulation, drill holes into a PVC pipe and insert it through the center of the pile.

SAFE AND SMART

➤ Never compost pet droppings—they may contain parasites or other harmful organisms. Manure from farm, zoo, and circus animals is safe to use as long as it hasn't been treated with pesticides. Always check before hauling it away.

➤ The leaves and growing branches of oleander plants contain a sap that can cause blindness. Keep them out of the compost pile.

➤ Compost piles that smell foul may either contain too much manure or may need air. Turn the pile thoroughly to aerate it, don't add manure, and mix in straw or soil to absorb the odors.

Hot spot. Compost piles heat up—to about 130°F—as they cook. If your compost feels cold, turn the material around the edges into the center with a fork every 3 to 5 days to incorporate air. Also mix in some manure or compost activator, add soil if it's too wet and water if it's too dry, or adjust the ratio of materials.

3 Keep adding garden debris to the pile. Also use vegetal waste, such as coffee grounds, vegetable and fruit peels, or nutshells. Try to achieve a ratio of 1 part high-nitrogen materials to 3 parts high-carbon ones.

4 To speed decomposition, keep the pile evenly moist, about the consistency of a damp sponge. Add 1 in. each of manure and soil on top of every 6 in. of debris. Turn the pile with a fork to bring material on the sides into the "hot" center. Poke holes in the pile with a broom handle to aerate it.

5 When the pile reaches the top of the bin, stop adding material. Keep it covered and let it "cook," turning and watering as needed. Depending on content and temperature, the pile will decompose in several weeks or months. Once the material turns crumbly, add it to the soil.

SAFETY AND SECURITY

Job ratings: Easy   Medium   Complex

Security measures. These days security is no longer a simple pursuit: leaving on a living room lamp and canceling the mail when heading off for the week won't fool an intruder worth his rap sheet. There is a science to being—and feeling—safe. Just look below. We've compiled 23 tips—14 for the outside of the home, 9 for the inside—that will tighten up security at your house.

Get a good look. Install a wide-angle peephole on the entry door. (6)

Outside

No place to hide.
Trimming back shrubs and other plantings near the house deprives prowlers of a place to hide. Strategically placed thorny plants—a hedge of rosebushes ringing the perimeter of the house, for example—can also be a deterrent. Consider putting gravel on pathways and under windows to prevent an intruder from approaching silently. (1)

Down and out. Protect basement windows with metal grates or bars or specially designed plastic bubbles. However, check local building and fire codes before blocking the exit from any window. (2)

Window of opportunity? Secure ground-level double-hung windows with keyed pin locks, which prevent the upper and lower sashes from being opened by pinning them together. Also install these locks on any upper-level double-hung windows that are accessible from garage roofs, shed roofs, etc. (3)

Bulk up the doors. Secure bulkhead-type basement doors from the underside with sliding crossbars. Recess the hinge barrels in concrete to protect them. (4)

Show them the door.
Placing lights on both sides of the entrance door should provide ample nighttime illumination, even if one light fails. For added security, consider converting at least one light on the front of your house to an emergency light, which flashes on and off when you flip the light switch twice. When the switch is flipped once, it functions as a regular light. Easy-to-install emergency light kits are available at hardware stores. (5)

Install deadbolt locks on all exterior doors, and on doors leading to the basement and the garage. If double-cylinder deadbolts are used, always keep a key within easy reach of the door to prevent being trapped in a fire. (7)

The strong, solid type.
Make sure all exterior doors are solid-core to strengthen them against intruders. (8)

Moving targets. Motion-detecting lights go on when someone approaches the house and enters the sensory field. Install them on your house's exterior so they illuminate areas that can't be seen from the street— back and side yards, for example, as well as areas that are screened by shrubs, trees, or other vegetation.

Place the lights high enough so they can't be reached without a ladder. (9)

Open-and-shut case. If you have an automatic garage door opener, consider replacing it with one that has a "rolling code." This defeats the "code grabbing" devices that thieves sometimes possess, and that allow them to access the electronic code that opens your door. To improve security and safety, you can also purchase remote-control devices that will open the garage doors and turn on interior and exterior lights— all without your having to get out of the car. (10)

Don't forget the garage. Reinforce the panels on wooden garage doors. If there are windows in the doors, consider replacing them with shatterproof glass. When going away for long periods, padlock the garage door track, or if it is an electric door, turn off the power. Electric garage doors should be the newer variety that reverses if it touches anything while closing. (11)

Grounding an intruder. Use vinyl rather than metal drainpipes, since vinyl is less likely to support a climber. Also, cut back tree limbs that a burglar could use to climb onto the roof. Place trellises and picnic tables away from the house. (12)

Sliding home. Secure sliding glass doors with keyed pin locks that are screwed into the inside frame. The fixed panel of the door should be also be screwed into the frame so it can't be lifted out. (13)

A well-lit path. Installing low-voltage ground lighting makes outdoor walkways safer at night. Place timers or light sensors on the lights so they go on automatically at dusk. (14)

Inside
If you smell gas, evacuate the house immediately. Call the fire department from a friend's house or pay phone—using the phone or any appliance can be dangerous when gas is in the air. (15)

Be savvy about smoke. Install at least one smoke detector on each level of the home, including the basement and attic, and in the garage. If bedrooms are more than 40 feet apart, place a smoke detector outside each bedroom. Smoke detectors are also needed at the top of stairwells and at the bottom of the basement stairs. Smoke detectors can be part of a whole-house security system that includes protection against break-ins. (16)

And about security. An electronic security system is a good idea. The most secure are the monitored systems, but unmonitored systems also help protect against burglary. Put a sign in front of the house indicating the presence of an alarm system or a watchdog. (17)

Quick call. Program the police and fire department numbers into your phone's autodial, or post the numbers on the wall. (18)

Put timers on lights and possibly on appliances such as the air conditioner, television, and radio so you can program them to go on and off while you are away. (19)

Store fire extinguishers in various locations in the house, most importantly the kitchen, basement, and any room where there is a fireplace. (20)

Store valuables in a fireproof, waterproof safe to protect them from theft, flooding, and fire. (21)

A well-planned escape. Make sure there is a fire escape ladder in each bedroom and in any other frequently used room above the ground floor. (22)

Carbon monoxide alert. Install a carbon monoxide detector on each level of the house, including the basement and attic, and in the garage. However, do not place a detector near a source of combustion, such as a furnace or gas stove. (23)

The sign of security.
Convicted burglars said they would be less likely to break into a house with a sign that warned of a guard dog or an alarm. A well-known alarm company name indicates a professionally installed system that may be monitored. But the threat of physical injury from a dog is probably the best deterrent.

The lived-in look. Arrange for someone to mow and water the lawns for the summer or to shovel walks and driveways in winter.

Trashy behavior. Empty garbage cans mean an empty house. Hide the cans in the basement, storage shed, or garage. Also, turn off the electric garage door opener, padlock the garage door, and lock the door that leads from the garage to the house.

Need a lift? Enlist a friend or call a car service to take you to the airport so you can leave your car in the driveway. Then have someone move the car once in a while to make it look as if it's being used. If your driveway will be vacant, ask a neighbor to park in it occasionally.

Shady business. Closed window shades or curtains are a sign that nobody's home. One night before your trip, take a walk around the house and note which blinds or shades are open or semi-open. Leave them like this so your house doesn't seem closed up.

Hard-wired timer systems control as many lights and appliances as you want from a central unit. Inexpensive and easy to install, these systems can be set to operate at random times or on several different cycles over a 24-hour period. Some can even be controlled from your personal computer.

The light stuff. Make use of the many timing devices for turning lights and appliances like radios on and off (see steps 1–4, facing page). Or try this low-tech method: simply leave a bathroom light on, since this is what many people do while they are at home.

Machine schemes. Never announce that you're away on your answering machine; instead say you have house-guests or are otherwise engaged and will return the call soon. Check the answering machine and erase messages frequently to ensure that the machine doesn't fill up.

Dead ringers. Turn the ringer on your telephone down or off: a ringing telephone that isn't answered alerts a burglar that nobody's around.

Tune the radio to an all-talk station with the volume set so it's a bit softer than normal conversation. You want someone listening from outside to hear voices without being able to distinguish the words.

Threatening sounds. Make a recording of a dog barking loudly, or buy a pre-recorded tape at a security equipment store. Plug the stereo into a random timer for a more realistic effect.

Key exchange. Give a friend an extra house key, a trip itinerary, and numbers where you can be reached. Also leave the numbers of your plumber, electrician, and utility companies. That way someone can handle an emergency, if one comes up.

FILE IT

Bon voyage: A smart checklist before you go away

Write up a point-by-point to-do list to ensure that you don't forget anything in the rush to get out the door. A good checklist might look something like this:

Make sure the oven is off.

Arrange for pet and plant care.

Fill prescriptions, and take copies with you in case you run out of or lose a medication.

Pack first-aid supplies and a sewing kit. Also take sunscreen and shades and electrical converters, if needed.

Clean the kitchen and bathroom and throw out the trash to make sure insects don't move in while you're gone.

Move light-sensitive objects out of the sun, and make sure rain can't enter through any window screens.

If you keep spare keys hidden under doormats or rocks, remove them. Don't leave keys to double-lock windows and doors near breakable windows.

Turn on security alarms and timers.

Tell a neighbor you'll be away.

And finally, lock all windows and doors, including garage doors and outdoor sheds.

Law on order. Call the local police to tell them you'll be away and for how long, and give them the name and number of people who have your keys. Some police stations may be able to arrange for a periodic patrol of your neighborhood to check on your house until you get back.

Miniature safes disguised as shaving cream cans, flowerpots, and books are good for hiding small valuables. Even if thieves are wise to this trick, they won't have time to inspect every ordinary-looking can. Just make sure your safes look like the real thing.

Read all about it. Newspapers piled up on your stoop let the world know you're not home. Cancel mail, newspaper, and other deliveries, or better yet, have someone stop by the house to pick these up each day.

Stash it. Move valuable items, such as expensive televisions or stereos, away from windows—especially windows that can be seen from the street. Store valuable jewelry, cash, and important papers in a safe-deposit box.

A trusty teen or neighbor may make a good house sitter. And they'll give potential burglars the very real impression that the house isn't empty.

Leave on the heating, air-conditioning, and ventilating systems to prevent damage to the house from excessive moisture or heat. You can safely turn off an electric water heater at the circuit breaker panel, and set the air conditioner to turn on at a slightly higher temperature and the heat at a slightly lower one. But too great an adjustment is an invitation to disaster.

Away for the winter? Avoid frozen pipes by draining the pipes and installing antifreeze. For shorter trips, shutting off the water at the main entry valve—or just to the toilet, dishwasher, and washing machine—will prevent leaks.

Unplug the toaster, the television, and other small appliances; they can catch fire even if they're not turned on, especially in areas that have frequent thunderstorms.

Out of the pool. Install a pool alarm so that neighbors will know if any curious children fall in or take a dip while you're away.

1 This light-sensing socket converter automatically turns a lamp on at dusk and off at dawn. Suitable for interior and exterior lights, it screws into any standard incandescent light socket.

2 A plug-in timer turns lamps, radios, or other appliances on and off twice a day to give your home a lived-in appearance. Just plug the timer into an outlet, and plug in the appliance cord. Move the colored tabs to set the times.

3 Replace a standard wall switch with a switch timer. Turn the dial to program it to turn the light on and off at set times. The timer also has a feature that memorizes and repeats your daily lighting pattern. There is also a manual override switch.

4 A motion-detecting light, installed outdoors, automatically turns on when someone enters its sensory field. You can adjust the sensor's direction, the size of the field, and the sensitivity of the system. Most models have a manual override switch.

Save on insurance. If you choose to install a monitored alarm system, consider adding smoke detectors to it. This can result in insurance discounts.

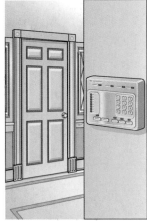

You're in control. Put the control panel near a door that you use a lot. If possible, put it out of sight. And make sure the panel can't be reached from the outside if a window is broken.

False startles. Most false alarms are triggered by users. Make sure you thoroughly understand your system. Choosing a simple coding sequence also helps.

Key to success. Another way to prevent false alarms is to choose a keypad that's easy to use. Opt for one that has large or backlit keys and will let you know when the buttons are fully depressed.

Place motion sensors where they have a good view of your house's access points (such as doors and windows) as well as the paths through the house that an intruder might take.

Sensors and sensibility. Infrared detectors are sensitive to light and should never be placed in a greenhouse or facing a fluorescent light or open window.

Common sensor. The most widely used motion sensor, the passive infrared motion detector, is more sensitive to motion across its field of vision than movement toward it. So if you want to protect valuable objects, place the sensor on a perpendicular wall, not right next to the possessions.

Hearing aids. Look for a keypad that starts buzzing when someone walks in the door and keeps going until the system is disarmed. Also, some systems use a digitized voice to let you know you've disabled it correctly.

Click on, click off. Some professionally installed systems come with a handheld remote that lets you arm or disarm the system, open the garage door, and turn on a porch light—all without getting out of the car. It also indicates whether there has been a fire or burglary.

Even more remote. Most high-end security systems can be controlled from a touch-tone phone—a useful feature should you forget to arm the system or if you want to let someone into the house during the day.

Installing a wireless home alarm

WHAT YOU'LL NEED

Wireless security system and desired accessories

Pencil or pen for marking

Awl

Screwdriver

Screws and wall anchors

Wire stripper

Electric drill

1 Follow the manufacturer's guidelines in deciding where to place the system console. Typically it should be near the main access door, unless a wireless keypad accessory is used. Locate the console where it can be heard at night and near a power source, but away from any large appliances. If there are glass panels on or flanking the door, locate the console several feet away from the door.

2 Install a sensor-transmitter at all ground-level and accessible upper-level door and window locations. Use the provided screws to secure the sensor-transmitter to the frame and the magnet switch to the door or sash (the magnet should be aligned with the sensor and no more than 1/2 in. away). Some alarm systems, such as the one shown here, use separate mounting plates.

In the future. If you plan to expand your security system later, choose an alarm that has terminals, so you can wire on additional components and sensors.

One room at a time. If you can't afford a whole house security system, protect isolated rooms with portable alarms. Placed on a table or shelf, a portable alarm scans the room with an infrared detector. If anyone enters the room, a loud alarm goes off.

Individual door alarms are available that can be hung on a doorknob or slid under the door like a wedge. You can also buy an electronic bar that slips into the track of a sliding door or window. These localized alarms aren't too loud, so use them only if there's an alert neighbor nearby.

Mix and match. When taking a more comprehensive approach, install a combination of magnetic contacts, which sound when a door or window is opened, and glass-break detectors, which respond to the shock frequency of glass breaking.

Screen out intruders. For added security, fit your windows with security screens. These look like ordinary windows screens but are interwoven with wires to form a protective circuit.

FILE IT

Dealer prep: What every security pro should have

Once you've narrowed down your list of home security installers, ask each of them if they have the following.

A license from the state (requirements vary).

Employees who have passed a background check.

Membership in the National Burglar and Fire Alarm Association.

General liability and workers' compensation insurance, as well as a policy known as "errors and omissions," which covers the installer if anything goes wrong with the security system.

An alliance with a professional monitoring firm that offers around-the-clock monitoring. Call your local consumer agency to check the firm's reliability.

Pet peeve. Minimize false alarms from roaming pets by purchasing sensors with "pet alley" lenses. These lenses cut off the sensor's field of vision so that motion within a few feet of the floor will not be detected.

A great combination. Motion detectors that use both microwave and passive infrared technology are less susceptible to false alarms than microwave-only detectors. Both units must detect motion in order to trigger the alarm.

3 Install shock sensors on glass doors and large-pane windows, and wire them to the sensor-transmitters. Adhere the shock sensors to the glass with the provided double-stick tape. Set all sensor-transmitter switches for either delayed or instant alarm, following the directions.

4 In order to group two or more windows together—or to provide dual protection for a sash you want to leave partially open for ventilation—install additional external switches, following the manufacturer's instructions. Wire them to the sensor-transmitter.

5 Add other accessories as needed—for example, motion detectors, smoke detectors, or an exterior siren, as shown here. The siren should be placed so that it is inaccessible to a burglar but can be easily heard by neighbors. Finally, program the security system according to your needs and the directions. Follow testing instructions after installation and periodically thereafter.

Installing deadbolt locks could save you a few dollars on your homeowner's insurance. Some insurance companies offer a 2 to 3 percent discount on homeowner's premiums if you install a deadbolt on every exterior door of your house.

Don't forget the back. Many people neglect to install deadbolts on back doors, side doors, and doors leading into the garage. Yet these entries are the most likely to be broken into, since they're often poorly lit and hidden from view.

One bolt or two? Deadbolts come in single- and double-cylinder models. Single-cylinder deadbolts are keyed on the outside and have a thumb turn on the inside. Double-cylinder types are keyed on both sides. The double-cylinder models provide more protection for doors that are flanked by glass. However, these locks have been known to trap people during a fire and are restricted by code in some areas.

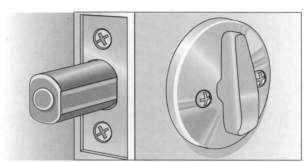

Throwing the odds. Thieves often break into a house by prying the jamb away from the door and freeing the deadbolt. Most deadbolts are equipped with a 1-inch throw, meaning that the deadbolt will extend 1 inch or more from the edge of the door when locked. If the deadbolt enters the framing lumber, it will be even stronger. Many older—and a few newer—deadbolts have less than a 1-inch throw. Check yours, and if this is the case, replace it.

Hollow-core doors are a poor choice for exterior doors, since they aren't as strong as their solid counterparts. But if you can't afford to change the front door, you can at least add a deadbolt. Install it close to the lockset because hollow-core doors are reinforced in this area.

Weighing your options. Though there are standards for classifying deadbolts, weight is a fairly accurate sign of quality. Look for heavy steel and a lock cylinder with a reinforced casing.

Installing a deadbolt lock

WHAT YOU'LL NEED

Deadbolt lock with template

Tape

Awl (or nail)

Electric drill and 1/8-in. drill bit

Hole saw

7/8-in. spade bit

Pencil

Hammer or wooden mallet and chisel

Wood scrap and clamps

Self-centering bit (optional)

Phillips screwdriver

Lipstick or grease pencil (optional)

1 Fold the provided template as instructed, and position it on the door about 6 in. above the doorknob's center; secure it with tape. Mark the centers for the lock and bolt holes with an awl or the point of a nail. Remove the template.

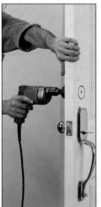

2 Drill through the center of the lock hole with a 1/8-in. drill bit. Bore the lock cylinder hole using a hole saw in an electric drill. Putting the pilot bit in the center hole, drill from one side halfway through the door, or until the pilot bit comes through. Repeat from the other side until the hole is bored out. Next, use a 7/8-in. spade bit to bore the bolt hole.

Strike one. A kick to the door can force the extended bolt right through the jamb. Prevent it by beefing up the strike, the metal plate into which the bolt slides. Strengthen the strike by removing the trim and adding wood between the jamb and the framing.

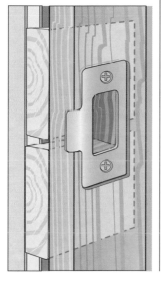

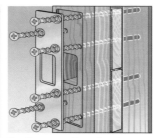

Strike two. Install a six-screw strike with screws long enough to penetrate the stud behind the jamb.

Strike three, you're out. Installing a strike box, a metal box recessed into the jamb, may provide some additional strength.

Put some spin on it. The spin ring, the large housing surrounding the outside of a deadbolt cylinder, protects the key cylinder from being removed with a pipe wrench or locking pliers. When buying a deadbolt, be sure to get one that has a solid metal insert for the spin ring, since hollow rings are easily crushed. The spin ring should also be beveled to prevent an intruder from getting a grip on it.

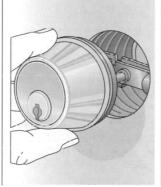

Totally keyless. Ever locked yourself out of the house? Keep it from happening again with a digital deadbolt. It works like a combination lock—you turn the dial to enter a personal code on a digital display. You can also change the lock's code to let repair people or others into the house when you want. If you're feeling nostalgic, you can always open the lock with a standard key at any time.

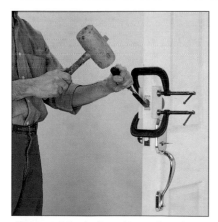

3 Insert the bolt and trace the plate outline on the door edge. Remove the bolt to chisel the plate mortise. Holding the chisel perpendicular with the bevel side in, cut around the perimeter. Then, holding the chisel at a 45° angle, make repeated cuts every 3/16 in. Chisel out the pieces. Clamp two pieces of wood to the door edges to prevent splintering.

4 Bore pilot holes for the screws with an awl or a self-centering bit; then install the bolt with the screws. With the bolt in the locked position, install the lock cylinder and reinforcing plate using the machine screws provided. Install the thumb turn, and test the lock operation with both a key and the thumb turn.

5 To locate the strike plate, paint the bolt end with lipstick, grease pencil, or pencil lead, close the door, and throw the bolt open. Hold the strike plate over the mark and trace its outline. Bore a 1-in. hole (or the recommended-size hole) for the bolt. Chisel a mortise for the plate and any reinforcing plate, as in step 3. Fasten the plate with 3-in. screws through the jamb and into the framing.

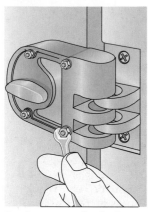

Beef up your rim lock.
Rim locks are effective, but they do have a weakness: they are usually secured by ordinary wood screws, which can sometimes be defeated by a few powerful blows or kicks. Remedy this by attaching the rim lock with carriage bolts secured by nuts. At the same time, strengthen the lock's strike plate by attaching it with flat-head screws that go into the framing.

Check the rating. A good sign of a lock's strength is its American National Standards Institute (ANSI) rating, listed on the package. The ANSI rating tells you a lock's resistance to forced entry and how difficult it is to pick. Grade 1 locks are meant for commercial use. Grade 2 models provide the best security for homes. Grade 3s shouldn't be installed on an exterior door.

Cylindrical is safer. Most residential locksets are classified as bored locks, which means they're installed by boring two holes in the door—one through the face and another into the edge. Cylindrical and tubular are the main styles of bored locks. Always choose a cylindrical type because its larger chassis provides more security than that of the narrower tubular style.

Mortise is safest. Help secure a wood entry door by putting in a mortise lock. Installed in a mortise, or recess, chiseled into the edge of the door, mortise locks are stronger and more durable than cylindrical locksets. Also, since the latch and deadbolt are in the same housing, it's possible to open both when you turn the interior knob. The downside: Mortise locks are expensive, and installation is best left to a professional.

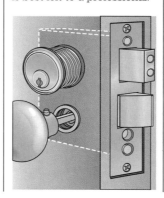

A single key. If you prize convenience, you can have all exterior locksets and deadbolts work with the same key. Locksets can usually be purchased to open with the same key, or a locksmith can rekey your existing locksets. Just remember that the locks must be from the same manufacturer.

A hand-tailored lockset.
Before buying a lockset, note whether the door is right-handed (knob on the right as the door opens toward you) or left-handed (knob on the left). Also note the lockset's size and heft, and see how it feels when you grasp it and make the motions of opening and closing it. This will help you choose the lock that best fits your door—and your hand.

Installing a rim deadbolt lock

WHAT YOU'LL NEED

Rim (surface-mounted) deadbolt lock with template and screws
Tape
Pencil
Awl or nail
Electric drill and drill bits
Hole saw
Screwdriver
Safety glasses
Two pairs of pliers
Hammer and chisel

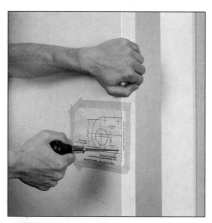

1 Fold and position the provided template on the door at least 6 in. above the doorknob. Use an awl or the point of a nail to mark the hole centers for the lock cylinder and the mounting bolts.

 Make sure the doorjambs are wide enough to install the strike plate.

2 Bore pilot holes for the mounting bolts and for the lock cylinder hole with a ⅛-in. bit (or whichever bit size is specified in your kit's instructions). Use a 1⅜-in. hole saw in an electric drill to bore the lock cylinder hole. Bore from one side until the pilot bit penetrates; then finish the hole from the other side. This is easier than drilling from one side, and it avoids damaging the door face due to tearout.

Maximum leverage.
Round knobs have long been the norm for exterior doors, but as barrier-free construction has gained in popularity, so have lever handles. These require less strength and agility to turn than knobs. Besides being a boon for elderly and handicapped people, levers can make life easier for anyone who routinely enters the house burdened by groceries or packages.

Going keyless? If you're thinking of installing a keyless lock system that opens with a combination, look for one that is battery-powered rather than hard-wired. The battery-operated model will remain locked even during a power outage.

Rekey or change all your locks at least once a year to help keep security up-to-date. If you are moving into a new home, change every lock prior to moving day.

An engaging solution.
If a door warps or bows, it may prevent the latch from properly engaging the strike plate. Fix this problem by moving the strike plate in the appropriate direction so that the latch catches.

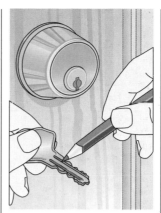

Lube the locks. Keep locks in good working order by lubricating them every 6 months. Use a commercial lock spray or powdered graphite. Or you can simply rub the point of a No. 1 or No. 2 graphite pencil along both sides of the key, then insert the key in the lock a few times.

Secure your sliders. Make sliding patio doors more thief-resistant with a patio door lock. This add-on is installed at the bottom edge of the inner door. The bar on the lock slides into a hole drilled in the outer door.

Room with a view.
A viewer, or peephole, is a must for even the best-secured doors; the newest ones come with wide-angle viewing. Another option is a swing bar, with a long piece on the door frame and a short piece on the door. It lets you open the door partway while still keeping it locked and is more secure than a chain guard, which can be easily pushed or kicked in. Either device is only as strong as the screws that mount it— they should be long enough to penetrate the framing.

3 Secure the lock cylinder and mounting plate to the door using a screwdriver and the bolts or screws provided. The tailpiece and the bolts or screws are grooved so that they can easily be broken to the right length using two pairs of pliers (inset). Wrap the jaws of one of the pliers with tape to avoid damaging the threads, and wear safety glasses to avoid injury.

4 Position the lock case so that the lock tailpiece engages the thumb turn, and secure it with screws. Make sure the key works in the lock.

5 Put the strike plate in position and close the lock. Use a pencil to mark the top and bottom screw holes on the jamb. Unlock and open the door. While holding the strike plate in position, mark all the screw holes with an awl. Drill pilot holes; then screw the strike plate in place. (If the strike plate needs to be mortised, draw the outline on the jamb; then mortise with a hammer and chisel as in step 3, p. 315.)

Air bag alert. Air bags are being redesigned to make them safer, but many cars still have the kind that inflate with great force, posing a danger to children and small adults. Reduce your chance of injury if you are in the passenger seat by sliding the seat back as far as possible, wearing a safety belt, and leaning back in the seat.

Thumbs down. The conventional wisdom of holding the steering wheel at the 10:00 and 2:00 o'clock positions turns out to be unwise if you have a driver's-side air bag. To reduce the risk of poking your eyes with your thumbs should the air bag inflate, hold the wheel at the 9:00 and 3:00 positions.

Safety seat smarts. Before installing a child safety seat, read the instructions carefully. If the car seat is secondhand and you don't have a manual, call the manufacturer. The safety seat must be compatible with your car seat and, especially, your seat belts. Some kinds of seat belts, including door-mounted and motorized models, are not intended to hold safety seats. Instead, you may need to use a special belt or clip.

Never in the front. Child safety seats—and young children, period—belong in the back, not the front, seat. This helps protect them from injury in case of an accident. Also, babies' safety seats should face the rear of the car. When baby gets bigger, turn the seat around or get a new one designed for a larger child. This will depend on the size of your child and on your particular safety seat; check the manual for specifics.

Hands on the wheel. For safety reasons, holding a cell phone while driving is a definite no-no. Keep your hands where they belong—on the wheel—by installing a cell phone holder. Most models feature a flexible arm that holds the phone in a convenient position while you talk.

1 A shoulder-belt adjuster is ideal for older children who have outgrown safety seats and boosters, as well as for short adults. The adjuster moves the shoulder belt away from the head and neck, and across the chest for a safer, more comfortable fit. It simply slides over the shoulder belt and can be moved back and forth for the best fit.

2 Childproof locking devices similar to this one come standard on most newer cars with rear doors, as well as minivans with sliding panel doors. Just flip the switch and the doors automatically lock from the inside when closed, making it impossible for a child to open them.

3 Replace your existing back-up light with a bright halogen bulb and an alarm that makes a beeping noise when putting your car in reverse.

In case of emergency.

Your car should always be stocked with jumper cables, flares, a flashlight, a spare tire, and a jack. A small air compressor or aerosol tire repair kit is also a good idea for temporary flat-tire fixes. If you will be driving off-road, add a tow rope, shovel, and jack board. For ice and snow, don't forget tire chains and some sand, salt, or cat litter for traction.

Cooler weather plays havoc with tire pressure. For every 10-degree drop in the temperature, tire pressure decreases about 1 or 2 pounds per square inch. Check the air pressure in your tires at least once a month; do it when they're cold—that is, before they've been run a mile. If the pressure is 4 pounds below the recommended level, the tires are underinflated.

A wrenching experience.

Many lug wrenches have handles that are too short, making them hard for even strong arms to operate. Slipping a 3-foot length of pipe over the wrench's handle will provide more leverage and ease the task at hand.

Take care of the spare.

Check the spare tire at least once a year to make sure it is sound and properly inflated. And if you do drive on the spare in an emergency, don't exceed the speed and distance indicated on the tire's sidewall. Repair the main tire ASAP.

Hot stuff. Before making a quick repair on a hot engine, slip your hand into a barbecue mitt to protect yourself from a nasty burn.

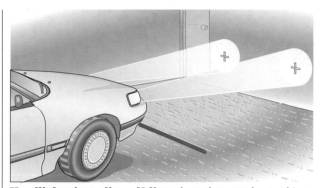

Headlights just aligned? Keep them that way by marking crosshairs at the center of the beams (you can check high and low this way) on the rear wall of the garage. Also mark the distance between the wall and the car on the driveway surface. Then check the alignment to see if it's right-on.

Rain, rain, go away.

Use wipe-on liquid polymers to coat a windshield with an invisible film that causes raindrops to bead up and roll off. Or get the same result by sprinkling some baking soda on a damp cloth and wiping it on the windshield.

To catch a thief. Many police stations around the country offer free antitheft services such as etching a vehicle identification number on your car's windows. If you enroll in such a program, check to see if your insurance company offers a discount on your premiums.

4 Installing an antitheft device on your steering wheel while parked protects your car by preventing a thief from turning the wheel. Just lengthen the device to fit your steering wheel and lock it with the provided key. For maximum security, install it behind the steering wheel as shown here, with the lock facing toward the windshield.

5 Locking gas caps come with keys to prevent anyone from siphoning gas or tampering with your gas tank. The caps come in different sizes, and in threaded and notched varieties. When purchasing a locking gas cap, take along the old cap to make sure you get the right size and type.

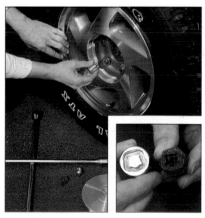

6 Wheel locks help protect your tires from theft. They replace existing lug nuts and require a special adapter to remove. (Make sure you keep the adapter handy, perhaps in the trunk or glove compartment.) It is necessary to replace only one lug nut per tire with a wheel lock.

Smoke gets in your nose, but the smell of it won't wake you if you're asleep. Don't rely on your senses—install smoke detectors.

Double detection. There are two basic kinds of smoke detectors: Ionization models are best at detecting fast-burning fires, while photoelectric detectors are more sensitive to smolder-ing, smoky fires. Installing both types will give you the best protection.

One on one. Install at least one smoke detector on each level of your home, including the basement and attic—more if you have a large house. If the bedrooms on one level are more than 40 feet apart, put a detector outside each one.

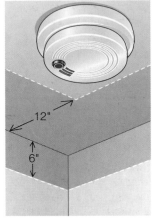

Give it space. To work correctly, a ceiling-mounted detector should be at least 12 inches away from a wall, a wall-mounted model at least 6 inches away from the ceiling.

Hot spots. The first-floor living room, the top of the stairwell to the second floor, and the bottom of the base-ment stairs are good loca-tions for smoke detectors.

Not spots. Don't place a smoke detector near a shower, where steam can set it off. Also avoid drafts and heating and cooling vents: moving air can blow smoke away from the detec-tor, rendering it ineffective.

Slow burn. Periodically test each smoke detector's sensitivity to slow-burning fires by blowing out a match or candle near the detector. The alarm should sound in about 30 seconds.

Time for a new battery. A smoke detector's batteries should be replaced twice a year. Change them when you change the clocks for daylight savings time.

Closed door policy. Sleep with the bedroom door closed to provide you with extra protection from heat and smoke. When leaving the house during a fire, close the doors behind you to buy getaway time and slow the spread of the fire.

Keep a flashlight nearby. It's a good idea to have a flashlight in each bed-room. The light will help occupants escape the house during a nighttime fire.

Fire extinguishers are classified by the kind of fires they're designed to quench. The best one for home use is labeled ABC.

Installing a 120-volt smoke detector

WHAT YOU'LL NEED

Line voltage smoke detector(s) with battery backup

Inductive voltage detector

Surface wiring raceway, ceiling box, backstraps, and other hardware

Approved electrical wire

Wire stripper and twist-on connectors

Electrical tape (if needed)

Screwdriver and screws

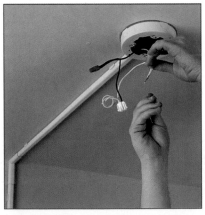

1 Choose a location for the smoke detector, and shut off the power to the circuit at the main panel. Use an inductive voltage detector to make sure the power is off (see p. 183). Install a detector using surface wiring (see pp. 186–187) or an unswitched electric box (consult an electrician). Connect the wires to the detector's pig-tail connector, white to white and black to black, with twist-on connectors.

2 Fold wires into the surface wiring ceiling box, black to one side, white to the other. Some pigtails have a third wire for interconnecting multiple units, all of which go off if one senses smoke. To interconnect, see step 4; otherwise, tape over the end of the wire and fold it into the box. The grounding wire may also be taped up and folded in—most detectors don't need to be grounded. Screw on mounting plate.

Snuff out electrical fires with a dry-chemical fire extinguisher. Always have a few handy in such places as the kitchen, basement, and workshop.

Where do you stand? When dousing a fire with a fire extinguisher, place yourself between the fire and the escape route. If you can't stop the flames within 2 minutes, close the door to the space where the fire is, get out of the house, and call the fire department.

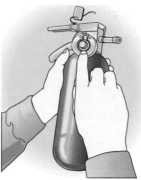

No pressure? Most household extinguishers have a test button or gauge that tells you if there's adequate pressure in the tank. When the pressure gets too low, replacing the unit usually costs less than having it repressurized.

Beef it up. If the door leading to your basement is a frame and panel or flush hollow-core type, replace it with a steel or solid-core door. These are better at slowing the spread of fire.

Don't lock yourself in. Double-cylinder dead-bolts—opened with a key from inside *and* outside—can trap people inside a house. Hide a key near the door and make sure everyone knows where it is. The same goes for windows with keyed locks.

Take care of your cords. Periodically check to see if extension cords are in good condition—a worn or overloaded cord is a fire hazard. So is a cord that runs under a rug or over a radiator.

Holiday leftovers. Wrapping paper and fragrant evergreens should be disposed of in the trash, not the fireplace. They burn like tinder and can throw off dangerous sparks.

Foam for your home. Spray expanding foam into the openings where ducts and pipes penetrate walls, ceilings, and floors. The foam seal will slow the spread of fire between rooms and will also reduce winter drafts.

Got the flue? Cracked older chimneys can direct flames into the house during a chimney fire. Fireproof an older chimney by having a qualified contractor install a flue lining.

3 Some detectors have a foam gasket that should be pressed over the mounting plate so that the mounting lugs are aligned with the slots in the gasket. Install the backup battery, and snap the pigtail connector into the back of the detector.

4 Secure the detector to the mounting plate with a clockwise twist. To interconnect units, a third set of wires must be connected to the pigtail (see step 1). Thread these wires out the other side of the surface wiring ceiling box (you may have to remove a knockout), and extend the surface wiring raceway to the next detector location. Repeat the installation procedure.

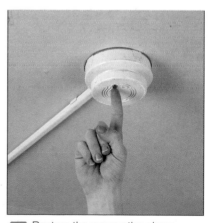

5 Restore the power; the alarm should beep once and a light should start blinking to let you know the detector is working. Test the detector every month by firmly pressing its test button.

Carbon monoxide detectors are not all alike. When you buy one, make sure that it is UL-listed, that it has a reset button, and that it won't go off at a safe CO level (15 parts per million) unless that level has persisted for 30 days. A detector that plugs into an electrical outlet is better than a battery-powered model, which can fail.

Check your furnace. A yellow flame in a gas furnace is a sign that the fuel isn't burning completely. In that case, carbon monoxide is probably being released into the air. Call your gas company to adjust the furnace's combustion.

Bag the carpet. Choose wood, ceramic tile, or vinyl flooring over carpets. Some carpets, especially those not made of wool, cotton, or nylon, emit high volatile organic compound (VOC) levels. Before bringing a carpet into the house, unroll it completely and let it air out for a few days.

Household ventilation. Any object with the "new smell" is probably emitting harmful fumes. Open windows to let fumes dissipate.

Test for radon. Don't rely on a neighbor's radon test to estimate the level in your home. Even houses that are next door can have very different radon levels. The only way to find the level of contamination in your home is to have it tested. Suggested EPA tests take from 2 days to around a year.

Sources of lead. If paint on a window is lead-base, the frame will create lead dust that is scattered into the house by air currents, or that collects on the windowsill itself. Many imported vinyl miniblinds purchased before July 1, 1996, have lead-base paint added to stabilize the plastic. Radiators that have been painted can also be a source of lead dust.

Get the lead out. If old paint is peeling from walls, wallboard or stucco them with joint compound to contain the spread of lead dust. Old paint in good condition can be sealed with shellac.

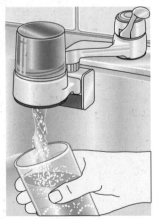

Save money by installing water filters only on the faucets from which you get your drinking water. Most water that is used in a home is not used for drinking water.

Lead-detecting kits are sold at hardware stores. When using such a kit, test every layer of paint all the way down to the surface. For detection of low levels of lead, check with your local health or housing authority.

If your municipal water tastes like chlorine, fill an open container and put it in the fridge overnight. Much of the chlorine will evaporate.

Store gasoline outdoors, in a closed container in a shed away from the house, never in the basement. Gas vapors are heavier than air, and tend to sink to the floor, where they could ignite.

Used oil filters can be recycled in many areas. Ask your local recycling center if they accept them.

Trashing latex paint. Mix old latex paint with cat litter or sawdust and leave off the lid. After the mixture dries, just put the can out with the trash.

Store it safely. Never store pesticides near food or in old food or beverage containers. And don't keep pesticides in an area where there could be flooding or a danger of them spilling or leaking into the environment.

FILE IT

Clean and green
Reduce your exposure to hazardous household cleaning products by choosing safer, less toxic substitutes.

Instead of	Try
Air freshener	A small dish of vinegar or lemon juice set out in a warm area
All-purpose cleaner	1 teaspoon liquid soap, 1 teaspoon borax, and 1/4 cup vinegar in 1 quart warm water
Bleach	Borax
Carpet cleaner	1 cup borax and 2 cups cornmeal or baking soda. Sprinkle on carpet stain; let stand 1 hour before vacuuming.
Detergent	Simple soap or phosphate-free detergent
Furniture polish	Almond or olive oil on oil-finish surfaces; dust with damp cloth and wipe dry.
Glass cleaner	2 tablespoons vinegar in 1 quart water
Grease remover	Baking soda paste
Stain remover	Cornstarch paste

Pesticide control. Clean up spilled pesticide quickly and safely by sprinkling the poison with sawdust, vermiculite, or cat litter and sweeping it up into a plastic trash bag.

Natural pest control. Nonchemical pest control has its advantages. Compared to pesticides, these are usually effective longer and don't create pesticide-resistant pest populations. Use natural insecticide made of pyrethrins, or try fighting pests with natural-born predators such as ladybugs.

Meant to be apart. Don't mix chlorine cleansers or bleach with ammonia, acids, or any other cleaning products. The combination could produce a deadly gas.

Less toxic cleaning. To limit the chemicals in your home, use pump sprays rather than aerosols, a plunger or metal snake instead of chemical drain openers, cedar chips or herbal sachets instead of mothballs, steel wool instead of rust removers.

Handling asbestos. The pipes in some older homes were insulated with asbestos. You can leave this insulation in place as long as it's in good condition and in an area where it won't be disturbed. If it's likely to be banged, rubbed, handled, or taken apart—especially during remodeling—hire a contractor to remove it.

Seal asbestos siding. Properly installed asbestos siding poses no health risk. However, if the siding is worn or damaged, use spray paint to seal in the fibers. If you want to remove it, hire a trained contractor.

Cleaning the air with houseplants? Occasionally cut back the lower branches to expose the soil's surface. This increases a plant's air-cleaning powers.

Plant a buffer. If pesticides are applied frequently near your home—for example, if you live next to a field that is regularly sprayed—consider planting a buffer zone of thick trees and shrubs to serve as a windbreak.

Installing a carbon monoxide detector

WHAT YOU'LL NEED

Carbon monoxide detector

Ruler, pencil, and level

Anchors and awl (if mounting on wallboard)

Screwdriver and screws

Plastic clips

Cigarette or incense stick (for testing)

1 Place the detector at least 6 in. from the ceiling. Measure the distance between the cutouts on the back of the unit and mark the wall. Install anchors, if needed, and insert screws until the heads are ⅛ in. from the wall. Install the detector.

2 Use plastic clips to attach the power cord to the wall. When possible, run cord along baseboard or molding. Or place the unit above a tall bureau or near curtains and conceal the cord, making sure the vents on the unit are unobstructed.

3 Test the alarm by holding the test button for 10–15 sec. A loud alarm should sound (you may want to cover the sounder opening with your finger). Periodically test the sensor by holding a smoldering cigarette or incense stick near the alarm for 5 min.

Electrical cords should be bundled up or tied up out of a child's reach. Cord organizers are available for computers and electronic systems that have multiple cords. There are also special devices for shortening cords. Or you can use cable ties to secure lamp cords to table legs, helping to prevent table lamps from tumbling down on junior.

Strings attached. Strings that secure the hoods on some babies' jackets can pose a danger. If the string gets caught on a snag while the child is climbing or crawling, it could wrap around the child's neck and choke him.

Medical advice. Store all medications, whether prescription or over-the-counter, in childproof containers. A small toolbox with a lock makes a good medicine chest; just keep it someplace where the child cannot get it.

Walk this way. When a child makes the transition from crawling to walking, he or she is likely to grab anything to steady themselves. Take a close look at your furnishings and eliminate tall, unstable items such as pole lamps, coat trees, and pedestal-type furniture. Also put away tablecloths and runners that hang off tables. They could become handholds for a curious toddler.

Basements and garages can be hazardous places for small children. Install self-closing springs on doors leading from the house to these spaces. As for electric garage doors, make sure yours is the newer variety that reverses if it touches anything while closing. And keep the remote control for the garage door out of baby's hands.

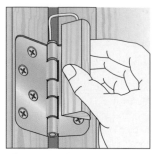

Finger-saving doorstop. Place a towel over a door to prevent it from closing on a child's finger. You can also buy special devices that keep doors from closing all the way, or make your own: Drive one end of a 6-inch length of coat hanger wire into the end of a 4-inch-long piece of 1-inch quarter round molding. Bend the other end of the wire to form a hook, and slide the wire over the top door hinge, with the molding positioned between the hinge leaves. This will prevent the door from closing all the way.

1 Place safety gates at the top and bottom of all stairways. A good stair gate, like this one, should be tall and sturdy, with strong mounting hardware and a release that is easy for adults—but not children—to operate. It should also swing in both directions. Avoid accordion gates, because a child's head could get caught. Pressure gates are not recommended for stairs.

2 Cover the slats of deck, porch, and staircase railings with sturdy mesh. Secure it with hooks, twine, or plastic wire ties. If there is a gap at the bottom of the railing, make sure you cover that, too, and secure it well.

3 There are many devices for securing doors. This suction device holds sliding glass doors in an open, closed, or partly open position. Just move the door to the desired position, then turn the lever that presses the suction cup against the glass surface. To move the door, turn the lever and release the suction cup. There are also doorknob covers and devices to prevent children from opening bifold doors.

Enclose open risers.
Porch and basement stairs in particular often have open risers. These should always be blocked off to prevent a child from falling through. An easy and inexpensive way to do this is to install a wooden bar lengthwise across the riser.

No climbing. Arrange furniture so children can't use items as stepping-stones to reach dangerous heights. For example, don't place a stool next to a chair next to a counter, or an active tot could climb all three.

Lose the loop. Cut the loop at the end of a window blind cord to prevent babies and toddlers from strangling themselves. Snip the cord above the tassel and remove the equalizer buckle. Then add a separate tassel to the end of each cord.

Up and away. Other safety options for window blind cords include wrapping them around cleats that you install on the window trim or wall. You can also secure them to hooks mounted high up. Or shorten the cords with special cord shorteners that snap open and shut, storing excess cord inside.

Cool it. Prevent children from burning themselves by installing covers on radiators, floor registers, and other heat sources. Also cool down your hot water while you're at it. Lower the water heater's thermostat to 120° from the standard 140°, and install antiscald valves on all sink faucets.

Tub tactics. Always test bathwater before allowing a child to get into it. Put cushioned covers over faucets, and face the child away from them while bathing; this will prevent the child from reaching for the hot-water tap. Place babies in special safety rings that are designed for the tub. Lastly, never take your eye off a small child in the bathtub.

Cushion your hearth.
Raised fireplace hearths should be padded in case of falls. Either buy a special elasticized cushion that fits all around the edge, as shown here, or create your own padding by folding a big fluffy blanket over the hearth. Remove either if you decide to light a fire, and watch baby at all times.

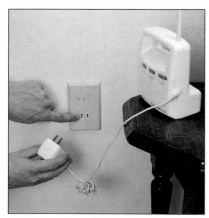

4 Different kinds of outlet covers are used for different purposes. The sliding type shown here is good for electrical items that are frequently unplugged. For items that are plugged in most of the time, use an outlet cover that shields the plugs as well, with openings at the bottom for the cords. For outlets that are seldom used, simply plug in outlet caps.

5 To prevent kids from playing with the stove's control knobs, use knob covers like the ones shown above. They come with instructions for easy removal when you want to use the burners or oven. And to keep children from opening the door to a hot oven, install a heat-resistant oven latch like this one. It, too, can be released by a knowledgeable adult, but not by a small child.

6 The magnetic key lock shown here is one of the most secure options for locking cabinets. The locking components mount inside the cabinet and can be released only with the magnetic key, which should be stored in a place accessible to adults, not to kids. Other options include cabinet latches that you disengage by opening the door slightly and pushing down, and locking devices that secure to the outside knobs.

Safe entry and exit. You don't have to be in a wheelchair to benefit from an exterior ramp. If you use a cane or walker or are just having a hard time navigating the steps, consider covering your outdoor steps with a wooden ramp that has sturdy rails on both sides. Check local building codes first.

Throw rugs are easy to slip on, especially if they have worn or curled corners or edges. They can also trip someone who is using crutches, a walker, or a cane. Get rid of them or back them with nonskid backing.

No-skid stairs. The stairway is one of the most dangerous spots in the house. To make falls less likely, place nonskid adhesive strips on uncarpeted interior and exterior stairs. Also consider marking the edge of each step with brightly colored paint or tape.

Add a handrail. If your stairway has only one railing, add a second one to the opposite wall. Having a railing on both sides makes climbing or descending the stairs much safer. When installing the new handrail, make sure it is the correct height and is anchored to solid framing. It should also curve in at the top and bottom to provide a tactile clue that this is the last step.

Lighten up. Because vision diminishes with age, it's important to keep rooms, as well as hallways and staircases, well lit. If you've always burned 60-watt bulbs in your lamps, upgrade them to 75 or 100 watts. But first make sure that the fixture can handle the extra load.

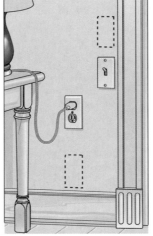

Plugged in. Installing electrical outlets higher on the wall—approximately 24 inches from the floor to the center of the outlet—makes it easier to plug in lamps or other electrical appliances. Similarly, light switches are easier to operate if they are installed lower on the wall; about 35 inches from the floor to the center of the switch is a convenient height. However, check local building codes before doing electrical work.

Light the way. To avoid having to fumble for a light switch when you enter a room, install motion-sensing wall switches. They automatically turn on lights when someone enters.

Night moves. Reduce the risk of nighttime mishaps and falls by putting night-lights in the bedroom, bathroom, and any other areas that you are likely to be entering after dark. There are also glow-in-the-dark light switches that are easy to find and that double as night-lights.

Electrical impulses. Switching from gas to electric appliances is often a good idea. As people age, their sense of smell isn't as acute, making it more difficult to recognize a dangerous gas leak.

Get a grip. For those who are a little unsteady on their feet, installing a handrail on the front of kitchen counters can provide an extra measure of support.

A safe step up. If you must use a ladder or step stool to access a high shelf, make sure it has a safety bar. Store overhead items in plastic baskets or boxes so they can't come tumbling down on you.

Out in the open. To make it easy to reach things in the kitchen, build an open shelf between the countertop and the top cabinets, and store your most frequently used items there. Also reorganize the kitchen cabinets to place often-used items within easy reach. Try not to keep everyday supplies in overhead cabinets.

Stay in touch. If there is more than one person living in the house, adding intercoms to the different rooms is a good idea. Inexpensive plug-in intercoms are available that transmit sound through the electrical wiring.

Hearing loss is a natural consequence of aging, but there are many measures you can take around the house to minimize its effects. Smoke detectors are available with strobe lights that flash in addition to the alarm to alert you to a fire. There are also devices that make the lights turn on and off if the telephone rings, and doorbells that ring loudly in every room in the house.

Curtain call. If you have a spring-type shower curtain rod, replace it with a screw-in model. If someone falls in the tub and reflexively grabs the shower curtain, a well-secured screw-in model is less likely to come down on top of them.

At your fingertips. Be sure to keep an easy-to-operate lamp and telephone next to the bed. The phone should have large numbers on the touch pads and a speed-dial feature for frequently called phone numbers as well as emergency numbers for the police, fire department, ambulance service, etc. For a person who may not be able to reach a phone, there are portable devices that alert a family member or a central monitoring service if there is a problem.

1 For safer stovetops, the control knobs should be on the front of the stove rather than on the back or the top. This way, there is no need to reach over hot burners or pots when using the controls. The knobs should also be easy to operate and read.

2 For a safer shower, install grab bars secured to studs. Also consider a shower enclosure with a nonskid floor and a bottom lip just a few inches deep, which makes for easy entrances and exits. Even better is a shower with no lip at all.

3 Sitting in the shower greatly reduces the chances of a fall. This shower has a built-in seat and grab bars for support. If your shower does not have a built-in seat, you can purchase a special shower stool and use it with a handheld shower.

4 Adapting the toilet seat is an inexpensive way to make the bathroom safer. These grab bars, which help you get up and down, can be installed on any standard toilet. There are also raised toilet seats that come with built-in arms.

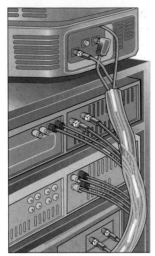

Out of sight, out of mind. Puppies and kittens tend to chew on electrical cords, which can cause shocks or burns. Prevent injury by tucking away cords and encasing them in a cord organizer. To prevent another pet hazard—cats pulling lamps or other appliances down on themselves—try a single cord shortener.

Rubber bands and string are favorite playthings for cats, in particular. Yet if swallowed, these can cause pets a lot of discomfort and may have to be removed surgically. If you see a string hanging from your pet's mouth, gently pull it out.

Choose plants carefully. Cats like to chew on houseplants, but many varieties, including poinsettia, can make them sick. If your cat or dog has eaten a plant and seems ill, call poison control with the correct botanical name of the plant. Better yet, don't keep toxic plants around the house.

Ditch the tinsel. Christmas tree tinsel can cause intestinal blockage if swallowed by a pet. Avoid the stuff altogether, or if you must use some, keep it out of chewing range.

Christmas trees are a favorite climbing target for cats. If you have an adventurous feline and are putting up a Christmas tree, make sure it is very secure at the base, and consider wiring it to the wall or ceiling as well.

Tag your pet. Dogs and cats should always wear identification tags. Some humane societies issue a tag and keep your name on file so they can contact you if the pet is found. Another option is to tag the pet with a microchip. About the size of a grain of rice, the chip is implanted beneath the pet's skin by a veterinarian. Later, should your pet be found, the chip can be scanned by a vet, an animal control officer, or the humane society.

Installing an invisible pet fence

WHAT YOU'LL NEED

Invisible fence kit (contains control unit, receiver, cable, boundary flags)

Screwdriver

Electric drill and suitable bit

Plastic conduit with angle fitting

Caulk and caulking gun

Spade or hand-operated or gas-powered lawn edger (a rental item)

Tamp

Safety glasses and dust mask

Circular saw with masonry blade (if needed)

Concrete patching compound or asphalt crack sealer (if needed)

Needle-nose pliers

1 Mount the control unit on a wall near an AC outlet. Bore a hole through the exterior wall, and install plastic conduit on the wall of the house. The conduit should enclose the wiring and extend from the hole to just below grade. Use an angle fitting at the top of the hole, and seal the hole with caulk. Feed the cable into the conduit, through the wall, and to the control unit.

2 Lay the cable on the ground, forming a loop that encloses the desired area and returns to the control unit. Starting at the conduit, use a spade or lawn edger to cut a narrow, 3-in.-deep slit in the ground next to the cable. As you proceed, bury the cable and tamp the soil closed around it.

Cold cats. In cold weather, watch out for cats that may have climbed up inside your car's wheel wells or engine compartment looking for warmth. If your cat or others in the neighborhood have access to your car, knock on the car's hood or honk the horn before starting the engine on wintry days.

No hot dogs. On hot days, it's better to leave a dog tied up at home in the shade than to take it with you in the car. The inside temperature of a car left closed in the sun can skyrocket to well over 100°F in 10 minutes. A dog left in the car could suffer brain damage or die from heat exhaustion. If you must leave the dog in the car, park in the shade, put the dog in a crate inside the car so that all the windows can be left open, and leave a supply of water.

Double up. When you go out, leave your pet two bowls of water. That way, if one gets knocked over in your absence, there will always be a backup.

Dehydration in pets is a serious health risk. Among the telltale signs are a dry mouth, sunken eyes, loss of skin elasticity, and exhaustion. To test for dehydration, gently pull the skin on your dog or cat's back. If the pet is dehydrated, the skin won't have its usual elasticity and won't snap back. Always seek a veterinarian's care.

Designing a doghouse. A good doghouse is large enough for the dog to comfortably lie down and sit up in, yet small enough that its body heat can warm the inside. You can put hay inside for insulation, but watch for allergic reactions. Make sure that the entrance is sheltered from the wind, and that the floor is raised to prevent dampness from creeping in.

Spilled antifreeze must be cleaned up immediately and completely from the garage or driveway. The scent and sweet taste can be attractive to animals, and even a small amount is enough to poison a pet.

Death by chocolate? Chocolate contains theobromine, which is toxic to dogs. Just one ounce of unsweetened chocolate can cause a small dog trouble. Symptoms of chocolate poisoning include hyperactivity, heavy panting, seizures, muscle tremors, vomiting, and diarrhea. If you suspect a pet has eaten chocolate, take him straight to the vet.

Police those butts. Puppies can get nicotine poisoning by chewing on cigar or cigarette butts. Don't leave ashtrays where a pooch can get to them.

3 If the cable crosses a concrete or asphalt walk or driveway, use a masonry blade in a circular saw to cut a 1-in.-deep slit. Wear safety glasses and a dust mask. Press the cable into the slit. Then fill the gap with concrete patching compound for concrete surfaces (see p. 260) or asphalt crack sealer for asphalt (see p. 266).

4 To complete the loop, run the remaining end of the cable through the conduit and attach it to the control unit. Keep in mind that the wiring leading from the perimeter to and from the house must be twisted together—otherwise, the wiring extending across the lawn could carry a charge. When the outdoor wiring is in place, install the boundary flags supplied with the kit.

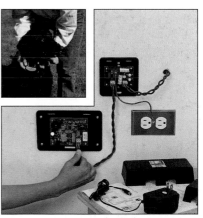

5 Complete the wiring according to the manufacturer's instructions, and plug in the control unit. Assemble your pet's receiving collar, and test it. If it works, put it around the animal's neck. Follow the manufacturer's pet-training instructions before allowing your pet to run free in the yard with the system activated.

Many of the tips in this book make use of discarded items, leftover materials you would store or throw away, or common household substances that you can put to new use. Here is a guide to these "recycling" tips, arranged alphabetically by material. Each entry gives the use, page number, and tip title.

A

Acorns
➤ Chipped and shredded, as garden mulch, p. 282, "From little acorns"

Aftershave
➤ Added to humidifier water, to purge the smell of chlorine, p. 219, "Catch a whiff"

Aloe plant
➤ Kept near a gas grill, in case you get a minor burn, p. 235, "A natural painkiller"

Alphabet blocks
➤ As drawer pulls for a child's dresser, p. 21, "Playful pulls"

Aluminum foil
➤ Wrapped around pillows, to keep cats off the sofa, p. 41, "Stay off the couch"
➤ As a tarp for covering exterior hardware when painting outdoors, p. 65, "A great coverup"
➤ For making a template when installing a flagstone patio or walk, p. 250, "Foiled flagstone"
➤ Wrapped around fruit-tree trunks, to repel climbing bugs, p. 289, "Foiling insects"

Ammonia
➤ For sprinkling in a garbage can to repel raccoons, p. 39, "Banish bandits"
➤ Poured into a pan, to keep squirrels out of the chimney, p. 39, "Squirrel in the chimney?"
➤ Sprayed on the compost bin, to repel pests, p. 305, "Pests be gone"

Animal figurines
➤ As drawer pulls for a child's dresser, p. 21, "Playful pulls"

Armoire, second-hand
➤ As a unit to hold the TV, VCR, and stereo equipment, p. 20, "Chic at cost"
➤ As a storage unit in the kitchen, p. 32, "Antique armoires"

B

Baby oil
➤ To remove burrs from a long-haired pet, p. 40, "Burrs are easier"
➤ To remove food or dried-on soap from the chrome parts of a dishwasher, p. 232, "The shining"

Baby-wipes container
➤ To store brushes used for finishing wood, p. 145, "Baby the brushes"

Bacon
➤ As mousetrap bait, p. 39, "Spicing up the bait"

Bag
➤ Mesh bag, to store children's bathtub toys, p. 31, "Bag bath toys"
➤ Plastic grocery bag, for slipping over a paint tray so you don't have to clean the tray when you're done painting, p. 65, "Slip a paint tray"
➤ Newspaper delivery bags, to cover ceiling fan blades when painting a ceiling, p. 120, "No fan of drips"
➤ Plastic bag, to cover the handset of a telephone so you can answer the phone when in the middle of painting, p. 121, "Call waiting"
➤ Nylon netting supermarket produce bag, to clean up the legs and spindles of wood furniture after stripping, p. 141, "Net gain"
➤ Sandwich bag, for mixing two-part epoxy, p. 148, "Knead epoxy?"
➤ Plastic grocery bags, to cover your boots when sealing the driveway, p. 266, "Save your soles"
➤ Long plastic bag, to cover your hand and arm when pulling up poison ivy or other rash-inducing plants, p. 273, "Don't be rash"
➤ Plastic bag, for catching seeds from plants that you are pulling up at the end of the season, p. 275, "Shake it up"
➤ Net bag, for storing bulbs until they are ready to plant, p. 278, "Shop early"
➤ Trash bags, draped over a tree stump, to kill it prior to removal, p. 290, "Stamping out stumps"

Baking powder
➤ As a cleanser for the canework of a spline-cane seat, p. 157, "When dirt is ingrained"

Baking soda
➤ For dousing range-top flames, p. 14, "Stovetop fires"
➤ To give an antique look to new roof shakes, p. 47, "Soda shakes"
➤ For a fresh-smelling kitchen waste disposer, p. 233, "A twist of lemon"
➤ Sprinkled on a damp cloth, to wipe on a windshield, causing raindrops to bead up and roll off, p. 319, "Rain, rain, go away"

Barbecue mitt
➤ Kept in the car, for hand protection in case you need to make a quick repair on a hot engine, p. 319, "Hot stuff"

Basket, large
➤ To store towels in the bathroom, p. 30, "Towel basket"

Baster
➤ To remove the gas remaining in a lawn mower tank at the end of the season, p. 299, "Run on empty"

Bed sheet
➤ For rag-rolling a wall, p. 128, "Try something different"

Belt
➤ To hang a ladder horizontally, p. 45, "Tightening the belt"
➤ As part of a caddy for tools when carrying them up a ladder, p. 65, "Buckle up"

Blanket
➤ For covering glass doors to protect them when working above them on a ladder, p. 44, "No way out"
➤ Placed over a fireplace hearth, as a child-safety measure, p. 325, "Cushion your hearth"

Bleach
➤ To refill a toilet-bowl cleaning device, p. 23, "It makes cents"
➤ For killing ticks picked off a dog, p. 40, "Killer brew"
➤ To remove ceiling stains caused by a leak, p. 46, "Coming clean"
➤ To remove mildew from a wall before painting, p. 121, "Mildew mistake"
➤ To lighten moldy or mildewy wicker, p. 155, "Brush-on brightener"
➤ For cleaning a portable humidifier, p. 219, "To kill bacteria"
➤ To kill algae spores in a refrigerator or freezer drain, p. 231, "Clean the drains"
➤ To remove mold and mildew from exterior brick, p. 254, "A shady situation?"

Blue jeans
➤ As polishing cloths, p. 145, "Blue-jean sheen"

Bonemeal
➤ For creating a barrier to keep carpenter ants out of the house, p. 39, "No entry"

Bottle
➤ Plastic soda bottle, to store plastic grocery bags, p. 17, "Pop-out bags"
➤ A piece of laundry detergent bottle, as a patch for repairing cracks in vinyl siding, p. 58, "Can't find scrap vinyl"
➤ Laundry detergent bottle, as part of a caddy for carrying tools when painting trim work at the top of the house, p. 65, "Buckle up"
➤ Dishwashing detergent bottle, for loading up a paint pad, p. 66, "Loading up"
➤ Plastic bottle filled with water, for saving water when you flush the toilet, p. 173, "No goldbricking"

Bread
➤ Rye bread, for removing stains from delicate wallcovering, p. 135, "Remove a spot"
➤ To stop a pipe from dripping while you solder it, p. 171, "White or whole wheat?"

Brush
➤ Paintbrush, to replicate the texture of an old plaster wall or ceiling when patching it, p. 83, "On the surface"
➤ Dust or shoe brush, instead of a stippling brush, p. 127, "On the dot"
➤ Paintbrush, as a glue brush, p. 149, "Born-again brush"
➤ Foam brush handle, as a paddle to mix cans of putty or epoxy, p. 149, "New life for old handles"
➤ Dog's grooming brush, to remove lint, string, and hair from a vacuum beater brush, p. 236, "Grooming the vacuum"
➤ Vegetable brush attached to the end of a leaf blower, to remove wet leaves from paved areas, p. 300, "One-step cleanup"

Bucket
➤ For retrieving items lost in the sink, p. 13, "Down the drain?"
➤ For collecting water flowing down an attic rafter, p. 13, "Wick it away"
➤ Paint bucket, as a garden hose reel, p. 35, "Hosing reel"
➤ As a caddy for tools when working on a ladder, p. 44, "An elevating thought"
➤ To lower loads of debris when cleaning a gutter, p. 53, "Attach a long rope"

Burlap
➤ For rag-rolling a wall, p. 128, "Try something different"

C

Cabinet, kitchen
➤ For use in a home office, instead of customized cabinets, p. 25, "Take stock"
➤ As a storage unit in attics, basements, and garages, p. 30, "Old kitchen cabinets"

➤ As a wine cellar, p. 32, "Wine cellar in a cabinet"

Cable ties
➤ To secure lamp cords to table legs, as a child-safety measure, p. 324, "Electrical cords"

Candle
➤ Jabbed into a jar of petroleum jelly, as a light source during a blackout, p. 12, "Happy birthday"
➤ For rubbing on painting or masking tape, to make it easier to remove, p. 65, "Easy-peel tape"
➤ For rubbing on double-hung windows, to make them easier to open and close, p. 101, "For slick sashes"

Can opener
➤ To widen plaster cracks that are too narrow to repair, p. 82, "Go wide"

Cardboard
➤ Corrugated cardboard, placed in a cookie sheet or jelly-roll pan, as a drip pan for a leaking car, p. 29, "Catcher in the carport"
➤ For test patches to decide what color to paint a shutter or door, p. 66, "Will an accent color clash"
➤ For making a wallboard patch, p. 85, "The hole story"
➤ Cardboard box lined with duct tape, as a holding box for small parts when repairing an appliance, p. 226, "Hold on"
➤ Cardboard box, to put food in when defrosting the freezer, p. 231, "Winter thaw"
➤ Cardboard tubing from rolls of carpet, as concrete pier footings, p. 259, "Free formwork"

Carpenter's apron
➤ As a tool belt for gardeners, p. 303, "Tools to go"

Carpet
➤ To protect a car from scraping against obstructions in the garage, p. 29, "Bumper room"
➤ For attaching to the steps and rungs of a ladder to avoid slips, p. 44, "Giving the slip to slips"

➤ Flame-retardant carpet placed under a clothes washer, to silence it, p. 228, "Washer rattling?"

➤ Slipped under a refrigerator, to make it easier to move, p. 230, "Your muscles thank you"

➤ Wool or cotton scraps, as weed-suppressing garden mulch, p. 283, "Roll out the carpet"

Cat litter

➤ To absorb spills in the kitchen garbage, p. 17, "Here, kitty"

➤ To eliminate musty odors on upholstery, p. 153, "A litter help"

➤ To absorb motor-oil stains on concrete floors prior to sweeping up, p. 260, "An absorbing job"

➤ Kept in the car, in case you get stuck in snow or ice, p. 319, "In case of emergency"

➤ For mixing with latex paint that you want to throw out, p. 322, "Trashing latex paint"

➤ For sprinkling on spilled pesticide, enabling you to clean it up safely, p. 323, "Pesticide control"

Ceramic tile

➤ For gluing over the damaged area of a countertop, p. 16, "Or hide a burned spot"

Chalk

➤ For placing in a toolbox to prevent tools from rusting, p. 36, "Discourage rust"

➤ Instead of paint, for covering up water spots on white ceiling tiles, p. 122, "Chalk up a good mark"

Charcoal

➤ For placing in a toolbox to prevent tools from rusting, p. 36, "Discourage rust"

➤ For creating a barrier to keep carpenter ants out of the house, p. 39, "No entry"

Cheesecloth

➤ For rag-rolling a wall, p. 128, "Try something different"

➤ For covering the nozzle of a vacuum when cleaning bureau drawers, p. 236, "Sucking up"

Chili powder

➤ For creating a barrier to keep carpenter ants out of the house, p. 39, "No entry"

Cigarette ash

➤ To remove white water spots from finished wood furniture, p. 141, "Out, damned spot"

Clothespin

➤ To mark your progress if you take a break when cleaning miniblinds, p. 100, "Pinning your progress"

➤ To hold a wood knob when you're applying finish to it, p. 144, "Neat knob finishing"

➤ As a wedge to hold prewoven cane in the seat groove when recaning a chair, p. 156, "In the groove"

➤ To spread out the branches of young fruit trees, p. 288, "Spaced-out fruit trees"

Club soda

➤ To remove food or dried-on soap from the chrome parts of a dishwasher, p. 232, "The shining"

Coffee can

➤ For overnight storage of a brush filled with oil paint, p. 67, "Overnight stay"

➤ Made into a sifter, for dispensing flour to mark out excavations for patios, etc., p. 248, "Flour power"

➤ To make a shaker for dispensing grass seed, p. 271, "Hit the spot"

Coffee can lid

➤ For keeping drips off your arm when painting overhead, p. 122, "Ceiling shield"

Coffee grounds

➤ To eliminate refrigerator smells, p. 17, "Overnight odor eater"

➤ To remove pet odors from a room, p. 40, "A deodorizing brew"

➤ Sprinkled on a concrete floor, to help catch dust and dirt while sweeping, p. 260, "Clean sweep"

➤ To use as mulch for the garden, p. 282, "Lighten up"

➤ To moisten compost, p. 304, "Liquid refreshment"

Colander

➤ To drain food scraps before throwing them away, p. 17, "Collect food scraps"

Cologne

➤ Added to the water in a humidifier, to purge the smell of chlorine, p. 219, "Catch a whiff"

Comb

➤ To replicate the texture of an old plaster wall or ceiling when patching it, p. 83, "On the surface"

Concrete block

➤ Placed on its side and filled with concrete, to support a freestanding outdoor outlet, p. 203, "Secure a freestanding"

➤ Placed on its side and filled with soil, as a patio planter, p. 263, "Growing in concrete"

Cookie sheet

➤ To smother range-top flames, p. 14, "Stovetop fires"

➤ As a drip pan for a leaking car, p. 29, "Catcher in the carport"

Cooking spray

➤ For spraying the underside of a lawn mower to prevent a buildup of clippings, p. 298, "A clean underdeck"

Cork

➤ To remove rust spots from a non-stainless-steel wok or frying pan, p. 237, "Rust relief"

➤ As compost, p. 304, "Making deposits"

Cornmeal

➤ As mousetrap bait, p. 39, "Spicing up the bait"

Cornstalks

➤ As compost, p. 305, "To help compost 'cook'"

Cream of tartar

➤ To remove rust stains on porcelain, p. 174, "Stain zappers"

Curtain rod
➤ Mounted on a windowsill, for making a window box, p. 30, "Windowsill solution"

D

Dartboard
➤ As a message board in the garage, p. 29, "Pinup board"

Dental picks
➤ For cleaning old stain from small crevices on wood furniture, p. 147, "Dental picks"

Detergent
➤ Dishwashing detergent, for adding to puddles to kill mosquitoes, p. 38, "Pesty puddles"
➤ Laundry detergent, as an ingredient in a solution for spraying away fungi on the roof, p. 47, "Good bye to fungi"
➤ Dishwashing detergent mixed with water, for removing food stains from flagstone., p. 251, "Are stains a pain?"
➤ Granular detergent mixed with hot water, for scrubbing away driveway stains, p. 266, "Oil be gone"

Dishpan, plastic
➤ As an under-the-stairs storage bin, p. 34, "Steps open at the back?"

Door handle
➤ Screwed to a wooden post, as a tamper for patching potholes in asphalt, p. 267, "Get a handle on it"

Doormat, rubber
➤ As a door for a doghouse, p. 41, "Shelter from the storm"

Drawer pulls
➤ For additional hangers for bathroom towels, p. 22, "More hang-ups"

Dresser drawer
➤ For under-the-bed storage, p. 31, "Down under"

Drinking glass
➤ For making a trap to kill silverfish, p. 39, "Go fishing"

➤ Placed near a sprinkler, to measure the amount of water your lawn is getting, p. 271, "Water wise"

E

Eggshells
➤ For sowing seeds prior to transplanting, p. 274, "Poor travelers"

Electric carving knife
➤ To cut high-density sheet foam padding when reupholstering, p. 152, "Just like butter"
➤ To cut rigid foam insulation, p. 215, "Kitchen power tool"

Electric mixer beater
➤ Chucked into a variable-speed drill, to mix paint, p. 147, "Beat it"

F

Fabric
➤ To create additional storage space under a bathroom sink, p. 22, "Skirt the issue"

Fabric-softener sheet
➤ Dabbed with rubbing alcohol, for cleaning and dusting a TV screen, p. 245, "Cleaning the screen"

Fertilizer
➤ For spraying on new exterior brickwork to create an aged look, p. 253, "Accelerated aging"

Film canister
➤ Secured to the plug of an extension cord, for holding grounding plug adapters, p. 37, "In the can"
➤ For storing leftover plant seeds, p. 285, "Until you plant again"

Fireplace ash
➤ As compost, p. 304, "Making deposits"

Fish bones
➤ As compost, p. 304, "Making deposits"

Fish hook
➤ To pull out a drain clog in a sink drain, p. 170, "Casting for clogs"

Flatware
➤ As drawer pulls, p. 19, "Accessorize a sideboard"

Flea collar
➤ For placing in a vacuum cleaner to prevent fleas from jumping out of the vacuum bag, p. 40, "Collared!"

Flour
➤ Dispensed from a coffee-can sifter, for marking out excavations for patios, etc., p. 248, "Flour power"
➤ For creating a map for your shovel to follow when laying out stones for a walkway, p. 250, "Take time to outline"
➤ Added to a fertilizer spreader, to help you see spots you have missed, p. 270, "When fertilizing"

Flowerpot, plastic
➤ For placing upside-down over the drain hole of a much larger flowerpot to reduce the amount of soil needed, p. 275, "Losing weight"

Flowers
➤ As compost, p. 304, "Making deposits"

Food dye
➤ For determining the source of a leak in a toilet, p. 172, "Is your toilet leaking?"

Fruit scraps
➤ Orange, grapefruit, and lemon rinds, to keep cats from digging up plants, p. 41, "Fruitful solution"
➤ As compost, p. 304, "Making deposits"

G

Garbage can
➤ With holes poked in it, as a compost bin, p. 304, "To bin or not to bin"

Garbage can lid
➤ As a form for molding concrete into stepping stones, p. 259, "Leftover concrete?"
➤ Placed on top of a cylinder of rolled stucco wire, as a storage bin, p. 265, "Leftover stucco wire?"

Garden fork
➤ As an anchor for a ladder, p. 44, "Secure the base"

Garden hose
➤ A small piece wrapped with sandpaper, as a sanding block for inside curves on wood furniture, p. 143, "Hose job"
➤ Instead of a plumber's auger, for unclogging a drain, p. 175, "If that didn't work…"
➤ Taped to the handle of a broom, as a way to clean the driveway, p. 266, "Speed-clean"
➤ Taped to an old broomstick to make a watering wand, p. 297, "Ready, aim, water"
➤ A split piece, as a cap for a chainsaw's teeth when not in use, p. 301, "Capping the teeth"
➤ A split piece placed over the shoulder of a shovel blade, as a cushion for your foot, p. 302, "Step softly"
➤ A split piece placed over the tines of an old rake, as a squeegee for cleaning patios, decks, etc., p. 303, "Old rakes never die"

Garden lattice
➤ Mounted on a basement wall, for storing long, narrow lightweight objects such as molding and spare pipes, p. 28, "Leftover lattice?"

Garlic
➤ For putting in pot soil to repel houseplant pests, p. 39, "To debug houseplants"

Glove
➤ For covering the top rail of a ladder, to prevent it from scarring shingles or siding, p. 44, "Damage control"
➤ Cotton gloves, for cleaning miniblinds, p. 100, "White-glove treatment"
➤ Cloth gardening glove, to wear when using a heat gun to strip paint from wood furniture, p. 141, "Too hot for comfort"
➤ Bicycle glove, to avoid getting blisters when using a screwdriver, p. 151, "Hand cushions"

Golf tee
➤ As a stopper for a tube of caulk, p. 63, "Tee time"

Grapefruit knife
➤ As a weeder, p. 302, "A grapefruit knife"

Grass clippings
➤ As garden mulch, p. 282, "Lighten up"
➤ For adding to the compost pile, p. 304, "Making deposits"
➤ As compost, p. 305, "To help compost 'cook'"

Gumdrops
➤ As mousetrap bait, p. 39, "Spicing up the bait"

Gutter brackets
➤ As hooks for extension cords, coils of wire, and garden hoses, p. 55, "Hang on to hangers"

Hair clippings
➤ Sprinkled in shrubbery beds, to deter deer, p. 286, "Oh, deer!"

Hair conditioner
➤ To soften paintbrushes, p. 67, "Tired of stiff brushes?"

Hair, dryer
➤ To thaw frozen pipes, p. 13, "Slow thaw"
➤ For warming up cracks before caulking, p. 62, "Make it stick"
➤ To make small patches of joint compound dry faster, p. 83, "Blow dry"
➤ To dry out a section of a basement wall when trying to determine the source of moisture, p. 92, "Divining dampness"
➤ To thaw frozen pipes, p. 171, "A new ice age"

Hammock
➤ To store bulky lightweight equipment in a garage bay, p. 35, "An old hammock"

Hardboard
➤ To clean a gutter, p. 53, "De-clutter the gutter"

Hassock
➤ For additional seating when company comes over, p. 18, "Have a seat"

Hose reel
➤ Mounted on a garage wall, to store long extension cords and make them easier to use, p. 35, "Reel organization"

I

Insulation, rigid
➤ To force between the walls of a concrete form in case you have to stop a pour before completion, p. 258, "Easy pour"
➤ To prevent a toilet bowl from "sweating" in humid weather, p. 173, "Bathroom condensation"

J

Jar, glass
➤ To store nails, screws, and assorted hardware, p. 36, "Just one look"
➤ For making a trap to kill roaches, p. 39, "Jar roaches"
➤ For overnight storage of a brush filled with oil paint, p. 67, "Overnight stay"

Juice
➤ To moisten compost, p. 304, "Liquid refreshment"

Knife holder, magnetic
➤ To organize tools in a workshop, p. 34, "Strip of tools"

L

Lace
➤ For rag-rolling a wall, p. 128, "Try something different"

Ladder, wood
➤ Secured to a workshop wall, as a storage unit, p. 45, "Instant storage"
➤ Laid flat and filled with soil, as a start-up herb garden, p. 285, "Instant herb garden"

Laundry lint
➤ As compost, p. 304, "Making deposits"

Lawn chair
➤ As the frame for a redwood chair, p. 159, "Redwood revival"

Leaves
➤ Chopped up, to use as mulch for the garden, p. 282, "Lighten up"
➤ For adding to the compost pile, p. 304, "Making deposits"
➤ As compost, p. 305, "To help compost 'cook'"

Lemon
➤ To remove food or dried-on soap from the chrome parts of a dishwasher, p. 232, "The shining"
➤ For a fresh-smelling kitchen waste disposer, p. 233, "A twist of lemon"

Linen
➤ For rag-rolling a wall, p. 128, "Try something different"

Linseed oil, boiled
➤ Instead of commercial wood preservatives, p. 60, "Boiled linseed oil"
➤ For applying to new interior brick to create an aged look, p. 253, "Fast patina"
➤ Mixed with turpentine, as a sealer for garage floors, p. 260, "Save money on sealer"
➤ Rubbed into wood tool handles, to seal areas where varnish has worn away, p. 303, "Preventing split ends"

Lip balm
➤ Instead of masking tape, when painting windows, p. 116, "Save time"

M

Mailbox
➤ Hung on a fence post or shed wall, as a place to store gardening tools, p. 302, "Stow gardening tools"

Manure
➤ As mulch for the garden, p. 282, "Use what?"
➤ As compost, p. 305, "To help compost 'cook'"

Margarine container
➤ For making a trap to kill wasps, p. 38, "Sweetening up wasps"

Milk carton
➤ For sowing seeds prior to transplanting, p. 284, "Recycled seed pots"

Milk crate, plastic
➤ As a soil sifter, p. 272, "Sifting the soil"

Milk jug, plastic
➤ As a patch for repairing cracks in vinyl siding, p. 58, "Can't find scrap vinyl"
➤ To store leftover paint so that you can see what color it is, p. 122, "Pour and store"
➤ Pierced with tiny holes and buried next to a plant, to create a homemade watering system, p. 297, "The buddy system"

Mirror
➤ For inspecting a car's front and rear lights, p. 29, "Night moves"
➤ Mirror tile, for mounting on the ceiling of a closet to see what is on the top shelf, p. 33, "A favorable reflection"
➤ To use when caulking the gap between a house's foundation and siding, p. 62, "Save your knees and back"
➤ Hand mirror, to help see when lighting or checking the pilot light of a water heater, p. 220, "Place a hand mirror"

Mittens
➤ For covering the top rail of a ladder, to prevent it from scarring shingles or siding, p. 44, "Damage control"

Mothballs
➤ For putting in garbage cans to repel flies, p. 38, "In mothballs"

Mouse pad, computer
➤ As a sander pad, p. 143, "Sander pad worn out?"

N

Nail polish
➤ To seal up small cracks or holes in a windowpane, p. 96, "Seal cracked glass"
➤ To repair small holes or tears in window screens, p. 103, "Mending the mesh"
➤ For applying to gouges in a clothes washer tub, p. 226, "A chipped tub"
➤ For dabbing on power tool bolts before retightening the nuts, p. 300, "Snug it up"

Nails
➤ A 10d nail, driven through a piece of dowel, as a handy jig for removing grout, p. 263, "Grouted out"
➤ A few 3d nails, pounded through a board, as a scratching rake for stucco, p. 265, "Make a rake"

Newspaper
➤ For wrapping up window screens when storing them for the winter, p. 103, "Winter storage"
➤ As garden mulch, p. 282, "Make your own"
➤ To make a mat for mulching the garden, p. 282, "If you are a newspaper mulcher"
➤ Shredded, to dry a compost pile and discourage pests, p. 305, "Pests be gone"

Nutshells
➤ As compost, p. 304, "Making deposits"

Oatmeal
➤ As mousetrap bait, p. 39, "Spicing up the bait"

Onion
➤ Chopped, in a container of water, to make the odor of brand-new paint disappear, p. 122, "Dislike that paint smell?"

Packing peanuts
➤ Placed at the bottom of a large flowerpot, to reduce the amount of soil needed, p. 275, "Losing weight"

Paint roller, power
➤ To remove wallcovering, p. 132, "Make a power peeler"

Pan
➤ Pizza pan, to smother range-top flames, p. 14, "Stovetop fires"
➤ Jelly-roll pan, as a drip pan for a leaking car, p. 29, "Catcher in the carport"
➤ Filled with ammonia, to keep squirrels out of the chimney, p. 39, "Squirrel in the chimney?"
➤ Pie pan, filled with water, to keep ants away from a pet dish, p. 40, "Starve 'em"
➤ Pie pan, to place under furniture legs when refinishing furniture, p. 141, "Do the pan-pan"

Pants hanger, wood
➤ To store paper bags, p. 33, "How to brown bag it?"

Pantyhose
➤ Filled with manure and steeped in water, for nourishing outdoor plants, p. 285, "Tea for the tomatoes"

Paper clip
➤ As a hook to pull the heating element of a space heater away from the reflector, p. 239, "It's shocking"
➤ To eject a floppy disk from a Macintosh computer, p. 242, "Floppy disk stuck?"

Paper plate
➤ For covering a paint can to avoid splashes when stirring paint, p. 122, "Spatter matters"

Paper towel tube
➤ To store plastic bags, p. 33, "Bag it"

Peanut butter
➤ As mousetrap bait, p. 39, "Spicing up the bait"

Pencil
➤ For temporarily sealing a small leak in a pipe, p. 177, "Making a point"
➤ For inserting into a videocassette's brake release hole to disengage the spring clip, p. 241, "Manual rewind"

Pennies
➤ Attached to the blades of a ceiling fan, to rebalance the blades, p. 210, "Cut the wobble"

Pet hair
➤ As compost, p. 304, "Making deposits"

Petroleum jelly
➤ In the jar, as a holder for a birthday candle, to lengthen the candle's life when using it as a light source during a blackout, p. 12, "Happy birthday"
➤ To rejuvenate the finish on wood furniture, p. 141, "Another spot remover"

Photo album
➤ For compiling a book of recipes, p. 16, "Store favorite recipes"

Pipe
➤ To provide more leverage when using a wrench, p. 37, "Getting leverage"
➤ PVC pipe, to slip over the loops on a long power cord, p. 37, "Cord control"
➤ PVC pipe placed over dowels, to make hose guides that prevent hoses from getting snagged, p. 297, "Let it roll"
➤ Metal pipe stuck in the ground, as a jig for straightening bent tool tines, p. 302, "Good tines"

➤ PVC pipe drilled with holes and inserted into a compost pile, for improving air circulation, p. 305, "For better air circulation"
➤ Slipped over the handle of a lug wrench, for better leverage when you're changing a tire, p. 319, "A wrenching experience"

Pitcher, heavy
➤ To hold kitchen utensils, p. 33, "Drawer space"

Place mat
➤ Slipped under a food processor, to make it quieter, p. 238, "Volume control"

Plant prunings
➤ As compost, p. 304, "Making deposits"

Plastic sheeting
➤ To cover a hole in the roof before making the repair, p. 13, "A storm-damaged roof"
➤ To capture water from a leaking roof, p. 13, "Catch a flood"
➤ For taping to siding to determine if the ground around the foundation is graded properly, p. 93, "Get a good grade"
➤ For piling dirt and sod so it cannot damage the grass, p. 248, "Pile dug-up dirt and sod"
➤ For covering a sand bed when paving is delayed because of bad weather, p. 248, "Sand sense"
➤ For covering concrete blocks to protect them from the elements prior to starting a building project, p. 256, "A dry run"
➤ To lay beneath sod if you have to store it before installing it, p. 270, "Storing sod"
➤ To spread beneath a tree or shrub before you start pruning, p. 290, "Smart cleanup"
➤ For covering a compost pile, p. 304, "To bin or not to bin"

Plastic tray with lip
➤ For catching parts when repairing a VCR, p. 240, "When repairing a VCR"

Plastic wrap
➤ For use in making custom weather-stripping for a drafty window, p. 104, "Barring drafts"
➤ For covering the pots of houseplants prior to going away, p. 297, "Going away?"

Plywood
➤ For creating furrows when planting the garden, p. 284, "Fast furrows"
➤ With wood dowels, as a tool for making holes in the ground to plant seeds, p. 302, "Sowing machine"

Pot lid
➤ To smother range-top flames, p. 14, "Stovetop fires"

Potato
➤ For smoothing caulk, p. 63, "Potato fingers"

Pot scrubber
➤ As a wallpaper remover, p. 132, "Glue removal II"

R

Radio, portable
➤ To keep raccoons out of the chimney, p. 223, "Raccoon remover"

Rag
➤ To pinpoint a frozen area of a pipe, p. 13, "Finding a frozen spot"
➤ To divert water flowing down a rafter in the attic, p. 13, "Wick it away"
➤ To prevent a mess when cleaning the gutter, p. 53, "When cleaning gutters"

Rake
➤ With the handle sawed off, hung on a garden shed wall, as a rack for tools, p. 302, "A handy hang-up"
➤ With a split piece of garden hose slid over the tines, as a squeegee for cleaning patios, decks, etc., p. 303, "Old rakes never die"

Report-cover spines, plastic
➤ As a safety cover for handsaw teeth, p. 36, "To keep saw teeth"

Rock salt
➤ Embedded in freshly poured concrete, to create a textured look, p. 258, "Salt in the earth"
➤ Kept in the car, in case you get stuck in snow or ice, p. 319, "In case of emergency"

Rubber boots
➤ To give a ladder skid-free traction, p. 44, "Solid footing"

Rubbing alcohol
➤ Dabbed on a fabric-softener sheet, for cleaning and dusting a TV screen, p. 245, "Cleaning the screen"

S

Salt
➤ For dousing range-top flames, p. 14, "Stovetop fires"
➤ As part of a cleansing solution for spline-cane seats, p. 156, "Salty cleanser"

Sander belt
➤ To sand spindles and other turnings on wood furniture, p. 142, "Reuse that belt"

Sand shovel, plastic
➤ For cleaning a gutter, p. 53, "Pick the bucket"

Saucer
➤ Placed upside down over a sink drain when repairing a faucet, to prevent small parts from going down the drain, p. 165, "Saucer savvy"

Sawdust
➤ As compost, p. 305, "To help compost 'cook'"
➤ For mixing with latex paint that you want to throw out, p. 322, "Trashing latex paint"
➤ For sprinkling on spilled pesticide, enabling you to clean it up safely, p. 323, "Pesticide control"

Scouring powder
➤ For improving the holding power of a screwdriver, p. 36, "Powder power"

Shaving cream
➤ For defogging a bathroom mirror, p. 23, "Defogging the mirror"

Shoe bag
➤ Hung on a garage wall, for storing miscellaneous small items, p. 35, "Got a hang-up?"

Shutters
➤ For a fireplace screen, p. 19, "Screen the fireplace"
➤ For making a screen behind which to hide kitchen appliances, p. 32, "Custom fit"

Snow saucer
➤ A child's snow saucer, as a means for hauling tools and supplies across the yard, p. 303, "Garden sled"

Soap
➤ For making double-hung windows easier to open and close, p. 101, "For slick sashes"
➤ Suspended in a mesh bag, for deterring deer from plantings, p. 286, "Oh, deer!"

Socks
➤ For covering the top rail of a ladder, to prevent it from scarring shingles or siding, p. 44, "Damage control"
➤ With the tip cut off, as a fingerless glove to keep paint from dripping down your arm, p. 66, "A free hand"
➤ For slipping over your shoes to absorb drips when painting, p. 121, "Shoe saver"

Sod
➤ As compost, p. 304, "Making deposits"

Soda holder, plastic
➤ For storing aluminum foil, wax paper, and plastic wrap under the sink, p. 32, "Free up drawer space"

Spacing wedge, nylon
➤ For aligning deck boards evenly, p. 27, "Spacing out"

Spaghetti
➤ To light the pilot light of an oven or gas grill, p. 234, "Got a match?"

Spatula
➤ Rubber kitchen spatula, to patch tiny cracks and nail holes in plaster, p. 82, "A putty spatula"
➤ Plastic kitchen spatula, instead of a metal scraper, for removing finish from wood furniture, p. 140, "Out of the kitchen"

Sponge
➤ To replicate the texture of an old plaster wall or ceiling when patching it, p. 83, "On the surface"
➤ For determining the original finish of a floor before refinishing, p. 89, "Finish up"
➤ Instead of paint stencils, p. 125, "Spongy variation"
➤ Sponge ball, as a shock absorber when using a chisel to make concrete repairs, p. 261, "Soften the blows"

Spoon
➤ As a tool for repointing mortar joints, p. 255, "Tooling along"

Spray can nozzles
➤ Stored in solvent, to use when new nozzles get clogged, p. 155, "Collect substitutes"

Squeegee
➤ To clean soap scum off shower walls, p. 23, "Run a squeegee"
➤ Notched, to create a decorative combed finish when painting a wall, p. 127, "Nice lines"
➤ To remove leftover wallcovering paste before installing the new wallcovering, p. 132, "Take off glue residue"

Steel wool
➤ To remove paint from a window frame, p. 64, "A glass act"
➤ To use in place of rust remover, p. 323, "Less toxic cleaning"

Stepladder
➤ To hold plants or other household items, p. 45, "If you're short on space"

Stones, flat
➤ As edging around the garden, to make mowing easier, p. 270, "Limit lawn edging"
➤ As markers for outdoor plants, p. 277, "Mark the spot"
➤ To provide stability when setting fence posts, p. 294, "Rock-solid footing"

Straw
➤ For adding to the compost pile, p. 304, "Making deposits"
➤ As compost, p. 305, "To help compost 'cook'"

Straw, plastic drinking
➤ Flexible straw, to attach to the nozzle of a caulking tube when working in tight spaces, p. 63, "Point and shoot"
➤ To scrape up hardened glue that has squeezed out of corners, p. 149, "Straw scoop"
➤ To feed phone wire through a wall horizontally, p. 198, "Use a drinking straw"

String, cotton
➤ Soaked in water and dipped in a pan of seeds, for planting lots of tiny seeds, p. 274, "When sowing tiny seeds"

Stucco wire
➤ Rolled into a cylinder and topped by a garbage-can lid, as a storage bin, p. 265, "Leftover stucco wire?"

Swim goggles
➤ To wear when sanding overhead, p. 85, "Visual effects"

T

Tea
➤ To moisten compost, p. 304, "Liquid refreshment"

Tennis ball
➤ To use as drawer pulls, p. 21, "Playful pulls"
➤ Slit, to make turning a screwdriver easier, p. 36, "Power steering"
➤ Wrapped with sandpaper, to sand inside curves on wood furniture, p. 143, "Curve ball"

Three-ring binder spine
➤ Mounted on a garage wall, for storing miscellaneous small items, p. 35, "Got a hang-up?"

Tire
➤ To protect a car from scraping against obstructions in the garage, p. 29, "Bumper room"

Toilet freshener cake
➤ For scattering over an area of the yard that a dog likes to dig up, p. 41, "The hole thing"

Toothbrush
➤ For working wood finish into crevices, p. 144, "Tooth tiny"
➤ For cleaning sap from a pruning saw's teeth, p. 303, "To quickly remove sap"

Toothpaste
➤ For dabbing on a scratched windowpane, p. 96, "Erase shallow scratches"
➤ To remove crayon marks on a wall before painting, p. 121, "Draw!"

Towel
➤ To contain water during a flood, p. 12, "Flood control"
➤ Spread on the bottom of the sink, to avoid breaking china and crystal when washing them, p. 17, "Cushion china"
➤ Dampened, to help tighten up the canework on spline-cane seats, p. 157, "Avoid a sag ending"
➤ For plugging up a sink drain when repairing a faucet, to prevent small parts from going down the drain, p. 165, "Saucer savvy"
➤ Placed over a door to keep it from closing completely, as a child-safety measure, p. 324, "Finger-saving doorstop"

Towel rod
➤ Mounted on a bedroom door, for hanging towels, p. 31, "Adding a bar"
➤ Mounted on the back of a cabinet door, for storing pot lids, p. 32, "Putting a lid on it"

Turpentine
➤ Mixed with boiled linseed oil, as a sealer for garage floors, p. 260, "Save money on sealer"

Twist tie
➤ For sealing a tube of caulk, p. 63, "Caulk-tube clogging"
➤ To gather wires from electronic components, p. 240, "Use twist ties"

U

Umbrella
➤ For catching drips when cleaning a chandelier, p. 191, "Clean a crystal chandelier"

Undershirts
➤ For rag-rolling a wall, p. 128, "Try something different"

V

Vegetable scraps
➤ For adding to the compost pile, p. 304, "Making deposits"
➤ As compost, p. 305, "To help compost 'cook'"

Velcro strips
➤ For attaching the satellite or TV remote to the TV, p. 245, "Close tabs"

Vinegar, white
➤ Instead of fabric softener, p. 23, "Faux softener"
➤ To deodorize a skunked pet, p. 40, "When a pet gets skunked"
➤ To remove pet stains from a wood floor, p. 40, "Floor exercise"
➤ To clean a brush that is hardened with oil paint, p. 67, "To revive a brush"
➤ As a wallpaper remover, p. 132, "Vinegary glue remover"
➤ For getting glue out of a bottle when the glue has hardened in the spout, p. 148, "Let it flow"
➤ For cleaning the sprayer head of a sink, p. 165, "To remove deposits"
➤ For cleaning the parts of a shower head, p. 174, "A trickle-down shower"
➤ To remove soap scum from a clothes washer, p. 227, "Detergent buildup"

➤ To freshen up a foul-smelling dishwasher, p. 232, "Washing the dishwasher"
➤ For a fresh-smelling kitchen waste disposer, p. 233, "Cleaning cubes"
➤ To prime an old concrete floor for a coat of new paint, p. 260, "Making it stick"

W

Wading pool, plastic
➤ To house a new litter of puppies or kittens, p. 40, "New babies in the house?"

Wallcovering
➤ To cover wastebaskets, lampshades, picture frames, window shades, shelves, books, and photo albums, p. 135, "Recycling the leftovers"
➤ As a wallpaper border, p. 137, "Make your own"

Wax paper
➤ To lubricate hard-to-remove vacuum hose connections, p. 236, "Slippery connections"

Weatherstripping
➤ For preventing chair legs from scratching the floor, p. 16, "Attach felt to the bottom"
➤ To increase a vacuum's suction, p. 37, "Shop vac not sucking up?"

Weed killer
➤ For spraying on exterior brick walls to remove moss, p. 254, "Gather no moss"

Window screening
➤ Installed beneath the floorboards, to prevent mosquitoes from getting into a screened-in porch, p. 27, "Mosquitoes invading"
➤ Placed over a chisel's handle, to prevent concrete chips from flying in your face, p. 261, "The chips are down"
➤ Placed over a flowerpot's drainage hole, to lessen soil leakage, p. 273, "Containment policy"
➤ Stapled to a wood frame, as a compost sifter, p. 305, "Spread compost whole"

Wire hanger
➤ To dislodge a blockage in a sink pipe, p. 170, "Digging a little deeper"
➤ To make pullers for removing pavers from walkways, etc., p. 249, "Paver pullers"
➤ Inserted into a piece of wood molding, to make a doorstop, as a child-safety measure, p. 324, "Finger-saving doorstop"

Wood block
➤ For extra leverage when removing nails with a hammer, p. 36, "Pulling a long nail"
➤ Placed beneath a VCR, to set it on top of a TV, p. 240, "A cool perch"

Wood dowels
➤ Covered in PVC pipe, as guides to prevent a garden hose from getting snagged, p. 297, "Let it roll"
➤ Inserted into a piece of plywood, as a tool for making holes in the ground to plant seeds, p. 302, "Sowing machine"

Wood molding
➤ As a guide when cutting sod for the lawn, p. 271, "To keep lawn edges neat"
➤ With a piece of wire hanger, to make a doorstop, as a child-safety measure, p. 324, "Finger-saving doorstop"

Wood pallets
➤ For making a compost bin, p. 304, "For a quick bin"

Wood planks
➤ Nailed to basement ceiling joists, for storing leftover building materials, p. 34, "The long view"
➤ As a fulcrum for a pry bar when removing exterior flagstones., p. 251, "The right way to pry"
➤ Cut to the desired size, for creating even grout joints between pieces of exterior flooring material, p. 263, "Space program"
➤ Cut to the desired size, to use as a spacer when positioning pickets on a fence, p. 295, "Even spacing"

INDEX

CONTRIBUTORS

Axonometric view and plan p. 292
Geoffrey Roesch

Consultants
Charles Avoles *Plumbing*
Philip Englander *Furniture*
Gene Falks *Electrical*
Mark D. Feirer *Around the Home; Exterior; Interior;*
Windows and Doors
Lori L. Gazzano *Painting and Wallpapering*
Carl Hagstrom *Stone, Brick, and Concrete*
Evan A. Powell *Electrical; Heating and Cooling; Appliances*
Rob Muessel *Safety and Security*
Rosemary G. Rennicke *Yard and Garden*
Dan Shon *Heating and Cooling*
Don Turano *Heating and Cooling*
Virginia White *Painting and Wallpapering*

Acknowledgments
Judge and Mrs. Salvatore A. Alamia
American Olean Tile Co.
Classic Residence by Hyatt
East Islip Paint and Wallpaper Co.
Wanda and Frank Haggerty
Erik Hansen
Homelite®/John Deere Consumer Products, Inc.
The Humane Society of the United States
The Invisible Fence Co.
Linear Corp.
Mary H. Packwood at Pet-Track
Sony Corp. of America
Catherine Steimle
Thomson Consumer Electronics/RCA
Veterans Chair Caning and Repair